Audiovisual Translation

Audiovisual translation is the fastest growing strand within translation studies.

This book addresses the need for more robust theoretical frameworks to investigate emerging text-types, address new methodological challenges (including the compilation, analysis and reproduction of audiovisual data), and understand new discourse communities bound together by the production and consumption of audiovisual texts.

In this clear, user-friendly book, Luis Pérez-González introduces and explores the field, presenting and critiquing key concepts, research models and methodological approaches.

Features include:

- introductory overviews at the beginning of each chapter, outlining aims and relevant connections with other chapters;
- breakout boxes showcasing key concepts, research case studies or any other relevant links to the wider field of translation studies;
- examples of audiovisual texts in a range of languages with back-translation support when required;
- summaries reinforcing key issues dealt with in each chapter;
- follow-up questions for further study;
- core references and suggestions for further reading;
- additional online resources on an extensive companion website, found at www.routledge.com/cw/perezgonzalez.

This will be an essential text for all students studying audiovisual or screen translation at postgraduate or advanced undergraduate level and key reading for all researchers working in the area.

Luis Pérez-González is Senior Lecturer in Translation Studies at the Centre for Translation and Intercultural Studies, University of Manchester, UK, where he teaches screen translation, translation theory and intercultural pragmatics.

'With this landmark volume, Luis Pérez-González gives audiovisual translation scholarship the means to generate its future. It is meticulously researched, intelligent, judicious, consummate in its ability to draw together the threads of AVT's intricate (multi)modalities, to challenge both our knowledge and our ignorance, and to give our theories and methodologies the robust grounding and mutual responsiveness they have hitherto missed. Work like this will help AVT to establish its authority in the twenty-first century.'
Marie-Noëlle Guillot, *University of East Anglia, UK*

'This is a fabulous, ambitious book that brings together research from far-flung disciplines – from fandom studies to neurolinguistics – to provide a comprehensive and insightful snapshot of audiovisual translation scholarship today. Skilfully analysing and illuminating this burgeoning area of study, it will appeal to students and researchers alike managing to combine accessibility with conceptual rigour.'
Tessa Dwyer, *University of Melbourne, Australia*

'Written by one of the leading scholars on the subject, *Audiovisual Translation: Theories, Methods and Issues* is an accessible and thorough introduction to the study of audiovisual translation in its different forms, providing a detailed examination of the concept of multimodality as well as a thoughtful exploration of fansubbing and other emerging practices, packed with examples and ideas to help students, professionals and general readers to become more informed and reflective about audiovisual translation.'
Yau Wai-ping, *Hong Kong Baptist University, Hong Kong*

'Luis Pérez-González successfully brings together distinct modes of audiovisual translation and offers a valid and systematic framework for their analysis. The robust and clear discussions of different theoretical models, research methodologies and tools of analysis for multimodal texts, accompanied by several resources such as interviews and follow up questions, represent an exciting and useful resource for undergraduate and postgraduate students, as well as researchers in this field.'
Alina Secară, *University of Leeds, UK*

AUDIOVISUAL TRANSLATION

Theories, Methods and Issues

Luis Pérez-González

Routledge
Taylor & Francis Group

LONDON AND NEW YORK

First published 2014
by Routledge
2 Park Square, Milton Park, Abingdon, Oxon OX14 4RN

and by Routledge
711 Third Avenue, New York, NY 10017

Routledge is an imprint of the Taylor & Francis Group, an informa business

British Library Cataloguing-in-Publication Data
A catalogue record for this book is available from the British Library

Library of Congress Cataloging-in-Publication Data
Pérez-González, Luis.
  Audiovisual translation : theories, methods and issues /
    Luis Pérez-González.
    pages cm
  1. Multimedia systems–Research. 2. Audio-visual equipment–
Technological innovations. 3. Translating and interpreting–
Technological innovations. I. Title.
  P306.93.P47 2014
  418'.03–dc23
                                                      2014004056

ISBN: 978-0-415-53025-5 (hbk)
ISBN: 978-0-415-53027-9 (pbk)
ISBN: 978-1-315-76297-5 (ebk)

Typeset in Joanna MT
by RefineCatch Limited, Bungay, Suffolk

To Iván

Contents

LIST OF FIGURES

LIST OF TABLES

PREFACE

There is no doubt that interest in audiovisual translation has grown significantly in recent years. The huge increase in the number of articles and volumes dedicated to the topic over the past decade alone testifies to this. And yet, most of the literature published by scholars of audiovisual translation, while unquestionably useful and welcome, has failed to engage other disciplines and lay the foundation for interdisciplinary research and critical theorizing. Understandably, perhaps, the priority has been to address practical needs, with training manuals and descriptive accounts of professional practice dominating the field.

This volume ushers in a new stage in the development of audiovisual translation as a key theme and research domain in the humanities. It constitutes the first sustained treatment of all forms of audiovisual translation as objects of research that can be examined from a variety of perspectives: as artistic, economic, social and political artefacts that now pervade all aspects of our lives. Far from being restricted to micro level textual analysis or macro level contextual analysis, it discusses and exemplifies the application of theoretical models and research methodologies that treat audiovisual products as semiotic wholes. Multimodal theory, for instance, is offered as one model that allows us to account for the full spectrum of sign systems deployed in audiovisual products, including speech, written language of subtitles, image, music, colour and perspective. The book's success in overcoming the fragmentation that characterizes much of the literature on translation studies is particularly evident in the final chapter, which brings together different threads of research and practice, and addresses scholarly as well as pragmatic considerations. The chapter offers invaluable guidance on designing both research and practical dissertations, exemplified with a variety of themes that can be fruitfully examined from a wide range of theoretical perspectives, from humour and cultural references to censorship and the participatory culture of fansubbing communities. The follow-up questions for discussion in all chapters are a mine of ideas for extended postgraduate essays, various types of dissertation, and (post)doctoral level research projects.

Combining the strengths and appeal of a student-friendly textbook and meticulous scholarly monograph, *Audiovisual Translation: Theories, Methods and Issues* offers an accessible introduction to the field and simultaneously provides seasoned researchers with powerful tools of analysis and novel theoretical perspectives. It promises to place audiovisual translation firmly on the scholarly map of the humanities.

Mona Baker
30 January 2014

Acknowledgements

I owe a deep gratitude to the international community of audiovisual translation scholars, whose past and present achievements have contributed to the advancement of this field. A number of them have read and commented valuably on various chapters of the manuscript. Although I have clung to some of my errors, there is no question that my book is markedly better for their advice.

I have benefited greatly from the opportunity to present insights contained in this book in a number of settings, particularly my own audiovisual translation courses at the University of Manchester and several sessions of the Translation Research Summer School held between 2005 and 2012 at Manchester, University College London, the University of Edinburgh and Hong Kong Baptist University. Among my doctoral students at Manchester, I have learnt particularly from Louisa Desilla and Dang Li, whose ideas have greatly influenced my understanding of multimodality and participatory audiovisual translation, and who have allowed me to quote their work extensively. I extend my affectionate gratitude to my colleagues at the Centre for Translation and Intercultural Studies at the University of Manchester, who have on every occasion shown themselves willing to offer assistance in various ways and, more generally, provided me with a supportive and stimulating environment in which to carry out my research.

My thanks go to Katherine Halls for her assistance with the transcription and translation of Arabic texts; Maria Freddi, Mary Erbaugh, Fotios

Karamitroglou and Jan Louis Kruger for permission to reprint copyrighted material listed in the Permissions section; Marie-Noëlle Guillot (University of East Anglia), Carol O'Sullivan (Bristol University), Amer Al-Adwan, Terence Murray and Nienke Brandsma for bringing different examples to my attention; Li-Wen Chang for her support with the development of audiovisual material for the companion website. I would also like to thank Sony Islam for allowing me to publicize his creative and valuable work in Chapter 7.

It is customary at this point in the acknowledgements section to praise your editors' unwavering patience and assistance. I have indeed benefited from large measures of both. My gratitude to Louisa Semlyen and Sophie Jaques, my editors at Routledge, however, is all the more sincere and heart-felt for their tact and support during and after a long period of illness, which put the book behind schedule.

Words cannot express how much I owe to my family, so I will try to work harder at showing it. Thank you for helping me see things in perspective.

My biggest debt of gratitude goes to Mona Baker, through whose work I first became interested in translation in the early 1990s. As a scholar, Mona continues to be a source of inspiration; as a friend, she has become an equally strong source of unqualified encouragement with her gifts of time and wisdom.

Luis Pérez-González
January 2014

PERMISSIONS

Every effort has been made to obtain permission to reproduce copyright material. Any omissions brought to our attention will be remedied in future editions.

The author and the publisher would like to thank the following copyright holders for their permission to reproduce a number of images and figures:

EuroparlTV for a screen shot of Daniel Cohn-Bendit's speech, as circulated via YouTube (www.youtube.com/user/zorbec68?feature=plcp) (Figure 3.1); *Cuaderno de Campo: Esclavos del Software Libre* for a screen shot (www.trebol-a. com/2006/09/01/galloway-en-youtube) of their website (Figure 3.2); *Al Jazeera* for a screen shot (www.universalsubtitles.org/en/teams/al-jazeera) of their website section on participatory subtitling (Figure 3.3); *Viki* (www.viki. com) for a screen shot of *Swallow the Sun*, episode 25 (Figure 3.6); Dr Fotios Karamitroglou (Athens University of Economics & Business) for the figure published in his 1998 online article 'A Proposed Set of Subtitling Standards in Europe' (www.bokorlang.com/journal/04stndrd.htm), reproduced in Box 4.1 of this book; Dr Jan-Louis Kruger (North-West University) for four samples of his analysis of *The Pear Stories* film published in his 2012 article 'Making Meaning in AVT: Eye Tracking and Viewer Construction of Narrative', *Perspectives: Studies in Translatology* 20(1): 67–86 (Figure 5.3); Dr Mary S. Erbaugh for four screen shots of *The Pear Stories* film, available via her website *The Chinese Pear Stories – Narratives Across Seven Chinese Dialects* (www.pearstories.org/docu/ research.htm) (Figure 5.3); Dr Maria Freddi (Università di Pavia) for the figure published on page 496 of her 2013 article 'Constructing a Corpus of Translated films: A Corpus View of Dubbing', *Perspectives: Studies in Translatology* 21(4): 491–503 (Figure 5.7); A-film for a screen shot of Joram Lürsen's *Alles is Liefde* (Figure 6.1); Warner Brothers/Hawk Films for a screen shot of Stanley Kubrick's *A Clockwork Orange* (Figure 6.9); Working Title Films/Universal Pictures for a screen shot of Beeban Kidron's *Bridget Jones: The Edge of Reason* (Figure 6.12); *Stop The Wall* and the itisapartheid.org collective for a screen shot of *Israeli Apartheid 5* (www.youtube.com/watch?v=0I-wFyQg32Y) (Figure 7.2); BBC for four screen shots of *Human Planet* (episodes 1 and 4) (Figures 7.3 and 7.4); Buena Vista International for two screen shots of Ola Simonsson's and Johannes Stjärne Nilsson's *Sound of Noise* (Figure 7.5); and Hartswoodfilms for two screen shots of *Sherlock* (episode 1, season 1) (Figures 7.6 and 7.7).

INTRODUCTION

There cannot be many people left on this planet whose life has not been, and continues to be, shaped by audiovisual texts. Their impact, it is fair to say, has not always been presented in the most positive light. Writing about films, the only form of audiovisual text available in his time, the influential literary critic F. R. Leavis notoriously asserted that motion pictures make 'active recreation, especially active use of the mind, more difficult' (1930: 20) – echoing earlier claims that audiences can only react to, but not reflect on what films show (Mann 1928/1978). This might explain why viewers of the Lumières' *Train Pulling into a Station* (1896) were so frightened by the sight of a life-sized train heading towards them and, reportedly, stampeded away from the screen (Loiperdinger 2004). One century later, our constant and routinized exposure to audiovisual texts would appear to have neutralized, to some extent, the 'affective response' that typically follows the advent of new media (Littau 2006: 3). Today, large sections of audiences all over the world still consume audiovisual texts in search of aesthetic experiences that tap into their emotions, memories or intimacy. However, it is also evident that the viewing experiences we derive from audiovisual texts have become more varied and sophisticated.

For oppressed communities all over the planet, global satellite and cable TV broadcasts are a unique opportunity to engage, for example, with representations of democratic life or public expressions of sexual identity that they subscribe to and identify with. For sensory impaired members of the community, access to media content enables their aspiration to be valued equally and to experience full inclusion in society. In the new media ecology, users of emerging audiovisual genres such as videogames crave traditional immersive experiences, while viewers of established audiovisual genres such as films lay claim to a more activ(-e/-ivist) role in the management of their own spectatorial experience – both as individuals or members of networked communities of like-minded individuals. Amid this broad canvas of motivations, practices and agendas, this book zooms in on an often neglected but vital aspect of the process of consumption and enjoyment of audiovisual material: translation. This book is about audiovisual texts that travel across linguacultures and examines how the creative genius of film directors, the commercial appeal of a mainstream drama series, the cult underground status enjoyed by certain actors, or the subversive potential of a narrative are mediated and reconstituted through different modalities of audiovisual translation.

AIMS OF THIS BOOK

Although published reflections on the vices and virtues of film translation date back to the early twentieth century, scholarly work on audiovisual translation only began to gain traction after the surge of translation studies in the 1990s. Intriguingly, this field was soon drawn into a dynamic of disciplinary devolution. While 'audiovisual translation' has remained a useful umbrella term around which to organize specialized postgraduate courses or conferences, published research has often focused on individual forms of audiovisual transfer. Nowhere is this trend more obvious than in the case of monographs, with books on subtitling, dubbing or voice-over already outnumbering volumes on the broader field of audiovisual translation.

This volume represents one of the first attempts by a single author to systematically chart and critique influential concepts, research models and methodological approaches in audiovisual translation studies. It hopes to offer a semblance of an integration of the vast territory formed by the sum of distinct modes of audiovisual transfer, and engender synergies to study the mediation of texts made up of verbal and non-verbal semiotics. Ultimately, the multimodal nature of the texts that lie at the heart of this field of practice and research presents translators and scholars with a common set of cognitive, epistemological and practical demands and challenges, irrespective of the specific modality of audiovisual translation they happen to specialize in. Marshalling this wide range of sources, approaches and debates to create my personal synthesis has been an arduous task that has, in some cases, pushed me to venture far afield from my core area of expertise.

Chief among the difficulties encountered in this conciliatory endeavour has been the tendency of audiovisual translation scholars to regard and present their work as a departure from previously existing research. In critiquing the discourse that typifies discussions of audiovisual translation, I have tried to tone down those novelty claims – providing readers with the means to gauge that originality by themselves. Anybody who has read Delabastita's (2013) 'B2B in Translation Studies: Business to Business, or Back to Basics?', an insightful essay exploring the impact of market forces and neoliberalism on translation studies, will understand the reasons for my unease in relaying these assertions of novelty. For these, Delabastita convincingly argues, are often meant to signal that one's own 'approach is indeed so different and so superior that it brushes aside or leaves behind anything that came before, and that critical dialogue with existing research in the field is therefore no longer required' (2013: 11). My synthesis thus aims to facilitate a

> different type of self-reflexiveness that . . . operates as a *common programme* on the collective scale of the research community, building on the individual scholar's determination to take full stock of the existing body of knowledge and to make a well-defined contribution to it with a maximum degree of logic and transparency throughout, the aim being to describe and explain, as well as we can, the things that happen and the things that people do, and how and why and with what effects they do them, and how we make sense of them.
>
> (ibid.: 16)

But this book is not confined to a comprehensive overview of audiovisual translation. A robust conceptual framework is woven into every chapter to facilitate the reader's critical engagement with the theoretical and methodological diversity of the field. The emphasis on conceptual rigour in this volume is particularly salient in discussions surrounding the multimodal make-up of audiovisual texts. Even though their polysemiotic nature has been widely acknowledged in the literature, attempts to operationalize the application of multimodal theory in audiovisual translation have been few and far between. In this book, readers are presented with a systematic formalization of the meaning-making resources at play in multimodal texts. For the purposes of clarity, I draw on abundant examples from various audiovisual genres, complete with accompanying discussions, to reveal how the distribution of meaning across different semiotics restrains the translator's mediation of multimodal texts. In widening the focus of audiovisual translation beyond debates on linguistic equivalence, which have tended to monopolize research in this field, I also expose readers to current developments outside the domain of commercial mediation practices. Non-professional practices are conceptualized here as an opportunity to monitor closely the crystallization of a new paradigm of mediation, driven by considerations other than the expectations of the media industry. The role of technological and socio-cultural change in the forging of alternative translation practices is subjected to detailed scrutiny, as are the changes in the contexts of production and reception of media content.

Significantly, this volume offers solid theoretical orientation and methodological direction to design new research projects in the field. For all these reasons, this volume should be of interest to students, reflective professionals and early career scholars in the field, as well as colleagues in the fields of media studies, cultural studies, and intercultural communication who, at some point of their research careers, find themselves investigating issues at the interface between language(s) and non-verbal semiotics.

FEATURES

All chapters of this book follow the same structure:

- **introductory overviews** outline the aims of the chapter and highlight the main concepts to be explored in the discussion;
- an **introductory video presentation** serves to further contextualize and highlight key issues pertaining to the topic of the chapter;
- **breakout boxes** are used to substantiate claims, showcase the contribution of leading scholars, refer the reader to relevant debates in the wider discipline of translation studies or in other disciplines. In some cases, breakout boxes simply provide anecdotal illustrations of the issue under scrutiny;
- **featured examples** sharpen the focus of the discussion and illustrate how theoretical insights can be applied in practical analysis. Examples are provided in a range of languages, including Arabic, Chinese, Dutch, English, Spanish, among others. The focus on the theoretical issues illustrated by those examples, and the use of detailed back-translations,

should make these examples accessible even to readers who are not familiar with the languages featuring in each example;

- **follow-up questions** provide readers with opportunities to reflect on and gain further insight into the concepts and arguments underpinning each chapter;
- **core references** and **suggestions for further reading** are provided at the end of each chapter to encourage and guide further exploration of specific topics and issues.

This volume can be used in combination with a comprehensive companion website, which contains additional resources for students and lecturers who may choose to use this book as recommended reading or as a course book for their audiovisual translation courses. Among these complementary materials, readers enjoy access to a significant body of secondary literature, in the form of journal articles, that I have drawn upon to develop my own narrative of how audiovisual translation emerged and continues to develop.

ORGANIZATION

The book consists of eight chapters divided into three parts.

Part I: Disciplinary and industrial foundations

Part I comprises three chapters. Chapter 1 charts the widening remit of audiovisual translation as a field of professional practice and research, as illustrated by (i) the numerous changes in the terminology used to designate audiovisual translation over the last 30 years; (ii) the growing number of transfer methods available to translate audiovisual texts; and (iii) the changing conceptualization of audiovisual texts within the translation studies literature, against the backdrop of gradual academization and institutionalization of the field.

Chapter 2 focuses on the genesis of traditional or representational translation practices in the media marketplace, as shaped by artistic, political and industrial developments throughout the twentieth century. Representational conventions have served as a basis for the spread of linear models of audiovisual content consumption and distribution, and for the consolidation of one-to-one correspondences between specific audiovisual genres and audiovisual transfer methods in most audiovisual markets.

Chapter 3 explores the emergence of interventionist practices prompted by ongoing changes in media business models and the emergence of new mediation agencies in our networked society. In our post-industrial economy, non-linear models of media distribution and consumption have paved the way for the formation of various translation cybercultures, whose approaches to audiovisual mediation aim to undermine the profit-ridden agenda of the industry's establishment.

Part II: Theoretical and methodological perspectives

Part II consists of two chapters. Chapter 4 examines the range of theoretical frameworks, or translation models, which have so far most informed audiovisual translation research. These include (i) process models – informed by psycholinguistic, cognitive and neurolinguistic approaches; (ii) comparative models, classified here into shift-based and corpus-driven approaches; and (iii) causal models, encompassing systems and norm-based approaches.

Chapter 5 focuses on the research methods that have proved most productive in the field. Starting with an overview of conceptual research methods, the chapter places particular emphasis on empirical research methods – as illustrated by observational, interactionist and documentary approaches.

Part III: New directions

Part III focuses on developments that are bound to shape most decisively the future of audiovisual translation scholarship. Chapter 6 surveys the theoretical apparatus of multimodality, focusing on a set of key notions, including medium, mode, core mode, medial variant, and sub-mode. A number of examples are drawn upon to explore how individual modes are integrated into the overall semiotic ensemble of original and translated multimodal texts. The relevance of new multimodal research methods, particularly multimodal transcriptions and multimodal corpora, to audiovisual translation is explored in some detail.

Chapter 7 focuses on the production and translation of self-mediated textualities by networked communities of fans, politically engaged citizens or, simply, reflective viewers. The discussion illustrates how these groupings prioritize non-representational practices of audiovisual translation, which thus becomes a platform for the expression of subjective spectatorial experiences.

Chapter 8, which brings the volume to a close, offers guidance for new scholars embarking on audiovisual translation research. Orientation is provided for readers working on theory-driven projects at postgraduate level and practical dissertations consisting of an extended translation project and a critical analysis or commentary. Specific advice is given on how to formulate research questions and hypotheses, identify relevant analytical tools, obtain copyright permissions and secure ethical approval for a research project.

Part I

DISCIPLINARY AND INDUSTRIAL FOUNDATIONS

1

MAPPING AN EVOLVING CONCEPTUAL NETWORK

For those with a philosophical disposition, there can be a depressing aspect to subtitling. Condensing sentences helps us to realize that it is possible to say almost anything using only a few words, to the extent that the human faculty of language is, if you like, superfluous. The pleasure of conversation, the exchange of ideas, everything can be reduced to simply a few grunts. The Stone Age, as we know it.

(Caillé 1960: 103, my translation)

Dubbing is a unique form of translation as it is blessed with the gift of total fidelity. It is the only type of translation that respects the written text, the life of words and the entire soul of language – both its visible and secret affections: diction, mimicry, gestures, demeanour, as well as intellectual and moral behaviour. If one wished to classify the different types of translation along hierarchical lines, would dubbing not deserve to be located at the apex of the pyramid?

(Cary 1969: 111, my translation)

In this chapter

Although it was first conceived to facilitate the international distribution of films, audiovisual translation is now used to mediate an ever more heterogeneous range of screen-mediated texts. The widening remit of audiovisual translation accounts for the wealth of terms that have been used to designate this field of practice and scholarly inquiry over the last thirty years, including but not limited to 'film translation', 'screen translation', 'multimedia translation' and 'audiovisual translation'. Today, audiovisual translation encompasses a variety of transfer methods, which are surveyed here under three major headings: **subtitling, revoicing** (incorporating **lip-synchronized dubbing, voice-over, narration, free commentary,** and **simultaneous interpreting**), and assistive forms of audiovisual translation (**subtitling for the hard of hearing, respeaking** and **audio description**) – which aim to facilitate access to information and entertainment for sensory impaired members of the community. Each of these modalities is defined and a brief overview of its features and development prospects is presented. The final section traces the changes in the way audiovisual texts have been conceptualized within the translation studies literature since the 1960s, as part of the processes of **academization** and **institutionalization** of the field.

▶ WATCH THE INTRODUCTION VIDEO

1.1 THE WIDENING REMIT OF AUDIOVISUAL TRANSLATION

During the last fifteen years, audiovisual translation has been the fastest growing strand of translation studies, as attested by the burgeoning body of domain-specific research literature, the development of undergraduate modules inducting students to relevant practices in the field, and the proliferation of specialized postgraduate courses, doctoral research summer schools and conferences – both academic and industry-oriented – all over the world. This exponential growth would appear to have been prompted by two main developments:

- communication technology has become an integral part of social life, as attested by the ever bigger impact and wider dissemination of audiovisual content vis-à-vis the circulation of literary texts and other materials published in the print media. Our increasing exposure to visual semiotics and different forms of interplay between verbal and non-verbal meaning-making resources is influencing and modifying our patterns of engagement with and reception of screen-based texts – whether they are produced and consumed for instrumental or contemplative purposes.

- the mutually shaping relationship between audiovisual translation and technological innovation has created a need for (i) robust theoretical frameworks to assist with the conceptualization of new text-types; (ii) new methodological approaches to guide the researcher through issues pertaining to the compilation, manipulation and analysis of samples of audiovisual data; and (iii) a better understanding of the new discourse communities formed around the production and consumption of established and emerging audiovisual text-types.

For all the academic hype surrounding audiovisual translation, there is ample evidence that the work of audiovisual translators and scholars remains poorly understood by society at large – including academics working in what may be regarded as neighbouring disciplines. By way of example, consider the two examples included in Box 1.1.

Box 1.1

Nornes (2007: 3–4)

Outside of film production and distribution, ideas and theories about film circulate the globe in translation, alighting in a certain place to be rejected, rearticulated, or assimilated. Furthermore, we must not neglect the role translation plays in canon formation, and the establishment, development, and maintenance of an academic discipline such as film studies, especially in its national cinema subfields.

However, despite the rich complexity of film translators' task and their singular role in mediating the foreign in cinema, they have been virtually ignored in film studies. Within translation studies, in contrast, there has recently been a proliferation of work, but it has almost exclusively concentrated on practical issues for translators, linguistic analysis, or the physiology of the peculiar brand of speed-reading demanded by subtitles. Scholars in either discipline have yet to explore in depth the historical, cultural and ideological issues I will attend to here.

Denison (2011: 453)

[W]ork on online anime fandom tends to be found in fields nominally separate from the study of both anime and fandom: in translatology and legal studies. Perhaps unsurprisingly, the former of these groups has been particularly concerned with mapping the practices of anime fan subtitlers (Díaz Cintas and Muñoz Sánchez 2006; Pérez-González 2006), while the latter has been concerned with the issue of copyright infringement (Daniels 2008; Hatcher 2005). Again though, and perhaps

> because of their clear reasons for focusing elsewhere, what is lacking in these studies is a sense of how fan subtitling groups relate to other kinds of anime fans, and how they present and perceive their work. Perceptions of fan subtitlers will be shown to play a role in broader community understandings of anime online, but there is potentially much more at stake in examining these fan subtitlers.

In these sample excerpts, Nornes (2007) and Denison (2011) reflect on the contribution of audiovisual translation studies to their respective scholarly fields, i.e. film studies and fandom studies. Despite the differences that exist between their disciplinary affiliations, both scholars share a common insight: the attention of audiovisual translation specialists tends to be focused almost exclusively on the practicalities of language mediation. As a result, Nornes and Denison argue, audiovisual translation specialists would appear to overlook the connections between the mechanical aspects of this mediation activity and the wider contexts in which audiovisual texts are embedded. As even newcomers to our field would agree, this is a rather narrow perception of what goes on in audiovisual translation, and one that the most cursory examination of publications on the different domains of the discipline should be able to dispel. The fact remains, however, that scholars in the field have not succeeded in communicating the wealth and relevance of their research beyond their own disciplinary constituencies.

I would argue that this relative failure is, to some extent, the result of the fast pace of technological progress witnessed since the beginning of the twentieth century, a period during which screen-based texts – ranging from films to videogames and the interface of software applications – have become increasingly ubiquitous. The successive stages of this expansion process can be traced by observing the changes in the terminology that specialists have used to designate this field of inquiry at different points in time (Chaume Varela 2004):

- Given the crucial contribution of audiovisual translation to the development of cinema as an art form (see Section 2.3), particularly during the formative years of film, it is only logical that the terms 'film dubbing' or 'film translation' gained so much currency in early studies on audiovisual translation (Fodor 1976, Snell-Hornby 1988/1995).

- The subsequent advent of televised broadcasting as a private commodity and its transformation into a mass medium of communication and entertainment provided new outlets for the dissemination of audio-visual translated texts. In keeping with this development in the global media ecology, terms such as 'film and TV translation' (Delabastita 1989) and 'media translation' (Eguíluz et al. 1994) came to feature more prominently in the specialized literature.

- More recently, the computerization of audiovisual texts, i.e. the popu-larization of electronic and/or digital media content to be viewed on the screen of a computer or a portable electronic device, has introduced some new terminology in the field. Terms such as 'screen translation' (Mason 1989, O'Connell 2007) and 'multimedia translation' (Gambier and Gottlieb 2001) are indicative of the extent to which audiovisual translation has grown far beyond its original disciplinary boundaries, bringing the investigation of ever new textual manifestations into its research remit.

- At different points during this period, specialists have also proposed terms that signal the medial restrictions (e.g. limited number of characters avail-able to translate a text) under which audiovisual translators operate, e.g. 'constrained translation' (Titford 1982, Mayoral et al. 1988). From a complementary perspective, others have opted to foreground the trans-formative dimension of audiovisual mediation, as translators often need to distance themselves from the original text to cater for new audiences – e.g. Gambier's (2003) 'transadaptation' – or preserve the immersive function of media content – e.g. Bernal Merino's (2006) 'transcreation'.

Amid this terminological inflation, Díaz Cintas and Remael have recently suggested that the term 'audiovisual translation (AVT) has been gaining ground in recent years and is fast becoming the standard referent' (2007: 11–12).

1.2 MODALITIES OF AUDIOVISUAL TRANSLATION

1.2.1 Subtitling

Widely regarded as an evolved version of the primitive intertitles (Section 2.2), subtitles are snippets of written text superimposed on visual footage that convey a target language version of the source speech. Conventionally, each of the snippets into which the original speech – whether in the form of dialogue or narration – is divided for the purposes of translation has to be delivered in synchrony with the corresponding fragment of spoken language. In communities where several linguistic constituencies co-exist, 'bilingual subtitles' convey two language versions of the same source fragment, one in each line of the subtitle (Gambier 2003).

Subtitling has been defined as a 'diasemiotic' or 'intermodal' form of audio-visual translation (Gottlieb 1997: 95), as it involves the shift from a spoken to a written medium. Given that 'people generally speak much faster than they read' (O'Connell 1998: 67), this shift has important consequences for viewers' experience of translated audiovisual texts. The empirical observation that, in order to match the temporalities of speaking and reading, subtitles can only accommodate 60 per cent of the source spoken text (de Linde and Kay 1999: 51) explains why they are normally worded as condensed, streamlined versions of the original dialogue (Karamitroglou 1998). These medial restrictions, that were first articulated in the 1930s (Section 2.3), dictate that the number of characters used in each subtitle should be commensurate with the duration of the corresponding speech unit and the reading speed of the target audience (Díaz Cintas and Remael 2007).

As discussed in Sections 2.4 and 4.5.2, the subtitlers' adherence to industry validated standards – notably, the condensation and synthesis of the original spoken dialogue – has been shown to compromise the **interpersonal pragmatics** of subtitled dialogue. For example, audiovisual translators tend to disambiguate instances of conversational ambiguity or indirectness that may have played an important narrative role in the original text (Hatim and Mason 1997, Mason 2001). It has also been suggested that conforming to these constraints often proves detrimental to the dynamics of dramatic characterization envisaged by the creator of the original audiovisual text, particularly in the case of films or TV drama (Remael 2003). As a result, characters' personalities may not be perceived by viewers as the film director had intended. It is therefore not surprising that independent film directors have raised criticisms against the creative limitations derived from these constraints (see Section 2.4). As illustrated in Box 1.2, deconstructing commercial subtitling standards represents an effective strategy for creators to signal their resistance to mainstream subtitling practices.

Box 1.2

As part of his study on 'accented' or diasporic films, Naficy (2004: 145–46) reviews the creative use of subtitles by Vietnamese film director Trinh T. Minh-ha.

Trinh's *Surname Viêt Given Name Nam* uses superimposed titles and subtitles extensively, graphically, and critically. Their large numbers and varied contents and layout give this film a truly calligraphic accent. Throughout, subtitles consisting of the translation of the film's dialogue and voice-over and of Vietnamese poetry and proverbs are displayed, as is customary, in the lower third of the screen. However, on many occasions, what the diegetic women say in Vietnamese or in heavily accented English is superimposed in different layouts, as blocks of English text on various regions of the film frame, including over the characters' faces. These graphic titles, or what Trinh calls 'visualized speech', act as traditional subtitles by aiding spectator comprehension. However, they also serve other graphic, critical, and deconstructive functions ... To these text-based complexities must be added Trinh's filming style that in *Surname Viêt Given Name Nam*, like in her other films, violates many of the norms of cinematic realism as a critique of those norms. For example, in some sequences she places the subjects on the margins of the frame or decentres them by panning away from them. Close-up shots that would normally show the subjects' full-face end up cutting off part of their faces. The film also subverts the accepted practices of lip-synching and title synchronization. Extra long or short duration titles draw attention to themselves and to the spectatorial readerly activities that are involved.

But the capacity to develop new subtitling conventions is not the sole privilege of text producers. Recent changes in the audiovisual landscape, notably the development of digitization techniques and new models of distribution and consumption of audiovisual products, have provided the impetus for the spread of transformational practices. Generally speaking, these new subtitling cultures aim to expose the expressive limitations of mainstream subtitling conventions. Fansubbing, namely the subtitling of television drama and films by networked fan communities, seeks to redress the shortage and cultural insensitivity of commercial translations (Section 3.3). Using a range of daring formal conventions, fansubbers produce and distribute their own subtitled versions through Internet-based channels and, in so doing, provide their fellow fans with a more 'authentic' and meaningful spectatorial experience. Subtitling is also being increasingly appropriated by groups of politically engaged amateurs to undermine the socio-economic structures that sustain global capitalism and/or to effect social and political change (Section 7.3). As is also the case within fansub-bing groups, members of politicized amateur cybercultures engage in complex negotiations of affinity: exploring their collective stance on aesthetic and political issues within their virtual communities brings them closer together.

In a separate development, technology-driven changes are increasing the need for subtitles and, by extension, creating a demand for a more 'efficient' approach to subtitling. This expansion is motivated by a number of reasons. For one thing, media content can now be accessed via a growing range of digital distribution channels, including video-sharing websites and on-demand Internet streaming media platforms. On the other hand, subtitling is now being used to mediate an expanding range of texts and genres. In addition to films and drama, subtitling is gaining popularity as the method of choice for the translation of utilitarian audiovisual texts, including promotional corporate films, videogames or documentaries. The fact that some of these screen-based texts make a relatively formulaic or routinized use of language represents an additional stimulus to automatize the production of subtitles.

Drawing on O'Hagan's (2003) pioneering work, Armstrong et al. (2006) have attempted to gauge the viability of Example-Based Machine Translation (EBMT) to the translation of DVD subtitles and bonus material for English-German and English-Japanese. Essentially, EBMT systems reuse examples of already existing translations, collected in the form of bilingual or parallel corpora, as a basis for the automated production of new translations. By combining real user evaluation studies with automatic metrics, Armstrong et al. concluded that 'the EBMT trained with homogeneous data [i.e. existing DVD subtitles] is likely to contribute to a higher translation quality than with heterogeneous data' (2006: 179). More recently, Volk et al. (2010: 53) have also presented a plausible rationale for the automation of subtitling in the Scandinavian context, where 'large amounts of TV subtitles are needed in Swedish, Danish and Norwegian'. Driven by the insight that subtitles are not always created independently for each language 'for efficiency reasons', the work of Volk et al. appraises the viability of automated subtitles generated by a statistical machine-translation system from Swedish to Danish and Norwegian. As was also the case with its EBMT counterpart, the statistical-machine translation system developed by Volk et al. is 'trained' by using large corpora of high-quality human translated subtitles in the different working languages, and assessed both by automatic metrics and real users.[1]

The production and reception of 3D subtitles is another area of professional practice and scholarly research influenced by technological and industrial advances that is bound to attract considerable attention over the next years. According to Kozoulyaev (n.d.), '3D subtitling calls for tectonic changes in all aspects of production and post-production of stereographic films and TV programmes', insofar as '[i]t requires new plots, new shooting approaches, new conventions and new workflows that will profoundly change the industry'. The basis for Kozoulyaev's claim is that working conventions developed for the delivery of 2D subtitles back in the 1930s are incompatible with the immersive viewing experience that 3D movies are meant to deliver. A straightforward application of 2D conventions may, for example, cause subtitles to collide with objects located within the three-dimensional diegetic space. In order to enhance the spectatorial experience and reduce eye strain, 3D subtitles should be dynamic, i.e. able to follow the main point of interest as it moves around the scene. Decisions pertaining to the depth position of 3D subtitles are equally important; in this environment, the size of subtitles should be scaled and adjusted to the different positions that subtitles occupy within the three-dimensional space at each point of the scene. As '3D subtitles interact with the film (and game) environment in a much stronger fashion than 2D subtitles and become elements of the action and shots themselves', Kozoulyaev (ibid.) argues, 3D subtitling constitutes 'a strong artistic undertaking'.

1.2.2 Revoicing

'Revoicing' is a generic term encompassing a range of spoken translation methods, including simultaneous interpreting, free commentary and narration (see Box 1.3) (Luyken et al. 1991, Baker and Hochel 1998). Although, technically speaking, voice-over and lip-synchronized dubbing are also types of revoicing, they are often dealt with and described separately.

In voiced-over or 'half-dubbed' (Gambier 2003: 173) material, the original and translated soundtracks co-exist and overlap. Typically, only the original voice track is audible at the beginning. A few seconds into the programme, however, the volume of the source dialogue or narration is lowered, while the translated voice track becomes acoustically salient until the end.[2] As the original sound remains vaguely audible throughout, this method of pre-recorded revoicing is widely considered to enhance the realism of voiced-over programmes (Luyken et al. 1991: 140). As a result, in

---

Box 1.3

Simultaneous interpreting is normally a live versioning method used to translate films or documentaries in settings where more elaborate forms of revoicing are not an option, typically due to time or funding constraints (e.g. film festivals). The interpreter, who may occasionally have to perform without accessing the relevant script, normally dubs the voices of the whole film cast (Lecuona Lerchundi 1994).

Free commentary, a revoicing technique performed on the spot by presenters or commentators broadcasting a high profile event, is 'clearly an adaptation [of the original voice track content] for a new audience, with additions, omissions, clarifications and comments' (Gambier 2003: 174). Delivered with a spontaneous tone, free commentary seldom aims to convey a faithful rendering of the original speech.

Narration is a live or pre-recorded form of oral transfer aiming 'to provide a summarized but faithful and carefully scripted rendition of the original speech'. Normally, 'its delivery is timed so that there is no clash with the visual syntax of the programme' (Pérez-González 2009: 16), as defined by the structural organization and the transitions between the constitutive units of the audiovisual text.

---

audiovisual markets dominated by subtitling and dubbing, voice-over is conventionally used for the translation of televised interviews, documentaries and other forms of audiovisual content where lip-synchronization is not of the essence.

Significantly, the fact that voice-over is 'a cheap alternative to dubbing' (O'Connell 2007: 124) explains why it is the audiovisual transfer method of choice for the translation of films in former Communist states and some countries in the Middle East and Asia (e.g. Iran or Thailand). The geographical dispersion of voice-over practices has resulted in a certain degree of variation as to the way in which this audiovisual transfer method is actually executed in each market. In Poland, for example, voice-over narrators or *lektors* 'provide a "whispering" translation, thus allowing the audience to hear the original voices to the greatest extent possible' (Szarkowska 2009: 187). Indeed, convention dictates that Polish (normally male) *lektors* should adopt a self-effacing presentational style and that no attempt should be made to mimic the prosodic and material features of the diegetic speech. By contrast, in Iran, where voice-over was originally used to revoice both Iranian and foreign films, the narrator's acting tends to be contagious and exuberant, as explained by Naficy (2003: 189):

> Since Iranian movies were usually not filmed in sync during production, skillful [sic] and versatile voice-over artists dubbed the actors' voices in postproduction. It can be safely said that approximately two dozen voice actors dubbed the majority of Iranian and foreign films shown in the country. Audiences drew special pleasure from hearing John Wayne and Jerry Lewis use expressions that Iranian tough guys or comedians used. Such intertextuality hybridized the diegeses and the characters who inhabited them. Also, because each voice-over artist often dubbed the voices of a number of different characters, strange cross-over resonances and dissonances would be set up between voices and characters, which could serve to confuse the mirror-phase identification with individual characters.

The wide range of perceptual and technical issues at stake in the production of voiced-over versions, and the varying conventions associated with the execution of this audiovisual transfer technique in different *locales* are explored in depth by Franco *et al.* (2010).

In terms of future research, voice-over scholarship is likely to benefit from parallel developments in the study of audio description, for both transfer methods involve the incorporation of an additional voice track to the multimodal ensemble. As Woźniak (2012: 226) notes,

> certain audio description principles could be applied successfully to voice-over to make it more unobtrusive and to reduce interference with the original soundtrack, while an in-depth analysis of . . . voice-over practices might have a positive impact on the study of audio subtitles and generally on media accessibility.

Ultimately, scholars in both fields are interested in understanding how narrators can best assist viewers in making narrative meaning from the film by themselves.

Once hailed as the supreme and most comprehensive form of translation (Cary 1969: 110), lip-synchronized dubbing involves 'the replacement of the original speech by a voice track which attempts to follow as closely as possible the timing, phrasing, and lip movement of the original dialogue' (Luyken *et al.* 1991: 311). When it was first developed in the 1930s (Section 2.3), the main priority for the film industry was producing target language dialogue that would perfectly fit the actors' lips, in what came to be known as voice 'doubling' and/or 'ghosting' (Ďurovičová 2003). For many years, this practice was surrounded by a certain mystique (Doane 1980). Intriguingly, voice was regarded as a revolving door between the diegetic and real worlds, on the one hand, and between the systems of values inscribed in the source and target cultures, on the other. To some extent, lip-synch dubbing still carries some of these connotations, as illustrated by the confusion surrounding Indonesia's audiovisual translation policies in the late 1990s. In 1996, the Indonesian government announced that 'foreign films on television should no longer be broadcast in their original language version with Indonesian summaries or subtitles but were to be dubbed into Indonesian' (Boellstorff 2003: 235). However, only a few months later, President Soeharto reversed his decision on the grounds that

> [d]ubbing can create gaps in family communication. It can ruin the self-image of family members as a result of adopting foreign values that are 'Indonesianized' [diindonesiakan] . . . This can cause feelings of becoming 'another person' to arise in family members, who are in actuality not foreigners . . . Whenever Indonesians view television, films, or other broadcasts where the original language has been changed into our national language, those Indonesians will think that the performances in those media constitute a part of themselves. As if the culture behind those performances is also the culture of our people.
>
> (Ali 1997:341–42, quoted in Boellstorff ibid.)

Over the last two decades, a number of studies (Herbst 1994: 244–45, Chaume Varela 2004: 155–65, Chaume Varela 2012) have widened the scope of dubbing scholarship beyond the impact of lip synchrony constraints – e.g. the tendency of dubbed language to neutralize markers of sociolinguistic and cultural variation present in the source text (Pavesi 2005). In addition to the industry's demand for equivalence between the original and translated speech, and for matching articulatory movements in the delivery of the source and target dialogue, today's dubbing specialists are urged to be mindful of the film's visual syntax, narrative pace, relevant medial restrictions and, more importantly, the multimodal distribution of meaning across different semiotics. This last aspect is explored in depth by Chaume Varela (2004), who argues that meaning is conveyed to viewers through the acoustic and visual channels along two clusters of semiotic codes. According to this specialist, three different codes or sign systems are realized in the acoustic channel: spoken language (what is said), para-verbal signs (how it is said) and non-verbal acoustic signs (e.g. music, special effects, incidental sound, etc.). For their part, the visual channel is shaped by signs pertaining to the photographic code (e.g. colour, light and perspective), the icono-graphic code (e.g. symbols and icons) and the mobility code – involving the positioning (proxemics) and movements (kinesics) of the film characters. Ultimately, Chaume Varela foregrounds the importance of the non-verbal dimensions of film and illustrates how the matching of non-verbal semi-otics in the original and target texts can make an important contribution to dramatic characterization and/or artistic integrity.

A large proportion of dubbing scholarship has shifted its emphasis away from the relationship of linguistic equivalence between the source and target text, focusing instead on the role and position of the target text as part of a dynamic system (translated fictional speech) of its own. Drawing on corpus-based models of translation (Sections 4.4.2 and 5.3.4), dubbing scholars have tried to gain a better understanding of the typicalities of dubbed speech and identify the defining features of 'authentic' or 'spontaneous sounding' dubbed dialogue (Romero-Fresco 2006, 2009; Pavesi 2009a, 2009b) vis-à-vis non-translated fictional speech. As Pavesi (2009a: 209) explains, these defining features are closely related to the structure of film discourse and 'norms emerging both in simulated spoken [language] and film translation'.

As was also the case with subtitling, advances in digital communication technologies have led to the emergence of amateur dubbing or fandubbing subcultures (see Section 7.1). Beyond this fandom-driven development, experimental work on speech and image synthesis technologies has explored the feasibility of (i) transferring the physical qualities of actors' voices across languages; and (ii) automating the production of audiovisual footage where actors are made to 'mouth' speech they did not actually utter (Box 1.4).

Box 1.4

Voxworks Technologies' ReelVoice system: voice morphing (Bloom 2002)

Voxworks Technologies' system creates . . . sound-alikes, solving a huge headache for those who create foreign-language tracks, have to cover up curse words or otherwise clean up and loop audio.

CEO Elio Zarmati says there's no bigger hassle in dubbing than finding sound-alikes. Normally, a studio must find a sound-alike for each actor to loop fill-in words for a film's TV-safe version. And when creating a foreign-language version, the sound-alike must also be fluent in that language, further narrowing the range of options. With Voxworks' ReelVoice, though, the voice-over talent need only be fluent in the translated language, and able to provide the actor's timing that distinguishes any talented performer. The technology takes care of the rest, 'morphing' the voice-over to sound like any or all of the original performers.

[. . .]

To work, the technology builds a library of phonemes, the little bits of words spoken in a performer's distinctive way, for both the star voice being morphed and for the voice-over actor. The technology then maps those two libraries of phonemes to each other.

Video Rewrite: visual morphing[3]

Video Rewrite uses existing footage to create automatically a new video of a person mouthing words that she did not speak in the original footage. This tech-nique is useful in movie dubbing, for example, where the movie sequence can be modified to sync the actors' lip motions to the new soundtrack.

Video Rewrite automatically labels the phonemes in the training data [i.e. previous recordings of actors uttering certain sounds] and in the new audio track [and] reorders the mouth images in the training footage to match the phoneme sequence of the new audio track. When particular phonemes are unavailable in the training footage, Video Rewrite selects the closest approximations. The resulting sequence of mouth images is stitched into the background footage. This stitching process automatically corrects for differences in head position and orientation between the mouth images and the background footage. . . . The new video combines the dynamics of the original actor's articulations with the mannerisms and setting dictated by the background footage.

1.2.3 Assistive forms of audiovisual translation

Over the last two decades, audiovisual translation has contributed to enhancing the social integration of minorities all over the world. Freely available subtitled programmes, for instance, have long helped immigrants to develop their proficiency in the language spoken by their host communi-ties. But the role of audiovisual translation as an empowerment tool has become particularly evident with the emergence and consolidation of relatively new forms of intersemiotic assistive mediation, such as subtitling for the hard of hearing or audio description, that aim to facilitate access to information and entertainment for sensory impaired members of the community. Capitalizing on the storage capacity of DVDs and Blu-ray discs, media companies are able to release audiovisual products aimed at mainstream viewers, while simultaneously allowing sensory impaired audiences to access the media content in assistive mode – i.e. viewing the film in combination with dedicated audio or video tracks. Similarly, on-demand Internet streaming media platforms and most TV sets also provide viewers with access to subtitles and audio narrations.

Subtitling for the hard of hearing provides a text display of the characters' speech interspersed with written descriptions of sound features from the diegetic action that would otherwise not be accessible to Deaf viewers. This transfer of information from speech to written subtitles involves the deployment of dedicated mediation conventions in relation to the colour, spotting and positioning of the subtitles (Neves 2005). Subtitles for the hard of hearing were originally available only for films and pre-recorded broadcasts. However, the enactment of a growing number of legislative and regulatory provisions since 1980 (Remael 2007) has set minimum quota requirements for the provision of live subtitling by broadcasters and subtitling companies. Against this backdrop, the audiovisual industry has spearheaded the development of live subtitling practices.

Real-time subtitling for the deaf and hard of hearing, often known as respeaking, is

> a technique in which a respeaker listens to the original sound of a live programme or event and respeaks it, including punctuation marks and some specific features for the deaf and hard of hearing audience, to a speech recognition software, which turns the recognized utterances into subtitles displayed on the screen with the shortest possible delay.
>
> (Romero-Fresco 2011: 1)

In addition to refining the workflow processes and the technological tools that shape and facilitate the respeaking process, a growing body of research is seeking to gain a better understanding of respeaking-specific translation techniques, e.g. the respeakers' reduction and omission of the original text (van Waes et al. 2013).

Audio description, a spoken account of those visual aspects of a film that play a role in conveying its plot, has become equally important in ensuring the accessibility of audiovisual products to the visually impaired. While transferring information from the visual to the acoustic channel – i.e. from images to the spoken narration that a voice delivers between the stretches of spoken dialogue – the audio describer 'engages in a delicate balancing exercise to establish what the needs of the spectator may be, and to ensure the audience is not overburdened with excessive information' (Pérez-González 2009: 16). Ongoing work on audio description has significantly widened the range of theoretical and methodological frameworks informing translation studies research; its originality and rigour are thus foregrounded in Sections 4.3.2 and 5.2.

1.3 AUDIOVISUAL TRANSLATION AS AN ACADEMIC DISCIPLINE

The **institutionalization** and **academization** of audiovisual translation,[4] two intertwined processes whose outcome is still uncertain and contested, have been arrested at different points by the dynamic nature of its object of study. The varying conceptualization of audiovisual texts in the literature is a good example of the obstacles found along the way:

- Consider the case of pioneering literature on audiovisual translation (Caillé 1960, Cary 1969), which predates the constitution of translation studies as a discipline in its own right. This body of literature was written at a time when films, the only consolidated form of mass entertainment, were presented as objects of artistic contemplation rather than simple cultural commodities. Audiovisual translation was thus conceptualized as an aesthetic form of mediation subject to a range of extra-linguistic constraints pertaining to the medium in which films are embedded.
- The consideration of audiovisual texts as hybrid textualities, influenced by both linguistic and extra-linguistic factors, is consistent with their treatment elsewhere – e.g. in early attempts to classify texts and formalize their functional characteristics as well as the translation methods typically associated with each text type. This is the case with the 'Audio-mediale Texte' category in Reiss' (1971/2000) taxonomy, although 'her definition seemed to refer more to fields such as advertising rather than film and documentary translation' (Munday 2012: 268).
- As recently as the late 1980s and early 1990s, new efforts to chart the map of translation studies (Snell-Hornby 1988/1995, Bassnett 1980/1991) placed audiovisual texts in the orbit of literary translation. Bassnett, for example, argued that the fourth category of her taxonomy, 'loosely called Translation and Poetics, includes the whole area of

literary translation, in theory and practice. Studies may be general or genre-specific, including investigation of particular problems of translating poetry, theatre texts or *libretti* and the affiliated problem of translation for the cinema, whether dubbing or sub-titling' (1980/1991: 8).

- Over the last fifteen years, the role of digital technologies as a catalyst for the emergence of innovative audiovisual textualities has attracted the attention of scholars focusing on the technological, industrial and pedagogical dimensions of audiovisual translation – as illustrated by the work of scholars working on the technologization of subtitling and dubbing that I have referred to in Section 1.2. It would be safe to argue that audiovisual translation has gained formal academic recognition with the inclusion of this field of professional practice and scholarly inquiry in translator training curricula in the mid-1990s. Through the institutionalization of audiovisual translation, scholars in the field have been able to access vital material resources, strengthen the field's research base and secure academic recognition.

Only fast changing landscapes such as the one presented in this section can accommodate strongly divergent opinions on such fundamental issues as the disciplinary status of a given scholarly field. Díaz Cintas' (2009: 7) assertion that audiovisual translation has 'now developed its very own theoretical and methodological approaches, allowing it to claim the status of a scholarly area of research in its own right', for example, was published only twenty years after Delabastita's description of the field as a 'virgin area of research' (1989: 202). Over the following seven chapters, I will try to shed some light on this and other key debates and discourses about audiovisual translation. I will show how, as audiovisual texts continue to proliferate and evolve, specialists have adapted existing theoretical models and developed new conceptual networks to drive the collection and description of their data sets. Similarly, I will present the reader with a range of methodological tools that audiovisual translation scholars have relied on to help the field remain abreast of its own needs. I will even attempt to draw readers' attention to specific areas of research that, I will argue, are bound to shape the future of audiovisual translation scholarship. The ground covered here is varied and diverse, as befits a volume that aims to provide a snapshot of an entire (sub?) discipline. The best place to begin is to ask why audiovisual translation is done the way we have been doing it since it was first engineered.

FOLLOW-UP QUESTIONS FOR DISCUSSION

- What terms are used to designate the field of audiovisual translation in the languages that you work with? Are any of these terms a literal translation of 'audiovisual translation'? Compare the set of terms you have collected with the terms outlined in Section 1.1. Can you find correspondences in your working languages for each of the English terms? If not, what do you think might be the reason for those differences? Do the terms that you have found in your working languages foreground the types of text that fall within the remit of audiovisual translation? Alternatively, do they signal the medial constraints that apply in the production and reception of audiovisual texts?

- How dominant/important is each of the modalities of audiovisual translation surveyed in this chapter in the media marketplaces that you have knowledge of? Are there relatively stable associations between audiovisual text types and audiovisual translation modalities? To what extent have assistive forms of audiovisual translation penetrated the audiovisual markets that you are familiar with? What is the regulatory framework in place regarding the need to meet minimum quotas in the provision of subtitles for the hard of hearing and audio described narrations? Are these assistive modalities confined to the public sector, or have they been embraced by private broadcasters, cinemas and translation services providers?

- How institutionalized is audiovisual translation in your country of residence and any other country you may know enough about? Are audiovisual translation course units available at undergraduate and/or postgraduate level? Are they mandatory or optative? What is their credit load vis-à-vis those of other specialized translation modules? Are there any specialized postgraduate programmes, both MA and PhD courses, available in those contexts? What is their disciplinary affiliation? Are they run by modern languages schools, translation schools or media studies schools, to give some examples?

- Are you familiar with audiovisual translation literature in languages other than English? Is the conceptualization of audiovisual texts in those academic traditions consistent with the changing scenario outlined in Section 1.3? If practicable, consult Gambier's (2008) overview of the main milestones and stages in the academization of audiovisual translation in Europe. Could you develop his account further, perhaps adding to the list of major conferences in the field? How would you rate the social recognition of audiovisual translation in the countries you live or have lived in? Are you acquainted with any professional association of audiovisual translators?

- Section 1.2 has referred to the growing popularity of amateur audiovisual translation subcultures such as fansubbing and fandubbing. Are you familiar with these developments? Have you come across any sample of fansubbing or fandubbing practices? What is, in principle, your stance on the existence of these communities and their impact on audiovisual marketplaces? What are the pros and cons of their intervention in the media landscape? Keep a record of your thoughts and consult it again once you have read Chapters 3 and 7. Has your opinion changed significantly?

NOTES

1   Volk *et al.* (2010) also deliver a useful overview of ongoing work on the production of semi-automated subtitles.
2   A detailed account of alternative voice-over practices is provided by Espasa (2004).
3   See http://mrl.nyu.edu/~bregler/videorewrite/ (last accessed 15 September 2013).
4   For a detailed chronology of the main milestones in the academization and institutionalization of audiovisual translation, see Gambier (2008).

CORE REFERENCES

Díaz Cintas, Jorge and Aline Remael (2007) *Audiovisual Translation: Subtitling*, Manchester: St Jerome.

Chaume Varela, Frederic (2012) *Audiovisual Translation: Dubbing*, Manchester: St Jerome.

Franco, Eliana, Anna Matamala and Pilar Orero (2010) *Voice-over Translation: An Overview*, Bern: Peter Lang.

Pérez-González, Luis (2009) 'Audiovisual Translation', in Mona Baker and Gabriela Saldanha (eds) *The Routledge Encyclopedia of Translation Studies*, 2nd edition, London and New York: Routledge, 13–20.

Romero-Fresco, Pablo (2011) *Subtitling Through Speech Recognition: Respeaking*, Manchester: St Jerome.

2

AUDIOVISUAL TRANSLATION AS A SITE OF REPRESENTATIONAL PRACTICE

Film art is the only art the development of which men now living have witnessed from the very beginnings; and this development is all the more interesting as it took place under conditions contrary to precedent. It was not an artistic urge that gave rise to the discovery and gradual perfection of the new technique; it was a technical invention that gave rise to the discovery and gradual perfection of a new art.

(Panofsky 1934/1999: 279)

It seems to me at the heart of the US policy of technological transfer and development aid for the Third World since the 1950s, was this notion of homogenization and synchronicity of the world within Western consumerist ideology. This is a shift from the earlier policy of diachronicity, promoted by colonists, which tended to keep the developed and the underdeveloped worlds apart. The emerging form of post-industrial capitalism sought synchronicity in the interest of creating global markets.

(Naficy 2003: 193)

In this chapter

This chapter begins by looking at the geography and sociology of the film industry at the beginning of the twentieth century. Amid the unprecedented degree of social penetration that films soon achieved, audiovisual translation became instrumental to the expansion of the film industry. On the one hand, it allowed for creative experimentation based on increasingly complex narratives; on the other hand, it paved the way for the international distribution of films. Given this intertwinement of artistic and economic interests, the development of audiovisual translation was closely monitored by the Hollywood industry. American studios imposed narrative patterns based on '**suture**' editing techniques – hiding the artifices of cinematic creation from the viewers. Over the first half of the twentieth century, totalitarian political regimes across Europe were quick to capitalize on the affordances of suture editing, favouring those modalities of audiovisual translation that allowed for a tighter control of the way in which foreign values were presented to local audiences. By contrast, it was market dynamics – based on variables such as the size of national markets or the costs associated with each form of audiovisual translation – that shaped the distribution of different modalities of audiovisual translation across more democratic countries. Whether for artistic, economic or political reasons, commissioners of audiovisual translation managed to impose homogenizing mediation strategies and monopolize the technology required to create new language versions of audiovisual products, as part of what I describe as the traditional or **representational approach** to audiovisual translation. Following developments in the media landscape, by the 1960s audiovisual translation had become a linchpin of the television industry and the **linear model of consumption and distribution** underpinning it. The one-to-one correspondence between specific audiovisual genres and the modalities chosen for their translation in different countries – a distinctive feature of such linear dynamics – would remain in place until the early 1990s.

▶ WATCH THE INTRODUCTION VIDEO

2.1 REPRESENTATIONAL PRACTICES IN AUDIOVISUAL TRANSLATION: CHOICES vs CONVENTIONS

Sergio Leone's *Spaghetti Westerns* have long been a guilty pleasure for film buffs all over the world. By subverting the stylistic and narrative conventions of the genre, Leone managed to leave a personal imprint on his films that did not go unnoticed by western fans. The alternation between extreme close-ups and wide-angled shots; the use of stylized acting, often interspersed with slow-motion effects to create a perception of expanded time; and the dominance of music over spoken dialogue within the overall conglomerate of film semiotics are some of the most recognizable features of Leone's 'visual style' (Cumbow 1985). But while acknowledging Leone's influence on later films and the Italian director's capacity to appropriate the ultimate American cultural idiom (Cumbow ibid.), film critics and genre purists have levelled trenchant criticisms at the artistic excesses of his anti-classicist style. Among these, it is Leone's idiosyncratic use of sound and dubbing that I intend to concentrate on in the coming paragraphs.

Leone's films belong to that rare breed of films shot in a foreign language and later dubbed into English for the enjoyment of mainstream American audiences. In his westerns, all dialogue was routinely re-recorded during the post-production stage for a number of reasons. For instance, the limited affordances of the cinematographic technology available in the 1960s significantly hampered Leone's attempts to imprint his own authorial style onto his films. The difficulties he encountered in trying to control the pickup of extraneous noise while filming wide shots prevented the Italian director from using synchronized sound to shoot a large number of scenes – which thus had to be dubbed during post-production (Agnew 2012). On a different note, Leone's films often involved multilingual casts, with actors performing and addressing each other in their respective languages (Kawin 1992). The implications of this multilingual set-up for the dubbing process have been discussed by American dialogue coach and screenplay translator Mickey Knox, who supervised the dubbing of a number of Leone's films (Barnes 2013).[1] As Knox explains, the process typically began with the production of a 'lip-synch script', i.e. the writing of English dialogue for what was, effectively, an existing multilingual film. Not only had the lip-synch script to 'fit the [actors'] lips': it also had to 'move the story along' (ibid.).

Notoriously, dubbed dialogue in Leone's films is poorly synchronized. This 'mismatch between sonic elements and the images over which they were artificially dubbed' has been widely presented as a major reason for the derision with which many an Anglo-American reviewer has treated Leone's films (Edmonstone 2008: 26). However, the critical unease surrounding Leone's commercial success in America suggests that the debate about the quality of dubbing in his films does not revolve exclusively around cosmetic considerations. According to Whitakker (2012: 294), there are reasons why films featuring post-synchronized sound may be potentially perceived as subversive by the American film industry, which has tradition- ally opted for 'directly recorded sound':

That the voice should be central to the coherence of Hollywood film is not surprising, given that it is one of the indices of the very individuality of the star. This was largely reinforced through the ideology of the Hollywood style of filmmaking, which through goal-oriented narratives, the development of the close-up and strong structures of narcissistic identification and moral allegiance, sought to articulate the American Dream of meritocratic individualism. In contrast, the voice in the post-synch film is no longer a private and personalised index of the body. Located from beyond the diegesis, both its provenance and presence create an ambiguity within the image.

Seen in the light of this logic, Leone's films appear to challenge Hollywood's steadfast adherence to **synchronous diegetic sound** – which Heath describes as 'a contract of thought [and] the expression of a homogeneous thinking subject' (1981: 191). As the argument goes, during the formative years of sound film, synchronization became a means to construct characters with an unambiguous voice, and hence to articulate a national identity based on individualism and meritocracy. But the implications of Hollywood's reliance on synchrony transcend the bounds of character construction. For example, synchronous sound has driven the technical and artistic evolution of film, transforming movies into commodities where the 'mise en scène, editing, sound and cinematography all function to advance the narrative and to create compositional unity so that the narrative represents a "cause-effect chain"' (Forbes and Street 2000: 37). Likewise, one should not overlook the financial implications of adopting synchronized sound and narrative transparency as fundamental means of cinematographic expression. Indeed, the universalist values inscribed in these 'transparent, easy to read, goal-oriented' narratives (ibid.) have facilitated the commercial penetration of foreign film markets by the American industry.

It is against this backdrop that poorly post-synched dubbing, as found in Leone's *Spaghetti Westerns* may be perceived to undermine the ideological, artistic and economic fabric of the US classical film. Ultimately, his disregard for accurate synchronization can be interpreted as a creative choice, an attempt to resist default conventions. The question then arises as to how, and at what point, synchronous diegetic sound became enmeshed with the cinematographic expression of a given set of values, the circulation of selected narratives and the promotion of certain industrial models. Even more relevant to the concerns of this volume is the question of how, and at what point, audiovisual translation practices became associated with the **commodification** of films. Indeed, to what extent did audiovisual translation conventions facilitate the emergence and consolidation of the forms of film production and consumption that have dominated the media marketplace until the advent of the digital culture?

The prominence given to film translation, vis-à-vis other forms of audiovisual translation, in this chapter is not accidental, for the connections between the media industry and translation were forged early in the twentieth century − at a time when motion pictures were evolving into the dominant form of mass entertainment. Likewise, my decision to focus this chapter almost exclusively on the developments that took place first in the American film industry is probably both justifying at this point. As is well-known, Hollywood consistently provided the main impetus for most of the artistic, technological and socio-economic innovations that surrounded the evolution of cinema during the twentieth century. Admittedly, most of the practices that originated in the American media marketplace have been inspired, adopted, refined or resisted by the work of filmmakers associated with other geographical contexts and filmic traditions, so my choice of focus should not lead readers to infer that I see the contribution of non-American models as being of lesser importance. Given the space constraints to which this chapter is subject, organizing my overview around the film industry with which most readers are bound to be familiar seemed a reasonable and effective way to proceed.

This chapter conceptualizes audiovisual translation, as executed by professionals since the birth of cinema, as a **site of representational practice**. It explores how the complex interweaving of ideological, artistic and economic factors played out during the formative years of film making and, by extension, of audiovisual translation. In so doing, it critically examines how dominant audiovisual cultures have attempted to 'construct' selected aspects of reality − including ethnic-, nation-, class- and gender-based identities − through the medium of film, and the extent to which these representations have been propagated by homogenizing audiovisual translation practices favoured by the industry. It should be noted that this retrospective account of the emergence and generalization of certain representational conventions in and through cinema, including those pertaining to the translation of film, is not meant to deliver a comprehensive or systematic overview of the history of film. The key milestones in the history of audiovisual translation have been extensively reviewed elsewhere (Izard Martínez 1992, Ballester

1995, Chaves García 2000, Nornes 2007) and are therefore not covered here.

2.2 SILENT FILMS: FROM 'PRESENTATIONALISM' TO 'DIEGESIS'

Nowhere is the impact of representational practices more readily observable than in silent films. In the absence of spoken dialogue, filmmakers had to rely primarily on visual semiotics to construct an experience of artistic expression for the benefit of their audience. These representational limitations of early cinema have been succinctly articulated by Nornes (2007: 89–90) as follows:

> This [early cinema] was a silent medium. Stories were told through visual means. The actor's only resource was his or her body. Acting was pantomimed by default. Where language entered in, it was to be found in codified gestures. As for the resources of cinema, the emphasis was on clarifying visual access to that body though the developing 'language' of narrative space . . . Directors, cinematographers, set and lighting designers, all conformed their work to these attitudes about cinema, rendering the expressivity of the actors' bodies as legibly as possible.

The stylization of gestures in silent cinema is widely regarded as 'a form of compensation' for the lack of speech (Doane 1980: 33), which 'had to be made dispensable by establishing an organic relation between the acting and the technical procedure of cinephotography' (Panofsky 1934/1999: 287). Effectively, this meant that, during the early history of film making, the means of production had to be subordinated to the means of representation. In other words, the affordances of the filming technology available at the time had to be strategically harnessed and used to accentuate and bring into sharp relief the actors' highly conventionalized gestures. Through this display of forcefully expressed emotions and the exploitation of visual semiotics (see Box 2.1), filmmakers were able to 'translate' the actors' feelings and subjective experiences into visual representations that viewers could disambiguate and interpret.

Box 2.1

The relevance of visual representation to early film characterization (Panofsky 1934/1999: 286, my emphasis):

> A less obtrusive method of explanation [of characters' roles in the film] was the introduction of a fixed iconography which from the outset informed the spectator about the basic facts and characters ... There arose, identifiable by standardized appearance, behavior, and attributes, the well-remembered types of the Vamp and the Straight Girl (perhaps the most convincing modern equivalents of the medieval personifications of the Vices and Virtues), the Family Man, and the Villain, the latter marked by a black mustache and walking stick. Nocturnal scenes were printed on blue or green film. A checkered tablecloth meant, once for all, a 'poor but honest' milieu; a happy marriage, soon to be endangered by the shadows from the past, was symbolized by the young wife's pouring the breakfast coffee for her husband; the first kiss was invariably announced by the lady's gently playing with her partner's necktie and was invariably accompanied by her kicking out with her left foot. **The conduct of the characters was predetermined accordingly**. The poor but honest laborer who, after leaving his little house with the checkered tablecloth, came upon an abandoned baby could not take it to his home and bring it up as best as he could; the Family Man could not but yield, however temporarily, to the temptations of the Vamp. As a result these early melodramas had a highly gratifying and soothing quality in that **events took shape, without the complications of individual psychology, according to a pure Aristotelian logic so badly missed in real life**.

But conventionalized expressions of subjectivism were not the only representational resources underpinning silent films. Early productions favoured '**presentationalism**' (Musser 1991) as the dominant mode of representation. Under presentationalism, artistic representations were constructed as 'diagrammatic' abstractions of the real world (ibid.) in at least three different ways:

- Early films drew, at least partly, on narratives that audiences were assumed to be familiar with. Although filmmakers only sketched out selected aspects of a story in the form of images, audiences still managed to derive a comprehensive spectatorial experience by viewing the film in relation to the narrative they already knew (ibid.).
- In silent cinema, film sets 'suggested locale' (ibid.: 8), rather than anchoring the story in a specific spatio-temporal setting. Although these conceptual and abstract representations of time and space undermined

the verisimilitude of the scenes, they facilitated the viewers' engagement with the incomplete or schematic narratives promoted by
presentationalism, as outlined in the previous bullet point.

- Silent films consisted of scenes built around 'tableau-like, static compo-
sitions' (ibid.) that were normally played through in their entirety
within the duration of the actual film. Rather than creating the illusion
of a real world, early productions distilled a whole narrative into a
limited number of carefully composed, stage-like scenes for the
purposes of 'monstration' or 'showing' (Testa 2002).

For all the simplicity of the representational practices used in silent movies,
where cinematic expression was modelled after other art forms such as
painting or theatre (Ellis 1995), large sections of the audience found it
sometimes difficult to understand speechless films (Panofsky 1934/1999).
The first attempts to facilitate and shape the audience's reception of motion
pictures – and hence, to 'translate' the artistic experience intended by the
film creator into preferred emotional responses on the part of the viewers
– involved the use of spoken language in the vicinity of the screen. Exhibitors
actively intervened in the mediation of cinematic representations by
arranging for the delivery of screen-side lectures (Musser 1991: 8). In-house
commentators, also referred to in the literature as 'explainers' (Panofsky
1934/1999) or 'lecturers' (Nornes 2007), were employed to enhance the
viewer's spectatorial experience in a variety of ways (Dreyer-Sfard 1965),
from giving 'explanations of the projection process (the workings of the
projector) to sharing gossip about the actors' or 'providing historical
background' (Cazdyn 2004: 408). Although the capacity of these explainers
to attract more viewers compensated for the costs incurred in employing
skilled lecturers, the long-term viability of live film narrations was compro-
mised by the exhibitors' difficulties in accessing film plot synopses, the
dearth of 'professional' lecturers, the rapid turnover of films and, more
generally, the fact that a significant number of films were, after all, fairly
intelligible without the complementary narration. Although it remained a
standard practice in Asia until the advent of the sound film, Europe and the
United States dropped the live narration of films during the second decade
of the twentieth century (Nornes 2007).

In America, the final decade of the nineteenth century saw the rise of
'talking pictures' as an extension of live narrations. What the term 'talking
pictures' denoted during the first decade of the twentieth century was very

different from what it would refer to after the advent of film sound (see Section 2.3). Essentially, companies specializing in providing film exhibitors with musicians and singers to entertain audiences before, during and after film projections began assembling groups of actors to stand off-stage delivering spoken dialogue to match, to some extent, the visual action. Musser's (1991: 400–401) overview of talking film reviews published before they reached the peak of their success around 1910 suggests that audiences felt these added dialogues made the stories more intelligible and added a significant degree of verisimilitude to filmic representations. Of particular relevance to this chapter is the extent to which 'talking pictures' increased the reliance of film on the spoken word, as distributors were forced to produce dialogues to be performed behind the screen (see Box 2.2). Broadly speaking, the decline of 'talking pictures' as a box-office attraction was due to the same reasons that led to the demise of live film narration. The crisis of 'talking pictures', however, was precipitated by other more-specific causes, including the varying quality of the dialogue written for screen characters by each producer, and the failure of back-screen dialogue to be universally adopted by all distributors. Effectively, this meant that film creators could not take for granted that spoken dialogue would be available as an additional representational resource during the projection of their films.

Box 2.2

Producer Will H. Stevens (Humanovo Producing Company) speaking on the training and management of 'speaking actors' in a 1908 interview quoted by Musser (1991: 399, my emphasis):

> 'I have to scratch through a great many films', said he, 'to find those that will stand interpretation by speaking actors behind the curtains. We now have twenty-two Humanovo troupes on the road, each consisting of three people. Each company stays at a theatre one week and then moves on to the next stand, traveling like a vaudeville act and producing the same reel of pictures all the time. They travel in wheels, so that a theatre has a change of pictures and company each week. It requires about four days to rehearse a company. First I select a suitable picture; then **I write a play for it, putting appropriate speeches in the mouths of the characters**. I write off the parts, just as is done in regular plays, and rehearse the people carefully, introducing all possible effects and **requiring the actors to move about the stage exactly as is represented in the films, so as to have the voiced properly located to carry out the illusion**'.

Towards 1910, filmmakers were torn between viewers' growing demand for heightened realism in cinema and the range of representational limitations surrounding the processes of film production and distribution. Experimental practices involving the use of speech as a supplementary expressive resource, e.g. live narration and back-stage dialogue, had enjoyed a warm reception by audiences. However, the novelty effect derived from the joint deployment of visuals and live narration/performance was not creatively and financially sustainable. The transformation of cinema into a form of mass entertainment placed considerations of creative and economic viability firmly at the centre of debates within the industry. Against this backdrop, producers set out to shape cinema as a site of representation that would allow audiences to understand the story without necessarily being familiar with the song, theatre play or news story the film may be more or less loosely based on; and without requiring any active *ad hoc* intervention on the part of exhibitors in the process of distribution, beyond the mere projection of the film.

According to Testa (2002), the transformation of cinema into a form of mass entertainment brought about the shift from earlier 'single image' or 'mimetic' motion pictures towards 'multi image' or **'diegetic' films**. During the era of presentationalism, films had been conceived primarily as pictorial representations: even when the film consisted of several scenes, these tended to be shot as discrete units. Unsurprisingly, the use of these static representational blocks became increasingly problematic. As filmic events unfolded in real time, 'overlapping action was frequent, temporal repetition common, and the narrative loosely constructed' (Musser 1991: 404). It was the development of editing techniques that allowed filmmakers to concentrate on plot and performance, over images and actions (Ellis 1995).

From a representational perspective, the shift from mimetic to diegetic films, and hence the construction of more efficient and complex film narratives, was facilitated by:

- The adoption of a rigorous linear temporal structure. This was achieved by enforcing a 'consistent forward movement of time' and the elimination of 'retrogressive elements' that could bring the action back to an earlier point of the narrative (Musser 1991: 404). On a related note, filmmakers began to contract temporality, i.e. they advanced the clock when presenting action that occurred off screen.

- The use of parallel editing, which allowed film creators to cut back and forth between two contemporaneous lines of action and provided further opportunities to move time forward.
- The popularization of the 'matching action' technique, whereby the director would cut from one shot to another that showed roughly the same action. The matching action technique allowed creators to smooth over the discontinuity of the editing process and create an illusion of logical coherence across individual shots. As Musser (1991: 405–6) puts it, '[a]ction now moved across shots, not within them'.

The diffusion and implementation of this rudimentary continuity style boosted the commercial dimension of film making. The editorial choices facilitated by the new representation of temporality made it possible to create films of standard length that could fit easily within the standardized schedules used in most cinemas. More importantly, continuity also led to 'the installation of the formal processes of **diegesis** as a dominant construct' in film (Testa 2002). Characters were, for the first time, presented as inhabiting a world of their own created by the story, different from the narrative space occupied by viewers. Through editing, 'telling or diegesis . . . become the controlling mode of film while [the earlier modes of] showing or mimesis becomes the servant of diegetic narration' (ibid.).

From a representational perspective, the logic of film editing, with its capacity to summarize, elide, abridge, or figurativize the action, has been compared with the building of a language (ibid.). Diegetic films did not just show what happened to the characters. Instead, through a series of editorial choices, the director could choose how to *tell* viewers what went on in the diegetic world. Indeed, events could be accentuated or glossed over, accelerated or presented in painstaking detail. Unsurprisingly, the shift from mimetic to diegetic films provoked mixed reactions. While the more complex narratives significantly enhanced the realism of the films, audiences found it much more difficult to understand the picture (Musser 1991: 403).

After a number of experiments involving the incorporation of dynamic text into the fabric of a film (see Box 2.3), directors began using on-screen texts or intertitles for the purposes of viewer orientation. Inserted between film shots, these texts 'commented on the action, attested to the accuracy of a setting, identified location, imparted information, explained difficult terms or abstract concepts (such as the passage of time), played on the

Box 2.3

Testa (2002) discusses Edwin Porter's pioneering use of dynamic intertitles in two films:

> The first film is *The Whole Dam Family and the Dam Dog* . . . Porter's film consists, first, of a series of close-ups of each of the Dam family, performed by actors' pulling faces. An accompanying caption appears at the bottom of the frame of each shot. The names play on 'Dam' – the daughter is 'Miss U.B. Dam' for example – that is, they play on the mild English-language profanity . . . One aspect of the film was a novelty: animated titles, which were called 'jumble announcements' and that Charles Musser describes as 'a hodgepodge of letters moved against their black backgrounds until they formed intertitles for the succeeding scene'. The Dam Family was successful and a fad for 'jumble announcements' continued for a while after this.
>
> In 1907, two years later, Porter directed *College Chums* that uses animated texts inside the frame space. Notable is the passage in which a young woman and man argue over the phone (about his 'other woman'): the two figures are seen in the sky over the town each in cameo and on the phone. Their words, animated in an undulating line, pass across the dark sky from one side to the other. When the conversation heats up, the words are seen to collide midair.[2] The more familiar uses of in-screen text of this kind occur in cartoons, both print-medium comics and film animations, notably in the case of *Felix the Cat*. It would seem that Porter was incorporating animation uses into his film.
>
> There are several ways these films might be discussed but I would like to isolate just two for brief comment. [In] *The Dam Family* . . . the portrait close-ups with captions extend the film using texts, identifying the figures (and punning on their names), and the jumbled announcements animate language. Both usages express a desire to incorporate text into the fabric of the film. This tendency deepens in *College Chums*, but here in an odder and more intense way, by making dialogue texts part of the image, as if it could be of the same substance as the analogue-picture. The uses in both cases became important selling points when the films were marketed. But the devices did not achieve extended application.

viewers' emotions, and expressed the characters' feelings or thoughts' (Dick 1990: 14–17).

For a number of years, directors who took the view that cinema was incompatible with the use of language – given the material differences that exist between images and written text – used intertitles sparingly.[3] But film reviewers soon began to call for the use of more frequent and informative intertitles to make the films intelligible (Musser 1991). By 1908, audiences had come to perceive the relationship between images and their linguistic supplement as one of representational unity. As Testa (2002) notes, '[i]nter-title language texts were almost now a compositional accomplishment, a convention that almost could be taken for granted'. The commercial implications of the popularization of intertitles were equally significant. For the first time, the film industry had managed to develop a set of representational conventions that placed control over the reception of the text firmly in the hands of creators and producers, rather than exhibitors. The standardization of intertitles ultimately 'allowed for a uniformity of information that was central to an industry based on mass production and consumption' (Musser 1991: 402).

During the following two decades, representational practices in film remained to some extent unchanged. Admittedly, 'refinements of visual expression in German films from 1919 to 1925 made possible a new intensity and unity of mood, emotion, and characterization' (Ellis 1995: 117). Likewise, during the late 1920s, the 'Soviets further explored the dynamic shot-to-shot relationship . . . and developed a systematic theory of editing which allowed an unprecedented eloquence and complexity of idea, feeling, and kinetic rhythm' (ibid.). Despite the increasing representational sophistication derived from the evolution of early editing techniques into complex *montage* conventions, the compositional unity of visual diegesis and accompanying snippets of written text remained as the cornerstone of film semiotics. Of particular relevance to this chapter is that these two sets of presentational resources continued to lack synchrony at two different levels. First, intertitles were inserted between, rather than superimposed on, images. As a result, they effectively separated the characters' speech from the visual representations of their bodies (Doane 1980). More widely, as explained earlier, the role of intertitles was not confined to 'translating' diegetic speech for the benefit of the audience. In many cases, intertitles served to contextualize, interpret or elaborate on certain aspects of the visual action.

It was not until the mid-1920s that the industry would witness the next major shake-up of filmic representational practices, involving the incorporation of sound tracks to silent features. Although the studios owning patented sound systems tried to make the most of this opportunity to incorporate sound special effects and musical underscores, large sections of the industry resisted this artistic and economic development for a number of reasons. The following objection, articulated by Ellis (1995: 119) is particularly relevant to the remit of this volume:

if the movies ever began to talk (a prospect vaguely foreseen), the long-term contracts with silent stars, foreign stars, and directors might prove frozen assets if those individuals couldn't adapt themselves to the altered medium or to the English language . . . If the marvellous esperanto of the silent film were sacrificed, audiences abroad would be curtailed: Whereas titles could easily and inexpensively be translated and re-shot, what could the Hungarians, for example, make out of conversations in English?

Amid this climate of debate, the commercial success of Alan Crosland's *The Jazz Singer* (1927), widely attributed to its 309 words of spoken dialogue, would soon force creators, producers and exhibitors to confront their worst fears.

2.3 TALKING FILMS: REPRESENTATIONAL IMPLICATIONS OF SYNCHRONIZED SOUND

The advent of sound had a significant impact on the semiotic fabric of the new 'talking pictures' or 'talkies'. Among other adjustments, filmmakers soon began to rein in the artistic expressiveness that they had managed to articulate through the *montage* of visual representational resources. Given the centrality of sound as a source of curiosity, the fact that the equipment available to record speech was stationary meant that the speaker, the hearer or both had to feature prominently in the shots. As Jacobs (1968: 435) notes,

the public, fascinated by the novelty, wanting to be sure they were hearing what they saw, would have felt that a trick was being played on them if they were not shown the words coming from the lips of the actors.

Consequently, the filmmaker was unable to vary the standard medium shot required to ensure that the microphone remained within adequate distance of the soundproof booth where the camera was located. Frustrated by these spatial restrictions, European directors soon expressed their fear 'that with sound, moviemakers would regress, forsaking the montage techniques peculiar to moviemaking for the anachronistic panning effects of filmed theater' (de Grazia 1989: 70). But talking pictures also imposed temporal restrictions on film creators. The fact that '[w]ords require natural time in which to be spoken, and they communicate much less in that amount of time than could images' (Ellis 1995: 123) often slowed down the pace of early talkies considerably. Likewise, the visual composition and the movement of the images in the film 'had to be related to the movement of sound – whether music, dialogue, or incidental noises' (ibid.: 125).

During the late 1920s, harnessing the creative potential of the interplay between sight and sound became the biggest concern for filmmakers. Talkies were no longer simply the sum of visual and acoustic stimuli, but the outcome of a multi-dimensional process of semiotic blending. Image, word, music and background noise could now be used as representational resources to construct the diegetic world, hence opening up new avenues for artistic expressiveness. For example, the voice had to be **spatialized** in accordance with the position of the actor in the scene, and music had to be incorporated in key parts of the narrative. According to film sound specialists, it was the need to marshal the affordances of these new multimodal ensembles that brought about the rise of synchrony as the key structuring principle in sound films. Whereas silent films had drawn on the asynchronous deployment of images and written language, representational practices in their talking counterparts were subordinated to the achievement of maximum synchrony between the different expressive resources. As Doane (1980: 34) aptly notes,

> [t]here is no doubt that synchronization (in the form of 'lip-sync') has played a major role in the dominant narrative cinema. Technology standardized the relation through the development of the synchronizer, the Moviola, the flatbed editing table. The mixing apparatus allows a greater control over the establishment of relationships between dialogue, music, and sound effects and, in practice, the level of the dialogue generally determined the levels of sound effects and music. Despite a number of experiments with other types of sound/image relationships . . ., synchronous dialogue remains the dominant form of sonorous representation in the cinema.

Although the synchronization and mixing of dialogue and sound effects 'reached a level of artistic maturity at least comparable to its technological adequacy' in the early 1930s (Ellis 1995: 127), the centrality of synchronous dialogue in talking films opened the door to a multitude of challenges for the film industry. For instance, the standardization of the relationship between image and voice led to a perceived loss of the film's artistic 'aura' on the part of the audience (Doane 1980) and the viewers' distrust of the embodied voice as the prevalent representational practice in talking films

> Box 2.4
>
> Lewin (1931: 48) vouching for the artistic integrity of post-synchronized dialogue editing and Hollywood's acceptance of 'voice doubling':
>
> > I would like to emphasize the fact that ordinary dubbing is not a form of faking, since, regardless of how many times a voice may be re-recorded for the purpose of adding sound effects, it still remains the actual voice of the person who is seen in the picture . . . The old practice of using 'voice doubles' to fake the speech of actors whose own voices were not suited for recording has been completely abandoned, and only those players who can record as well as act have survived the complete transformation which the microphone has wrought in the motion picture industry.

(see Box 2.4). But the popularization of synchronous dialogue posed a much bigger threat to the film industry, as it soon began to undermine its financial viability.

The advent of sound was a major commercial blow for film industries such as Hollywood which, until the early 1920s, had enjoyed a sound financial position based on their growing export capacity and exerted a significant artistic influence on other national industries. Although the incorporation of written language into the semiotics of silent films had undermined the universality of early films to some extent, translating and recording intertitle cards was easy and cheap. This explains why, by the early 1920s, American pictures had 'seized over 50 per cent of the market in a number of European countries and over 80 per cent in Britain and in Italy where a once flourishing industry was nearly destroyed by the competition' (Novell-Smith and Ricci 1998: 3). The obstacles to international expansion that talkies presented to Hollywood producers and distributors were, however, of a different magnitude altogether, to the extent that they 'temporarily arrested American domination of the European film industries' (Forbes and Street 2000: 10).

Hollywood soon began to experiment with new representational practices to satisfy the demands of foreign audiences for films spoken in their respective languages. Examples of such practices that failed to reassert Hollywood's former dominance of film markets all over the world included, for example, the use of the cumbersome 'dunning process' (Ballester 1995: 4) or the expensive **multilingual filming method**. The production of multiple-language versions of the same story 'with separate and/or multilingual casts' was soon abandoned because 'usually only one version, the original, had a dynamic life of its own, the others being merely dutiful copies' (Ellis 1995: 124).

For the first time in the history of film, representational advances were being driven by the need to articulate new strategies to translate dialogue. One of such strategies capitalized on the post-synchronization technology that the industry had originally developed to enhance the quality of outdoor filming. Indeed, post-synchronized dubbing was first conceived as a means to facilitate '**doubling**' (Ďurovičová 2003), i.e. the revoicing of poor dialogue recordings in the same language; the adjustment of incidental noise volume; and/or the incorporation of music (Whitman-Linsen 1992: 57, Chaves García 2000: 30) during the post-production stage. However, the industry soon saw the potential of this technology to revoice the original dialogue with a translated version thereof, a practice that would become the immediate forerunner of lip-synchronized dubbing as we know it today (Box 2.5). In a further important development,

> [c]oncurrent advances in the manipulation of celluloid films during the 1920s allowed distributors to superimpose titles straight on the film strip images through optical and mechanical means (Ivarsson 2002). By the late 1920s, it had become customary to use this evolved version of the primitive intertitles to provide a translation of the source dialogue in synchrony with the relevant fragment of speech, thus paving the way for the development of modern subtitling.
>
> (Pérez-González 2009: 14)

The enmeshment of audiovisual translation within the representational realm of cinema was thus prompted by the need to safeguard the sustainability of an industrial model that was now dominated by the use of synchronous sound. The perfection of subtitling and dubbing techniques, and their growing acceptance by audiences all over the world, would soon allow American producers to regain a market share of 70 per cent in Europe and Latin America by the mid 1930s (Chaves García 2000) – ending the moratorium on Hollywood's control of European markets that the popularization of film dialogue had effectively managed to impose for over a decade (Forbes and Street 2000).

Box 2.5

Ďurovičová (2003: 14) refers to the German dubbing of Brenon's *The Lummox* (1930) to illustrate how this representational practice first became dominated by the principle of synchronized sound:

> [T]he veteran German [dubbing] director [Friedrich Zelnick] gave absolute priority to the expressive aspect of language, affording maximal respect to the actors. No doubt driven by the key economic imperative of eliminating any 'doubling', i.e. repetition of performances to facilitate lip-synching, in particular in close-ups, Zelnick left the image track intact. With absolute priority allotted to the lip movement, he then rewrote the German dialogue so as to conform, as much as possible, with the English lip movements, regardless of semantic consequences (presumably thus the English 'hat' as the German 'hat' (= [s/he] has)). Judging from the press (as well as from Zelnick's subsequent interviews), the catastrophic reception of the film was directly related to the near-nonsense of the German dialogue so produced. Another way of putting this would be that language was here treated more as expressive than as communicative, more akin to, say, an echo than as speech. However, the basic premise of such 'squeezing' of the translated words into the pre-shaped mouth of the original speaker on screen is of course au fond not different from the basic convention of dubbing still in use today. Any semantic 'truth' of the dialogue still remains fundamentally 'captive' to its visible evidence, its sound shape. So, though Zelnick's method fell short because it granted words all too much arbitrariness (as if taking seriously the point that sound/image relationship is one of merely conventional fidelity), its ruthlessly mechanistic innovation lies precisely in treating language as no more and no less than a category of noise, untrammelled by inwardness, projection or any ruse of 'character'.

The second wave of American domination not only threatened the viability of other national film industries. In modern talking pictures, the powerful representational force of language, combined with an enhanced visual sophistication and narrative depth, was often used to articulate aspirational lifestyle messages, complete with the promotion of the political and ideological values inscribed in the diegetic action.[4] The clash between the cultural identities and political values represented in American films and the socio-political make-up of some of the importing markets – which between the mid-1930s and the 1970s ranged from democratic systems to fascist regimes and other forms of totalitarian rule – played out on a number of fronts. For further discussion on and examples of the impact of censorship on audiovisual translation, see Sections 4.5.2 and 5.3.3.

The significance of Hollywood's interest in the global distribution of its films showed in their treatment of different aspects of filmic material. The characterization of other ethnic groups, for example, 'demonstrates particularly clearly the connection between the American film industry's representational strategies and its wider political, diplomatic, and economic agendas' (Vasey 1992: 617–18). After a number of incidents in which Hollywood's vilification of characters with recognizable national characteristics led affected countries to place an embargo on the films produced by certain companies, most producers agreed to industry-wide regulation of the themes presented in their films. Making concessions in their representation of other national or ethnic groups became an effective way of securing favourable trade agreements for the film industry. For example, when Japan threatened to curb the influx of American films in 1938, the American negotiators 'warned the Japanese that if they did not constitute a reasonably lucrative market they might find themselves singled out to wear the black hats in American movies' (ibid.: 631). Eventually, the Motion Picture Producers and Distributors of America (MPPDA) became directly involved in monitoring the studios' treatment of issues that could upset major target markets, urging companies to 'correct their movies before release' to avoid 'censorship intervention and truncated distribution' (ibid.: 621).

For their part, importing countries tried to counteract America's influence and preserve their own national industries through different means, including protectionist measures. The **cartelization** of European companies was one of the most important developments on this front. Companies formed alliances to control international competition, favouring exchanges with certain countries who agreed to open their borders to films from partner nations (Gomery 1980). In some cases, these powerful cartels operated by securing shared sound film patents. Effectively, this split the global market into different areas, with foreign film companies having to pay royalties every time they tried to distribute their films outside the company's own territory. Where the inflow of foreign films could not be truncated, censorship mechanisms became the protectionist strategy of choice (Novell-Smith and Ricci 1998). In addition to cropping or removing scenes, censors often relied on subtitling and dubbing to amend or replace sensitive parts of the original dialogue. The adoption of preferred forms of audiovisual translation by certain countries (see Box 2.6), for a range of nation-specific agendas, is thus another example of the extent to which the mediation of film dialogue has become ingrained in the representational fabric of cinema.

Box 2.6

Pérez-González (2009: 18) on the rationale for the emergence of 'dubbing countries', 'subtitling countries' and 'voice-over countries':

> Lip-synchronized dubbing, the most expensive method of audiovisual trans-
> lation, has traditionally been the preferred option in countries with a single
> linguistic community – and hence a large potential market to secure a size-
> able return on the investment. In some cases (e.g. France), the dissemina-
> tion of a single dubbed version across the length and breadth of the national
> territory has been instrumental in achieving linguistic uniformity, to the detri-
> ment of regional dialects or minority languages (Ballester 1995). On the
> other hand, the predominance of dubbing in Germany, Italy and Spain in the
> 1930s and 1940s was fostered by fascist regimes. Revoicing a whole film
> became an effective instrument of censorship, enabling the removal of
> inconvenient references to facts and values that clashed with the official
> doctrine (Agost 1999). Voice-over, on the other hand, became the transfer
> method of choice in most Soviet bloc countries and other Asian markets (e.g.
> Thailand), either because the national language was unchallenged (Danan
> 1991) or because budget constraints made the cost of lip-synch dubbing
> simply prohibitive (Gottlieb 1998). Subtitling, on the other hand, thrived in a
> group of rich and highly literate countries with small audiovisual markets
> (Scandinavian countries) and bilingual communities (the Netherlands and
> Belgium), as well as in other states with lower literacy rates but much poorer
> economies (Portugal, Greece, Iran and most Arab countries), for whom
> other forms of audiovisual translation were unaffordable.

2.4 SUTURING TRANSLATIONS IN THE ERA OF MASS MEDIA

Despite the technological changes witnessed by the industry during the
second half of the twentieth century with regard to film production and
distribution, the use of audiovisual translation as a core representational
resource in cinematic texts has remained basically unchanged since the
1930s (James 2001):

* On the one hand, the subtitling apparatus imposed by the industry
  continues to prioritize maximum synchrony between the display of
  written subtitles, 'the temporality of utterance and the temporality of
  reading' (Sinha 2004: 175). As the rate of speech delivery is much
  higher than the average viewer's reading speed, subtitles normally
  contain up to '43% less text than the original [spoken] dialogues' (de
  Linde and Kay 1999: 51). The need for subtitlers to delete, condense and
  adapt the original spoken dialogue to comply with technical constraints

of shortage of screen space and lack of time has been found to have important representational implications, including 'the acculturisation or domestication of the source text in line with dominant conventions and expectancies prevailing in the TC [target culture]' (Ulrych 2000: 130) (see Section 4.5.1 for examples). As a result, non-mainstream identities, and their individual speech styles, tend to be standardized or ironed out of the subtitled narrative (Fawcett 2003), which 'can make a character come across as more abrupt, or unfriendly and thereby change characterization' (Remael 2003: 236) (see Section 4.5.2 for examples).

- On the other hand, dubbing remains trapped within representational practices shaped by 'the hegemony of synchronous sound and the strict alignment of speaker and voice' that the industry requires' (Naficy 2001: 24). This concern with synchronization has often resulted in 'compartmentalized' translations. By focusing exclusively on the need to produce translated dialogue that matches screen sounds, as embodied by lip movements, translators focus on short bits of dialogue at a time – which often proves detrimental to the overall 'naturalness' and 'contextual appropriateness' of the dubbed speech (Herbst 1997: 305, Pérez-González 2007a) (see Section 4.5.2 for examples).

The professional and academic discourses that have enjoyed more currency in the field of audiovisual translation over the last decades, particularly in instructional settings, have accounted for the restrictions that lie at the heart of these representational practices as the result of 'technical constraints of shortage of screen space and lack of time' (O'Connell 1998: 67). As the argument goes, assisting in the construction of reality through film is only possible if translators adhere to the representational practices imposed by the hegemony of synchronous sound. In recent years, however, film studies specialists have questioned this premise. As I will discuss in the remainder of this section, they argue that the strict alignment of speaker and voice in commercial cinema is motivated by economic, rather than artistic considerations.

For all the rhetoric that surrounded the birth of cinema, pertaining to the status of films as innovative and distinctive art entities that sought to facilitate new experiences of visual enjoyment (Ellis 1995), the evolution of this form of entertainment has always been steered by entrepreneurism. As explained in Section 2.3, the advent of sound was capitalized on as an opportunity to impose linear, goal-oriented narratives to 're-establish that dynamic contact between art production and art consumption which [. . .] is sorely attenuated, if not entirely interrupted, in many other fields of artistic endeavor' (Panofsky 1934/1999: 280). Since the 1930s, the commercial success of films has thus been predicated on their compliance with a set of standardized conventions regarding the organization of the narrative or the overall duration of the film, to give a couple of examples. Top among these conventions is the widely accepted 'assumption that what we see on the screen and the words we hear on the soundtrack should be related in obvious ways that smooth the development of narrative action' (MacDonald 1995: 5). From this perspective, Hollywood's imposition of synchronous sound can be regarded as a means to impose global narrative conventions and, in so doing, to exclude alternative narrative traditions from mainstream distribution circuits (Berliner 1999: 6).

The contribution of synchronous sound to narrative clarity has been critiqued by scholars working in different strands of film studies. For Minh-ha (2005), Hollywood favours the use of synchronous diegetic sound because it is part of an aesthetic of objectivity that provides 'unmediated access to reality' (2005: 129). In other words, in Hollywood's classical cinematic apparatus, synchronous sound manages to shift viewers' attention away from the tools and relations of production – i.e. from the spaces between image, sound and text. In so doing, films reduce the margin for subjective viewing experiences and are able to impose preferred interpretations on their audiences through the deployment of '**suturing**' practices (Heath 1981: 76). By adopting this style, the Hollywood classical cinematic apparatus manages to keep audience members absorbed in the fiction and 'maintain an efficient, purposeful and uninterrupted flow of narrative information' (Berliner 1999: 6). Driven by these evolving conventions, Hollywood narratives gradually shifted

> from what had been called a 'cinema of attractions' to the self-contained diegetic world. The latter conception of cinematic textuality is based on a new kind of realism that closed the world of the story off from the space of the audience, demanding narrative motivation for everything on screen.
>
> (Nornes 2007: 115)

Adherence to suturing conventions dictates that creators and technicians should not make their presence felt in the films they shoot. This self-effacing presentational style achieved by making the cinematic apparatus invisible is reflected in and reinforced through translation. According to Minh-ha (1992), for instance, the hegemonic structure of the Hollywood narrative imposes 'suture subtitling' practices aiming to 'collapse, in subtitling, the activities of reading, hearing, and seeing into one single activity, as if they were all the same' and hence 'to naturalize a dominant, hierarchically unified worldview' (quoted in Nornes 1999: 18). For his part, Nornes (2007) contends that the willingness of subtitlers to comply with 'a method of translation that conspires to hide its work – along with its ideological assumptions – from its own readers-spectators' (2007: 155) represents a form of corruption, for they end up presenting their audiences with incomplete and distorted experiences of the foreign. In Nornes' view, **corrupt subtitles** fail to explore those spaces of generative cultural and linguistic multiplicity that emerge in any instance of cross-cultural transaction precisely because they smooth over cultural differences on the grounds of medial constraints and hide their presence through restrictive rules. As a result, those 'textual and cinematic effects that exceed the creation of a narrative-focused equivalence' (ibid.: 180) and could favour experiences of spectatorial distantiation by providing unmediated access to the source culture are sacrificed. A similar line of argument is pursued by Mowitt (2004) with regard to lip-synchronized dubbing. Drawing on his thorough analysis of a number of documents produced by key figures in the Hollywood establishment in the 1940s, Mowitt claims that the development of edited, synchronous film soundtracks (from which all traces of film work have been effaced) has served to impose the linear narrative patterns of classical Hollywood cinema on other cultures and to hamper the penetration of conventions from other world cinematic traditions into the mainstream market.

The range of technological, artistic, economic and socio-political developments outlined in this chapter have contributed to shaping audiovisual translation as a site of representational practice during the twentieth century. Throughout that period, this context of production and consumption of translated media content advanced hand in hand with the ever expanding film industry, although in the 1960s it widened its sphere of influence to incorporate the subtitling and dubbing of televised broadcasts (Delabastita 1989). In both domains, the representational approach to audiovisual translation has contributed to naturalizing the world of the story, making it self-contained and confining it to the space of diegesis. In other words, only the voices of characters inhabiting the world created by the story – and, by extension, any narratorial voices bringing the diegetic space to the viewers' own one – are subtitled or dubbed. In purporting to represent the diegetic reality, audiovisual translation practices convey a **presumption of faithfulness**. In other words, translators are meant to deliver approximate linguistic representations of the original dialogue.

The organization of audiovisual translation as a site of representational practice has been inextricably intertwined with **linear models of communication** (McNair 2006), which account for the organization of the media industry in terms of top-down, elite-controlled structures. In this context of analogical media production and consumption, corporations (i) decide what is to be translated and choose the outlets for the distribution of those translations; (ii) hold in monopoly the technological means required to subtitle or dub audiovisual material and to display them in conjunction with the visuals; and (iii) rely on groups of translation professionals working under close surveillance of distribution companies. For all these reasons, media corporate structures are able to exercise a significant degree of political and ideological control over the reception of their audiovisual products, including their translated versions. To a large extent, this control is facilitated by the fact that, for decades, the boundaries of audiovisual markets have tended to map onto those of nation-states. Within each audiovisual market/nation, the configuration of audiences as culturally homogeneous constituencies has allowed the film and television industries to perpetuate the deployment of representational conventions that were forged over several decades within each geographical context; and to endorse the dominant or preferred status of specific methods of audiovisual translation at the expense of others (e.g. the case of dubbing, subtitling and voice-over in Spain, Portugal and Poland, respectively). The one-to-one correspondence between specific audiovisual genres and the modalities chosen for their translation in different countries – a distinctive feature of such linear dynamics – would remain in place until the early 1990s.

The dynamics of audiovisual translation as a site of representational practice reflect the cultural and economic logics of the era of mass media technologies, prior to the advent of digitization and networking technologies. Although these representational logics are still at the centre of translation practices undertaken in the context of commercial settings, the emergence and spread of the digital culture has brought about important changes to the organization of the audiovisual landscape, including the shift from linear to non-linear models of distribution, the blurring of the boundaries between the production and consumption of translated media content, and the reconfiguration of audiences into audienceships (see Section 3.2.2). The evolution of audiovisual translation into a site of interventionist practice, driven by participatory and co-creational activities of mediation, will be extensively discussed in Chapter 3.

FOLLOW-UP QUESTIONS FOR DISCUSSION

- The expansion of Hollywood's cinematic apparatus has been challenged at different points in time by resistant practices. Shohat and Stam (2006), for instance, report on activist films (e.g. *La hora de los hornos – The Hour of the Furnaces*, 1968) that 'incorporate[d] into the text programmed interruptions of the projections to allow for debate concerning the central political issues raised by the film', thus opening the cinematic apparatus 'to person-to-person dialogue in a provocative amalgam of cinema/theatre/political rally' (2006: 111). Naficy (2003), on the other hand, reflects on his own experience as a young film viewer in Iran, where Western talkies were introduced in the 1930s. As Naficy explains, film viewing was a communal experience, often punctuated by vocal expressions of enthusiasm or disappointment; during the projection, 'screen readers and student translators' translated 'the inter-titles, the subtitles of the foreign language dialogue in real time', often making use of 'colourful Persian stock expressions, which indigenized and enriched the film experience' (2003: 189).

  What points of connection can be drawn between these two contexts of reception, considering that the example provided by Shohat and Stam does not actually involve translation across languages? Consider the ways in which each of these contexts of reception deviates from the individualized viewing experience promoted by commercial cinema, where both the duration and preferred reception of films are controlled by the industry. Can you identify similar contexts of reception in other cultures/regions you are familiar with? What role does audiovisual translation play in those contexts? To what extent can their existence be accounted for only on the basis of artistic considerations? Are there any other constraints, whether political, religious or ideological, that may shape those sets of representational practices?

- Section 2.3 explains how the American industry put in place a self-regulatory framework to ensure that the representations of other nationalities or ethnic groups in Hollywood films did not cause offence in their most lucrative markets. In *The Collaboration* (2013), for example, Urwand draws on extensive documentary evidence to show that 'once Hitler ascended to power in 1933 the major Hollywood studios tacitly agreed not to portray Germany in an unfavourable light or to mention its persecution of the Jews', in what reviewers have presented as 'a shameful policy of compromise and kowtowing on the part of the studio bosses'.[5] Against this backdrop, consider the following case reported in Cronin (2009: 11), concerning the censorship by colonial powers of films watched by viewers in Northern Rhodesia:

> One of the paradoxical effects of paranoid censorship in imperial settings was that the narrative or storyline was continually disrupted by the anxious cuts of colonizers. Vulnerable natives were thus unlikely to be affected by the meanings of narratives that the censors' shears had rendered illegible [. . .] [T]he vast majority of showings of films in the Copperbelt were out of doors and the noise levels were such that the soundtrack was not often audible. Even if it had been, this would have made little difference as the miners and their families with limited access to formal education would not have been able to follow extended dialogue in British English or colloquial American English.

How can the distributors' decision to remove sensitive material (e.g. scenes depicting riots or sexual encounters, to give but a few examples) while retaining the dialogue in English be interpreted in terms of Hollywood's representational priorities?

NOTES

1   Barnes, Mike (2013) 'Mickey Knox, Actor and Sergio Leone Writer, Dies at 92', *The Hollywood Reporter*, 22 November. Available online: www.hollywoodreporter. com/news/mickey-knox-actor-writer-sergio-leone-dies-658437 (last accessed 15 September 2013).

2   A still image illustrating this moment of the film can be accessed at www. moma.org/collection/browse_results.php?criteria=O%3AAD%3AE%3A32341 &page_number=6&template_id=1&sort_order=1

3   This argument would be taken up by directors belonging to the 1920s French avant-garde, whose attempt to free films from the influence of language included the abandonment of intertitles. As Testa (2002) reports, other films such as *Un chien Andalou* (1929) by Spanish director Luis Buñuel opted to make a subversive use of intertitles. By 'scrambling temporal indicators' and

'accenting the madness of their concatenation' throughout the film, Buñuel managed to enhance the surreal aesthetics of the film.

4   According to American magazine *Collier's Weekly*, '[t]he American moving picture [was] [. . .] familiarizing South America and Africa, Asia and Europe with American habits and customs. It [was] showing American clothes and furniture, automobiles and homes. And it [was] subtly but surely creating a desire for these American-made articles' (quoted in Forbes and Street 2000: 10).

5   Quinn, Anthony (2013) 'The Collaboration: Hollywood's Pact with Hitler by Ben Urwand', *The Guardian* 16 October. Available online: www.theguardian.com/books/2013/oct/16/collaboration-hollywood-hitler-ben-urwand (last accessed 15 September 2013).

CORE REFERENCES

Cronin, Michael (2009) *Translation Goes to the Movies*, London and New York: Routledge.

Ellis, Jack C. (1995) *A History of Film*, 4th edition, Boston and London: Allyn and Bacon.

Nornes, Abé M. (2007) *Cinema Babel: Translating Global Cinema*, Minneapolis and London: University of Minnesota Press.

3

AUDIOVISUAL TRANSLATION AS A SITE OF INTERVENTIONIST PRACTICE

As we settle into an era in which the channels of media transmission are greater in number and more diverse and easily accessible than ever before, it is becoming increasingly apparent that the routes of cultural exchange are becoming more complexly entangled, fragmented and collaborative. While the rise of massive global commercial media enterprises leads to renewed discussion of the dominance of the 'West' upon the 'Rest', the increasing portability, transmitability, and reproducibility of media has helped to generate a grassroot globalization of migrant populations, pop cosmopolitans, and other groupings that do not fit so neatly into pre-given categories.

(Li 2009: 9)

The media landscape will be reshaped by the bottom-up energy of media created by amateurs and hobbyists as a matter of course. This bottom-up energy will generate enormous creativity, but it will also tear apart some of the categories that organize the lives and work of media makers . . . A new generation of media makers and viewers are emerging which could lead to a sea change in how media is made and consumed.

(Blau 2005: 3–5)

In this chapter

The 'de-materialization of space' resulting from the digitization of audiovisual commodities has led to highly consequential transformations in the conceptualization and practice of audiovisual translation. On the one hand, we are witnessing the compartmentalization of traditional national audiences and the emergence of niche audiovisual markets oriented towards specialized constituencies. On the other hand, these emerging niche markets are turning into fluid and decentralized **audienceships** of unprecedented accessibility and diversity. Thanks to digitization and the widespread availability of information and communication technologies, appropriating audiovisual commodities, translating them and disseminating the output of this mediation process – both within and outside commercial circuits – is becoming increasingly easier and affordable. These technological developments have also brought about important changes in media business structures. In the new post-industrialist, networked economy, **non-linear models of media distribution and consumption** are coming to the fore. As part of this devolution of power from media corporations to consumers, the involvement of viewers or media consumers in the process of translation (**co-creational practices**) is growing apace. Most crucially, the growing visibility of these (often politically, ideologically or aesthetically engaged) **cybercultures** has brought about a deliberately **interventionist approach** to audiovisual translation that seeks to undermine the profit-ridden agenda of the industry's establishment.

⏵ WATCH THE INTRODUCTION VIDEO

3.1 AUDIOVISUAL INTERVENTION

Digital technologies are transforming traditional processes of media production, consumption and distribution. This chapter examines how these transformations are changing the relationship between the agents involved in those processes and the audiences they work for. In tracing those changing intersections between old and new forms of mediation, I will argue that audiovisual translation, formerly a site of representational practice, is quickly becoming a site of interventionist practice.

The transition into the second decade of the twenty-first century will long be remembered for its relentless socio-political and financial volatility, as illustrated by what have come to be known as the 'Arab Spring' and Eurozone 'Sovereign Debt Crisis', respectively. In May 2010, amid fears of a possible default on Greece's debts, Eurozone countries approved a multi-billion 'rescue package' for the country, bringing about ever-deeper spending cuts and pushing Greece to the brink of economic and social collapse. Against this backdrop, the speech delivered by Franco-German lawmaker Daniel Cohn-Bendit, a French MEP affiliated to the the Greens/ European Free Alliance, during a plenary session of the European Parliament resonated strongly with critics of austerity measures across Europe. While publicly urging Greece to make harsh public spending cuts, Cohn-Bendit alleged, France and Germany were bullying Prime Minister George Papandreou to honour massive arms deals signed by previous Greek govern-ments.[1] Despite the seriousness of these allegations, Cohn-Bendit's speech largely failed to make the headlines of Europe's mainstream media.

For critics of the austerity-driven approach to resolving the debt crisis, Cohn-Bendit's speech was a source of legitimization. It gave greater visi-bility to those voices resisting the EU's neo-liberal orthodoxy from within and exposed cracks in what the institution presented as the only way to solve Greece's debt problems. Unfortunately, it soon became clear that the patchy journalistic coverage of the speech in the European mainstream media was insufficient for austerity detractors to gain political momentum and establish their stance more firmly in the European public consciousness. In the era of networked technologies, however, tech-savvy 'netizens' know how to get around the dictates of the media establishment and kick-start the transnational flow of selected media content. Zorbec le Gras, a Greek blogger critical of the savage austerity measures imposed on his country, is indeed one of such individuals.[2] Drawing on downloadable footage of the speech available on the European Parliament's website, Zorbec took only two days to produce a Greek subtitled version of Cohn-Bendit's speech, which he proceeded to upload to his own blog and YouTube account. Within the following three weeks, Zorbec worked in partnership with like-minded 'translators' to create four more language versions of the speech – i.e. Spanish, English, German and Italian (Figure 3.1) – that he made available via the same video-sharing website.[3] On the whole, the subtitled versions produced and circulated by Zorbec and his 'ad hoc' subtitling partners were viewed by more than two million YouTube users. As viewers shared their experience via Facebook, Del.icio.us, Twitter and a range of personal or collective blogs, the interview became diverted into new audiences at every step along the way.[4] Two years after being first uploaded, a viewer of the Spanish version wondered '[w]hy is this video not playing around the media everywhere? [sic] ... Spread the word, millions have already seen this but it's not near enough!!' (Nokael1, 7 June 2012).[5]

Figure 3.1 Screen shot from Daniel Cohn-Bendit's speech on YouTube (Spanish subtitled version)

In choosing to subtitle Cohn-Bendit's speech, this group of amateur translators acted as self-appointed commissioners and distributors, showing no concern over their perceived subjectivity in trying to advance an overtly political cause. The subtitling of Cohn-Bendit's speech by subtitling activists thus illustrates a number of developments that have brought about a shift from representational towards interventionist forms of mediation in the media landscape over the last decade. Having examined the dynamics of audiovisual translation as a site of representational practice in the previous chapter, attention now turns to the interplay between the forces of globalization and technological progress and the way in which that interaction is shaping transnational media flows and the mediation thereof along more interventionist lines. The scope of this impact will be examined in terms of a set of defining features which are briefly outlined here.

- The extent to which advances in digital communication technology have empowered ordinary citizens to become involved in the production, manipulation and circulation of media content is one of such features. Formerly entrenched divisions between producers and users are becoming increasingly blurred, and forms of active spectatorship are emerging as individuals become involved in subtitling and dubbing activities – only two of the wide range of participatory practices that are proliferating around the transnational flow of digital media content. Seen in this light, Zorbec and his fellow subtitlers are good examples of those **consumers-turned-producers** who capitalize on the affordances of digital technologies to work collectively on the promotion of their political allegiances and values.

- The second key feature pertains to the changing relationships between audiovisual mediators and the media industry. As the growth of networked technologies continues to foster the development of collaborative media practices, audiovisual translation is now also used to mediate genres of ephemeral interest whose commercial distribution would be hardly viable. The subtitling of news interviews or speeches like Cohn-Bendit's – two examples of such genres of ephemeral interest – are therefore bound to call for the development of new subtitling conventions and shift the media user's experience away from commercial distribution to a multi-stop circulation of content. Indeed, active media users living in the digital culture are able to intervene in the texts at each of these stops, often by incorporating elements that foster subjective viewing experiences and deviate from industry conventions.

- Finally, audiovisual translation is becoming increasingly conceptualized as a reterritorializing force in the media marketplace. Amid the growing mobility of individuals, either motivated by forced dispersal or voluntary displacement, immigrant and diasporic communities are decoupling the notion of audience from that of national market. More importantly, collaborative technologies are contributing to the formation of transnational networked collectivities, and hence re-defining the traditional boundaries of nation-based cultural and linguistic constituencies. Ultimately, the configuration of these transnational communities of interest as spaces of participation and collaboration is bringing to the fore the intersectionality and fluidity of cultural identities.

As the notion of national audience, the conventional process of media content distribution and the traditional relationships between the agents involved in the production and consumption of media content have become subject to revision and reformulation, audiovisual translation is beginning to move beyond existing means of analysis and critique.

3.2 KEY CONCEPTS FOR THE STUDY OF INTERVENTIONIST AUDIOVISUAL TRANSLATION

Recent technological developments have led to a growing compartmentalization of media audiences. Such advances include, for example, the advent of digital terrestrial television platforms, with the consequent increase in the number of channels available for the distribution of media content, and on-demand Internet streaming multimedia providers, whether on a free or a subscription-based basis. Powerful global corporations have so far preserved their commercial viability by resorting to strategies of corporate concentration, i.e. placing the ever growing number of mainstream media in the hands of a relatively small number of industry players. As Compaine (2005) explains, diversifying their revenue streams and strengthening their presence in different segments of the marketplace has allowed most global media players emerging from corporate consolidation processes to enhance their economic efficiency while increasing viewers' choice.

The transition to a digital media culture has also contributed to the fragmentation of audiences in other ways. Spurred by recent legislative provisions aiming to accelerate progress towards universal media access,[6] the affordances of digital technology have acted as a catalyst in the development of new forms of **intersemiotic assistive mediation**. These include forms of translation where information is transferred across different types of signs (primarily from images to written or spoken language), such as subtitling for the Deaf and hard of hearing and audio description for the blind, respectively. The new interactive features available in digital TV sets, on the one hand, and the growing ubiquity of infrared audio description equipment or induction loops in cinemas, on the other, are helping spectators adapt their viewing experience to their specific needs and/or preferences. The generalization of these new modalities of audiovisual transfer have contributed decisively to mainstreaming entertainment for sensory impaired members of the community, albeit at the expense of atomizing media audiences into additional subgroups (Gambier 2003).

While the gradual immersion into the digital culture is having profound effects on mainstream media structures, the significance of these changes to audiovisual translation lies elsewhere. Advances in communication technology are amplifying and accelerating the mediation of media practices and experiences, bringing about a worldwide 'shift of all culture to computer-mediated forms of production, distribution, and communication'

(Manovich 2001: 19). As they 'enable consumers to archive, annotate, appropriate and recirculate media content in powerful new ways' (Jenkins 2004: 33), networked technologies are ultimately giving viewers more control over their user experience.

Featured example 3.1: The Galloway interview (2006)

In the summer of 2006, Sky News broadcast an interview with the British MP George Galloway against the background of the ongoing military conflict between Lebanon and Israel. The interview took place following Hezbollah's rocket attack on northern Israel in early August, approximately one month after the beginning of the fighting.[7] Covering the invasion of Lebanon from Israel, Sky News presenter Anna Botting introduced George Galloway as 'a man not known for sitting on the fence', who 'passionately opposed the invasion of Iraq' and believed that 'Hezbollah was justified in attacking Israel'. Botting's decision to begin by asking Galloway how he could justify his support for Hezbollah and its leader Sheikh Hassan Nasrallah set the tone for a very tense interview. In his responses, Galloway tried to present Hezbollah's attack as a response to Israel's aggression, argued that only Rupert Murdoch's media (including Sky News) regarded the militant group as a terrorist organization and went on to accuse Botting personally of believing that 'the Israeli blood is more valuable than the blood of Lebanese or the Palestinians'.[8] Overall, Galloway's stance clearly reflected his hard-line stance against the 'War on Terror' narrative and Israel's foreign and security policies vis-à-vis neighbouring Arab countries.

Although the interview could be accessed via the Sky News website and remains available through the news broadcaster's YouTube account, the footage was posted in this and other video-sharing platforms by many ordinary citizens. In Jenkins' terms, this involves an exercise of media content **appropriation** and **recirculation**. Securing their own copy of the interview and sharing it through their own blogs and social networking sites allowed these individuals to exploit the interview through and for their own means. Indeed, access to the interview is normally contextualized or rather 'framed' using catchy headlines and blurbs (e.g. 'George Galloway Savages SKY NEWS! George Galloway on his usual warpath, this time about the Israeli/Palestine Battle. Sky News is the current target'; 'George Galloway Embarrasses Sky News: George Galloway is interviewed by a woman on Sky News and points out the hypocracy [sic] of Rupert Murdoch news reporting'[9]). This form of **annotation** has a clearly strategic objective, as it serves as a basis to construct a virtual community of affinity with other like-minded individuals. By posting comments and video responses, viewers articulate spaces of engagement with and participation in ongoing political debates on the Israel–Palestine conflict. A cursory inspection of YouTube uploads featuring this interview reveals that, empowered by networked technologies, ordinary citizens involved in this form of remediation were able to bring this content to millions of users.

The text annotation aspect of this process is of particular interest to audio-visual translators scholars. As some of the issues addressed in this broadcast –

e.g. the Arab–Israel conflict(s), the effects of American/British foreign policy in the Middle East or even the editorial line of Murdoch's media empire on the post 9/11 terrorist threat – have global reach, the interview soon became part of the global media flows described in Section 3.1. At different stops in its travels around the world, 'consumers-turned-producers' intervened in the text by subtitling it into a number of languages. *Cuaderno de Campo* bloggers represent a clear example of the interventionist dimension of subtitling in the era of the digital culture. On 11 August 2006, UK-based Mónica posted an entry on this collective Spanish language blog,[10] drawing readers' attention to the availability of the interview on the Sky News website and noting that, due to its interest, she would soon be circulating a transcription and Spanish translation of the interview. Drawing on her translation, it took fellow blogger Trebol-A one day to create a full subtitled version of the programme. In one of the comments featuring as part of this blog entry, Trebol-A noted that, due to the constant overlaps between the participants, he had opted to 'privilege the interviewee's speech over the interviewer's'. Thus the interventionist nature of this group's subtitling venture not only had to do with their role of 'selectively appropriating' (Baker 2006) British media content for release within the Spanish blogosphere, but also with the way in which they flaunted their subjectivity as mediators.

The comments posted by readers illustrate the impact that subtitling, as part of the wider process of **remediation** (i.e. the remix of old and new media content) by ordinary citizens, has on the creation of sites for affinity-driven interaction between audiences and texts. Spanish readers express their surprise at the vehemence of Galloway's responses, appreciating their apparent disregard for political correctness and orthodoxy; heated discussions about political developments on the Middle East are also prompted by this interview, with a large section of viewers commenting either on the failure of mainstream media to provide reliable information on the different conflicts or the subordination of news providers to Zionist agendas. Interestingly, many viewers remark on this subtitling exercise as a liberating media consumption experience, i.e. an antidote against 'conventional disinformation'. Most importantly, a significant proportion of contributions demonstrate and celebrate the power of networked communication, referring to sites with similar content or featuring other subtitled versions of the same interview, and reporting that they will be putting a link to the interview on their own blogs.

On 1 September 2006, three weeks after the release of their Spanish subtitled version of the Galloway interview, *Cuaderno de Campo* bloggers posted a new entry (Figure 3.2)[11] reflecting on the success of their initiative. Their subtitled video ranked among the top 100 most popular videos in YouTube's News&Blogs section, with the original English version ranking third on that same list. On behalf of herself and her fellow bloggers, Mónica thanked their viewers for their support and for having actively contributed to circulate their work through hyperlinked connections across sites. *Cuaderno de Campo*'s version is the only subtitled Spanish interview that is still available online. The group's decision to host the video within their own server and share it via a dedicated media player – an instance of what Jenkins labels as **archiving** – as opposed to simply embedding

Cuaderno de Campo

Esclavos del software libre

Galloway en youtube
■ Viernes, 1 de septiembre de 2006

El video subtitulado de Galloway en Skynews que tradujimos hace 3 semanas bate records. Ayer recibió en youtube.com el **"Honor"** de figurar entre los 100 videos más vistos en la sección de News&Blogs con **22877** vistas en 21 días. El puesto 96 de los 100 primeros ó el puesto 96 de 183.835 videos que hay en esa sección, les dejo elegir, al fin y al cabo han sido todos ustedes los culpables.

¿Sorprendente? Pues no tanto si tenemos en cuenta que el mismo video en su versión original está en 3 lugar de la misma lista con **282.608** vistas en el mismo periodo, solo superado por un abuelo bitacorero y un reportaje titulado ¿Es Bush Idiota? (que cada cual saque sus conclusiones).

PD: Aprovecho para daros las gracias a todos por la difusión que habeis dado al video y las muestras de apoyo, tanto en los comentarios del apunte de Mónica como en las webs en que se ha enlazado (demasiadas para ponerlas aqui).

Figure 3.2 Screen shot from *Cuaderno de Campo* blog entry: 'Galloway on YouTube'

their original YouTube upload within the blog pages, appears to have so far protected this content from copyright claims.

Featured example 3.1 reveals the co-existence of 'a top-down corporate-driven process and a bottom-up consumer-driven process' in the production and consumption of digital media content that Jenkins has labelled as **media convergence** (2004: 37). Digital communication technologies are therefore not only allowing global media corporations to reinvigorate their business models, but also fostering new forms of collaborative citizenship (Von Hippel 2005, Hartley 2009, Green and Jenkins 2009) based on viewers' participation and interactivity (McChesney and Schiller 2003). This emerging participatory environment, where translation plays a very important role, has 'a cultural logic of its own, blurring the lines between economics (work) and culture (meaning), between production and consumption, between making and using media, and between active or passive spectatorship of mediated culture' (Deuze 2009: 148). The remainder of this section explores the implications of media convergence for audiovisual translation, re-conceptualizing three main aspects of this form of mediation in the era of the digital culture: audiovisual media translators, audiences and markets.

3.2.1 Audiovisual media consumers-*cum*-translators

Banks and Deuze (2009: 419) use the term **co-creation** to describe the 'phenomenon of consumers increasingly participating in the process of making and circulating media content and experiences' that have become 'significant sources of both economic and cultural value'. So while all professional audiovisual translators can be regarded as co-creators involved in the adaptation and modification of media content (Barra 2009), the term 'co-creational practice' has taken on a new significance in the context of media convergence. Following the advent of collaborative technologies, the study of audiovisual translation can no longer be based on the premise that the field is exclusively in the hands of professional mediators. The boundaries that have traditionally prevented media consumers (in this case, viewers) from taking on the role of amateur co-creators, either by collaborating with other professional agencies throughout the life-cycle of a project or by modifying what professionals have previously produced, are no longer enforceable. Also worthy of note is that, in the era of media convergence, the involvement of amateurs in the process of co-creation is not restricted to the manipulation of media content. As illustrated in example 3.1, co-creation often spans from the selection of media content to the circulation of re-mediated broadcasts (Section 7.2.2).

According to Banks and Deuze (2009), studies on the proliferation of co-creational practices may be arrayed on a continuum, with **development** and **dependency theories** at the poles (ibid.: 422). Development theory scholars (e.g. Bruns 2008 and Benkler 2006) regard the involvement of users in co-creational practices as a democratizing and empowering force, which facilitates associative relations between individuals around their cultural practices. For their part, dependency theory scholars (e.g. Terranova 2004, Scholz 2008 and Ross 2009) postulate that amateur co-creators are often exploited by neo-liberal media corporations keen to capitalize on what has been variously termed as 'immaterial labour, affective labour, free labour and precarious labour' (Banks and Deuze 2009: 424). The involvement of reflexive consumers in the translation of audiovisual global flows has received little scholarly attention to date. The remainder of this subsection therefore concentrates on a relatively under-explored aspect of participatory audiovisual translation, i.e. the motivations that fuel viewers' participation in the translation of media content.

Most instances of co-creational audiovisual translation practices – overwhelmingly by amateurs or ordinary citizens[12] – documented in the literature so far have been theorized as a product of 'the dialectical relationship between media technologies and the participatory practices these technologies enable' (Chouliaraki 2010: 227). Koskinen (2010), for example, reports on the European Union's Governance 2.0 strategy, intended to stimulate citizens' interest and participation in its institutional activities through the creation of a range of web-based communication spaces, including dedicated channels in social media networks and video-sharing platforms. Despite the EU's notable efforts to foster a culture of active European citizenship, Koskinen explains, ordinary people have failed to engage in communication with the institution. Interestingly, more recent attempts by the EU to 'communicate Europe' acknowledge that the institution needs to move away from the 'administrational e-democracy' paradigm, aiming to stimulate *active* participation, towards new forms of engagement that promote *affective* participation. While the former sought to design the audience that the EU had in mind and wished to target, 'affective citizenship in a sense turns this around; affection makes you *wish to be addressed* or *accept* the role of the addressee, creating a dialogic or sympathetic relationship or bond' (Koskinen 2010: 145; emphasis in the original). From the perspective of audiovisual translation practitioners and scholars, the most interesting implication of this change in orientation is the EU's new interest in the 'audiovisualization' of its interaction with citizens. This emphasis on audiovisual texts, and the fact that citizens are invited to subtitle their content, is now regarded as a more effective means of promoting active affective citizenship (Box 3.1).

Box 3.1

Koskinen on the impact of amateur subtitling on the training of audiovisual translators in Europe

According to Koskinen, the involvement of ordinary citizens in the subtitling of the EU's audiovisual broadcasts has contributed to widening the participation of European citizens in the institution's virtual forums. Their affective-driven approach to subtitling should, therefore, inform the training of future subtitlers as audiovisual texts become more central to the institution's communication strategy:

> The emphasis on multimodal web-based communication requires new translator competences for those working for the European Union [. . .]

> These new skills profiles create challenges for recruitment and training. The DGT has taken an active role in training by introducing the concept of a European Master's in Translation (EMT) [. . .] However, in its present format the EMT model is too narrow and too traditional to accommodate the challenges posed by Governance 2.0. The competences expected from the graduates, and the model curriculum, offer little if any support for working with social media and only pay lip-service to audiovisual translation. In addition to the technical skills of using web-based communication tools and combining audio and visual elements (e.g. subtitling for institutional purposes), the translator needs enhanced skills on drafting affective and personalized messages . . . The training of translators (and their continuing professional development) will need to be geared to an 'EMT 2.0' model.
>
> (Koskinen 2010: 152–53)

But the involvement of ordinary citizens in co-creational subtitling is also being encouraged by a growing number of companies and organizations of different kinds. Since April 2007, non-professional organization TED (Technology, Entertainment, Design) has been circulating 'free knowledge from the world's most inspired thinkers, and also [building] a community of curious souls to engage with ideas and each other' through its website.[13] In 2009, with the sponsorship of a global telecommunications company and the technological support of free online subtitling tool dotSUB, TED launched an *Open Translation Project* that brought 'TEDTalks beyond the English-speaking world by offering subtitles, time-coded transcripts and the ability for any talk to be translated by volunteers worldwide'.[14] Hundreds of amateur subtitlers – including speakers of less-dominant languages – have been empowered by TED to partake in the co-production of media content, but their work is constrained by the organization's standards of translation accuracy and style guidelines for translators. Through their work, TED subtitlers contribute to the market penetration of dotSUB's enterprise solutions and, by extension, maximize the spread of **crowdsourcing** as a business model for the translation of corporate online content (Ray and Kelly 2011).

Feature example 3.2: Al Jazeera amateur subtitlers

Qatar-owned independent broadcaster Al Jazeera also relies on amateur subtitlers for the translation of citizen media footage from Syria, Tunisia and other Arab spring hot spots, as part of a project blurring the traditional boundaries between media producers and consumers.

Amateur subtitlers join teams of individuals with similar linguistic expertise through a dedicated website (Figure 3.3)[15] and engage in collaborative work using Amara – an online toolset and community facilitating both the subtitling and circulation of subtitled videos – to complement Al Jazeera's news output from around the globe. Amara is one of the tools developed by PCF (Participatory Culture Foundation), a 'non-profit organization, . . . dedicated to supporting a democratic media by creating open and decentralized video tools and services and . . . working to eliminate gatekeepers and empower communities around the world'.[16] The synergies between PCF's work towards an open and collaborative world and Al Jazeera's initiative – born out of a desire to give visibility to the medi-ated participation of Arab ordinary people in global media – are clear and provide a robust platform for this participatory process of media convergence. Unlike other co-creation projects, however, amateur subtitlers involved in this venture are constrained by the technical limitations of the subtitling tool and the range of texts made available for translation – which ultimately serve Al Jazeera to construct and circulate a specific narrative of events in the Arab world on a global scale and, arguably, to promote the brand worldwide.

The co-creational forms of amateur subtitling favoured by EU, TED and Al Jazeera are heavily constrained by their organizational agendas and the specific technological tools that they make available to their constituents/users/viewers. Insofar as the latter's 'monitored' or 'guided' involvement in subtitling practices reproduces, to some extent, the institutional power relations that participatory media practices seek to challenge, they instantiate a context of cultural production that Foucault (1982) has labelled as **technologization of democracy**. The dominance of technologization over democratization in these sites of amateur subtitling manifests itself, for example, in the restrictions that organizations place with regard to what needs translating. The EU only allows citizens to subtitle pieces of 'infotainment'; similarly, engaged viewers willing to collaborate with TED or Al Jazeera can only choose among broadcasts that have been previously selected for translation by these organizations. Using digital communications technology to foster a participatory environment for the mediated participation of ordinary people in public culture while, at the same time, restricting the range of discourses and genres available for the implementation of such co-creational practices represents an important change in the traditional dynamics of the audiovisual market. As far as professional audiovisual translators are concerned, these emerging forms of amateur medi-ation undermine the sustainability of creative industries and the social percep-tion of their 'symbolic capital' (Bourdieu 1977), understood here as the social recognition of these workers' expertise and professional latitude as assets

Figure 3.3 Screen shot from Al Jazeera's participatory subtitling project website

worthy of remuneration. From the stance of scholars subscribing to the dependence-based understanding of co-creation, the growing social recognition of consumers-turned-producers ultimately represents a threat to the stability of traditional labour structures within the media industries.

Mónica and her fellow *Cuaderno de Campo* bloggers (see Featured example 3.1), however, do not fall under the category of citizens whose subtitling practices are monitored by specific institutions or organizations. In line with other radical forms of citizenship found across different cultural industries (Deuze 2006), their amateur subtitling work contributes to articulating 'novel discourses of counter-institutional subversion and collective activism' (Chouliaraki 2010: 227) rather than advancing organizational agendas. While their involvement in amateur audiovisual translation is also shaped by the dialectic between technological ubiquity and the growth of participatory culture, the primary impetus behind this instance of co-creational work is on the democratizing potential of collaborative media technologies or, to put it in Foucault's terms, the **democratization of technology**. Scholarly interest in participatory subtitling of audiovisual media flows within this dimension of the dialectic has so far revolved around two main areas of mediation, **aesthetic** and **political** activism, and brought to the fore the role that networks of engaged amateur translators are playing in terms of cultural resistance against global capitalist structures through inter-ventionist forms of subtitling. These new agencies of amateur audiovisual translation are relatively under-represented in the literature; they will be examined in some depth in Section 3.3.

3.2.2 Audiences and audienceships

Technological developments and, in particular, the digitization of audio-visual content, have allowed media to overcome spatial barriers and speed up the circulation of information and knowledge. This 'de-materialization of space', in Cronin's (2003) words, is responsible for the creation of supra-territorial and interconnected audiences and accounts for the centrality of 'transworld simultaneity' and 'instantaneity' (Scholte 2005) in the contem-porary media landscape. Zorbes and his fellow subtitlers (Section 3.1), for example, are part of a supraterritorial audience made up of different linguistic constituencies scattered around the world but bound together by shared values, beliefs and practices (Deuze 2006: 71).

Box 3.2

Examples of comments by viewers of the German, Italian and Spanish versions of Cohn-Bendit's speech

Even a cursory inspection of the comments posted under the three amateur subtitled YouTube uploads reveals similarities that signal common concerns across linguistic collectivities. Examples include:

- Appreciation for Cohn-Bendit for 'telling it like it is' (unlike conventional politicians):

    finalmente qualcuno che dice la verità. peccato che nessuno in tv mandi in onda questo video, è troppo scomodo pare . . .

    Finally someone says the truth. It's a pity that nobody on TV broadcasts this video, it's probably an inconvenient truth . . .

    Ser político y humano es posible gracias a personas sinceras como esta. Si la Unión Europea fuera democrática y su presidente fuera elegido por todos, yo le votaría a este hombre.

    Being a politician and a human being is possible thanks to sincere people like these. If the EU was democratic and its president was elected by us all, I would vote for this man.

> Ednlich [sic] jemand der die wahrheit sagt. hätte nicht gedacht dass es menschen gibt die es noch zugeben dass in europa keine demokratie herscht.
>
> Finally someone says the truth. I did not expect that there would be somebody prepared to admit that there is no democracy in Europe.

- Vilification of Germany:

  > Hasta cuando la fürher Merkel y su socio Sarkozy, van a estar aprovechándose del resto del pueblo europeo ... Mientras que las demás naciones europeas tengan a dirigentes ineptos, pues siempre ...
  >
  > Until when will Führer Merkel and her partner Sarkozy carry on exploiting the rest of Europeans? ... Forever, as long as other nations continue to choose useless leaders ...
  >
  > E' [sic] una vergogna, la Francia e la Germania con la loro politica stanno rovinando l'Europa!
  >
  > Shame on them! With their policies, France and Germany are ruining Europe!
  >
  > ich finds [sic] traurig dass wir Deutschen bei der englischen Version dieses Videos in den Kommentaren als Übeltäter dargestellt werden. Die Nazivergleiche da sind wohl mehr als unpassend und ungerechtfertigt.
  >
  > I find it sad that we Germans are presented as villains in the comments posted under the English versions of this video. The comparisons with the Nazis are completely inappropriate and unjustified.

Unlike the era of mass media technologies, where the boundaries of audiences and audiovisual markets could often be mapped onto the borders of nation-states, digital technologies allow citizens to reach beyond their immediate personal and professional environment and become active members of global collectivities – clustered on the basis of mutual affinity and chosen affiliations – to articulate and promote shared cultural values and practices. In other words, 'the combination of intense local and extensive global interaction' or 'glocalization' that lies at the centre of these networked groupings (Wellman 2002: 11) facilitates the engagement of individuals in the construction of 'unimaginable communities' (Kumar 2005) that have superseded traditional cultural realizations of national identity. The role of audiovisual translators in this process is crucial. As global flows reach a new locale, bilingual viewers take on the role of co-creators, appropriating media content, subtitling it and releasing the new translated version within one or more new linguistic constituencies – thus allowing flowing broadcasts to take on new resonances as they reach newer audience segments. The significance of these developments for audio-visual translation is aptly articulated by Li (2009: 9):

> These newly visible media users are themselves circulating and engaging with media across political borders, market segments, and language barriers, creating deterritorialized social imaginaries that not only tran-scend national boundaries, but signal the emergence of new discursive spaces of audienceship that cannot be adequately described by the estab-lished models of global media culture.

Within these geographically dispersed communities of interest, audience members – including those who occasionally choose to become involved in co-creational practices – participate in the negotiation of mutual affinity by sharing aspects of their identity. The collectivities that emerge by reflexively assembling and circulating their own representations of reality through media, often by intervening in the conventional dynamics of the audio-visual markets, can thus be described as sites of participation and encounter around an audiovisual text. Drawing on Punathambekar (2008), Li (ibid.) contends that traditional conceptualizations of audiences as groupings clustered around traditional categories of cultural politics (including nation and language) are no longer helpful to understand and describe the practices and connectivities at the centre of emerging transnational commu-nities of media co-creators. The complexity of these new imaginaries, Li argues, can only be accounted for in terms of a shift from audiences to **audienceships**:

> [W]hereas an 'audience' is typically defined in terms of subject position, of the context of the viewers, 'audienceship' describes a context for the viewing process. Audienceship helps steer us away from the audience as a category of person, and towards audience as a situation that describes particular sets of practices and engagements with texts and cultural mater-ials. This is not to understate the importance of historically situated under-standings of audiences and media engagement, but to interrogate the prospect of any absolute alignment between any single factor or condition

and how texts are viewed and meanings made . . . This is especially true as media moves across national and cultural borders, resulting in increasingly complicated negotiations of cultural identity and citizenship. The notion of audienceship seeks therefore to orient the discussion around not simply *who* the audience is, but *how* it is – the practices, encounters, the discursive processes through which audiences are formed.

(Li 2009: 12–13)

Box 3.3

From audiences to audienceships . . .

One of the instances of media translation that best illustrates the shift from traditional audiences to audienceships is the co-creation of Japanese animation cinema, or *anime*, for fan communities in the US during the second half of the twentieth century.

Anime films first arrived in the US market during the 1960s, often packaged as amalgamations of unrelated anime series cobbled together into a single story and aired as such on commercial TV channels (Pérez-González 2006). The fact that, for almost two decades, imported anime films were primarily aimed at children favoured dubbing as the most effective means to Americanize the stories and characters and adapt them to the expectations of their intended conventional audiences.

The second stage in the internationalization of anime begins in the 1980s, with the release of a number of successful (predominantly science fiction) animation films oriented towards a more adult audience (Sato 2002). During this period,

> [t]he fandom grew through screening sessions at science fiction conventions and through the efforts of Westerners who traveled to Japan. Anime videotapes and laser discs were imported and distributed among club members and later by small companies formed by fans. When through such means Western fans became aware of the extent to which these texts had been altered for American audiences, distribution practices within the fan community were aimed at gaining access to the original versions of the programs.
>
> (Cubbison 2005: 48)

During this second stage, American anime audiences began to organize themselves to demand their right to experience the cultural 'otherness' behind anime films. The increasing sophistication of the storylines and the ever more crucial impact of cultural references on the viewer's appreciation of the plot enhanced the fans' awareness of their own idiosyncratic expectations. As anime communities became more engaged, their strategy shifted away from the circulation of original versions to the production of fan-translated copies facilitating their immersion in the unique imagery of the genre. It was towards the end of this second stage that American anime audiences began their transition towards audienceships, with growing numbers of viewers taking on co-creational tasks, in an attempt to strengthen the binding affinity of anime fandom through their translations. Subtitling thus became a space of participation seeking to favour specific forms of connectivity around the text.

During the third stage of internationalization, which began with the advent of digitization and led to the consolidation of anime fandom as the most influential paradigm of amateur audiovisual translation, the fan communities completed their reconfiguration into audienceships, as will be explained in Section 3.3.

The viability of audienceships is predicated on two main premises:

- Firstly, the capacity of these geographically dispersed communities to capitalize on their **collective intelligence** (Levy 2000): co-creators operate within virtual knowledge communities pooling their linguistic or technological skills and, in sharing these, extend their knowledge, influence or internal cohesion. The pooling of knowledge, particularly when it is shared online, provides a strong drive for the emergence of new transnational collaborative audienceships. *Cuaderno de Campo* bloggers (Featured example 3.1) are an excellent case in point. Mónica, a bilingual UK-based blogger, is responsible for the translation of the Galloway interview, while Trebol-A – a Spanish 'techie' affiliated to the same community – incorporates the subtitles onto the clip and makes it available online for the rest of the *Cuaderno de Campo* audienceship. More importantly, the connectivity of the blogosphere allows *Cuaderno de Campo* members to reach multiple other audienceships, inspiring like-minded individuals to subtitle media content and acting as mentors for other consumers-turned-producers or 'prosumers' (Iwabuchi 2010, Denison 2011) in a number of ways – not least the posting of online tutorials on the practicalities of subtitling.[17]

- The second requirement is inextricably connected to the previous one. Media co-creators must possess relevant **genre knowledge** (Dwyer 2012), i.e. expert skills gained through their familiarity with the values, practices and expectations of fellow group members to enhance collaboration and foster interaction within a given audienceship. The involvement of community members in translation tasks represents an important manifestation of genre expertise (O'Hagan 2008) that enhances the internal cohesion of audienceships. By 'augmenting' (Denison ibid.) both (i) the original texts through the incorporation of subtitles; and (ii) the social imagery of commercial media flows through the free circulation of amateur content within alternative geopolitical and linguistic constituencies, audienceships are shaping new discourses between prosumers and the companies that originate their media objects of political support or contestation, on the one hand, or fandom, on the other hand. Whereas national audiences revolved around market-driven commercial broadcasts and physical media copies, audienceships gravitate around socially motivated 'markets' where digital flows are bound by non-traditional models of distribution.

3.2.3 Cultural logics of the new audiovisual marketplace

Section 3.2.1 has examined the threat that the advent of co-creation – and, specifically, the proliferation of immaterial labour in the era of media convergence – represents for the social recognition of audiovisual translators' professional expertise. This involvement of amateur mediators in the translation and circulation of media content has been theorized as a form of intervention that disrupts traditional labour structures in the media industries. This section focuses on the interventionist role that collaborative networks of amateur translators are playing within the global audiovisual marketplace and the challenge they are mounting to the control that media corporations have traditionally exerted over the distribution and consumption of their products.

In their capacity as self-appointed translation commissioners, amateur translators are responsible for a displacement of commercial media content both in space and time:

- **Spatial displacements** occur as the flow of broadcasts originally released for commercial distribution in certain constituencies of the deterritorialized digital sphere is redirected by co-creational networks to reach new audienceships. The subtitling of Cohn-Bendit's speech and the Galloway interview are two cases in point. When displaced media content is brought to intersect with alternative communities of values, beliefs and practices, it often takes on new resonances, either by heightening a sense of affinity with and among the viewers, or becoming a site of social contestation. The capacity of co-creators to intervene in the circulation of media content and, hence, contribute to the spatial displacement of audiovisual texts has been boosted by the development of technologies for the 'aggregation and curation' of media flows (Li 2009: 46). While the term **aggregation site** designates a range of gateways providing easy access to torrent tracker engines (see Pérez-González 2006 for a discussion of Animesuki's torrent list), direct download aggregators or multimedia streaming sites, **curation platforms** refers to 'wikis, blogs, postings, and communities devoted to the recommendation and discussion' of amateur subtitled content, i.e. sites that 'provide information, criticism, commentary and general recommendations and direction' for potential consumers (ibid.: 47).

• Overall, the proliferation of aggregation sites and curation platforms means that the media industries are gradually losing control over where the content is to be received; however, it also brings to the fore the interventionist nature of amateur co-creational practices in relation to the temporal dimension of media consumption. Along with the ease of retrieval and storage of audiovisual texts, digitization has created the conditions for their **asynchronous** and **iterative consumption** (Crewe *et al.* 2005).

Media sociologists have accounted for the shift from a distribution towards a circulation-driven flow of media content in terms of a distinction between **linear** and **non-linear** models of communication (McNair 2006). The era of the mass and electronic media was bound by a linear model of communication: the distribution of content was controlled by top-down, elite-controlled structures, which were thus able to exercise a certain degree of political and ideological control over their national audiences. In the era of digital media, however, a non-linear model of communication prevails. This emerging context of media circulation – which exhibits unprecedented diversity and unpredictability, both in terms of the variety of content available to audiences and the increasingly atomized receiving communities – can be best described as

> a movement from a *control* to a *chaos* paradigm; a departure from the sociologist's traditional stress on the media's functionality for an unjust and unequal social order, towards greater recognition of their capacity for the disruption and interruption, even subversion of established authority structures . . . The chaos paradigm acknowledges the *desire* for control on the part of elites, while suggesting that the performance, or exercise of

control, is increasingly interrupted and disrupted by unpredictable eruptions and bifurcations arising from the impact of economic, political, ideological and technological factors on communication processes.

(McNair 2006: 3; emphasis in the original)

New audienceships, including the networks of subtitlers at their core (i.e. 'agents of chaos'), represent 'unpredictable eruptions' of resistance against the media industry and the socio-political structures they represent (i.e. 'control culture'). The multi-stop circulation of content associated with the era of media convergence provides these collectivities with abundant opportunities for the aggregation, curation and augmentation (through translation) of commercial media content — independently of whether these forms of intervention are driven by fandom, grassroots or political agendas. Non-linear models of communication are therefore central to the articulation of these audienceships or affinity spaces that constitute 'highly generative environments, from which new aesthetic experiments and innovations emerge' (Jenkins et al. 2006: 9) and have been hailed as an important engine of cultural and economic transformation (Blau 2005). The final section of this chapter turns to survey one instance of such generative experimental environments in amateur audiovisual translation.

3.3 AUDIOVISUAL TRANSLATION CYBERCULTURES

The final part of Section 3.2.3 referred to a relatively under-researched dimension of the dialectic between collaborative technologies and participatory practices: the democratization of technology. The final section of this chapter focuses precisely on one of the **cybercultures** of collaborative audiovisual translation that has emerged within this context of cultural production: **aesthetic subtitling**. Another of these subcultures, **political subtitling**, has been used as a running theme throughout the chapter and provided a comprehensive basis for discussion across different sections. These two collaborative subcultures, which aim to advance the agendas of media fans and grassroots movements, respectively, illustrate the nature and scope of interventionist audiovisual translation in the era of media convergence.

Aesthetic subtitling is primarily associated with **fansubbing**, i.e. the subtitling of television drama and films by fans involved in collaborative co-creational practices as part of networked, often transnational collectivities (see Box 3.3). The origins of fansubbing are inextricably interlinked with the early internationalization of Japanese animation cinema, or anime, which predates the advent of digital technologies. As anime audiences grew worldwide,[18] fans became increasingly unhappy about the shortage and cultural insensitivity of commercial translations of Japanese anime productions. As Dwyer (2012: 229) puts it, fans felt that 'professionally translated *anime* tended to involve extreme "flattening" or domesticating textual strategies that performed a culturally "deodorizing" function, removing its distinctly Japanese flavour'. By making selected productions of their favourite genre available to the global anime fandom community, fansubbers engaged in a form of **aesthetic activism** – resisting commercial subtitling conventions and intervening in the circuitry of anime distribution – that illustrates the trend towards cosmopolitanism in today's global media landscape (Leonard 2005).

The body of literature published on early, anime-driven fansubbing has tended to focus so far on the formal manifestations of this cyberculture's interventionist mission. The rationale for the expression of fansubbers' activism through aesthetic experimentation has been articulated, among others, by film studies scholar Abé Nornes (1999, 2007). According to Nornes, the adherence of professional translators to the commercial subtitling conventions examined in Chapter 2 – and their willingness to accept the widespread omission and suppression of meaning that the latter entail – represents a form of **corrupt mediation**. To preserve the synchronicity between the temporality of spoken dialogue and the temporality of subtitle presentation on screen, traditional subtitles convert foreignness into easily consumable information, thus depriving viewers of the possibility of getting to understand 'the Other'. Through formal experimentation and the breach of mainstream subtitling standards, however, fansubbing has emerged as a new paradigm of **abusive mediation** (see Box 3.4). Greater cognitive demands are placed on viewers, who are expected to process more information displayed in less predictable formats and in non-conventional regions of the frame. Their effort is, however, rewarded. As a form of **abusive subtitling**, fansubbing 'does not present a foreign divested of its otherness, but strives to translate from and within the place of the other by an inventive approach to language use and the steady refusal of rules' (1999: 29).

Box 3.4

Nornes on the abusive turn

The abusive subtitler uses textual and graphic abuse – that is experimentation with language and its grammatical, morphological and visual qualities – to bring the fact of translation from its position of obscurity, to critique the imperial politics that ground corrupt practices while ultimately leading the viewer to the foreign original being reproduced in the darkness of the theatre. This original is not an origin threatened by contamination, but a locus of the individual and the international that can potentially turn the film into an experience of translation.

(Nornes 2007: 177)

Hatcher (2005), Kayahara (2005) Díaz Cintas and Muñoz Sánchez (2006), and Pérez-González (2006, 2007b) have provided some of the most comprehensive accounts of the experimental conventions developed by fansubbers to date. Pérez-González's (2006, 2007b) account is the basis for the summary provided in Figure 3.4.

The two most salient formal features of early fansubbing, however, are the use of 'headnotes' and the 'dilution' of written text within the pictorial semiotics of the audiovisual text. In fansubbed content, traditional subtitles conveying the translation of diegetic[19] speech often compete for attention with other written textual elements displayed at the top of the frame. These **headnotes** complement traditional subtitles and provide audiences with a 'thicker'[20] translation of the audiovisual text. For example, they define 'untranslatable' Japanese words mentioned by the characters, gloss the cultural connotations of visible objects and actions performed on screen (see Section 5.3.2), or draw viewers' attention to contextual aspects of the narrated events, e.g. speakers' accents, geographical idiosyncrasies of landscapes, etc. Their combination of authoring (creation of traditional subtitles) and commentary (use of headnotes with glossing function) reflects the extent to which the distinction between consuming a text and re-authoring it is blurred by the practices of these interventionist communities of co-creators. Ultimately, headnotes introduce a non-diegetic dimension into the interlingual and intercultural mediation process. By including in the frame snippets of written text that do not convey the translation of dialogue between the characters, headnotes enhance the visibility of fansubbers as translators and maximize the interventionist potential of this subculture even further.

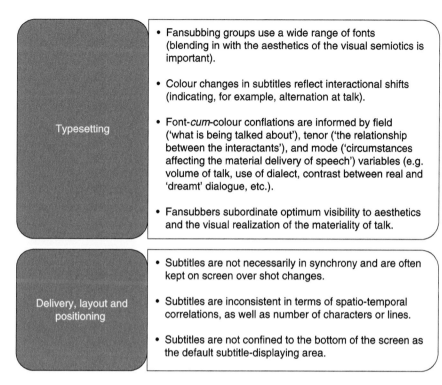

Figure 3.4 Selected formal features of fansubbing (based on Pérez-González 2006, 2007b)

But fansubbers transcend the boundaries of written language to intervene also in the visual modes of the audiovisual text (see Section 7.3). Insofar as fansubbing places particular emphasis on the affective dimension of its mediation practices, subtitles often intrude into the visual fabric of the text. In the fansubbed version of *Burst Angel* (Figure 3.5), for example, the English titles that Lunar fansubbers have inserted in different regions of the frame are styled to ensure that the aesthetics of the chosen fonts and colours blend, as much as possible, with the original language text (e.g. 'CRIMINAL', 'ARMED AND DANGEROUS'), or indeed replace the original (e.g. 'WANTED', 'REWARD') while retaining their instrumental purpose. Their genre expertise and familiarity with the expectations of the audienceship they belong to and work for drives amateur subtitlers to enhance the pictorial dimension of the subtitles. By creatively exploiting the semiotic affordances of submodes (see Section 7.4) such as colour, font,

Figure 3.5 Pictorial subtitles in fansubs by Live-Evil (Lunar's fansubs of *Burst Angel* 2005, ep. 1)

perspective and other compositional variables, Lunar fansubbers ultimately draw on these pictorial subtitles to articulate an immersive spectatorial experience for their viewers.

As the involvement of ordinary citizens in co-creational practices continues to grow apace, fansubbing has been effectively decoupled from the subtitling of anime, and become co-terminous with any form of 'subtitling made by fans of foreign films' from and into an increasing range of languages (O'Hagan 2008: 161, Barra 2009, Fernández Costales 2011). Dwyer's (2012) study of fansubbing for the Korean Viki website,[21] an online platform for the streaming of Asian drama subtitled by amateurs wishing 'to spread the love', outlines recent developments in this co-creational subculture. New trends in fansubbing have, to a certain extent, traded 'the experimentation (and attendant regulation) enabled by niche *anime* markets for broad accessibility and a more open if chaotic model of participation' (ibid.: 220). So while post-anime fansubbing is less experimental in its use of fonts or the positioning of subtitles, the involvement of fans in the processes of translation and curation has never been easier. Neither has been the nature of their mediation more unpredictable. The Viki site incorporates a subtitle editor enabling its translational audienceship to take part in the creation of subtitles without becoming formally affiliated to a fansubbing network. Unlike traditional collaborative subtitling, where translation and curation were two completely separate processes, Viki fansubbing conflates both dimensions of the co-creational process within the frame. Through the 'discussion band available for viewers to activate by clicking on a button that appears when the mouse rolls over that part of the screen' (ibid.: 231) (Figure 3.6), users vote on their favourite subtitled version – among the several proposed by fellow fans. But when enabled, the discussion band also displays fans' comments that are 'overwhelmingly devoted to celebrity gossip, and emotional responses to onscreen characters, fashions and narratives'. As Dywer notes, this 'formally and textually disruptive device . . . is used more as an emotive community-building tactic than to increase awareness of the role and production of translation itself' (ibid.).

In this chapter, I have explored the transformations that audiovisual translation has experienced following the advent of digital communications technology and discussed the implications of these changes to fundamental aspects of the audiovisual industries – including audiences, markets and the very agencies of translation. Consumers-turned-producers are opting for different forms of networked participation in the era of media convergence. Some choose to provide their free subtitles for companies and institutions they have an affinity with. Others set out to undermine the traditional dynamics of the audiovisual industry, hoping their attempts to displace

Figure 3.6 Viki fansubs (*Swallow the Sun* 2009, ep. 25)

commercial media content in space and time will contribute to effecting aesthetic, social or political change. This chapter has paid particular attention to this second group and demonstrated that, whether amateur subtitlers are driven primarily by fandom or political engagement, audiovisual translation is central to the formation of collectivities that are 'not created and self-maintained through connected devices and access alone'; they also have 'self-referential properties in that certain values, beliefs, and practices are preferred over others' (Deuze 2006: 71). The discussion of these practices brings to the fore the extent to which, after having been monopolized by a small group of professional translators during the best part of the twentieth century, audiovisual translation has now become a fluid and decentralized arena of unprecedented accessibility and diversity that is fast moving beyond existing means of analysis and critique.

FOLLOW-UP QUESTIONS FOR DISCUSSION

- Engagemedia is 'a non-profit media, technology and culture organisation' that uses 'the power of video, the Internet and free software technologies to create social and environmental change'. Engagemedia believes that 'independent media and free and open technologies are fundamental to building the movements needed to challenge social injustice and environmental damage, as well as to provide and present solutions' (www.engagemedia.org/about-us). Familiarize yourself with their volunteer subtitling initiative (www.engagemedia.org/lingua) and consult their 7 Tips on Best Practices for Subtitling (http://blog.universalsubtitles.org/2011/08/09/best-practices-for-subtitling-videos/). To what extent do the recommended subtitling practices abide by or deviate from mainstream commercial conventions? One of the sources for Engagemedia's subtitling tutorial is a guide on fansubbing. How can the use of conventions developed by fans to subtitle drama be justified in the case of Engagemedia's videos? Is Engagemedia's subtitling initiative an example of democratization of technologies? Alternatively, does it instantiate the context of production known as technologization of democracy? Before you make a final decision, note that Engagemedia's subtitling initiative is powered by Amara, 'the largest, most powerful captioning and translation platform in the world' (www.universal subtitles.org/en/) that provides corporate solutions and relies on volunteers to translate its own website (http://blog.universalsubtitles.org/volunteer/).

- Against the current expansion of postgraduate courses on audiovisual translation worldwide, consider the following excerpt from the introduction to a special issue of a leading translation studies journal on the phenomenon of non-professional translation:

> [O]ver the last four decades large sections of translation scholars have ... tried to establish the importance of professional translation/ interpreting expertise in the public consciousness by focusing on issues pertaining to translation pedagogy, translation quality assessment and criticism, as well as the observance of professional ethics and norms ... The public perception that translators and interpreters lack a systematic body of 'exclusive' knowledge remains a major obstacle for the social recognition of these occupations as professions.
> (Pérez-González and Susam-Saraeva 2012: 150)

Does the exponential growth of amateur subtitling threaten to undermine the social recognition of professional audiovisual translators even further? Alternatively, may this new development complement and enrich the work of professionals? In articulating your response, you may want to consider Dwyer's (2012) and Denison's (2011) accounts of the ways in which amateur subtitlers are beginning to enjoy commercial success and, in some cases, place professional translators out of the market.

- According to Nornes (2007), abusive subtitles manage to maintain the visibility of the original and encourage viewers to 'work off' the original semiotic ensemble (dialogue and image) while they process a profusion of titling elements all over the frame. To what extent do these proposed reading practices resemble those described by Cazdyn (2004) in relation to running subtitles on television? In his paper, Cazdyn (ibid.: 405) argues that running subtitles are necessary to process the 'unmanageable surplus of meaning' conveyed by media texts. Can abusive subtitling practices be conceptualized as forms of conveying an unmanageable surplus of meaning? What similarities and differences can you find between Nornes' and Cazdyn's accounts of modern subtitling practices?

NOTES

1 An interpreted English version of this speech is available via the European Parliament's website: www.europarl.europa.eu/ep-live/en/plenary/video?end-

date=20120611&idmep=1934&page=2&format=wmv&askedDiscussionNu mber=9 (last accessed on 15 September 2013).

2   Zorbec's blog, BLOGiokommenos, is available at http://zorbec.blogspot. co.uk/ (last accessed on 15 September 2013).

3   Zorbec's YouTube account, containing links to all the subtitled versions of the speech, is available at www.youtube.com/user/zorbec68?feature=plcp (last accessed on 15 September 2013). Viewers can also navigate their way into a different language version by clicking on any of the direct links superimposed on the frame at the beginning of the clip.

4   A comparison of the viewing figures at the time of writing revealed that the Spanish subtitled version was watched almost six times more than the Greek version, the second most popular language, and over three times more than all the other language versions put together. To some extent, this reflects the high public and media profile of the Spanish version's author. Dr Pedro Olalla, a Spanish academic and broadcaster based in Athens, used his website (http://pedroolalla.com) – structured as an aggregation site, providing the user with access to his profiles in different social networking sites – to give maximum visibility to his work and the political narratives he subscribed to. The release of his subtitled version was complemented by the posting of a blog entry on Cohn-Bendit's speech (http://pedroolalla.com/index.php/es/blog/ 75-parrhesia) and a number of media appearances discussing its implications for European policies. These dynamics of production and circulation account for the notably higher popularity of the Spanish subtitles vis-à-vis other language versions and demonstrate the impact of networked media in the digital culture.

5   See www.youtube.com/watch?v=nqno8H-mjeY&feature=plcp (last accessed on 15 September 2013).

6   For a comprehensive overview of such legislative advances in Europe, see Romero-Fresco (2012).

7   Israel originally justified its 34-day invasion of Lebanon during July–August 2006 on the grounds that, following an anti-tank missile attack by Hezbollah militants on two military vehicles patrolling the Israeli side of the border fence, three Israeli soldiers were killed, two injured and two more abducted into Lebanon. Over the course of the conflict, Israel's bombardments of Lebanon were criticized by the British government for not being sufficiently 'proportionate and restrained' (see Macintyre and Silver 2006 in *The Independent*). The premise that proportionality was necessary for Israel to win the 'political battle' represented an acknowledgement of the lack of support that Israel's stance (and, by extension, that of most Western governments behind it) drew from important sectors of the public opinion worldwide. Chomsky (2006), one of the many members of civil society with a progressive political agenda who regarded the Western posture as 'cynical fraud' (ibid.), provided an alternative analysis of the reasons for this conflict, placing it in the wider context of the Israel–Palestine conflict.

8   The interview is available via the Sky News YouTube profile at www.youtube. com/watch?v=hbyF1Mp-fHk (last accessed on 15 September 2013).

9   At the time of writing, these two interview uploads were available at www. youtube.com/watch?v=249JalaubVw&feature=related and www.youtube.com/ watch?v=E_tbj6v1KVs&feature=fvwrel, respectively.

10 Available at www.trebol-a.com/2006/08/11/585 (last accessed on 15 September 2013).

11 Available at www.trebol-a.com/2006/09/01/galloway-en-youtube/ (last accessed on 15 September 2013).

12 For a detailed discussion of the complexity surrounding the distinction between professional and amateur forms of translation, see Pérez-González and Susam-Saraeva (2012).

13 Available at www.ted.com/pages/about/ (last accessed on 15 September 2013).

14 Available at www.ted.com/pages/view/id/287/ (last accessed on 15 September 2013).

15 Available at www.universalsubtitles.org/en/teams/al-jazeera/ (last accessed on 15 September 2013).

16 Available at www.pculture.org/pcf/about/ (last accessed on 15 September 2013).

17 A subtitling tutorial provided by Trebol-A is available at www.trebol-a. com/2006/08/12/ksubtile/ (last accessed on 15 September 2013).

18 For a comprehensive historical account of the success and consolidation of anime in the US, see Cubbison (2005) and Pérez-González (2006).

19 'Diegetic' is understood here as 'belonging to the fictional world narrated in an audiovisual text'. The term 'extra-diegetic', on the other hand, designates the sphere of reality inhabited by the audience.

20 The notion of 'thick translation', discussed extensively in Hermans (2003), normally designates the use of supplementary textual material, traditionally in the form of footnotes, to provide readers with key information on the context of production of the primary text, normally with a view to enhance their reading experience.

21 Available at www.viki.com (last accessed on 15 September 2013).

CORE REFERENCES

On co-creative and participatory media practices:

Banks, John and Mark Deuze (2009) 'Co-creative Labour', *International Journal of Cultural Studies* 12(5): 419–31.

Chouliaraki, Lilie (2010) 'Self-mediation: New Media and Citizenship', *Critical Discourse Studies*, 7(4): 227–32.

Jenkins, Henry (2004) 'The Cultural Logic of Media Convergence', *International Journal of Cultural Studies*, 7(1): 33–43.

On co-creation and participatory audiovisual translation:

Barra, Luca (2009) 'The Mediation is the Message: Italian Regionalization of US TV Series as Co-creational Work', *International Journal of Cultural Studies* 12(5): 509–25.

Denison, Rayna (2011). 'Anime Fandom and the Liminal Spaces between Fan Creativity and Piracy', *International Journal of Cultural Studies*. DOI: 10.1177/1367877910391865.

Dwyer, Tessa (2012) 'Fansub Dreaming on ViKi: "Don't Just Watch but Help when you are Free" ', in Sebnem Susam-Saraeva and Luis Pérez-González (eds) *Non-professionals Translating and Interpreting: Participatory and Engaged Perspectives*, special issue of *The Translator*, 18(2), 217–43.

O'Hagan, Minako (2012) 'From Fan Translation to Crowdsourcing: Consequences of Web 2.0 User Empowerment in Audiovisual Translation', in Aline Remael, Pilar Orero and Mary Carroll (eds) *Audiovisual Translation and Media Accessibility at the Crossroads*, Amsterdam and New York: Rodopi, 25–41.

Pérez-González, Luis (2006) 'Fansubbing Anime: Insights into the "Butterfly Effect" of Globalisation on Audiovisual Translation', *Perspectives: Studies in Translatology* 14(4): 260–77.

Part II

THEORETICAL AND METHODOLOGICAL PERSPECTIVES

4

AUDIOVISUAL TRANSLATION MODELS

The professionals of film translation claim that subtitling and dubbing are not translating and therefore, by implication, cannot be dealt with by translation theory. Rowe, for example, writes that 'The activity is a bastard offshoot of phonetics and has nothing to do with translation'. This may, of course, be no more than a protective move, a case of getting one's retaliation in first, in order to ward off criticism of the work they do, but it is a problem for theory, which has to decide if there is a phenomenon here that it can deal with.

(Fawcett 1996: 67)

[T]he study of A[udio]V[isual]T[ranslation] has by now developed its very own theoretical and methodological approaches, allowing it to claim the status of a scholarly area of research in its own right. This new-found autonomy of AVT is evident in the fact that specific research frameworks have been developed for the study of dubbing and subtitling . . . In addition, AVT has become the main topic of books, postgraduate courses and international conferences focusing on the specificity of this field.

(Díaz Cintas 2009: 7)

In this chapter

The move from practice to theory in audiovisual translation has been relatively recent. The body of literature on different forms of audiovisual transfer has grown exponentially in the last two decades, but specialists have regularly raised concerns over the lack of systematic theorization that has plagued the expansion of this area of translation studies. In particular, the reliance on **allochthonous translation models** (approaches imported from the wider context of translation studies or beyond) to the detriment of **autocthonous** ones (developed from within and for audiovisual translation studies) has been identified as a challenge for audiovisual translation specialists. This chapter delivers a survey of the main theoretical models of translation that have so far propelled the disciplinary enlargement of audiovisual translation. **Process models** – informed by **psycholinguistic, cognitive** and **neurolinguistic approaches** – provide us with a better understanding of how the translator's mind functions during the mediation process. **Comparative models**, classified here into **shift-based** and **corpus-driven approaches**, set out to chart relations of correspondence between aspects of source and target texts. Finally, **causal models** of audiovisual translation shed light on why the translation looks the way it does. Causal models include **systems** and **norm-based approaches**, which examine how the interaction of power, prestige and other market factors has shaped the way audiovisual translation is used in different contexts. Against the backdrop of increased attention to processes of contextualization, discourse and ideological approaches investigating the impact of gender, ideology and power differentials on audiovisual translation decisions also lend themselves to causal readings.

▶ WATCH THE INTRODUCTION VIDEO

4.1 FROM PRACTICE TO THEORIZATION

What a difference a decade makes – or so would the juxtaposition of the two introductory quotations suggest. Poised on the cusp of a dramatic cultural and technological shift, i.e. the beginning of the transition from the electronic to the digital culture, Fawcett (1996) brings into sharp relief the precarious position that audiovisual translation occupied in academia until the mid-1990s. At a time when translation studies was beginning to establish itself as a 'scientific' discipline, audiovisual translation practitioners were still sceptical about the 'theorizability' of the decisions they made in the exercise of their professional discretion – effectively raising 'the question of what translation theory can make of such an aleatory phenomenon' (ibid.: 65). But practitioners' reservations were not, according to Fawcett, the only factor hampering the 'academization' of audiovisual translation at the time.

The most significant obstacles encountered by scholars in the 1980s and early 1990s can be summarized under the three headings in Figure 4.1.

The extent to which audiovisual translation had evolved by the end of the noughties can be gleaned from the second introductory quotation. It is reasonable to posit that the emancipation of audiovisual translation as a 'scholarly area of research in its own right' (Díaz Cintas 2009: 7) is partially predicated on the growing ubiquity of digital communication technology. By facilitating the 'reproducibility' and 'manipulability' of audiovisual material, networked mediascapes have minimized some of the material difficulties that had previously beset audiovisual translation research.

Changes in the make-up of the profession, on the other hand, have also played a significant role in keeping prescriptivism at bay. A growing number of audiovisual translation practitioners are now translation graduates with the capacity to reflect critically on their translational decisions and the range of interdisciplinary factors that inform their chosen mediation strategies.

However, one of the most significant driving forces behind the consolidation of audiovisual translation has been the gradual expansion of the definition of translation 'to encompass a wide range of activities and products that do not necessarily involve an identifiable relationship with a discrete source text' (Baker 2014: 15). As a result, the term 'translation' is no longer restricted to designating processes of linguistic mediation that involve rendering spoken text into an 'equivalent' oral or written version in another language. Having received formal training in translation, the new generation of professionals is better placed to contribute to and benefit from this re-conceptualization of translation as well as the sophisticated strategies of mediation that it now incorporates within its remit (see Chapter 7).

But are these developments significant enough to support Díaz Cintas' contention that audiovisual translation has become a fully fledged discipline for which 'specific frameworks have been developed' (2009: 7)? A selective survey of the literature reveals evidence for and against his argument. Having fleshed out the rationale for Díaz Cintas' stance in previous paragraphs, I now present a sample of opinions that would seem to urge more caution in weighing the available evidence:

> Apart from descriptive studies on dubbing and subtitling, . . . there does exist rather more literature dealing with the problems of general translation, analysed in the corpora of audiovisual texts . . . Strictly speaking, then, we should not consider those works which centre on literary aspects

Material difficulties

- Analysing audiovisual material is time-consuming. Iterative viewing of data is often required to gauge the viability of a research project, support or refute hypotheses, or respond to a set of research questions. Similarly, conventions and protocols for the transcription of multimodal texts are less standardized and systematic than those used in the analysis of written texts.

- Working with audiovisual material requires access to and familiarity with specific technological processes and equipment, and raises complex copyright issues. The extraction and reproduction of audiovisual fragments for the purposes of illustration may not be universally endorsed by fair use policies. On a related note, the presentation and dissemination of research findings can be challenging, particularly in traditional publication outlets that rely primarily on printed written text.

- Building homogeneous corpora of comparable audiovisual material – including different language versions of one text in one or more audiovisual translation modalities – is expensive and rarely viable. This can result in 'random' corpora and, by extension, dubious results.

Prescriptivism

- Working with audiovisual material requires the capacity to engage with concepts and insights pertaining to a range of disciplines, including semiotics and film studies. Audiovisual translators should be able to account for the impact of their mediation on the redistribution of meaning across different semiotic resources during the translation process.

- The acquisition of professional translation skills is often driven by prescriptivist judgements not always based on research. This often results in a tendency to anecdotalism and over-reliance on personal intuition and habits.

Mediality

- Synchronization is central to commercial audiovisual translation. The technological apparatus developed by the film industry in the twentieth century (Chapter 2) demands adherence to the synchronous diegetic sound principle in certain modes of audiovisual translation. In these contexts, the nature and scope of the chosen translation strategies will be subordinated to the degree of spatio-temporal synchrony required by the commissioner.

- 'Audiovisual translation' is an umbrella term encompassing a wide range of audiovisual transfer types. Each of these involves specific combinations of semiotic resources and varying synchronization demands across different geographical contexts and markets (Section 2.4) – which exacerbates the excessive reliance on anecdotalism and intuitive decision-making.

Figure 4.1 Obstacles to theorization in audiovisual translation (based on Fawcett 1996)

of novels adapted for the cinema, on mechanisms of cinematographic adaptation, on the sociological or political aspects of an audiovisual text with the excuse of its translation, or those centred on concrete cases such as the translation of film titles of proper nouns in certain films, and so forth, to be studies on audiovisual translation.

(Chaume Varela 2002: 1–3)

If we want our area of research to be given the consideration it deserves, more analyses are needed with a more theoretical and less anecdotal approach. I personally believe that D[escriptive]T[ranslation]S[tudies] offers an ideal platform from which to launch this approach. For translation scholars, this catalogue of concepts is a heuristic tool that opens up new avenues for study, strengthens the theoretical component and allows the researcher to come up with substantial analyses. Scholars then belong to a research community, minimising the risk of coming up with approximations that are too intuitive or too individual and subjective . . . To work within a school – that does not have to be static or rigid – helps to avoid a possible and menacing diaspora of knowledge.

(Díaz Cintas 2004: 165)

When read in succession, these stances reflect a shifting and fragile consensus on the robustness of audiovisual translation as a field of scholarly inquiry. Do descriptive studies represent an established canon of research in the field, as Chaume Varela appeared to suggest at the turn of the century? Or do they constitute, as Díaz Cintas contended only two years later, the much-needed platform to agglutinate future research on audiovisual translation? Delimiting the scope and remit of the discipline emerges as another area of concern expressed by both scholars, although each of them approaches this issue from a different angle. Chaume Varela's essentialist stance advocates the exclusion from the emergent discipline of any study that fails to address explicitly the semiotic idiosyncrasies of audiovisual material – whatever the theoretical framework(s) informing the research. On the other hand, Díaz Cintas' programmatic prescription to place descriptive translation studies at the centre of audiovisual translation ultimately articulates an opposing view: it is by sanctioning specific theoretical frameworks (rather than research topics) that organic disciplinary growth obtains.

This section has exposed a range of inconsistencies in the discourses that circulate around the status of audiovisual translation studies as a (sub) discipline within the wider domain of translation studies. As shown here, disciplinary progress is still varyingly gauged by different scholars relying on seemingly overlapping terms – including 'research framework', 'theoretical approach', 'theoretical component', '(research) school' or even 'descriptive studies'. This chapter aims to make a more systematic contribution to the debate and reveal the full scope of theoretical innovation seen in audiovisual translation studies over the last three decades. Having illustrated the extent to which laxity in the use of technical terms has led to what outsiders may perceive as divergent appraisals of scholarly achievements in the field, I will now seek to establish a level playing field for the discussion of such developments.

4.2 AUTOCHTHONOUS VERSUS ALLOCHTHONOUS MODELS OF AUDIOVISUAL TRANSLATION

Chesterman on Translation Theories and Translation Models

'Theory' and 'model' are slippery concepts. The recent *Dictionary of Translation Studies* (Shuttleworth and Cowie 1997) refers only to the following as theories: skopos theory, polysystem theory, and the interpretive theory of translation. The only entries containing the word 'model' are on the ethno-linguistic model of translation (Nida) and the operational model (Bathgate). This is interesting: some approaches are designated as theories and others are not (there is a manipulation school), and some models but not others seem to have attained proper-name status. There is obviously much conceptual work still to be done in translation studies on clarifying what we mean by a theory or a model.

(Chesterman 2000: 15)

As discussed in the previous section, the disciplinary status of audiovisual translation has grown as scholars in the field have articulated new ways of theorizing those forms of semiotic transfer observed in materials that co-ordinate text, images and sound. But how can we gauge the originality of these theorizations vis-à-vis other developments in the wider domain of translation studies? Drawing on Andrew Chesterman (2000), I would argue that elusive concepts such as **translation theory** and **translation model** have an important role to play in this debate.

The choice of one or more theories is central to the structuring of a research project. The conceptual network and suppositions underpinning the chosen theory shape the way(s) in which data is to be interrogated, and give us a logical framework to ask questions about the primary object of investigation, respectively. However, not all the frameworks that help us orient ourselves when trying to account for different aspects of translation exhibit the same degree of abstraction or sophistication. Indeed, as Chesterman notes,

- the term 'theory' designates 'a set of concepts and statements (claims, hypotheses) that provides a systematic perspective on something, a perspective that allows us to understand it in some way, and hence perhaps to explain it' (ibid.: 15);
- the term 'models of translation' refers to 'preliminary, pretheoretical ways of representing the object or research' (ibid.).

While theories are configured as idealized representations of the object of study and calculated to have the maximum explanatory power, models have a more practical dimension. In Chesterman's own words, models 'are often understood as being intermediate constructions, between theory and data' and used to 'illustrate a theory, or part of a theory' (ibid.: 15). For example, in applying polysystem theory to the study of audiovisual translation (Section 4.5.1), scholars may choose different models, depending on whether they are interested, for example, in how dubbed language has developed features that differentiate it from spontaneous interaction in the target language; or in the extent to which the prestige or relative power of a given language on the international scene has led to the prevalence of a specific modality of audiovisual translation in the country where it is spoken.

On the basis of these definitions, it is reasonable to posit that a fully fledged theory is yet to emerge within and for audiovisual translation studies. As Chaume Varela (2002: 1) aptly highlights, the onus remains on 'teachers and researchers to draw our attention precisely to those aspects which mark it [audiovisual translation] as different from other modalities, whilst the effort is made to ensure that the global theoretical framework of our discipline can include the peculiarities of this modality'. Instead, the burgeoning body of audiovisual translation studies published over the last three decades reveals the extent of the field's reliance on **allochthonous models of translation** (approaches imported from the wider context of translation studies or beyond), to the detriment of their **autochthonous** counterparts (developed from within and for audiovisual translation studies).

The remainder of this chapter delivers a survey of the main models that have so far propelled the academic development of audiovisual translation, drawing on the three model types proposed by Chesterman (2000):

- **process models** of translation: dynamic representations seeking to capture and formalize the different phases of the translation process;
- **comparative models** of translation: constructions developed in positing relations of similarity between source and target texts, with an emphasis on the description of translation products;
- **causal models** of translation: representations of translation aiming (i) to unveil how different 'levels of causation' – including cognitive, situational and socio-cultural issues – influence the production of the target text; and (ii) to identify the effect that the target text has on its readership.

Of note is the fact that comparative and process models may be causally implicit. In comparative models, 'a particular equivalence relation can be read as a cause-effect sequence' when a given element or feature of the target text can be demonstrated to follow from the presence of a similar one in its source counterpart. Likewise, causality is present in process models in those cases where the translator's choices can be shown to be 'determined by what was done in a preceding phase, or indeed the purpose of the translation' (Williams and Chesterman 2002: 53).

The overview of scholarly work provided in the following sections is not meant to be exhaustive. Given the wide remit of audiovisual translation studies as currently configured and the ready availability of syntheses of theoretical trends (Gambier 2006b, O'Connell 2007, Pérez-González 2009, Chiaro 2009, Remael 2010, Baker and Pérez-González 2011, Chaume Varela 2013, Díaz Cintas 2013, Gambier 2013, among others), this chapter will thus rely on a selection of studies that best illustrate the contribution of process, comparative and causal models to the expansion of audiovisual translation over the last three decades.

4.3 PROCESS MODELS OF TRANSLATION

Among the range of scenarios where Williams and Chesterman (2002: 52) envisage the use of process models of translation, two of them appear to recur in audiovisual translation studies: studies seeking to make inferences about the functioning of translators' minds – on the basis of the source language input and the target language output; and research work investigating the 'sequential relations between different phases of the translation process'. Studies based on process models of translation that are surveyed here deal with:

- applications of psycholinguistic theories to optimize information processing in subtitling and respeaking;
- the contribution of figure/ground alignments to minimize the arbitrariness of current audio description guidelines;
- the articulation of cognitive metrics to maximize the match between films and audio described films – i.e. between visuals and their verbalizations;
- the impact of sensory stimuli on the comprehension and perception of original and translated media content;
- the feasibility of translating audio description across languages and cultures;
- subtitlers' handling of implied language.

4.3.1 Psycholinguistic models

Audiovisual translation has traditionally relied and continues to draw on sequential constructs and assumptions originally developed within psycholinguistics and information processing studies. From these disciplinary perspectives, subtitling can be conceptualized as the reshaping of linguistic information over a number of stages. To begin with, the source language speech is transformed into a target language written representation: starting with the choice of words, subtitlers proceed on to form phrases, then clauses and, eventually, assemble complete 'information units'. In the case of dubbing, the shift towards the target language also takes place early in the reshaping process: the source language acoustic input is initially transformed into a target language phonological representation, which is manipulated in various ways to create translated speech. Viewers' processing of subtitles or dubbed conversation follows the opposite direction: the starting point is the form of words, which are then mapped onto meaning.

The fact that linguistic information in audiovisual material has to be assembled and processed under pressures of time adds further complexity to the production and reception of translations, respectively. Psycholinguists (Wray 2002) have posited that understanding written or spoken language effectively under these medial constraints is feasible because frequently occurring groups of words are stored in the mind as pre-assembled chunks. When watching a subtitled film, psycholinguists argue, viewers are able to recognize and anticipate these structures – and hence process them faster. In sum, audiences can keep apace of the filmic action because subtitles contain pre-packaged structures whose parts need not be parsed individually.

The insight that most of these pre-assembled chunks can be mapped on to grammatical phrases has helped scholars to operationalize the role of information processing theories in practical subtitling. Karamitroglou (1998), for example, postulates grammatical phrases as the 'lowest syntactic' nodes with the capacity to influence the internal segmentation of subtitles (Box 4.1).

Box 4.1

Syntactic nodes and subtitle segmentation (Karamitroglou 1998)

The subtitled text should appear segmented at the highest syntactic nodes possible. This means that each subtitle flash should ideally contain one complete sentence. In cases where the sentence cannot fit in a single-line subtitle and has to continue over a second line or even over a new subtitle flash, the segmentation on each of the lines should be arranged to coincide with the highest syntactic node possible. For example, before we segment the phrase:

'The destruction of the city was inevitable.' (44 characters),

we first have to think of its syntactic tree as follows:

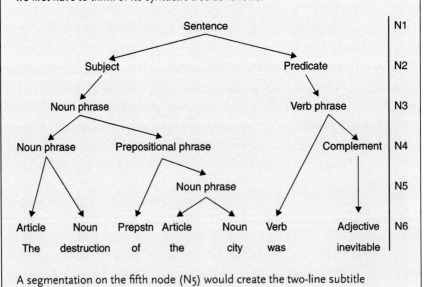

A segmentation on the fifth node (N5) would create the two-line subtitle

'The destruction of the
city was inevitable.'

A segmentation on the second node (N2) would create the two-line subtitle

'The destruction of the city
was inevitable.'

Out of the two segmentations, it is the second that flows as more readable. This occurs because the higher the node, the greater the grouping of the semantic load and the more complete the piece of information presented to the brain. When we segment a sentence, we force the brain to pause its linguistic processing for a while, until the eyes trace the next piece of linguistic information. In cases where segmentation is inevitable, therefore, we should try to force this pause on the brain at a point where the semantic load has already managed to convey a satisfactorily complete piece of information.

Recent eye-tracking studies (Rajendran *et al.* 2013) have corroborated the key role of segmentation in speeding up the comprehension of subtitles and provided us with a better understanding of the psycholinguistic mechanisms that influence the processing of written language in the context of subtitled audiovisual material. Earlier experimental studies (d'Ydewalle and Van de Poel 1999) concluded that subtitle reading tended to dominate the viewing experience to the detriment of the visuals. This is the case, according to d'Ydewalle and Van de Poel, whether or not viewers are used to watching subtitled material; they need the subtitles to understand what is going in the film or programme, even when information is being provided through the acoustic channel. The work of Rajendran *et al.* (2013: 18), however, reveals some nuances that had not been gleaned in earlier studies, showing that 'text chunking by phrase or by sentence reduces the amount of time spent on subtitles, and presents the text in a way that is more easily processed'. This is particularly important in the context of respeaking, a modality of audiovisual translation where viewers rely heavily on subtitles.

Indeed, the fact that effective subtitle segmentation is still attracting considerable scholarly attention is reflective of the rise of assistive forms of audiovisual transfer such as subtitling for the hard of hearing, respeaking and audio description. It is precisely the need to facilitate the access of sensory impaired members of the audience to visually and acoustically conveyed meaning that has driven the proliferation of research informed by cognitive linguistics.

4.3.2 Cognitive models

Audiovisual translation specialists are becoming ever more interested in exploring the relevance of **gestalt perception** theories to audiovisual translation. The logic behind the principle of gestalt perception is as follows: when presented with a visually complex object, the human eye focuses on the object as a whole before focusing on its individual constituents. The implication of this principle is that the meaning conveyed by the object in its entirety is greater than the sum of its parts.

One of the experiential aspects of gestalt perception that has found increasing favour within audiovisual translation research is the dialectic between the constructs of **figure** and **ground**. This strand of cognitive research contends that, when viewing a given scene, members of the audience will invariably single out certain elements as prominent figures, while relegating others to the less salient status of ground. Talmy's (2000) application of these notions shows that perceptual stimuli typically selected as figures tend to be geometrically simpler, smaller and more movable than ground entities. It is because of the strong associations between figure entities and mobility that other specialists such as Tyler and Evans (2003) use the terms **trajector** and **landmark** to refer to figure and ground elements, respectively.

Perceptions of **prominence** or **salience**, as conceptualized within the field of cognitive linguistics, are beginning to yield interesting results in the study of audio description. Audio describers have so far tended to select the information they convey to their blind audience by relying on their own intuitions as to what their viewers require to enjoy the narrative (Orero 2008). To a large extent, this arbitrariness stems from the fact that '[e]ven after watching the same film, different people have different recollections and interpretations, and in some cases some details are observed by some while going unnoticed by others' (Orero and Vilaró 2012: 297–98). Grasping the impact of this variability is the main impetus behind Kruger's (2012) contribution to this research strand. By relying on eye-tracking technology (see Section 5.3.1), he sets out to determine the extent to which variable perceptions of visual saliency influence the effectiveness of audio descriptions. The analysis of eye-tracking data is meant to reveal those visual elements of a film that are more prominent for sighted viewers; provide a better understanding of the role that visually salient entities play in the development of the narrative; and yield a systematic insight into the mechanisms of 'cognitive construction' used by sighted viewers. On the basis of his results, Kruger concludes that audio describers' capacity to 're-narrativize film more effectively for blind viewers' (ibid.: 69) is contingent on their ability to gauge both the **visual prominence** and **narrative saliency** of specific entities (see Box 4.2).

Box 4.2

Kruger (2012: 82–83)

[I]t would appear that the audio narrator has to be attuned firstly to the narrative saliency of the different visual elements before selecting which elements to convey in the A[udio]N[arration], and not attend only, or mainly, to those elements with high visual saliency. It may very well imply that there will be cases where elements with a high visual saliency but a lower narrative saliency will have to be sacrificed, something that may not sit that well with some practicing audio describers, and something that holds the danger of alienating partially sighted viewers because of something like a visual 'gossip effect'. And, as in all AVT contexts, the competition between different codes is such that selection is often based on the prioritization of information, which means that when faced with a situation in which there are more than one visually salient elements that also have high (but not equal) narrative saliency, the narrative saliency will have to take priority.

Vandaele also relies on a cognitive theoretical framework to examine how audio describers identify those discourse elements that produce narrative force with a view to 'attain a degree of narrative equivalence between source film and audio described film' (2012: 87). According to Vandaele, **narrative force** is made up of two intersecting planes: discourse and story: '[D]iscourse constructs story content for the reader's or audience's mind, and the action-logical nature of this content makes the mind generate predictions and evaluations which may (or may not) be confirmed by the narrational discourse' (ibid.: 90). Suggestive 'discursive triggers' can thus give rise to specific narrative states of mind – such as suspense, surprise or curiosity. Insofar as these triggers prompt viewers to hypothesize about the narrated world, they play a significant role in the reception of the story – hence the importance of selecting narratively relevant information. Difficulties inherent to this process are compounded by the time constraints under which audio describers operate. Ultimately, it is their capacity to discriminate between 'visual information [that] (co)creates realized and hypothesized action' (ibid.) that distinguishes an effective, fully narrative audio description from a mere 'action summary'.

Vandaele's study of film **renarrativization** also aims to gauge the similarity between film images and the mental imagery that audio describers produce through their verbalizations. Drawing on the widely held view that thinking processes revolve around 'imagistic cognition', and the concomitant premise that language evokes image-based representations of reality, Vandaele contends that effective audio descriptions are bound to be informed by **embodied** or **grounded models of cognition**. In other words, to achieve equivalence between film images and the mental imagery that re-creates them in audio described narrations, it is necessary to incorporate a perspectival reading of time and space, where events and locations are described with reference to the viewer. According to Vandaele, metrics originally developed by cognitive linguists – e.g. Langacker (1987), Talmy (2000), Herman (2009) – can help audio describers to optimize the match between film images and their verbalizations (Box 4.3).

Box 4.3

Metric to describe the imagery of verbal narrative (or construal) (adapted from Vandaele 2012: 96–97):

- **selection**: how much of the filmic scene is incorporated in the narrated scene that one is construing;
- **perspective**, which includes:
  - **figure-ground alignment**, foreground-background relations;
  - **viewpoint** = vantage point + orientation within a directional grid consisting of vertical and horizontal axes;
  - **deictic expressions**: they incorporate some reference to the 'ground' or situation of utterance;
  - **subjectivity/objectivity of a verbal narrative**: the more the ground is included, the more objectivized the verbal narrative.

- **abstraction**: pertains to the degree of granularity (level of detail) of a verbal narrative;
- **location of a perspective point** within a 'referent scene';
- **distance of a perspective point** from the regarded scene (distal, medial, proximal);
- **perspectival mode**, including

  - **motility**: whether the perspective point is stationary or moving;
  - **mode proper**: synoptic versus sequential viewing.

- **direction of viewing**: 'sighting' in a particular direction (spatially or temporally) from an established perspective point.

Although they do not always acknowledge the theoretical influence of cognitive science so explicitly, many other studies have recently set out to formalize different aspects of the cognitive construction processes at the heart of audio description practices. Salway (2007), for example, draws on basic assumptions of **cognititive narratology** to postulate the importance of selecting appropriate material as a basis to construe objective verbal narratives. Audio describers, Salway argues, use a 'special language characterized by a preponderance of linguistic features that are idiosyncratic in comparison with everyday language' (ibid.: 154). A classification of the main types of information provided by audio describers is then proposed on the basis of a semi-automated, corpus-based analysis of narratives in over 90 films. But cognitive narratology is also central to other qualitative studies focusing on the analysis of narratives from an 'audience-oriented, story-reception perspective' (Vercauteren 2012: 212). Unlike traditional structuralist approaches, cognitive narratology 'tells us how audiences process stories and how they prioritize information' (ibid.), including the audio description of time in film.

4.3.3 Neurolinguistic and pragmatics-based models

Although neurolinguistics has traditionally been dominated by research on language disorders, this interdisciplinary field of study has widened its scope to account for the impact of factors such as sensory stimuli, 'emotions, multimodality, body movements and actions' on the relationship between language use and brain activity (Ahlsén 2011: 469).

Recent work on the influence of sound effects on the comprehension of video content illustrates how the widened remit of neurolinguistics can inform audiovisual translation research. Vilaró *et al.* (2012), for example, argue that the perception of a given visual clip can vary if this is viewed in combination with different audio tracks. Changes in acoustic stimuli would appear to influence the gaze trajectories and the foci of the viewing experience. The insight that sound proves to be as important as images in shaping viewers' perception and comprehension of audiovisual content has important implications for the study of audio description, as noted by the authors of the study (Box 4.4).

But even if the impact of auditory stimuli on the perception of audiovisual texts is confirmed by further research, the question arises as to whether that influence is the same across different languages and cultures. For example, can an English audio description informed by heatmap visualizations and other data on gaze trajectories be readily translated into other languages? Alternatively, should the narration be developed from scratch in each language in recognition of potential differences in the way different cultures categorize and perceive those stimuli?

Box 4.4

Implications of neurolinguistic research for the production of audio description (AD) guidelines (Vilaró *et al.* 2012: 62–63):

AD describers can view sighted participants' gaze data (heatmaps) as a means of guiding their own description of the scene (for participants who may have trouble viewing the scene due to problems with their own sight). If, given different classes of viewers, their gaze data does not show any significant difference (there is indeed little variation), then audio describers can use the heatmap visualization as a kind of visual indicator of what to describe. There have been a few AD examples where the AD talks about a character's dress, or other scene elements, whereas it is the emotion on the character's face that is most relevant to the story – in such cases viewers' gaze points tend to coalesce atop the face with little variation.

If, on the other hand, the aggregated gaze data does show significant differences, one may then probe further into what has driven the disparity, e.g. culture, translated audio track, or something else? In this case, the AD describers may choose to follow one set of gaze points, or attempt to provide a description of multiple visual attractors.

According to Gronek *et al.* (2012), the viability of repurposing audio descriptions across linguacultures can only be established by comparing the **culture systems** (Floros 2003) that underpin different language versions of a given narration. Cultural systems are understood here as categorizations of background cultural knowledge that viewers need to be acquainted with and rely on in order to comprehend audiovisual content. Each cultural system manifests itself through a set of features known as **concretizations**, which can be bundled into groups of interrelated features known as **holons**. In their study, Gronek *et al.* (ibid.) compare the concretizations of the 'help and thanks' holon (Table 4.1) that feature in English and German narrativizations of the same clip:

In the film scene that is part of the analysis, a boy is riding a bike, falls down, and the pears that he is transporting on his bike fall on the ground, as does his hat. A group of three boys come along and help him to collect the pears. The boy drives away on his bike and shortly after that the kids whistle at him, since they had found the boy's hat. One of the three returns it to the boy, whereafter the boy gives him three pears without saying anything. The overall context leads to the hypothesis that this gesture is a way to say **thank you** for the previous **action(s) of 'help'**.

(Gronek *et al.* 2012: 48–49; my emphasis)

The concretizations of the 'help and thanks' holon are, according to this study, more frequent in the English version; in other words, the expression of 'thanks' following an 'action of help' is less explicit in the German narrative. It therefore follows that neglecting the connection between 'help' of 'thanks' in English audio descriptions – for example, when these are translated from German – may result in a 'coherence gap' hampering comprehension of the clip by English-speaking audiences. By contrast, the unnecessary expression of thanks in German audio descriptions translated from English may result in information overload and constrain the viewers' interpretative space. This insight, the authors conclude, 'strengthen[s] the argument that translating an AD into another language is inadequate from a cultural point of view' (ibid.: 43).

Albeit not theorized in terms of culture systems, viewers' reliance on background knowledge as an aid to the comprehension of translated audiovisual material is also central to recent pragmatics-based studies on interlingual subtitling. Desilla (2009, 2012), for example, builds on the insight that opaque or indirect meaning – arising from the mismatch between what speakers say and their underlying communicative intention – is central to the enjoyment of (translated) film dialogue. When interpreting **implicatures**, understood as what the dialogue indirectly suggests, viewers draw on

Table 4.1 Sample German and English narrations

Sample German narration (back-translated into English)	Sample English narration
Three boys come by and **help** the pear thief to collect his pears. One boy **helps** him to get up and knock off the dust. Then the boy mounts his bicycle and rides off. One of the boys finds the floppy hat and whistles loudly. The boy on his bicycle stops and waits until the other boy has brought him his hat. He **gives** him three of his pears and rides off.	3 boys say what happened and **helped** the boy pick up his pears. As they were walking away 1 of the boys found the other child's hat and gave it back to him. **To say thank you, the boy gave** them 3 pears (1 each).

Source: adapted from Gronek *et al.* 2012: 50

a 'background of expectations which may be revised or elaborated as the utterance unfolds' (Wilson and Sperber 2004: 615).

Instances of conversational indirectness or implicatures are particularly difficult to elucidate in multimodal environments, for the construal of implicatures in audiovisual texts often involves the combined use of spoken language and salient non-verbal cinematic signifiers. Drawing on the theoretical apparatus of **relevance theory**, Desilla hypothesizes that viewers work out implicatures by (i) retrieving background knowledge in the form of **implicated premises** (i.e. the most readily accessible assumptions guiding the addressee towards a relevant interpretation in that context); and (ii) selecting the information readily conveyed via the film's image and sound as **immediate contextual premises**. Box 4.5 reproduces a fragment of Desilla's (2009) discussion on a specific example from *Bridget Jones: The Edge of Reason* (2004), based on the analysis of a **multimodal transcript** containing both verbal and non-verbal data (Section 8.2.3).

Box 4.5

Working out implicatures in filmic dialogue (Desilla 2009: 199–200)

Bridget [Jones] and [her fiancé] Mark are having tea with her parents. Pam [Bridget's mum] asks them when they are going to name the day. Bridget and Mark are rather taken aback by this question and feel uneasy. There is an awkward silence for about six seconds during which the characters merely exchange glances. It is Mark who breaks this silence saying that he and Bridget 'are certainly not thinking about that yet'. Then he turns for confirmation to Bridget, who, quite surprised, chuckles nervously and finally agrees. Her disappointment and heartache are palpable in the subsequent close-ups. These shots pave the way for the conversation between Bridget and Mark in the car. Bridget asks Mark if he meant 'the thing' that he said. Mark insists that he does not know what thing Bridget is talking about. Although Bridget starts to lose her patience she strategically avoids being more explicit; she merely refers to 'the thing, thing'. Bearing in mind Bridget's reaction to what Mark said about their non-existent marriage plans in her parents' house, the audience can infer that what she actually wants to know is whether Mark wants to marry her (implicated conclusion). However, marriage is usually considered a rather risky subject at the first stages of a relationship (implicated premise). Bridget does not pursue the topic openly, presumably because she is afraid of rejection. Communicating obliquely seems to be safer in this case. As in the previously examined examples Bridget appeals for Mark's empathy, demanding that he understands her intimations, only to be disappointed again. Bridget faint-heartedly enriches her own utterance in a feeble attempt to make him co-operate. Yet, Mark's silence indicates that he does not wish to have this conversation now, and Bridget eventually gives up bitterly frustrated. Needless to say, the emotional music and the rainy weather intensify Bridget's sadness.

Admittedly, conversational indirectness is costly, as it requires a great processing effort on the part of the viewer. In some cases, audiences may misunderstand the intended implicature – by selecting a context more or less different from the one intended by the film creators – or simply fail to identify the relevant implicated premises. But difficulties in the pursuit of implicature recovery are even more significant when filmic dialogue is subtitled into a different linguaculture. Target language viewers may lack the necessary background knowledge to work out implicatures that presuppose familiarity with aspects of the source culture. Consider Desilla's (2009) example below, where Bridget Jones' mum (Pam) compares herself to Australian-born, British feminist writer and academic Germaine Greer while expressing her regrets about her lack of power, career and sex life (*Bridget Jones's Diary* 2001):

PAM: Darling, if I came in with my knickers on my head he wouldn't notice. I've spent thirty-five years cleaning his house, washing his clothes, bringing up his children . . .
BRIDGET: I'm your child too.
PAM: To be honest, darling, having children isn't all it's cracked up to be. Given my chance again, I'm not sure I'd have any. Now it's the winter of my life and I haven't actually got anything of my own. I've got no power, no real career, no sex life. Got no life at all. I'm . . . I'm like the grasshopper who sang all summer. Like Germaine sodding Greer.

The question thus arises as to how source language implicatures are relayed in the target language subtitles. Do subtitlers simply retain the original's conversational indirectness across languages or do they, to a greater or lesser extent, spell out the implicatures through processes of 'explicitation' (Shuttleworth and Cowie 1997: 55)? Desilla's analysis of her data sample, consisting of English films and their corresponding Greek subtitled versions, suggest that implicatures tend to be preserved in subtitles – either because medial constraints make it impossible to spell them out in the subtitles or on account of viewers' preference for indirect communication in certain filmic genres. The frequency of partial or total explicitation would appear to be higher in the case of implicatures that are endemic to the source culture, and 'whose recovery presupposes familiarity with specific aspects of the source culture' (Desilla 2009: 220).

The range of psycholinguistic, cognitive, neurolinguistic and pragmatics-based approaches surveyed in this section ultimately reveal how the human mind functions while engaged in the process of audiovisual translation, whether at the producing or receiving end. A set of widely shared assumptions pertaining to the assembly and storage of language in the brain and a widening network of conceptual tools and knowledge resources – including, among others, notions such as implicature, figure/ground alignment, embodied cognition, cognitive construction, cultural system, and holon – are improving our understanding of the processual interplay between verbal and non-verbal semiotics, particularly in the context of emergent forms of assistive audiovisual translation. To a large extent, the growing contribution of process models to the expansion of audiovisual translation studies is being driven by the advent of new methods and technologies for measuring and visualizing cognitive and neurolinguistic phenomena.

4.4 COMPARATIVE MODELS OF TRANSLATION

Comparative models are some of the earliest and simplest formalizations and representations of knowledge about translation. Typically more static than their process counterparts, comparative models focus on translated output (products) to chart relations of equivalence or, more loosely, correspondence between source and target texts. From an essentialist standpoint, comparative models can be regarded as a logical extension of contrastive linguistics: instead of language systems, however, comparative models of translation put original and translated texts under contrastive study (Chesterman 2000).

As first noted in Section 4.2, there is a considerable degree of overlap between comparative and causal models. Any relationship of equivalence or correspondence between texts can be ultimately accounted for in terms of a cause-effect sequence based on discernible correlations between certain source text elements and specific target text features. Given the importance of directionality in traditional conceptualizations of translation, source text entities have been normally regarded as the causes for the occurrence of their target text correlates. Despite having an in-built causal dimension, the range of comparative studies surveyed in this section place their emphasis on the description of similarities and differences between original texts and their translations – rather than on the causes why translations look the way they do.

Studies based on comparative models of translation surveyed in the following subsections address the following issues:

- the productivity of the notion of shift in articulating and classifying similarities and differences between originals and translations, at different levels of textual organization;
- the use of different types of computer-held corpora as a benchmark against which certain features of translated audiovisual texts (e.g. naturalness) can be measured.

4.4.1 Shift-based models

For the last two decades, scholars have been preoccupied with the challenge of defining audiovisual translation and delimiting their object of study in different ways. The strength of this definitional impulse during the late 1980s and early 1990s was indeed justified, given the lack of a scholarly consensus about the place of audiovisual texts and audiovisual translation within the wider discipline of translation studies (see Section 1.1). During this period, most attempts to investigate the idiosyncrasy of audiovisual translation as a form of intersemiotic mediation involved the development of a systematic record of translation strategies used in the field – often drawing on case studies based on the translation of a single film. By cataloguing recurrent translation strategies and formalizing the differences between source and target texts that such strategies brought about, audiovisual translation scholars attempted to generalize certain translational trends and features as inherent to subtitling, dubbing or other forms of audiovisual transfer (Karamitroglou 1998, Díaz Cintas 2003).

Comparative models seeking to systematize the differences between original and translated audiovisual texts have been mostly driven by shift-based theoretical frameworks, typically associated with the early stages of translation studies and, more specifically, with the linguistic turn – i.e. the period during which linguistics was the discipline that most informed translation studies research. Proponents of linguistic approaches to the study of translation (Vinay and Darbelnet 1958/1995) initially sought to capture the differences that arise between source and target texts during translation by developing typologies of translation strategies. By mapping out such strategies, Vinay and Darbelnet brought to the fore the range of textual adjustments that translators have to make when there is no exact structural, lexical or even morphological equivalence between the source and target languages. Catford (1965) then put forward the generic notion of **shift** to designate any such 'departures from formal correspondence in the process of going from the S[ource]L[language] to the T[arget] L[anguage]' (1965: 73) due to structural incompatibilities or anisomorphisms in the translation interface between both languages.

In the case of audiovisual translation literature, these departures – normally prompted by medial (spatio-temporal) constraints and asymmetries between the source and target cultures – have also been accounted for in terms of typologies of translation strategies. Díaz Cintas and Remael's (2007) classification (summarized in Figure 4.2) is a good example of how comparative models have informed not only the conceptualization of audiovisual translation itself, but also translator training practices. In Díaz Cintas and Remael's typology, translation strategies are essentially conceived as shifts involving a formal departure from the source text. At a higher level of abstraction, translation strategies can be grouped together under broader headings corresponding to two larger-scale shift categories: text reduction shifts and shifts pertaining to the translation of culture-bound terms. In Figure 4.2, translation strategies are illustrated with a 'source' subtitle in English (e.g. 'He's gonna be just the same'). Each of these subtitles is then contrasted with an 'edited' version of itself, also in English ('He won't change'). This comparison between the source and edited versions is meant to reveal the scope of the shift under study.

As the linguistic turn in translation studies became superseded by its cultural and sociological counterparts, the notion of shift gradually widened to cover aspects other than language. Early in this process, Popovič (1970) extended the concept of shift to designate 'all that appears as new with respect to the original, or fails to appear where it might have been expected' (ibid.: 79). Shifts, as defined by Popovič, result not only from linguistic constraints but also from other non-linguistic differences between the context of production and the context of reception, which are 'governed by differing social and literary situations' (ibid.). To systematically investigate and evaluate shifts, as understood by Popovič, it is necessary to take into

Text reduction shifts

Aims of text reduction:

- Eliminating what is not relevant for the comprehension of the message
- Reformulating what is relevant concisely

1 Condensation and reformulation

1.1 Condensation and reformulation at word level
- Simplifying verbal periphrases with shorter verb forms ['He**'s gonna be** just the same' > 'He won't change']
- Generalizing enumerations ['You lied to us, son. **Your own mother and father**' > 'You lied to us, your parents']
- Using a shorter near-synonym or equivalent expression ['He's got **lots of money**' > 'He's rich']
- Using simple rather than compound verbal tenses ['Her father **had thrown** her out' > 'Her father threw her out']
- Changing word classes, e.g. adjective into verb ['That's **an expensive weapon**' > 'That costs a lot']
- Using short forms and contractions

1.2 Condensation and reformulation at clause/sentence level

- Turning negative or interrogative clauses into affirmative sentences ['**Can't you hear** the difference' > 'Listen!']
- Changing indirect into direct questions ['**Did I tell you** there's a party Friday?' > 'There's a party Friday']
- Simplifying indicators of modality ['I understand that it **may be** the best result, politically, that can be delivered just at the moment' > 'That is the best political solution right now']
- Turning direct speech into indirect speech ['**I often tell myself**: Good thing she went' > 'Sometimes I'm glad she went']
- Manipulation of theme and rheme ['**The laundry, the ironing**, your grandmother did all that' > 'Your grandmother did all the chores']
- Turn long and/or compound sentences into simple ones
- Turning active sentences into passive or vice versa
- Use of pronouns and other deictics to replace nouns or noun phrases ['There is no food **in this high mountain**' > 'There's nothing to eat here']

2 Omissions

2.1 Omissions at word level ['A **cup of** coffee, **please**' > 'A coffee']

2.2 Omissions at clause/sentence level ['**Why did she leave? If she left**, it's because she had some reasons!' > 'She must have had a reason']

Shifts pertaining to culture-bound terms

- **Loan**: a source text word (e.g. perestroika) is transferred to the target text
- **Calque**: literal translation (e.g. translating 'Secretary of State' into Spanish as 'Secretario de Estado', instead of the more idiomatic 'Ministro de Asuntos Exteriores')
- **Explicitation**: translating via specification (using hyponym) or generalization (using hyperonym or superordinate)
- **Substitution**: 'when spatial constraints do not allow for the insertion of a rather long term, even if it exists in the target culture' ('goulash' > 'stew') (Díaz Cintas and Remael (2007: 206)
- **Transposition**: replacing a cultural concept from source culture into a concept from target culture
- **Lexical recreation**: use of neologisms in the target language when words are made up in the source one
- **Compensation**: 'making up for a translational loss in one exchange by overtranslating or adding something in another' (ibid.: 206)
- **Omission**: used when the target language does not have an equivalent for a culture-specific term in the source language
- **Additions**: when comprehension might be at stake ['Now you can send him to the chair' > 'You can send him to the electric chair']

Figure 4.2 Classification of subtitling strategies/shifts (based on Díaz Cintas and Remael 2007)

account a range of constraints on translation choices. These include the translator's personal preferences, translational policies or wider organizational norms influencing the translator's environment (Shuttleworth and Cowie 1997). Shifts can thus arise from 'cultural considerations' (ibid.: 153) which are in turn a result of situational and convention-driven constraints with a bearing on the translation process. Insofar as this conceptualization of shifts places more emphasis on the causes of the changes than the effects derived from the latter, I will discuss them in more depth in Section 4.5.1. But the insight that shifts are often prompted by extra-linguistic factors has driven abundant, primarily comparative studies on audiovisual translation that I critique in the remainder of this subsection.

Of particular relevance are Delabastita's (1990) and Lambert and Delabastita's (1996) contributions to the theorizing of shifts, for they address an aspect often neglected by shift-based studies: how meaning is re-distributed across verbal and non-verbal semiotics during the translation process. In Delabastita's model, audiovisual texts convey meaning through the combination of signs pertaining to a number of acoustic and visual codes: verbal (consisting of linguistic and paralinguistic signs), narrative, vestimentary, moral and cinematic. Drawing on classical rhetoric, Delabastita identifies several types of semiotic shifts across codes:

- **Adiectio**, where the translation of the source text involves the incorporation of additional signs, whether they are 'new images, sounds, dialogue or spoken comments' (Delabastita 1990: 102). Adiectio is common in fansubbing. The use of fansubbers' headnotes (Section 3.3), for example, allows target language viewers to appreciate culture-specific nuances that the original text conveys exclusively through non-verbal means.
- **Detractio**, where the translation results in a reduction of the verbal and non-verbal semiotics deployed in the source text. Detractio is increasingly common, for example, in the localized versions of Hollywood blockbusters released in China. Faced with the prospect of censorship by China's State Administration of Radio, Film and Television (SARFT), US distributors often choose to remove potentially offensive or sensitive scenes and/or expressions from their films.[1]
- **Substitutio**, i.e. replacing one sign with a (more or less) equivalent one, from a different code. Subtitling, for example, may involve a partial

substitution of visual and non-verbal signs by verbal signs conveyed through the visual channel (Lambert and Delabastita 1996: 40). Similarly, in dubbed films the original visuals are preserved but the source dialogue is substituted by a different set of verbal spoken signs, i.e. translated dialogue.

Box 4.6

Sample research questions articulated on the basis of Lambert and Delabastita's shift classification (1996: 41–42):

- Is the target version a direct translation of the source text, or is it based on other intermediary texts – among other possible scenarios?
- How does the translator address the problem of linguistic variation, whether it is caused by geographical differences (dialects), social differences (jargon, register, slang), or individual features (idiosyncrasies, tics, faulty elocution)? In sum, what is the conception of language informing their discourse, in particular in relation to the differences between written and spoken language?
- How does the translator deal with instances of literary and filmic intertextuality in the source text (allusions, citations, parody, subversion of genre-specific conventions, etc.)?
- How does the translator mediate the political and ideological aspects of the source text?
- Has the translator manipulated the narrative structure underpinning the source text (text segmentation, narration and focalization, characters, etc.)?
- Has the translated text made more explicit what was left implicit or unsaid in the source text?
- How does the translator deal with local difficulties such as wordplay or the prosodic features of the source text?

Lambert and Delabastita (ibid.: 41) argue that this categorization of shifts provides a more systematic insight into the semiotic configuration of audiovisual texts. Contrastive studies informed by this classification of shifts are thus meant to reveal the full range of translation strategies that can be deployed to transfer meaning across the visual and acoustic channels. Ultimately, this categorization allows scholars to gain a better understanding of the priorities behind the translators' choices. Indeed, Lambert and Delabastita stress that their classification of shifts should serve as a springboard for more detailed analyses of the textual relations between original and translated speech. Box 4.6 lists a number of research questions that, according to Lambert and Delabastita, can be addressed by drawing on their classification of shifts.

In more recent years, rhetoric has continued to inform research on the translational relevance of shifts. However, this notion is no longer confined to the study of textual readjustments that arise when subtitling or dubbing audiovisual texts. Cattrysse (2004), for example, argues that the notion of **narrative shift** can be productively applied to gauge the impact of different audiovisual translation strategies on the commercial success of exported films. From Cattrysse's standpoint, shifts may take place when filmic narratives travel between two linguacultures that favour different rhetorical features.

Indeed, in order to ensure that domestic audiences follow a filmic narrative through and enjoy it, film makers place more or less emphasis on the protagonists as individuals (rather than on the values they embrace); give varying weight to what viewers may perceive as worthwhile dramatic goals; and rely to a greater or lesser extent on antagonists and obstacles hampering the achievement of such goals. When films are exported to other markets, however, the rhetorical conventions underpinning the original narrative may not be necessarily consistent with the expectations of target language viewers. The 'distance' between the source and target audiences can be measured in terms of the number of differences or shifts between the rhetorical features of the original and translated narratives. The range and scope of such shifts will determine whether a film can be dubbed/subtitled (when the rhetorical structures of the source narrative roughly match their target counterparts); remade (when the rhetorical features of the original narrative deviate significantly from the expectations of the receiving culture); or excluded from the circuits of international distribution (when the rhetorical mismatches are too large).

In Cattrysse's (2004: 49) view, the comparative analysis of source and target narrative structures, and the scrutiny of rhetorical shifts arising during translation should

> enlighten us on the relative importance of the various parameters with respect to the general translation policy within that specific time-space context. Also, [. . .] a comparative study of these parameters and the use of language could determine the relative importance of the latter in the international and cross-cultural functioning of filmic narratives.

4.4.2 Corpus-driven models

Traditional comparative research continues to yield useful insights into a wide range of transfer strategies prompted by linguistic and cultural differences among major audiovisual markets. But relying more or less explicitly on the notion of shifts has its drawbacks. Notably, shift-based models often stop short of addressing the implications of the formal departures that translated texts tend to exhibit vis-à-vis their source counterparts.

Unsurprisingly, scholars working in the field of dubbing studies have led the way in exposing the limitations of traditional comparative models. Most contrastive descriptions of translation shifts have been developed from the analysis of written data, thus overlooking the specific difficulties involved in translating spoken language. Understanding the idiosyncrasies of dialogue translation, however, is particularly important in the context of multimodal texts such as films. Indeed, the authenticity of translated fictional dialogue, as perceived by viewers, is held to have an important impact on the reception and success of films (Kozloff 2000). As may be expected, traditional contrastive research has attempted to articulate how 'naturalness' can be achieved in dubbed dialogue (Pérez-González 2007a, Pavesi and Freddi 2009). However, these studies have only managed to provide piecemeal evidence that dubbing tends to bring about a shift toward a neutral uniform written standard. As part of this shift, those features of sociolinguistic variation and orality present in the original dialogue are significantly eroded. Overall, the dearth of major quantitative studies on the specificities of dubbed language has so far hampered our understanding of how translated film dialogue deviates from real dialogue exchanges.

As Chesterman (2000: 17) notes, **corpus-based studies** are 'a more recent variant of the comparative model'. The growing availability of electronic corpora in translation studies research has opened up new ways of looking into the authenticity of dubbed dialogue. Computer-held collections of texts, which can be processed using concordancers and other software applications (Olohan 2004), help scholars to identify typicalities (Baker 1993) of translated language through comparison with original texts. This development has encouraged attempts to capture the defining features of 'authentic' or 'spontaneous-sounding' dubbed dialogue. If viewers are to identify themselves with the fictional world portrayed on the screen, dubbing scholars contend, realistic dubbed speech should display features of naturally occurring conversation. As Pavesi (2009a: 198) notes, '[t]o which degree such truthfulness is achieved and, more feasibly, which features are involved deserve quantitative and qualitative in-depth investigation in line with recent approaches within both linguistics and translation studies'.

Box 4.7

Corpora used for the study of naturalness in Spanish dubbing language (Romero-Fresco 2006, 2009):

- **Parallel corpus**: this collection of source language texts and their translations in the target language is commonly used to identify translational shifts across languages. Romero-Fresco's parallel corpus consists of transcripts of the American TV series *Friends* (ST) and their dubbed versions in Spanish (TT) (300,000 words approximately).
- **Comparable corpora**, made up of two independent collections of texts. One of them 'consists of original texts in the language in question and the other consists of translations in that language from a given source language or languages' (Baker 1995: 234). These monolingual corpora help analysts to pinpoint typical linguistic features of translated texts through comparison with originals belonging to the same genre or sharing one/more communicative functions. Romero-Fresco's comparable corpus includes transcripts of the Spanish dubbed version of Friends (TT) and the Spanish sitcom *Siete Vidas* ('Seven Lives') (1999–2006) (300,000 words approximately) – as both sitcoms feature similar settings, plots and protagonists.
- A **reference corpus**: this comprehensive collection of texts, belonging to a specific variety of the language (e.g. spoken language,) is used as a benchmark for comparison with some other variety of the same language (e.g. written language) or the same variety of some other language. Romero-Fresco uses the spontaneous speech section of CREA, the 12-million contemporary Spanish corpus compiled by Real Academia Española de la Lengua (Royal Spanish Language Academy).

Romero-Fresco's (2006, 2009) work on naturalness in Spanish dubbing language illustrates the basic premises of corpus-driven research in audiovisual translation. As is also the case with other researchers in the field (Pavesi 2005, 2009a, 2009b; Freddi 2009; Bruti 2009), Romero-Fresco relies on different types of corpora, as summarized in Box 4.7.

Comparisons between the two sections of his parallel corpus indicate that dubbed scripts exhibit 'a prefabricated orality that bears a great resemblance to that of the ST' (Romero-Fresco 2009: 58). While aiming to sound spontaneous and idiomatic, dubbed conversation also abides by the conventions of fictional dialogue. But using a parallel corpus also reveals significant differences between the original and translated versions. Take the case of phraseological units (PUs), i.e. multi-word units with idiomatic meaning and often associated with spontaneous speech. Romero-Fresco (2006) finds that the translator often 'takes advantage of the different codes, whether visual (changes of shot) or acoustic (overlapping dialogues or cases of voice out)' to 'intentionally add PUs that are not present in the ST' in an attempt to enhance the naturalness of the dubbed text, as illustrated in Table 4.2.

Romero-Fresco (2009) also compares dubbed Spanish conversation with fictional dialogue originally written in Spanish (comparable corpus) and with naturally occurring spoken Spanish (reference corpus). In the case study under consideration, the analysis focuses on the frequency of intensifiers (i.e. Spanish equivalents of 'really', 'seriously', 'honestly', etc.) and discourse markers (i.e. Spanish equivalents of 'OK', 'well', 'let's see' or 'all right', among others) in each corpus. The rationale for the choice of these features as objects of study is twofold: 'their importance in real conversation' and their 'key role in providing fictional dialogue, and especially dubbing dialogue, with naturalness' (2009: 60). Romero-Fresco's results indicate that the frequency of intensifiers and discourse markers in the comparable corpus (*Siete Vidas*) and the reference corpus (CREA) is similar. By contrast, the occurrence rates of such items in the two sections of the parallel corpus (original and translated scripts) are rather erratic. Translators choose to use intensifiers and discourse markers even when these are not present in the source text, and vice versa. According to Romero-Fresco, this is indicative of translators' tendency to adhere to the idiosyncratic

Table 4.2 Findings from parallel corpus research in dubbing studies

Context: Chandler walks into a café and exchanges greetings with his friends – all of whom, except for Ross, appear in the frame. The Spanish dubbed version incorporates an additional turn at talk: Ross delivers the PU '¿Qué hay?' ['What's up?']. According to Romero-Fresco (2009), '[t]his seems to be a personal choice of the translator [. . .] to add phraseological idiomaticity and, given the register and meaning of '¿Qué hay?', also makes the TT very idiomatic'.

Chandler: Hey!	Chandler: ¡Hola!
All: Hello!	All: ¡Hola!
	Ross: ¡Hola! **¿Qué hay?**

Source: Romero-Fresco 2006

conventions of dubbed language (see Section 4.5.1). While it may be detrimental to the naturalness of Spanish dubbing language, this 'genre-effect' (ibid.: 66) makes it easier for viewers to suspend disbelief in relation to the stilted orality of filmic dialogue.

Comparative models have spearheaded the study of audiovisual translation since the inception of this field of study. The notion of shift, originally developed to account for the textual readjustments that arise during the translation of written texts, has evolved to encompass more substantial departures from the source text. This section has examined two of them in some detail: **multimodal shifts**, involving the redistribution of meaning across semiotic channels and codes during the translation process; and adaptations of filmic narratives oriented to satisfy the rhetorical preferences of target audiences. Despite enjoying a great deal of analytical purchase, criticisms have been levelled at the limitations of shift-based approaches – in particular, their incapacity to inform systematic quantitative analyses of translated audiovisual texts. Corpus-based dubbing studies have gone some way towards allaying such concerns. Research conducted so far has revealed the existence of idiosyncratic language features used in dubbed dialogue to convey orality. According to Pavesi (2009a: 209), such distinctive traits 'cannot all be accounted for as shifts in level or formality or moves towards the written form of the target language. Rather, these features may have to do with different factors such as film discourse structure and norms emerging both in simulated spoken [language] and film translation'.

4.5 CAUSAL MODELS OF TRANSLATION

Both process and comparative models lend themselves to a causal reading (Chesterman 2000). Relations between successive phases of the translation process can be described, from a causal standpoint, as cause-effect sequences where each stage shapes the following one. Similarly, comparative approaches view certain features present in translated texts as prompted by specific structures in the corresponding originals. However, as Chesterman (ibid.: 19) notes, 'in the above two types of model, causality is not overt, not central, and not explicit'. Unlike its comparative and process counterparts, causal models 'help us to explain why the translation looks the way it does, or what effects it causes' (ibid.).

In the remainder of this chapter, I survey studies based on causal models of translation that address the following issues:

- asymmetries between the international status of source and target film cultures and the impact of such differences on translation flows, both from a quantitative and qualitative point of view;
- the prevalence of normative behaviour in the audiovisual translation industry;
- the tendency for translators to prioritize propositional over interactional meaning and its consequences in terms of audience reception;
- the role of ideology and power differentials on the translators' mediation of audiovisual texts.

4.5.1 Systems and norm-based approaches

The relevance of causal concepts to the study of audiovisual translation is particularly discernible in studies driven by Even-Zohar's (1979) theorization of culture as a **polysystem**. This fluid heterogeneous structure is made up of various interconnected **systems** (such as language, economy, politics or ideology) which, in turn, consist of a number of **sub-systems**. Extending Even-Zohar's theory to cover our object of study, the dynamics of the filmic system can be accounted for as the product of the interplay between its various sub-systems: institutionalized genres, non-canonized forms of expression and, most importantly from our perspective, translated films.

From a polysystemic perspective, translations are shaped by the interaction between different filmic sub-systems and bound to cluster around two poles. **Source-text oriented film translations**, on the one hand, involve a relatively straightforward linguistic recoding, with minimal adaptations of culture-specific meaning. In this regard, source-text oriented film translations are widely held to foster formal and conceptual innovation in the receiving culture. By contrast, the linguistic and cultural configuration of **target-text oriented film translations** is the result of an effort to conceal the translated nature of the target text through processes of cultural realignment and adaptation. Target-text oriented films thus act as a conservative force by pandering to the conventions that prevail in the receiving context. Whether film translations play an innovative or conservative role in each case is ultimately determined by the continuous tension between systems – e.g. films, economy and language – at a higher hierarchical level in the polysystem. The relevance, potential and application of polysystem theory to the study of audiovisual translation are best illustrated by Delabastita's (1990) set of programmatic research questions listed in Box 4.8.

Box 4.8

Investigating the systemic position of film translation (adapted from Delabastita 1990: 103–5):

- What is the position of the target culture in an international context? Is it prestigious or peripheral? Does it entertain frequent relations with the source culture or with other cultures?
- What is the position of the source culture in an international context? Does it enjoy high prestige or is it perceived as a minor culture, relatively devoid of interest?
- Does the target audience impose particular restrictions on the translator in terms of literacy (films for children, for instance, for seniors, for immigrants, films shown in the context of literacy campaigns)?
- Does the genre that the source film belongs to exist in the receiving culture? Does the source film's models (linguistic, stylistic, cultural, filmic) find a counterpart in the target culture?
- What cultural status does the source film genre claim?
- What degree of openness does the target culture display towards other cultures? Does it entertain relations of dominance, subordination, competition – or any relations at all? Does the target culture constitute a stable system or does it find itself in a period of rapid change?

The literature has extensively documented the overwhelming dominance of the American film industry over the last century. During this period, the US has established itself as the world's largest film exporter (Novell-Smith 1998) and, by extension, as the default source culture in most processes of transnational audiovisual transfer. The consequences of these monopolistic dynamics for audiovisual translation practices have been explored from various, sometimes clashing, perspectives. Duro Moreno (2001) and Gómez Capuz (2001), for instance, argue that the influence and prestige of American films lie behind the widespread occurrence of Anglicisms and calques (from English) in European **dubbese** – a term that 'negatively connote[s] the linguistic hybrid that over the years has emerged as the "standard" variety of [a number of European languages] spoken by characters in dubbed filmic products for both TV and cinema' (Antonini 2008: 136). By importing linguistic and culture-bound elements from the source linguaculture into their respective varieties of dubbese, most receiving cultures display their openness towards American filmic conventions – thus entertaining a relationship of subordination vis-à-vis the US industry (Nedergaard-Larsen 1993).

But not all scholars analysing translations of US films regard the influence of the American industry as an unassailable undercurrent of cultural quasi-colonialism. Perego (2004) demonstrates that not all audiovisual translations of US films result in source-text oriented translations. Indeed, she goes as far as to advocate the 'unobtrusive manipulation and use of target culture frames . . . to orient viewers and provide them with an effective cognitive framework that enables them to interpret new realities consciously, and process them quickly and easily despite their foreignness' (ibid.: 161).

The existence of target-text oriented film translations can also be accounted for in polysystemic terms. The expansion of dubbing in nationalist and fascist regimes 'at its formative moment' (Nornes 2007: 191) – which allowed target cultures with a less prestigious or visible role on the international media scene at the time to appropriate and exploit US films for their own political ends – is a good case in point. The tensions between the filmic and political systems afforded valuable opportunities for censorship and manipulation of the original narratives (see Section 2.3) with 'deracinating, deodorizing, imperial' consequences (Nornes 2007: 192).

Significantly, the dominance of American filmic discourses and aesthetics is more palpable in those comparatively few instances of transnational flows where foreign films find their way into the US market. Unsurprisingly, the reluctance of American audiences to watch films in other languages has significant implications for the commercialization of such commodities (Rich 2004). Of particular importance among the strategies used to disguise the foreign origin of films is the generalization of 'no-foreign-tongue trailers' since the mid 1980s (ibid.: 156). To ensure that subtitled or dubbed dialogue do not deter American viewers from going to cinemas, trailers dropped dialogue completely. This move brought about other formal changes, such as the quickening of the trailer's pace through the introduction of multiple shot changes, which allowed for the juxtaposition of carefully selected scenes. The examples of trailers discussed by Rich (see Box 4.9) reveal to what extent '[t]he blinders imposed by monolingualism and cinematic illiteracy [a term that Rich uses to designate the resistance of US viewers to subtitles] have created a nation prone to global illiteracy, bound by linguistic leashes to a univocal universe, impervious to subjectivities not their own' (Rich 2004: 164).

Box 4.9

The 'bait and switch' tactics (Rich 2004: 157–60)

In 1985, the folks at Orion (today Sony Picture Classics) were trying to figure out how to market Akira Kurosawa's *Ran* to US audiences . . . So they did something that was so brilliantly obvious that it's hard to believe it wasn't already commonplace, something that instantly became the norm: they had a trailer made for *Ran* that omitted the Japanese and thus rendered subtitles unnecessary. They marketed the film, in other words, with the hope that it might be mistaken for an English language picture.

[. . .]

One of the most memorable trailers of this period was the one introducing audiences in the summer of 1995 to *Il Postino* (The Postman): it used the voices of movie stars reading Pablo Neruda to imply that the voices declaiming in English were somehow excerpted from the Italian language, subtitled film. The campaign for *Shall We Dance?*, the Japanese film about a salaryman who falls in love with ballroom dancing classes and his teacher, went even further. The trailer showed a couple dancing but made their race indeterminate, sustaining the illusion of the non-existent dialogue; unlike *Ran*, it didn't allow the audience to peg nationality visually. . . . A universal picture, indeed, especially with the characters pictorially decapitated and reduced down to fancy; and of course inherently non-verbal, footwork.

Evidence of the use of audiovisual translation by American distributors to posit a monocultural world is also yielded by the proliferation of subtitling and dubbing practices that are mostly circumscribed to the US as a receiving culture. These include **adaptive dubbing**, an extreme form of domestication[2] involving a significant departure from the source text and, in some cases, the reconfiguration of non-verbal components of the audiovisual text (see Box 6.2). The polysystemic dynamics behind adaptive dubbing can be illustrated with reference to the broadcast of Japanese anime series on US television networks during the 1980s. As Nornes (2007) explains, most early imports fell short of the minimum number of episodes required to fill a standard season in American channels. This problem was compounded by the mismatch between the internal narrative structure of Japanese episodes and the rigid timing for the insertion of commercial breaks on US networks. In order to meet what was 'basically a demand and precondition of the televisual distribution in the first place' (ibid.: 195), adaptive dubbing challenged traditional perceptions of translation. Fragments from different short shows would be repackaged and repurposed to form new episodes of a single series. As a result, characters that had originally inhabited different fictions and dramatic spaces would be brought together by new narratives and the deployment of new visual transitions. The translator at the centre of Nornes' example 'would watch the series with the volume off and imagine the narrative transpiring'. Significantly, in adaptive dubbing '[t]his imaginative narrative would become the object of translation' (ibid.).

Building on polysystem theory, proponents of **descriptive translation studies** led by Toury (1995) have invoked the sociological concept of **norm** to propose hypotheses as to why translations read the way they do, and hence gain a better understanding of the causal dimension of translational behaviour. As defined by Toury, norms are 'the translation of general values or ideas shared by a community – as to what is right or wrong, adequate or inadequate – into performance instructions appropriate for and applicable to particular situations' (ibid.: 55). Normative principles governing what is regarded as an adequate translation are thus bound by temporal, geographical and cultural constraints.

An important specificity of Toury's approach vis-à-vis polysystem theory is its target-orientation: translations are considered to be facts of the target culture, their characteristics being conditioned by target culture forces. By familiarizing themselves with the constraints operating in a given historical target context, scholars stand a better chance of successfully formalizing the different norms that lie behind translators' choices. While norms may be notions of approved behaviour that have prescriptive force within a community, for norm theorists, they are to be analyzed as objects of study.

Although it is not framed explicitly in terms of norms theory, Nornes' (2007) discussion of dubbing practices in the Japanese industry aptly illustrates the relevance of Toury's notion of **initial norm** to audiovisual translation. The initial norm determines the global approach of the translator with respect to the following two polar alternatives: adhering to the textual relations and norms embodied in the source text (**adequacy**); or complying with the linguistic and rhetorical norms of the target language and culture (**acceptability**). Faced with the proliferation of swearing and obscenity in American films produced from the 1970s, Japanese translators chose to deploy repressing and self-censoring translation strategies – thus taking on a role that Hollywood's studio system had traditionally played during the film pre-production stage. In prioritizing acceptability over adequacy,

> film translators confront a 'dirty word' by either cleaning it up or replacing it with terms so highly conventionalized that they have lost the force of their obscene power ... Japanese translators would deny their prudishness, pointing to various theories to justify their actions. These theories are explicated, defended, and naturalized through pedagogy and publishing. These discourses basically call for a kind of rarefied, literary language for film translation, which is why obscenity is cleaned up ... When the subject of obscenity is taken up, it is usually dismissed as 'untranslatable' in Japanese language.
>
> (Nornes 2007: 216)[3]

This section has explored two interconnected causal models of research. Polysystem theory facilitates macro-contextual research, theorizing translations as the effect of the interplay between source and target culture forces. Norm theory, on the other hand, attempts to map such contextual forces onto a set of normative principles governing translational behaviour in the receiving community. Both polysystem theory and the sociological notion of norm drive Karamitroglou's (2000) research into what dictates the choice between dubbing and subtitling when translating television programmes in Greece. In order to establish the rationale behind such preferences, Karamitroglou's comprehensive study scrutinizes the following elements:

- human agents, including 'spotters, time-coders, adapters, dubbing director, dubbing actors, sound technicians, video experts, proof-reading editors, translation commissioners, film distributors and finally the translator him/herself' (ibid.: 71);
- translated material – dubbed or subtitled programmes;
- recipients and users of audiovisual translations;
- translation mode – the semiotic environment moulded by the technical constraints that operate on audiovisual texts;
- individual and institutional players in the production of dubbed and subtitled material;
- the market – outlets involved in distributing, screening or broadcasting dubbed or subtitled programmes.

Karamitroglou interrogates these factors at three different levels of contextual abstraction. At the lower or case-specific level, audiovisual content is examined against its specific situational context of production. The middle level facilitates the study of the relationships that hold between such specific contexts and the overall audiovisual scene. Finally, the connections between Greece's audiovisual translation context and the general literary system are analysed at the upper most level.

Although questions have been raised as to whether he 'needed such an elaborate theoretical basis' to establish that 'in Greece most TV programmes are dubbed and most films are subtitled unless aimed at younger children with limited reading skills' (Munday 2012: 175), Karamitroglou's pioneering application of this theoretical framework has greatly contributed to the perception of the descriptive paradigm by audiovisual translation scholars as 'a heuristic tool that opens up new avenues for study, strengthens the theoretical component and allows the researcher to come up with substantial analyses' (Díaz Cintas 2004: 31).

4.5.2 Discourse and ideological models

Audiovisual translators have traditionally aimed to achieve equivalence at micro-structural level by translating the content of each turn at talk in the original dialogue into a similar structural unit in the target language. But making local decisions that are not necessarily informed by the overall picture of what is going on outside the turn at hand can have significant effects on dubbed and subtitled material. The compartmentalization of the source text during translation accounts for the tendency of dubbed speech towards neutralization and standardization (Herbst 1997: 305). It also has homogenizing effects on subtitled dialogue, with subtitlers often opting to prioritize propositional content over 'dialogue's oral and interactional features' (Remael 2004: 105).

Until the turn of the twenty-first century, audiovisual translation studies were primarily focused on 'linguistic phenomena spanning up to one turn-at-talk or the relationship between immediately contiguous turns' (Pérez-González 2007a: 11). However, such (mostly comparative) research 'tended to overlook the mechanisms that enable the achievement of naturalness and appropriateness over a whole scene' (ibid.). Over the last decade, a range of studies adopting a causal stance have postulated that industrial constraints on dubbing and subtitling practices tend to undermine the interpersonal aspects of the original dialogue. In other words, the translator's mediation often brings about changes between the relations that characters develop with each other through conversation in the source language and the social relations that these same characters develop in the target dialogue.

- Pérez-González (2007a) gauges the impact that compartmentalized translation practices have on the interpersonal dimension of dubbed dialogue by drawing on the systemic-functional notion of **telos**. This strand of research starts from the premise that films and TV dramas normally exhibit a high incidence of 'mood telos' – whereby conversational exchanges between actors' lines are neatly structured, often organized as a series of straightforward question-answer pairs. Although this may result in stretches of stilted interaction, relying on mood telos is an effective strategy to propel the narrative forward. By contrast, audiovisual narratives seeking to recreate more realistic conversational dynamics tend to deploy 'appraisal telos' resources – e.g. evaluative lexis, interactional disagreements and overlaps, etc. – for characterization-enhancing goals. Pérez-González's case study reveals that the translation of conversation 'triggers off shifts from appraisal telos (in the source text) to mood telos (in the target dialogue). The upshot of this is that the spontaneous-sounding fragments of the original dialogue are occasionally neutralized by the overall artificiality of the interactional dynamics in the target language' (ibid.: 34).
- Compliance with industry standards – specifically, the need for condensation and synthesis derived from spatio-temporal constraints – tends to jeopardize the interpersonal dimension of subtitled dialogue. This is the argument that Hatim and Mason (1997) and Mason (2001) put forward drawing on **politeness theory**. Their data set indicates that the prevalence of reduction in subtitled interaction can significantly alter the interpersonal dynamic of the original dialogue. The main effect of this interpersonal shift is that 'the purpose of the communicative interchange can be "read" in a much clearer way in the subtitles' (Hatim and Mason 1997: 89), which promotes a single linear narrative in the eyes of the viewers.

Remael (2003) corroborates that subtitling tends to bring about changes to the interpersonal pragmatics of fictional dialogue, as illustrated by the example presented in Table 4.3. This fragment of Mike Leigh's *Secrets and Lies* (1996) features Roxanne arguing with her uncle (Maurice) about her mother's decision not to reveal that she had another daughter in her youth.

Table 4.3 Example of interpersonal shift in *Secrets and Lies*

Maurice:	Well, I always . . . Thought she'd'ad a boy . . .	Ik dacht dat ze'n jongen had. Gloss: *I thought she had a boy*
Roxanne:	She's a slag.	– Ze is een snol
Maurice:	No, she's not.	NO SUBTITLING
Roxanne:	Yes, she fucking is.	NO SUBTITLING
Maurice:	She loves yer. We all Love yer. You comin'back?	Ze houdt van je. Wij allemaal. Kom je terug? [idem]
Roxanne:	No.	NO SUBTITLING
Maurice:	You got to.	Je moet.
Roxanne:	Why should I?	NO SUBTITLING
Maurice:	You gotta face up to it!	Je moet 't onder ogen zien
Roxanne:	Face up to what?	NO SUBTITLING

Source: Remael 2003: 242–43

The right-hand column displays the Dutch translation segmented into the subtitles. Arguably, the omission and condensation of parts of the source text (mostly Roxanne's contributions) in the Dutch subtitles would appear to enhance the clarity of the unfolding narrative. Indeed, the subtitler of this excerpt deletes those turns at talk that challenge Maurice's representation of events and hence minimizes Roxanne's confrontational and uncompromising stance. Ultimately, the subtitled version presents the target audience with a simpler, linear interactional episode.

But Remael's study goes beyond merely identifying the tendency of subtitled dialogue to streamline fictional dialogue. Based on the analysis of other examples from the same film, Remael reveals that the simplification of diegetic interaction often jettisons secondary narratives and voices, particularly those that subscribe to less mainstream values and narratives. Subtitled dialogue, Remael argues, tends to reinforce established conventions, uphold traditional power relations and minimize the contribution of dissenting voices. So while most research driven by discourse models concentrates on the effects that the mediation process has on the naturalness and interpersonal dynamics of translated dialogue, Remael offers important new insights into the ideological implications of audiovisual translation.

Attempts to gain a better understanding of the role of ideology and power differentials as causal constraints in dubbing and subtitling provide the impetus behind a growing body of scholarship in the field of audiovisual translation. Drawing on theories from neighbouring disciplines (including, but not limited to historiography, sociolinguistics and gender studies), these studies conceptualize translations as the product of the interplay between dominant and subaltern socio-political forces that shape the production and reception of audiovisual content. Research on the ideological dimension of audiovisual translation has clustered around three main themes: (self-)censorship, gender and sociolinguistic variation.

(Self-)censorship

Numerous scholars have investigated audiovisual translation through the lens of history and revealed how the consolidation of different film translation modes went hand in hand with the emergence and institutionalization of totalitarian regimes, particularly in Europe. In most of these studies, audiovisual texts are conceptualized as extensions of hegemonic socio-political agendas during specific historical periods. Against this backdrop, translations are viewed as the product of **censorial interference** by the relevant governmental boards (Ballester 1995, 2001; Gutiérrez Lanza 1997, Camus 2007, Guidorizzi 1999, Merino Álvarez 2008, Mereu 2012).

Other studies underpinned by causal models are based on the premise that audiovisual content is imbued with ideological connotations, some of which may be potentially sensitive or outright offensive in the target culture. In these cases, audiovisual translators deploy self-censoring strategies (e.g. cultural substitution or euphemization) to avoid clashes with the censors, or simply to ensure that translations are aligned with the preferences and expectations of mainstream audiences (Chen 2004, Scandura 2004, Al-Adwan 2009). Significantly, recent studies show that self-censorship is not restricted to the mediation of fictional audiovisual narratives; the process of digital games localization would also appear to bring about self-censoring translational decisions to maximize their commercial return, particularly when the censorship mechanisms in the target culture are not sufficiently transparent (Zhang 2012).

Gender

In fictional audiovisual narratives, whether they mirror reality or unfold in imaginary diegetic worlds, stereotypes and perceptions of gender differences and sexual identities significantly contribute to characterization. As in any other form of translation, the various modes of audiovisual transfer offer ample opportunities to redress or perpetuate the gender divide. While De Marco's (2012) study of dubbed and subtitled dialogue provides evidence that translation can exacerbate gender stereotypes already present in the original films, Baumgarten's (2005) analysis of dubbed German shows how the sexism embedded in the original versions of James Bond films can be diluted through a series of translational micro-shifts.

Recent publications have also attempted to gain a better understanding of how filmic representations of 'transgenderism' and 'gayspeak' are mediated by audiovisual translators. Asimakoulas (2012: 47) explores the textual manifestations of what he presents as the 'queering tactics of transsituated discourse'. Transsexualism, Asimakoulas argues, constructs an identity of its own by selectively appropriating expressive resources of mainstream discourse and reversing their semiotic function in the dominant culture. As a result, those appropriated resources acquire subversive connotations within the context of the transgender culture. Asimakoulas' insight that subtitling brings about 'recurrent shifts in the semiotic load of these resources' (ibid.: 55) is consistent with Ranzato's (2012) findings on the transformations that 'gayspeak' undergoes during the dubbing process. Drawing on a range of examples from anglophone audiovisual productions, Ranzato puts forward a causal reading of such alterations. 'The lack of an Italian vocabulary rich in homosexual terms of common usage' hampers the translators' work and is ultimately responsible for the neutralization of gayspeak in the Italian versions. From Ranzato's standpoint, this lexical deficit can be ultimately accounted for as the result of 'the bias and precon-ceptions of a culture, the Italian, which has opened up to homosexual themes much more slowly than the Anglosaxon world' (ibid.: 382).

Sociolinguistic variation

The debate on whether it is feasible to transfer **sociolectal**, **idiolectal** or **dialectal differences** at the centre of audiovisual narratives has traditionally split specialists into two groups. Some take the view that recreating socio-linguistic variation (in particular, where dialectal markers are foregrounded) in a different linguaculture is incompatible with the industry's emphasis on readability and standard language usage (Gambier 1994), while others advo-cate adopting a more creative approach (Federici 2011). Experimental attempts to mediate instances of geographical variation through subtitles may involve the use of a 'dialect-for-dialect' strategy (Mével 2007: 54), whereby the original variety is replaced with an existing or made-up equivalent in the target language (Salmon Kovarski 2000, Jäckel 2001, Nadiani 2004). The dialect-for-dialect approach also prevails in the dubbing industry, where scholars have documented attempts to establish correspondence across languages by relying on target language dialects or fabricated varieties (Heiss and Leporati 2000, Alemán Bañón 2005).

But among the different manifestations of language variation found in audiovisual texts, **diglossia** is attracting increasing attention for its capacity to influence translational behaviour (Gamal 2007). Indeed, the interaction between two markedly different varieties of a language or two different languages ('high language' and 'low language') in a single linguistic community has been often exploited for the purposes of dramatic characterization in audiovisual narratives. As high and low languages tend to be associated with formal contexts and informal settings, respectively, diglossic material facilitates the multimodal realization of power differentials in society and plays an important role in moving the plot forward. The widely held assumption that translators should attempt to recreate the original's diglossic dynamics in the target language means that, effectively, the deployment of each and every translation strategy to this end lends itself to a causal reading.

Murray's (2012) analysis of English subtitled versions of Taiwanese films featuring bilingual diglossia – where Mandarin acts as the high language and Tai-gi as its low counterpart – reveals that English subtitles conveying Mandarin speech tend to exhibit more markers of formality than those rendering Tai-gi speech. In doing so, subtitles would appear to act as a transparent medium, mirroring linguistic behaviour both in the diegetic and extra-diegetic worlds. Yau (2012), on the other hand, explores the rhetorical function that subtitles can fulfil in diglossic contexts. Translators, Yau argues, may actively work to subvert traditional power relations inscribed in the hierarchy between Standard Chinese (high language) and Cantonese (low language) by creating new hybrid target language varieties. Subtitles are crucial to articulate and disseminate these self-asserting varieties, based on a combination of 'the standard and the non-standard, the spoken and the written, the current and the archaic' (ibid.: 572). Yau's data set suggests that subversive subtitles can be used for a range of purposes, not least the construction and empowerment of Cantonese identity and the way this is represented in audiovisual texts.

Overall, causal models of research have been primarily used in our field to investigate whether and how translation influences the perceived authenticity of audiovisual texts in the target culture. As illustrated in this section, causality accounts for the growing shift from compartmentalized approaches towards sequential studies of subtitled or dubbed dialogue. In this sense, recent scholarship postulates that translations informed by the trajectory of the overall conversational encounter, rather than just the content of one conversational turn at a time, are bound to be perceived as more natural. But this causality-driven widening of the translator's perspective is not confined to the analysis of textual material. In audiovisual texts, naturalness is also contingent on the translator's capacity to reproduce in translation the socio-linguistic make-up of the diegetic world portrayed in the original text. The strategies deployed by translators to recreate social asymmetries through selected sociolectal, ethnolectal and idiolectal features are difficult to account from a purely comparative perspective. Instead, it is the systemic position of the audiovisual genre at hand within the source and target cultures, and the translator's decision to adhere to or deviate from translation norms prevailing in the target culture that ultimately help scholars understand why translated texts look the way they do.

This chapter has surveyed a range of translation theories and models that audiovisual translation scholars have imported from the wider discipline of translation studies or other disciplines to develop new conceptualizations and representations of their object of study. These translation models need to be operationalized and tested through the choice of suitable research methods. It is therefore to an exploration of such methods that I turn my attention in the next chapter.

FOLLOW-UP QUESTIONS FOR DISCUSSION

- In her monograph on the history of Japanese cinema, McDonald (2006) discusses the impact of the country's strong theatrical tradition on the narrative structure of early Japanese films. McDonald contends that such influences were responsible for the delay in the formation of a specifically cinematic grammar and in the development of distinctive narrative conventions in films. As McDonald explains,

    > [t]he center-front long shot was a natural outcome of cinema's first view of itself as a camera-eye spectator of ongoing stage performance.

> Most early footage showed what theater audiences saw: entire scenes shot in one long take showing actors full-length. This fixed approach to camera work remained a defining characteristic of Japanese cinema even after the long shot and long take were joined by other more specifically cinematic devices.
>
> (2006: 2)

But as Japanese directors became increasingly attracted to Western editing techniques, old conventions lost popularity and were replaced by imported practices.

Similarly, in her overview of the evolution of Korean cinema, Chung (2007: 1) makes the point that the Korean film tradition has no indigenous genres: the emergence and development of the latter were influenced by Western and other Asian film genres. Significantly, one of the biggest hindrances to the construction of Korea's own cinematic conventions and modes of representation had to do with timing: the advent of cinema as an art form in Korea coincided with Japan's colonization of its Asian neighbours. As a result of Japan's control,

> the Korean melodrama was an exact copy of Japanese shinpa films to the extent that they were called 'namida (tears, なみだ)' films, adopting the Japanese term for a tearjerker. Even after liberation, when Japanese films were strictly forbidden in Korea, plagiarism paradoxically persisted until the government allowed Japanese films back in 1998.
>
> (ibid.: 3)

How useful is polysystem theory in examining the role that Western techniques and genres played in driving early developments in the Japanese film industry? Can the logic of your response to this question be extended to account for the triangular relationship between Western, Japanese and Korean traditions? Consider the list of research questions proposed by Delabastita (1990) (see Box 4.8) and discuss their relevance to the evolution of Japanese and Korean cinematic conventions. Is the technical and rhetorical influence of Western practices justified in terms of America's and Asia's respective positions in the international context at the turn of the twentieth century? In addressing this question, you may want to give some thought to the interaction between the different systems that make up each of these cultures. On the basis of the findings of studies surveyed in Section 4.5.1, how might the dynamics of the relationship between Western and Asian film traditions have shaped the audiovisual translation industry in Japan and Korea? As a result of this relationship, are Japanese and Korean translators more likely to aim at source- or target-text oriented film translations?

• Written and directed by Dany Boon in 2008, Bienvenue chez les Ch'tis (Welcome to the Sticks) tells the story of Philippe Abrams, a postal worker transferred from Southern France to the northern town of Bergues. Upon arrival, Philippe is initially confounded by the dialect of his local co-workers. Speakers of the Ch'ti dialect pronounce the French [s] sound as [ʃ]. For example, in the line 'Bah ici c'est pas les spécialités qui manquent' ('Well, there are lots of delicacies here'), 'c'est' (/sɛ/) would be pronounced as 'ch'est' (/ʃsɛ/). But Philippe is also troubled by his negative stereotypes of the townspeople. Indeed, the ch'timi dialect is often regarded as a language of farmers and coal miners rarely used in school or heard on the television (Harrod 2012). Gradually, Philippe is won over by the town as he learns the dialect and forgets his false preconceptions about his hosts.

When subtitling or dubbing this film, opting for a standard variety of the target language, i.e. following a conservative approach, would be easier than relying on a dialectal one (see Section 4.5.2). However, this conservative approach would be hardly feasible in this case. In the first encounter between Philippe and Antoine, for example, the former – who is not familiar with the ch'ti dialect being spoken by Antoine – assumes that Antoine's pronunciation in French is the result of a jaw injury. Insofar as it is central to the plot of Bienvenue chez les Ch'tis, omitting the dialectal variation in the target text would necessitate a quite dramatic change to the plot of the film.

A more experimental approach to the translation of dialect in this film would involve finding an equivalent dialect in the target language. By translating into an existing target culture dialect, viewers would be able to draw on their pre-conceived notions of speakers of this dialect. Further, this strategy of localization may appeal to certain viewers who find the familiarity of a local dialect renders the film less obscure and as such more relatable. Finding a suitable dialect, though, would present a major difficulty to translators.

A third option open to a translator would be to translate the ch'ti into an invented variety. Under this strategy, more specific features of the source text dialect could be relayed into the target text. Lexical, phonological and grammatical characteristics could thus be replicated in the target language, allowing similar puns and language humour to be conveyed from the original to the target text. But while this strategy also aids in the individualization of characters, marking their divergent geographical or social origins, it has some drawbacks. An invented dialect, for instance, does not carry any authentic sociolinguistic meaning. Consequently, it would not trigger any preconceived notions of class or cultural stereotypes in the target audience. Language variation is a valuable tool used in films to draw characters quickly (Lippi-Green 1997: 81) and this would have to be compensated for through plot lines and dialogue.

Consider these options from the perspective of your own language pair. Which would be the most suitable approach? You may want to give some consideration to the way in which other films featuring a conspicuous dialectal variety have been subtitled or dubbed into your target language. Which type of translation model is more likely to assist you in accounting for your decision: comparative or causal ones?

- As explained in Section 4.3.3, neurolinguistic approaches to the study of audio description suggest that the perception of combined visual and acoustic stimuli may be influenced by culture-specific factors. The argument goes as follows: if differences in perception among cultures are confirmed by future research, new versions would have to be developed from scratch for audio described narrations to be effective in different linguacultures.

The following example allows for further reflection on this argument. According to Shafik (2007), Arab cinema is dominated by language. As she notes,

> many Arab directors and authors trust the signifying power of words more than the visual arrangements. Consequently, they prefer to fix the meaning of symbols by giving clear linguistic indications. Some even 'translate' literary metaphors, images and expressions without further ado into the visual (e.g. 'working like a donkey').
>
> (ibid.: 87)

For Shafik, this emphasis on language arises from the Arab tradition of state-produced films aimed at largely illiterate audiences who are primarily used to oral narrative forms. This fixation on verbal meaning minimizes the presence of ambiguous subtexts in audiovisual narratives, which facilitates their use for the purposes of political indoctrination.

Consider the idiosyncratic features of Arab film semiotics against the core premises of neurolinguistic research, pertaining to potential differences in perception between cultures. How may neurolinguistic translation models contribute to researching audio description from and into Arabic? In trying to address this question, you may want to familiarize yourself further with this research strand, and the way in which it is systematizing the impact of different semiotic configurations on culture-specific perceptual habits. Also, how would causal models complement neurolinguistic insights? Finally, note Shafik's causal reading of the tendency for Arab films to rely primarily on verbal signs: films are instrumentalized as platforms for the circulation of political and ideological propaganda. Against this backdrop, what could be the forces responsible for the emergence and consolidation of other narrative conventions and practices, possibly more reliant on non-verbal semiotics?

- Buffy the Vampire Slayer (1997–2003) was a TV series following Buffy Summers, the latest in a line of young women known as 'slayers' who fight the supernatural evil that plagues her alternative reality. This show has long been considered a feminist series: it defies patriarchal stereotypes by empowering women, offering them independence, agency, and active roles to attack gender assumptions (Byers 2003). 'Although the traditional hero of mythology is inarguably male, with Buffy the heroic becomes not just reconciled with the feminine but ruled by it' (ibid.: 171). Wilcox makes the important point that the creative use of language in the show is itself 'symbolic' (2005: 18) and contributes to uphold the feminist principles underpinning the series. Indeed, 'Buffyspeak' has been defined as a kind of slang, with characters using the English language in an innovative fashion. Through a combination of neologisms and jargon, affixation, changing parts of speech, truncation, syntactic change, semantic shift and pop-culture references (Kirchner 2006), users of Buffyspeak deviate morphologically, lexically and syntactically from standard usage (Adams 2003). Overall, this experimentation is considered to underline Buffy's 'violence against language' as a feminist counter-attack against male domination (Craigo-Snell 2006).

What similarities can you find between the strategy deployed to articulate language-driven feminism, as manifested in Buffy the Vampire Slayer, and Asimakoulas' account of the construction of transsexual identities in audiovisual texts (as outlined in Section 4.5.2)? Which translation models would be more useful to identify the linguistic features of Buffy's subversive idiolect? Consider the relevance of polysystem and norm theories to the analysis of subtitled and dubbed versions of Buffy. To what extent can the interplay between the systems of translation, religion and education within different recipient polysystems, for example, affect the way Buffyspeak is recreated in the relevant target languages?

NOTES

1   For more information on this manifestation of *detractio*, see http://uk.movies.yahoo.com/how-hollywood-films-were-censored-for-the-chinese-market-163134985.html (last accessed on 15 September 2013).

2   The relevance of Venuti's well-known 'domestication/foreignization' dichotomy to audiovisual translation has been explored in some depth by Ulrych (2000). Medial constraints imposed on audiovisual translation professionals, Ulrych argues, lead to 'the acculturisation or domestication of the source text in line with dominant conventions and expectancies prevailing in the TC [Target Culture] and, more often than not, to the translator's effacement or invisibility' (2000: 130). Central to Ulrych's critique is her characterization of audiovisual translators as 'subservient scribes' failing to take a proactive stance in the act of cross-cultural mediation. 'In assuming and accepting such a position', Ulrych contends, 'translators endorse the positive and negative effects of both foreignising and domesticating processes and do nothing to improve standards in the film translation industry' (2000: 140).

3   Nornes goes on to recount how the convention whereby Japanese translators subject themselves to the norms of the target culture played out during the translation of Stanley Kubrick's *Full Metal Jacket* (1987) into that Asian language. Notorious for his direct involvement in the translation of his films, Kubrick commissioned a translation of this film from an established Japanese translator, who removed all the obscenity featuring in the original film. A second translation was then commissioned from a film maker who was largely oblivious to the conventions of film translation. The second version prioritized adequacy over acceptability. Apart from preserving obscene language, the translator 'proved willing to make his audience work, using imagery

and phrases that may not have made crystal clear sense, but which had the tremendous force of the original' (Nornes 2007: 217).

CORE REFERENCES

On translation models:

Díaz Cintas, Jorge (2004), 'In Search of a Theoretical Framework for the Study of Audiovisual Translation', in Pilar Orero (ed.) *Topics in Audiovisual Translation*, Amsterdam and Philadelphia: John Benjamins, 21–34.

Chesterman, Andrew (2001) 'A Causal Model for Translation Studies', in Maeve Olohan (ed.) *Intercultural Faultlines: Research Models in Translation Studies I: Textual and Cognitive Aspects*, Manchester: St Jerome, 15–28.

Munday, Jeremy (2012) *Introducing Translation Studies*, 3rd edition, London and New York: Routledge.

Examples of different audiovisual translation models: Causal models

Remael, Aline (2004) 'A Place for Film Dialogue Analysis in Subtitling Courses', in Pilar Orero (ed.) *Topics in Audiovisual Translation*, Amsterdam and Philadelphia: John Benjamins, 103–26.

Yau, Wai-Ping (2012) 'Power, Identity and Subtitling in a Diglossic Society', *Meta* 57(3): 564–73.

Comparative models

Delabastita, Dirk (1990) 'Translation and the Mass Media', in Susan Bassnett and André Lefèvre (eds) *Translation, History and Culture*, London and New York: Pinter Publishers, 97–109.

Pavesi, Maria (2009a) 'Dubbing English into Italian: A Closer Look at the Translation of Spoken Language', in Jorge Díaz Cintas (ed.) *New Trends in Audiovisual Translation*, Bristol: Multilingual Matters, 197–209.

Process models

Orero, Pilar (2008) 'Three Different Receptions of the Same Film', *European Journal of English Studies* 12: 179–93.

Vercauteren, Gert (2012) 'A Narratological Approach to Content Selection in Audio Description. Towards a Strategy for the Description of Narratological Time', in Rosa Agost, Pilar Orero and Elena di Giovanni (eds) *MONTI 4: Multidisciplinarity in Audiovisual Translation*: 207–31.

5

RESEARCH METHODS IN AUDIOVISUAL TRANSLATION

A central problem with research in translation studies is that so few scholars are fully trained in the research methods necessary for the field. This is not surprising. Because the cross-temporal, cross-cultural concept translation is a cluster concept and because the concept is so diverse and open, the skills required for translation research are themselves enormously diverse and open.

(Tymoczko 2007: 140–41)

The field of film translation is not easy to research for a number of reasons: the reading net [. . .] must be cast wide to take in sources which are not normally associated with translation studies and which are not always easily available; the researcher must be multidisciplinary, with a knowledge not only of language, but also, amongst other things, of psychology, aesthetics and economics; the materials may be hard to de-randomise, with the researcher having to use what falls to hand rather than being able to build a homogenous corpus, a situation which may cast doubt on the validity of the results.

(Fawcett 1996: 66)

In this chapter

This chapter provides a comprehensive overview of established and emerging **research methods** in audiovisual translation studies. Starting with **conceptual research**, i.e. studies that prioritize the exploration of ideas over the interrogation of data, the overview places particular emphasis on **empirical** research methods. **Observational** research methods, illustrated by eye-tracking studies, address the perceptual and cognitive aspects of audiovisual translation, with a view to inform professional practices and achieve a better understanding of how viewers process information in screen-based environments. **Interactionist** research methods, involving the use of questionnaires or interviews, bring to the fore important considerations pertaining to the reception of audiovisual translations. **Documentary** methods have traditionally taken the form of archival research, but they are now also at the centre of new netnographic methodologies – which require the immersion of the investigator as a participant in online translator communities. Finally, computer-held corpora provide the main focus of the exploration of quantitative research methods in audiovisual translation scholarship. The overview of research methods presented here showcases the complementarity of different research methods; and brings to the fore the growing importance of reception-oriented studies in the field.

▶ WATCH THE INTRODUCTION VIDEO

5.1 RESEARCHING AUDIOVISUAL TEXTS

Audiovisual texts can be reconfigured across languages and cultures in multiple ways, as outlined in Chapter 1. Traditional forms of audiovisual translation, such as subtitling and dubbing, remain primarily anchored to discourses on correspondence or equivalence between source and target texts. Emerging assistive varieties such as audio description, on the other hand, call for an alternative understanding of translation as mediation – thus acknowledging the active role that audio describers play in selecting what needs to be transferred to their sensory impaired viewers and how best to do so on a case by case basis. Consequently, audiovisual translation accommodates **multiple ontologies**, i.e. different answers to the question 'what is audiovisual translation'. According to Chesterman (2006: 10), this co-existence of ontological views under a common label calls for a concept of translation that has a 'flexible cluster shape rather than a prototypical form'. Understanding translation as a **cluster concept** thus allows for a productive interplay between multiple theorizations that foreground different aspects of the translation phenomenon.

In turn, the ontological diversity at the heart of audiovisual translation engenders **epistemological plurality**. In other words, researchers' assumptions on 'what can be known' determine their judgement on 'how best to investigate it'. Just as audiovisual translation scholars choose among different translation models representing their objects of study (see Chapter 4), they must select the most appropriate **research methods**, i.e. particular strategies for the collection of evidence in order to build or test each theory. As Chesterman notes, the choice of 'any model of translation has specific methodological consequences: translation models constrain research models, and hence the construction of translation theories' (2000: 16).

The purpose of the present chapter is to provide a comprehensive overview of research methods used in the field of audiovisual translation, both established and emerging ones. The rationale for this springs from the widely endorsed view that only a relatively low proportion of scholars are equipped with the multiple and wide-ranging skills required to undertake research on the cluster concept of translation. As Tymoczko observes, many specialists 'lack basic training in hypothesis formation and testing, recognition and determination of margins or error or uncertainties in research conclusions, protocols facilitating replicability of results, and interrogation of the researcher's perspective and presupposition' (2007: 142). But the motivation for the overview that follows is further hinged on the particularly exacting demands of audiovisual translation as a field of research (Fawcett 1996). For specialists coming to translation studies with a background in the study of modern languages, analysing meaning that is conveyed partially or totally through non-verbal semiotics is particularly challenging. Indeed, the very selection of issues worthy of investigation is not without problems. As Fawcett claims, audiovisual translation,

> even more than the standard forms of translation, is a perfect case of the Quantum Mechanics principle that the observer and the process of observation influence the observed. Many translations are accepted without any sense of problem by the intended readership until someone decides to look at them not as an 'offer of information', as German theorists call it, but precisely as a translation. The process of analysis alters our focus and what we find, so the results we are looking at are not those perceived by a non-analytic reader or spectator. In this sense, it may well be the case that much of what is written about translation is actually beside the point.
>
> (1996: 69–70)

The remainder of this chapter examines the contribution of methodologies aligned both with conceptual and empirical research to the expansion of audiovisual translation in recent decades. Given the sustained dominance of the former in the literature published until the turn of the century, I will place particular emphasis on recent empirical developments and the ways in which they can help the field remain abreast of its own needs.

5.2 CONCEPTUAL RESEARCH

Concepts are central to both objectivist and subjectivist research traditions, as instantiated by empirical and conceptual methodologies, respectively. Objectivists regard conceptualization as a preliminary stage of the research process. From their perspective, concepts assist scholars in articulating research questions and hypotheses, which are in turn used as a reference point for interpreting empirical data (Leuzinger-Bohleber and Fischmann 2006). For subjectivists, however, concepts are the subject of the research itself. From their standpoint, knowledge is not an objective truth waiting to be discovered. Instead, it is researchers' own conceptualization of a given subject that allows them to construct knowledge and gain a deeper insight into their research object. Ultimately, proponents of conceptual methodologies acknowledge that 'different people may construct meaning in different ways even with regard to the same phenomenon' (Xin *et al.* 2013: 66).

In the context of translation studies, **conceptual research** has been generally used to develop new concepts or to reinterpret existing ones, to set up new classification systems, and to come up with better definitions of the categories to be used in the analysis of one's research topic.

Giorgio Curti's (2009) conceptualization of the subtitle as a dynamic affective force within film semiotics (Figure 5.1) is a good case in point. The impetus behind Curti's concept of **living subtitles** is the growing crisis of film as a means of representation (Aitken and Dixon 2006). Emerging narrative forms, Curti claims, problematize traditional assumptions that there is only 'one' reality to be captured and mirrored in films. Rather than attempting to mimic the extra-diegetic reality, a growing number of films set out to present viewers with aspects of different, sometimes clashing, realities. Under this new paradigm, subjectivity plays a crucial role in shaping the spectatorial experience: audiences are prompted to take part actively in the process of constructing meaning and articulating their own

Featured example 1: conceptual research (Curti 2009)

What is the purpose of this research?

Curti seeks to reconceptualize the contribution of subtitles to film semiotics. Films are now demanding viewers' involvement in the construction of their spectatorial experience; in this context, a creative approach to subtitling is crucial to ensure that the expressive, affective dimension of the viewing experience is adequately mediated when a film is translated into another language.

What are the key concepts used here?

Living subtitles, i.e. snippets of text prioritizing the affective force of the speech over the accuracy of the translation they deliver.

Scapes, i.e. the different loci or sources of semiotic meaning (e.g. sound, colour, light or perspective).

Assemblages, i.e. multimodal textualities resulting from the combination of different scapes.

What are the implications of this research?

Theoretically, it forges more robust connections between audiovisual translation and other disciplines such as multimodal theory and non-representational theory.

At a practical level, it provides a conceptual platform for the investigation of transformational subtitling practices (see Section 7.3).

Figure 5.1 Conceptual research: the 'living subtitle' (Curti 2009)

interpretation of reality. In this context, films set out to provide viewers with a platform for the expression and recognition of mutual affectivity – both with film creators and fellow spectators.

Box 5.1

Williams and Chesterman on conceptual research in translation studies:

Conceptual research (conceptual analysis) often takes the form of an argument. You might argue, for instance, that a particular concept should be understood or defined in a particular way: that it should be classified in a given way; that it should be related to certain other concepts in certain ways; or that it should be replaced by some other concept. One of the key words in

> conceptual analysis is (in English) the word 'as' . . . To interpret something, i.e. to understand it (so the argument goes), is simply to see it 'as' something else, usually as something more familiar . . . Conceptual arguments need to show that they are in some way more convincing than alternative or preceding analyses of the concept in question.
>
> (Williams and Chesterman 2002: 59)

The manifold aspects of reality presented to viewers are articulated through a range of **scapes** – such as sound, colour, light or perspective – that interact with one another within the wider **filmic constellation** or **assemblage**. It is by engaging with these different scapes that viewers explore their subjectivity and reflect on the manifestations of 'multiplicity, affect, openness, embodiment and expression' embedded in the film (Curti 2009: 202).

So what happens when the 'language projected by films and ears viewing film do not match up' (ibid.: 201)? Will subtitles, understood as linguistic approximations of the meaning conveyed by speech in the original language, not undermine the construction of spectatorial subjectivity? According to Curti, contemporary experiences of film reception call for living subtitles that are able to challenge the dominance of the visual and to become a fully ratified component of the film. When considering these subtitles, the question to ask

> is not 'what is their meaning' or 'what are they representing', but 'what are they accomplishing?' That is, are they good – do they cause or permit the spectator to think and act simultaneously with and through different(iating) assemblage(s)capes of filmic content and expression? Or, are they bad – do they inhibit spectators, limit them, neglect differences of thought and action for a return of sameness and redundancy?
>
> (Curti ibid.: 205–6)

Living subtitles are not bound primarily by what the original speech actually says; their ultimate aim is to enhance the viewer's enjoyment or alignment with the film. Living subtitles do not set out to relay pre-existent experiences, but to create new ones. In fleshing out the concept of living subtitle, illustrated with examples of creative subtitling found in Timur Bekmambetov's Nochnoi Dozor (2004),[1] Curti departs from traditional accounts of film semiotics in at least two respects. First, he brings into sharp relief the unexplored scope available for film creators and translators to experiment with multimodal semiotics during the production and reception of audiovisual texts.[2] Second, Curti delivers a sophisticated critique of the role that subtitles can play in that process of experimentation – for they should no longer be confined to providing a faithful representation of the original speech through static written representations in the bottom regions of the frame. At a more practical level, Curti's work on living subtitles provides a conceptual framework for recent research on transformational subtitling practices, whether these are referred to as 'authorial titles' (Pérez-González 2012), 'integrated subtitles' (Fox 2013) or 'creative subtitles' (McClarty 2013). The implications of such transformational practices are explored in some depth in Section 7.3.

As Williams and Chesterman (2002: 60) note, a scholar's 'selection and interpretation of concepts, metaphors and theories' is 'seldom value-free, entirely objective'. Curti's conceptualization of living subtitles, for example, is indicative of his cinematic taste and the degree of intellectual effort he is willing to put into the viewing experience. Given its subjectivist epistemology, however, the results of Curti's conceptual research cannot be validated by an appeal to empirical data. Understandably, scholars who prioritize the interrogation of data over the exploration of ideas do not regard conceptual work as autonomous research; instead, they argue the case for an interplay between conceptualization and empiricism in the creation of knowledge.

5.3 EMPIRICAL RESEARCH

Empirical research is data-driven, and hence capable of being verified by observation (naturalistic inquiry) or experiment (experimental inquiry):

- **Naturalistic inquiry** involves observing how translators behave when mediating audiovisual texts in real life settings, and aims to develop context-specific statements about the multiple, constructed experiences of participants in the translation process. 'The observer', Williams and Chesterman note, 'tries not to interfere with the process (as far as possible), but simply observes it and notes certain features of it' (2002: 62). Admittedly, naturalistic research is **interpretive** in nature.

This means that proponents of naturalistic inquiry try to gain a better understanding of translation practices or the use of translated material from the point of view of observed participants, and to articulate relevant **idiographic interpretations**.[3] These accounts try to make sense of how individual events situated in specific socio-historical contexts work; therefore, insights derived from idiographic studies can only be applied tentatively outside the actual settings under study. In practical terms, the flow of naturalistic research normally requires the use of qualitative methods (e.g. interviews, questionnaires, or eye-tracking analysis of viewer behaviour) and purposive sampling (i.e. concentrating on a limited number of issues or participants that represent a larger group).

- **Experimental inquiry** requires immediate, first-hand access to data and often involves taking deliberate steps to stimulate the production of the desired information. Scholars involved in experimental research tend to begin by developing a working hypothesis and setting up carefully designed experimental designs to prove or refute it. The researcher thus 'deliberately interferes with the natural order of things in order to isolate a particular feature for study and, as far as possible, eliminate other features that are not relevant to the research' (Williams and Chesterman 2002: 63). Empirical research, often associated with quantitative methods, is therefore particularly appropriate when proof is sought that certain variables have an impact on other variables. Evidence collected through experimental studies is widely regarded to provide the most robust and objective corroboration for a given hypothesis.

The remainder of this chapter delivers a survey of naturalistic and experimental research methods – both quantitative and qualitative in nature – that have been undertaken over the last decades in the field of audiovisual translation. As was also the case with the overview of theoretical frameworks presented in Chapter 4, the research methods survey provided in the following sections is not meant to be exhaustive. Instead, the selection of studies delivered here is primarily intended to illustrate the growing epistemological diversity of audiovisual translation. Although most of the methods examined below are often used in combination with others, they will be explored separately here for the sake of expositional clarity.

5.3.1 Eye-tracking methods

Watching and making sense of audiovisual texts is a cognitively complex process facilitated, among other actions, by eye movements. To process the wealth of visual information that these texts make constantly available to us, we rely on **saccades**, i.e. ballistic scanning movements that occur typically three or four times every second (Bridgeman 1992). Insofar as their onset and offset coincide with **fixations**, i.e. pauses during which our eyes remain static over an area of interest, saccades allow us to inspect small portions of the visual world in a rapid sequence. Effectively, saccades filter the unlimited visual stimuli we are exposed to, reducing them to a manageable amount. So while our eyes are constantly surveying our entire visual field, we only receive detailed information from a small region known as **fovea** that has the size of a 'thumbnail at arm's length' (Levi et al. 1985). The volitional, more or less conscious, control of saccades, which has been shown to be closely related to attentional mechanisms, can now be monitored through eye-tracking technology with great precision (Figure 5.2). It is therefore unsurprising that the potential to enhance our understanding of the cognitive processes involved in watching translated audiovisual texts has attracted increasing interest from scholars in our field, particularly those drawing on cognitive models of translation (see Section 4.3.2).

As Kruger (2012) acknowledges, eye-tracking methods are being increasingly used in audio description studies to establish how 'the audio describer is able (or can be enabled) to identify and isolate from [the] coherent whole [of film] the information which is not available to the blind audience but essential in constructing a similar coherent whole' (Braun 2007: 3, quoted in Kruger 2012: 68). Kruger's own attempt to answer this question is driven by his insight that audio narrations should not be confined to descriptions of visually salient elements of the filmic narrative. In his view, effective audio narrations are those that empower visually impaired viewers to 'map the narrative cognitively, to immerse themselves in the fictional world, to experience the narrative as directly as possible' (Kruger 2012: 68). To enhance the viewing experience of partially sighted and/or blind audiences, audio narrations should incorporate references to seemingly unobtrusive visual features of the film, as these significantly foster the capacity of viewers to make narrative meaning from the film by themselves (see Box 5.2).

Featured example 2: eye-tracking Study (Kruger 2012)

What is the purpose of this research?

Kruger monitors the visual behaviour of participants in his study using eye-tracking technology to understand better how they make sense of narrative content presented through audiovisual texts. By comparing participants' actual behaviour with their written account of what happened in the film, Kruger concludes that visually unobtrusive elements of the film can play a key role in the comprehension of the narrative.

What kind of method is being used here?

Eye-tracking is, in principle, a naturalistic methodology: it allows for observation without interference. Depending on how controlled other variables (e.g. age and background of participants, time constraints, etc.) are, eye-tracking technologies can be used along more experimental lines.

Eye-tracking is combined in this study with an introspective research method: reconstructive memory reporting – participants are asked to report on what they have watched.

What are the conceptual domains at stake in this study?

Narrative analysis, **narrative cognition**, **narrativization**, **visual** vs **narrative salience**

Audio description, (re-)narration

Saccade, fixation, area of interest, scan path, focus map, heat map

What are the implications of this research?

Theoretically, investigating how we process elements with different degrees of narrative and visual salience helps us understand better the needs of partially sighted viewers.

At a practical level, eye-tracking studies aim to inform audio description practices, and supplement the intuition of audio narrators. As Kruger (2012: 69) puts it, 'we would like the blind audience to share in the enjoyment of decoding a narrative – not patronising them by interpreting the scene for them'.

Figure 5.2 Naturalistic research: eye-tracking methods (Kruger 2012)

Box 5.2

Kruger on the construction of narrative meaning through audio description:

> Films are constructed in specific ways to draw our attention to specific filmic elements that are visually salient and to which our attention is guided almost involuntarily – bottom-up demands. For the most part this is true. But there are times when our interpretation of a scene is not necessarily based on such salient filmic features, but also on minor visual details; in particular, when what is visible on screen is shaped into a narrative through the way it is shown, or how the what is shown, and an audience has to apply top-down attention in order to make sense of what they see.
>
> (Kruger 2012: 69)

In order to gain a better insight into how sighted viewers make sense of narrative sequences, Kruger sets out to monitor the visual behaviour of a group of individuals as they watch a scene of Wallace Chafe's *Pear Stories* (1975).[4] The scene in question shows a boy stealing fruit from a pear picker working atop a tree. Despite their physical proximity, *mise-en-scène* suggests the worker is oblivious to the boy's opportunistic actions, underscoring the 'tension of possible discovery'. As Kruger puts it, '[t]his understanding is not derived only from the objective visual information (*what*), but more specifically from the way in which the information is presented (the man seen in medium shots from a low angle, intent on his pears, and the boy, with the baskets that tempt him so, in unobstructed full shots)' (ibid.: 75). Kruger hypothesizes that this sophisticated understanding requires a high degree of cognitive depth on the part of the viewers who, in addition to visually salient aspects of the narrative, must also be aware of visually peripheral elements such as the baskets.

Eye-tracking technology helps Kruger to identify the main areas of interest in the scene by quantifying the number of fixations that they attract and measuring the overall dwell time spent processing those areas. His chosen eye-tracking tool allows him to visualize:

- **scan paths**, i.e. series of fixations and saccades that participants have followed when watching the film (Figure 5.3, Screenshot A);
- **areas of interest**, i.e. regions or spaces attracting attention, as delimited by entering and exiting saccades (Figure 5.3, Screenshot B);
- a **focus map**, where the frame has been blacked out to highlight only those areas that received viewers' attention – and, by extension, what they did not focus on (Figure 5.3, Screenshot C);

- a **heat map** featuring coloured spots over the areas of the frame that received the most attention from participants during the experiment. The core of such spots, corresponding to the stimuli attracting more interest, are shown in red; yellow and green/blue denote areas prompting medium and little attention, respectively (Figure 5.3, Screenshot D).

Kruger then correlates his eye-tracking data with narrative reports on the scene produced by participants in the experiment – thus illustrating the advantages of combining different research methods within a single study. A subjective cognition score is awarded to each report on the basis of whether its delivers simply a description (lowest score) or a full narrativization of the action (highest score). By correlating those reports exhibiting the highest cognition scores with specific patterns of viewing behaviour around key areas of interest, Kruger concludes that 'the less visually salient element of the baskets, in combination with the more visually salient elements of the man and the boy, had a decisive impact on the narrative cognition' (ibid.: 81). More importantly, his findings lead him to postulate that audio narrations should prioritize narrative salient elements over their visually prominent counterparts.

Further reading on eye-tracking studies:

- Jensema *et al.* (2000a, 2000b)
- Lång et al. (2013)
- Orero and Vilaró (2012)
- Vercauteren and Orero (2013)

5.3.2 Questionnaires and interviews

Kruger's decision to correlate the findings of his eye-tracking experiment with written input from the participants in his study is highly representative of research trends in audiovisual translation. In our field, eliciting views and gauging perceptions of audiences, practitioners and scholars are common ways of securing data, often in combination with other research methods, whether as part of quantitative or qualitative projects.

Grouping questionnaires and interviews under the same heading acknowledges the important similarities that exist between two of the most

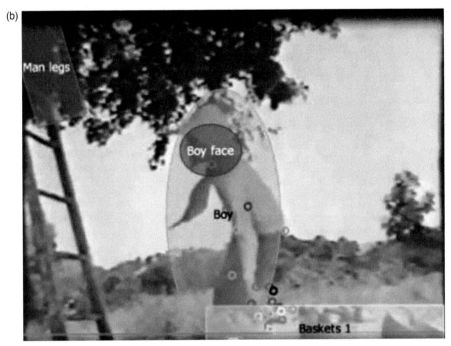

Figure 5.3a–d Monitoring viewing behaviour using eye-tracking technology

(c)

(d)

common methods used by scholars to interact with their informants. For instance, when using questionnaires and interviews, decisions have to be made as to whether it is more appropriate and/or effective for the researcher to rely on open-ended or leading questions or, indeed, whether to build in mechanisms for in-depth probing at certain points in the series of written or spoken questions. On the other hand, the need to secure ethical approval has now become an essential part of research protocol in projects relying on either of these two methods. This section draws on selected examples of published research to illustrate how audiovisual translation scholars – mostly proponents of process (Section 4.3) and causal models of translation (Section 4.5) – have designed their survey work and interviewed their respondents.

Caffrey's (2009) doctoral thesis (Figure 5.4) investigates the impact that the use of **pop-up glosses** has on viewer perception of **culturally marked visual nonverbal cues** in anime series broadcast on television. Pop-up glosses, a sub-type of the headnotes described in Section 3.3, are snippets of target language text placed anywhere on the frame to complement the content of standard or dialogue subtitles located at the bottom of the screen (e.g. Figure 3.5).

Box 5.3

Caffrey's definition of 'positive cognitive effect' with reference to subtitle viewing behaviour:

> [I]n the context of the present study a positive cognitive effect is defined as a worthwhile difference to the individual's representation of the world evidenced by that individual's ability to retain and retrieve new information on the basis of some input. Using this definition of positive cognitive effects, it is possible to determine whether the use of pop-up gloss in an excerpt will result in more subjects experiencing positive cognitive effects than subjects watching the same excerpt with no pop-up glosses.
>
> (Caffrey 2009: 53)

In this study, Caffrey gauges whether and to what extent the use or non-use of pop-up glosses superimposed on culturally specific visual items is beneficial or detrimental to the viewing experience of non-Japanese audiences. On the one hand, it is acknowledged that pop-up glosses place additional cognitive strain on the audience. As they have to be read at the

Featured example 3: questionnaire-based study (Caffrey 2009)

What is the purpose of this research?

Caffrey sets out to investigate whether/how the use of pop-up glosses interferes with viewing behaviour. The information provided by such glosses is key for English-speaking viewers to make sense of culture-specific visual signs used in the Japanese original material. However, processing those glosses while watching the visuals and reading standard subtitles is cognitively taxing. The question then arises: how beneficial/detrimental are pop-up glosses in terms of their contribution to viewers' enjoyment of anime?

What kind of method is being used here?

Questionnaires allow for the efficient collection of highly relevant data from selected participants as part of an **experimental research project**. Using two experiment conditions, the use and non-use of pop-up glosses while viewing anime reveals what participants think they understand, and what they actually understand.

The use of questionnaires is combined in this study with an observational research method, **eye-tracking** – which helps to corroborate or challenge empirically participants' declared perceptions.

What are the conceptual domains at stake in this study?

Pop-up glosses, culturally marked visual nonverbal cues, positive cognitive effect, processing effort

Questionnaire, experiment conditions, independent variable, dependent variable, open-ended questions, scaled questions

What are the implications of this research?

As new audiovisual translation practices emerge, it is necessary to gain an empirical understanding of their impact on spectatorial experiences.

Questionnaires allow for a highly targeted and relatively cheap collection of data, as long as they are well constructed and institutional requirements for ethics consent are met.

Figure 5.4 Experimental research: questionnaires (Caffrey 2009)

same time as dialogue subtitles, and processed contemporaneously with the images, pop-up glosses are likely to require a greater **processing effort** on the part of viewers. On the other hand, pop-up glosses provide useful information to elucidate the meaning of culturally marked visual content, which is bound to have a **positive cognitive effect** (see Box 5.3), and enhance both the viewers' comprehension and enjoyment of the subtitled material.

As part of his two-pronged experimental study, which also involves the use of an eye-tracker to measure viewers' processing effort in terms of pupillometric measurements, Caffrey administers a questionnaire to appraise his subjects' experience of positive cognitive effects empirically. Questionnaires are thus used to establish whether the information conveyed by pop-up glosses in Caffrey's chosen anime excerpts has been retrieved and retained.

There are a number of clear advantages to the use of questionnaires in Caffrey's study. Although the design and construction of the questionnaires may be time-consuming, data elicited and collated through this instrument is bound to be highly relevant to the research questions at the centre of the study. Likewise, questionnaires are easily adaptable to the relatively small scale of the project at hand. In this case, and given the abundance of complementary data secured through the eye-tracking analysis, only 20 subjects were required to take part in the study. Participants in Caffrey's experiment were asked to watch 11 excerpts of anime series featuring culturally marked visual nonverbal cues. Excerpt 5, one of fragments tested by Caffrey, will be used here to illustrate how this questionnaire was constructed.

The culturally marked visual nonverbal cue at the heart of excerpt 5 is an image of a photo frame wrapped in a black ribbon. The spoken dialogue delivered while the photo frame is shown ('いきなり殺すな') has been subtitled into English as 'Don't kill her off already!' Participants viewed this excerpt under two different experiment conditions:

- **normal condition**: excerpt 5 displayed no pop-up gloss and there was no reference to the culturally marked visual nonverbal cue in the standard or dialogue subtitle either;
- **treatment condition**: excerpt 5 contained a pop-up gloss with reference to the culturally marked visual nonverbal cue, in addition to the standard or dialogue subtitle. The text of the gloss was as follows: 'In Japan, the photo frame for a deceased person's picture is decorated with a black ribbon'.

The section of Caffrey's questionnaire appraising viewers' understanding of the culturally marked visual nonverbal cue in excerpt 5 is reproduced in Figure 5.5.

Excerpt 5 questionnaire

1 What does the girl tell the old teacher he'd better *not* pull out a picture of?

2 Do you know what the photo frame surrounded by the black ribbon represents?

    Not at all   1☐   2☐   3☐   4☐   5☐   6☐   *Completely*

3 What is a photo frame with a black ribbon used for in Japan?

4 How did you find the speed of the main dialogue subtitle in this excerpt?

    Too slow   1☐   2☐   3☐   4☐   5☐   *Too fast*

(Caffrey 2009: Appendix E)

Figure 5.5 Measuring actual and declared positive cognitive effects through questionnaires (Caffrey 2009)

- Questions 1 and 3 are examples of **open-ended questions**. These allow respondents to contribute individual points of view and detailed information. Open-ended questions queried the participants' understanding of the dialogue subtitle and the culturally marked visual nonverbal cue. Correct responses to these questions were held to provide evidence of *actual* positive cognitive effects.
- Questions 2 and 4 are examples of **scaled questions** based on the Likert scale. In this case, respondents were prompted to express their (dis) agreement with a statement by choosing one among a range of proposed scores – each of which articulates a specific shade of opinion. Insofar as Likert scales are primarily used to elicit opinions rather than facts, they are commonly known as 'opinionaires'. Respondents' scores to these scaled questions were held to provide evidence of *declared* positive cognitive effects (i.e. how good participants *thought* their comprehension was).

Caffrey's analysis of participants' responses to questionnaires on the 11 excerpts can be summarized as follows. Under the treatment condition, participants provided more correct responses to the open questions. In other words, when respondents watched the excerpt with pop-up glosses, the rate of positive cognitive effects was significantly higher. Questionnaire data also revealed that, under the treatment condition, participants declared higher positive cognitive effects in response to the scaled questions. Viewers thus felt more confident about the amount and accuracy of information they had been able to retain about the culturally marked visual nonverbal cue when they had access to the pop-up glosses while watching the excerpts.

Pop-up glosses are a good example of innovative mediation practices originally developed by amateur and fan subtitlers outside the influence of the media industry. Amid the ongoing fragmentation of audiences and identities, however, these emerging practices are being gradually co-opted by commercial distribution companies (Denison 2011). By releasing multiple dubbed and subtitled versions of their audiovisual commodities, drawing on both established and unorthodox conventions, distributors seek to appeal to different segments of the audience – and hence to maximize the return on their investment. But while the adoption of new practices by the media industry is gathering momentum, we remain oblivious to the significance and impact that innovative forms of mediation have on viewers. As illustrated in this section, Caffrey's study brings to the fore the importance of empirical research at a time when the ever growing digitization of audiovisual texts and advances in communication technology are driving a diversification in translation conventions.

Further reading on questionnaire-based studies

- Antonini (2005)
- Antonini and Chiaro (2005, 2009)
- Bucaria and Chiaro (2007)
- Chiaro (2004, 2007a)
- Fresno (2012)
- Fuentes Luque (2000, 2003)
- Gottlieb (1995)
- Jensema (1998)

With the proliferation of sociological approaches to the study of translation and the consequent borrowing of research methods from social sciences, interviews have become an increasingly ubiquitous tool for the collection of research data. The tendency to make use of interviews is 'expected to continue as the discipline', including audiovisual translation studies, 'expands beyond the realm of linguistics, literature and cultural studies, and takes upon itself the task of integrating the sociological dimension of translation' (Saldanha and O'Brien 2013: 168). Interviews have a number of advantages:

- they are often experienced by participants as highly personal encounters, so they can be conducive to a frank exchange of views, knowledge and experiences;
- unstructured or semi-structured interviews allow researchers to maintain a certain degree of control over the encounter, while at the same time giving participants room for free individual expression;
- interviews prioritize attention to participants' personal circumstances and attitudes towards the topics under investigation over standardized techniques of data collection.

In the field of audiovisual translation studies, the role and significance of interviews vis-à-vis other participant-driven research instruments (e.g. questionnaires) remain relatively unexplored. Karamitroglou's (2000) research on the norms that determine the choice between revoicing and subtitling in Greek TV channels (Section 4.5.1) represents a notable exception. His study delivers an in-depth and rigorous account of the relevance of interviews to the study of 'human agents' in the context of audiovisual translation, conceptualized as a 'target language literary system'. In their capacity as norm creators and enforcers, Karamitroglou argues, human agents operate at different levels of the interface between individual translations and the systems in which they are embedded (Box 5.4).

Box 5.4

Karamitroglou's (2000: 70) categorization of 'human agents' in the Greek system of audiovisual translation

- Upper level human agents influence the relationship between Greece's literary system and its audiovisual translation sub-system. Interviews can be used at this level to investigate the 'attitude of agents (commissioners, translators, etc.) towards the translation of literary products in general'.
- Middle level human agents mediate the relationship between the audiovisual translation scene and specific translation projects. Interviews can be used at this level to investigate the 'attitude of AV translation agents (commissioners, translators, spotters, etc.) towards overall AV translation'.
- Lower level human agents deal with individual projects, setting them against the relevant context of production. Interviews can be used at this level to investigate the 'status and attitude of a particular AV translation product's agents (commissioners, translators, spotters, etc.) towards the particular AV translation product'.

In his search for the most effective interview format to unveil the translators' motivations for choosing a specific form of audiovisual translation over others, and to gain a better understanding of the conventions constraining their decisions as human agents, Karamitroglou weighs up the advantages and disadvantages of interactionist and positivist interviews (Silverman 1993):

- The epistemology of **interactionist** interviews is more constructive and draws on a conceptualization of interviewees as meaning makers. Therefore, interactionist interviews tend to yield valuable insight into authentic personal experiences, from which general interpretations can be derived.
- **Positivist** interviews, on the other hand, regard interviewees as 'passive conduits for retrieving information from an existing vessel of answers' (Holstein and Gubrium 2001: 83) and tend to involve a much higher degree of standardization.

Karamitroglou indicates his intention to interrogate the role of human agents in the Greek audiovisual landscape by relying on a positive epistemology. With their emphasis on facts, positivist interviews are meant to facilitate the comparison between individual responses (ibid.). However, Karamitroglou's positivist orientation ultimately leads him to ditch interviews for questionnaires as his primary research method. It is only after the preliminary analysis of his questionnaire-based findings has been completed that Karamitroglou holds 'unofficial mini-interviews', both face-to-face or over-the-phone encounters. Interviews thus serve to confirm the validity of his interpretations and the conclusions he draws from his data set. Through these interviews, Karamitroglou clarifies, 'human agents had the chance to reformulate, elaborate and clarify points they had expressed when filling the questionnaires but were not so clear after all' (2000: 116).

Although Karamitroglou gives serious consideration to the use of interviews, his decision to switch to questionnaires as the primary tool for data collection is reflective of a wider trend within audiovisual translation studies. The terms 'interviews' and 'questionnaires' are often used interchangeably (Widler 2004). When an explicit distinction between them is made, interviews are effectively deployed as a complementary instrument to confirm or elaborate on the results gathered through questionnaires (Fuentes Luque 2000). Even in those cases where scholars go some way towards reporting what is discussed in their interview (Martí Ferriol 2006), full transcriptions of the encounters are rarely made available. Overall, the treatment of interviews in audiovisual translation remains mostly anecdotal, as rigorous accounts of the methodological rationale for their use are few and far between, as illustrated by Chiaro (2007b).

5.3.3 Archival methods

In audiovisual translation studies, doing **archival research** has typically involved three major steps: locating, inspecting and interpreting documentary sources accessible only through large collections held in major libraries or in the archives of public bodies and institutions. Originally collected for other purposes, these materials are normally consulted and scrutinized by audiovisual translation scholars for reasons different from those that prompted their compilation in the first place. As shown in Chapter 2, examples of such purposes include tracing the historical origins and consolidation of early modalities of audiovisual translation, and studying the impact of the socio-political landscape on subtitling and dubbing practices at their formative moment. By asking new questions of old data and drawing together evidence from disparate sources, researchers have been able to gain a better understanding of the contexts of production and reception of translated audiovisual material over the last century.

The traditional reliance of historical research on manuscripts and artefactual sources (including copies of old films) has contributed to ingraining conventional methods of undertaking background research, interpreting and consulting original documents within the scholarly environment of major libraries and archival search rooms. It is thus common for archival research to be driven primarily by **paratextual elements**, as understood by Genette (1983 [1980]).

Gutiérrez Lanza's (2007) detailed account of the design and compilation of TRACEci – a database of film translations censored during Franco's dictatorship in Spain – is a case in point. In addition to copies of original and translated (subtitled or dubbed) films and their corresponding written scripts (including censored versions thereof), Gutiérrez Lanza draws on a wide range of paratextual documents housed at the archive of the Spanish Ministry of Culture, Spain's General Archive (Archivo General de la Administración) and the Library of the Spanish Film Institute (Filmoteca

Española). Examples of paratexts include film dossiers assembled by a range of censorship boards and collectable information sheets published by specialized periodicals. These documentary sources provide detailed particulars on the circumstances surrounding the translation and reception of foreign films in Spain at the time, such as film titles in the source and target languages, details of the dubbing studio responsible for the production of each dubbed version, dates and venues of film premières, information on the duration of the film's run on commercial screens, plot synopses, church and governmental censorship classifications, film reviews published after theatrical release, and predictions of the box office revenue that films were likely to attract, to give but a few examples. The development of an electronic database with information distilled from these paratexts allows Gutiérrez Lanza to identify censored films that are worthy of in-depth analysis.

But advances in communication technologies are bringing about fundamental changes as to what researchers now regard as archival information, as well as the ways in which they access archival collections and interpret archival sources. Consequently, the traditional understanding of archives as physical, spatially localized field sites is fast becoming outdated. Nowhere is this more evident than in netnographic research. Practitioners of **netnography** investigate communities and cultures created through increasingly sophisticated forms of computer-mediated social interaction. These virtual groupings, netnographers argue, deserve scholarly attention because they 'form or manifest cultures, the learned beliefs, values and customs that serve to order, guide and direct the behaviour of a particular society' (Kozinets 2010: 12). Netnography thus represents a methodological extension from the study of co-located, face-to-face encounters to technologically mediated interactions in networked environments. Through their immersion and direct participation in those virtual communities, i.e. by observing, analysing and interpreting cultural practices within the culture itself, netnographers are able to articulate a 'thick description' (Geertz 1973) of their research site. From the perspective of archival research methodology, it is worth noting that observations gathered through direct participation in a networked community can be greatly enhanced by the availability of previous computer-held data of social interaction within the community under scrutiny. As Kozinets (2010: 104) notes, netnographic research often involves

> large amounts of conversational cultural data collected from archives. These data are unaffected by the actions of the netnographer. Archival

cultural data provide what amounts to a cultural baseline. Saved communal interactions provide the netnographer with a convenient bank of observational data that may stretch back for years or, in some cases, well over a decade. Netnographers benefit from the prior transcription of posted text, images, and other messages. Collecting and analysing these archival data is an excellent supplement to cultural participation. These can be used analogously to the way that archival and historical data are used in ethnographies to extend and deepen the knowledge of a cultural context.

Li's (2014) netnographic study of *The Last Fantasy* (TLF), one of the most influential fansubbing groups in China, is a good example of this new methodological trend in audiovisual translation studies (Figure 5.6). As part of her investigation into the role that amateur subtitlers play in the Chinese digital media landscape, Li analyses how TLF members make use of communication technology to produce and share subtitled material; build and maintain relationships with other group members performing different roles within this participatory network; and articulate a collective voice and sense of identity. To explore each of these aspects of TLF's activity, Li immerses herself in the group as a participant. The fieldnotes she makes contemporaneously with her participation in TLF's work are complemented by two strands of archival data:

- subtitle files previously produced by TLF. The analysis of subtitled output is intended to reveal the set of discursive strategies that fansubbers deploy to construct and articulate their collective identity through their voluntary involvement in subtitling activities;
- messages posted by TLF members through the group's different online forums. The analysis of their posted messages is meant to provide Li with a better understanding of the roles that amateur subtitlers adopt in the context of a 'self-organizing' participatory network, where no external governance mechanism is in place.

From an archival perspective, netnographic studies such as Li's highlight the relevance of **genetic criticism** (Hay 2004) to audiovisual translation scholarship – in keeping with developments on archival research within the wider discipline (Bollettieri Bosinelli and Zanotti 2011). The availability of access to electronic records of interaction between TLF members acting as

Featured example 4: archival research (Li 2014)

What is the purpose of this research?

Li aims to understand the reasons for the ever growing involvement of Chinese amateur translators in fansubbing communities and the consequent changes in media consumption practices in the country. Can this phenomenon be accounted for in terms of a shared identity, a set of common experiences expressed through this participatory phenomenon? If so, how does technology facilitate the display and perception of mutual recognition?

What kind of method is being used here?

Fieldnotes made during Li's participation in the activities of a fansubbing group are complemented by the **analysis of archival data**. These include subtitles created for previous projects and records of computer-mediated interactions between group members.

Questionnaires help Li to elicit information on members' perceived roles in the group and provide fans with a platform to articulate their expectations and values.

What are the implications of this research?

Translation studies has generally been regarded and presented as a discipline largely concerned with professional translation. In the era of the digital culture, however, the relationship between the media marketplace and audiovisual translation is changing. Non-professionals are increasingly taking on the role of audiovisual translators to pursue and promote different agendas (see Chapter 8).

Networked communities of non-professional practice are self-organizing, horizontal structures. Their intervention in the co-creation and reception of media content challenges the traditional role of media corporations as translation patrons/commissioners. The researcher's immersion and participation in the activities of such communities is crucial to construct new theorizations of these new structures of media production/consumption.

Figure 5.6 The role of archival research in the era of the digital culture (Li 2014)

subtitlers, revisors, technical specialists and fellow fans enables researchers to reconstruct the subtitling process and offers them insights into the rationale for the translational decisions made throughout it.

With traditional conceptualizations of patronage struggling to harness the changing dynamics of translation in the informational society, it is imperative to find new ways of studying emerging collaborative, commons-based peer production structures and the way in which they organize themselves.

As the involvement of these networked communities in audiovisual translation and other forms of media co-creation continues to grow apace, genetic criticism, as enabled by netnography, is bound to play an ever more influential role in audiovisual translation studies. From the perspective of genetic criticism, audiovisual translations are best conceptualized as 'palimpsestic' forms of mediation. Ultimately, the abundant records of computer-mediated interaction available within networked communities assist researchers in unveiling original translations that may have been effaced to make room for later versions; establishing at which point modifications were incorporated; and articulating the rationale for the introduction of such changes.

Further reading on archival studies in audiovisual translation:

- Lindgren (2013)
- Antonini and Chiaro (2005, 2009)

5.3.4 Corpus-based methods

Corpus-driven findings derive from the analysis and interpretation of **corpora**, i.e. large collections of computer-held texts, using powerful processing software. Although these software applications also allow for qualitative analyses of linguistic structures with reference to the local contexts in which they occur, corpus-based studies are chiefly quantitative in orientation. The vast amounts of data required to identify idiosyncratic patterns of language used in translated texts are therefore widely regarded, in and by themselves, as sufficient evidence for the validity and generalizability of computer-based findings.

Corpora represent a growing research method in the field of audiovisual translation. As explained in Section 4.4.2, they have been so far closely associated with comparative models of translation. By contrasting dubbed fictional language with original dialogue, both in the source and target languages, scholars have been able to identify features of dubbed conversation that set it apart as a linguistic variety worthy of study in its own right – rather than in terms of its equivalence to the source text. As Weizman and Blum-Kulka (1987: 72) note,

> The identification of a text as a translation product implies that deviations from cultural norms are not judged as intentional, and therefore are not assigned any 'hidden' meanings. In this respect, the perception of 'translationese' plays a significant role in the process of text interpretation.

Unlike in Section 4.4.2, the emphasis here is placed on the methodological aspects of corpus-based research over its theoretical counterparts, with a view to illustrate the specific ways in which corpus-driven research is being operationalized in audiovisual translation studies. Within this disciplinary area:

- corpora consist of naturally occurring texts, i.e. actual translations compiled specifically for the purpose of systematic analysis;
- corpora are compiled in some principled way, and hence contain carefully selected texts on the basis of clearly stated criteria;
- corpora lend themselves to manipulation by allowing for different ways of data sorting, display and annotation;
- corpora are commonly exploited through KWIC (key word in context) concordances (lists of all the occurrences of search words or expressions in a corpus, set in the middle of one line of context each) or frequency lists of words in a corpus (identifying common lexis in a corpus or isolating unusual or creative items).

Concordance-driven analysis of corpora

Concordances are central to the exploitation of the Pavia Corpus of Film Dialogue (PCFD), as reported by Freddi (2013). Designed to facilitate the study of sociolinguistic and pragmatic features of dubbed Italian, PCFD is made up of three sections (Figure 5.7):

- Sub-corpus 1 (BrE/AmE Source Texts) consists of the orthographic transcriptions of 24 films shot in British and American English (approximately 258,000 words);
- Sub-corpus 2 (IT Target Texts) holds the orthographic transcriptions of the dubbed Italian versions of the 24 English originals (approximately 240,000 words);
- Sub-corpus 3 (IT Source Texts) is made up of the orthographic transcriptions of six Italian original films (approximately 60,000 words) that are comparable to their British and American counterparts in terms of genre affiliation and critical success, among other criteria.

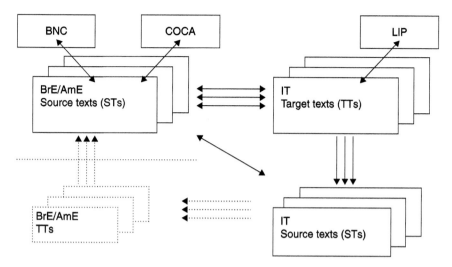

Figure 5.7 The Pavia Corpus of Film Dialogue design (Freddi 2013: 495)

The contrastive scrutiny and exploitation of sub-corpora 1 and 2 as constitutive components of a **parallel corpus**[5] allow for comparisons between
selected sociolinguistic and pragmatic features of original (English) and
dubbed (Italian) filmic dialogue. Similarly, sub-corpora 2 and 3 on the one
hand, and sub-corpora 1 and 3 on the other, can be exploited by way of
comparable corpora. While the comparison of sub-corpora 2 and 3 sheds
light on the similarities and differences between dubbed and original
fictional dialogue in Italian, insights afforded by the comparison between
sub-corpora 1 and 3 help the analyst to pinpoint cross-linguistic sociolinguistic and pragmatic correspondences of original English and Italian
fictional speech.

In turn, each of the sub-corpora included in PCFD can be potentially
subjected to comparative analysis with other collections of spontaneous
non-fictional conversation data, which act as **reference corpora**. Sub-
corpus 1 (original film dialogue in English), for instance, can be compared
with the spoken sections of BNC (British National Corpus) and COCA
(Corpus of Contemporary American English). Sub-corpus 2 (dubbed Italian
speech), on the other hand, can be studied contrastively with the LIP
(Lessico di frequenza dell'italiano parlato) corpus of spoken Italian.[6] Finally,
'[t]he dotted part [of Figure 5.7] points to the fact that the corpus is
unidirectional, reflecting the asymmetry in the AVT practices of the

countries involved in the comparison (the UK and US are not dubbing countries)' (Freddi 2013: 495).

Freddi's work exploits the configuration of PCFD to maximum effect, both from a source-oriented perspective (placing the emphasis on how the source text has been translated) and a target-oriented perspective (focusing on dubbed language as a distinct language variety):

- The first of these approaches is illustrated through the analysis of how the source language pragmatic marker 'listen' is dubbed into Italian. Evidence gathered in the form of concordances from sub-corpora 1 and 2 indicates that, when used as a pragmatic marker in turn-initial position, 'listen' is predominantly translated into Italian using different forms of the verb 'sentire' such as 'senti' or 'senta' (see Box 5.5).
- Under a source-oriented perspective, the analysis can also begin at the target text end. Having established the relative prominence of 'sentire' and its inflectional variants as pragmatic markers in the target language sub-corpus, Freddi uses these items as search words to interrogate the source language sub-corpus. This analytical direction unveils relatively stable patterns of correspondence between the selected Italian discourse markers and a number of source language 'utterance launchers' (e.g. 'you know what', 'hey, well' and 'I mean').
- Adopting a target-oriented perspective, Freddi contrasts the sub-corpora of dubbed and original Italian fictional dialogue (sub-corpora 2 and 3, respectively) to establish the relative frequency of the Italian pragmatic markers 'senti' and 'ascolta' in each of these language varie-ties. Ultimately, this strand of analysis contributes to yield a better understanding of translational language (dubbed Italian) as a variety of the wider target language (spoken Italian).

Box 5.5

Freddi's (2013: 496–97) example of corpus-based analysis from a source-text perspective:

Source Text: ERIC: **Listen**, erm, I'm really sorry about all the fuss. I'm really sorry, yeah. I really don't know what got into me, nurse.

> Target Text: ERIC: Ah, **senta**, mi dispiace molto per il casino che ho combinato, io . . . non lo so che cosa mi è preso, infermiera.
> Back-translation: Ah **listen**, I'm really sorry about the mess I've made, I . . . don't know what was wrong with me, nurse.

Overall, the combined exploitation of the three sub-corpora from both source- and target-oriented perspectives assists Freddi in uncovering a distinctive structural feature of dubbed language. Translators' awareness of this range of Italian expressions that share a common 'pragmatic function as turn initiating devices with an interpersonal function' should allow for a more objective assessment of 'the quality of translated texts as products circulating within a target culture' (ibid.: 499–500). Similarly, a comparison of the frequency of these pragmatic markers in the sub-corpora of original English film speech and its Italian counterpart (sub-corpora 1 and 3, respectively) should have beneficial effects both on the production and translation of fictional dialogue. Indeed, the development of corpus-driven guidelines on the production and mediation of this form of spoken interaction could 'be instrumental for professional translators/dialogue writers to increase their knowledge of the linguistic and textual conventions of the genres and cultures at stake and develop appropriate target language phraseology' (ibid.).

Frequency-based analysis of corpora

Frequency lists also have an important role to play in driving audiovisual translation research forward. Salway's (2007) corpus-based analysis of audio description is a good case in point. Working on the premise that the language of audio description is strongly influenced by its distinctive narrative function, Salway hypothesizes that 'audio describers use a special language that is shaped by the communicative needs of its users' (ibid.: 152). Compiling corpora of audio description scripts and interrogating these collections of text using corpus processing software, Salway argues, could potentially help scholars to identify idiosyncratic linguistic features of audio descriptions and, more significantly, to automatize the production of such narrations.

Salway sets out to test his hypothesis empirically by compiling lists of the most frequent words in the 618,859-word TIWO (Television in Words) Corpus, comprising 91 audio description scripts. TIWO-based lists are then compared with frequency lists drawn from corpora of general English. By doing so, Salway aims to single out those words that appear in the special language (SL) of audio descriptions much more frequently than in general language (GL). As he put is, '[i]f a word has a high SL/GL ratio, it suggests idiosyncratic usage in a special language corpus and therefore demands closer inspection' (2007: 158).

Concordances for 'unusually frequent' words, i.e. lexical items that exhibit a high SL/GL ratio, are then compiled and scrutinized to uncover the wider phrases and expressions that they are embedded in. By bringing together and cross-checking the findings derived from the analysis of frequency lists and concordances, Salway identifies a range of commonly occurring phrases that can be grouped under the five headings presented in Figure 5.8.

As Salway notes, corpus-driven developments have the potential to play

Characters' appearances	• *Woman in/man in* + item of clothing • *Woman/man wearing* + item of clothing • *Woman/man with* + distinctive physical feature • *A + adjective* [pertaining to physical appearance] *man/woman*
Characters' focus of attention	• Character *looking at, looks up at, looks around, stares at, glances at, gazes at, watches*, etc.
Characters' interpersonal interactions	• Character *turns to, shakes hands, sits next to, their eyes met, puts hand on, gaze into each other's eyes* • Character *smiles at* + adverb, *nods* + adverb, *shakes his head* + adverb
Changes in location of characters and objects	• Character (*stands up* and) goes *to/into/off/out, walks away/off/ out/over to, steps towards/into/onto, opens/closes doors* • Vehicles *pull up, drive off* • Characters *pick up/pull out* an object, *put* an object somewhere
Characters' emotional states and reactions	• Character *looks/is looking* + adjective (*confused, shocked, surprised, thoughtful, troubled, uneasy, annoyed, puzzled*, etc.) • Character *smiles/stares/looks/walks* + adverb/adverbial phrase (*contentedly, fondly, happily, sadly, curiously, in disbelief, anxiously, stiffly*)

Figure 5.8 Commonly occurring phrases in audio narrations (Salway 2007: 160–161)

an important assistive role in the production of semi-automated audio narrations. Nowhere is this potential more obvious than in the interface of the software applications used to prepare, record and synchronize audio description scripts. These applications, Salway contends, should provide users with direct 'access to previous descriptions in order [for professionals] to see how certain things have been described before, either for inspiration for their description or to ensure consistency with previous descriptions within a TV series or film' (2007: 167). Consistency can also be enhanced through the targeted interrogation of corpus resources enabled by advances in processing software. In exploiting corpus-based resources, describers may choose to draw only on those sections of the corpus that hold comparable descriptions. For instance, they may opt to scrutinize only past narrations that match the current project in terms of filmic genre, linguistic register or dramatic characterization; or use as a reference past descriptions that were commissioned by the same institution. Narrations that are modelled directly on selected previous narrations are bound to adhere to generic conventions or institutional guidelines more effectively. More widely, the growing reliability and flexibility of corpus processing technologies are envisaged to bring about the customization of audio narrations at a relatively low cost. Consequently, future users of this mode of audiovisual translation 'may be able to choose alternative description tracks, or access more detailed descriptions whilst pausing a film' (ibid.: 168).

Multimodal corpora

Most corpus-based approaches to the study of audiovisual translation have so far revolved exclusively around collections of written text, i.e. orthographic transcriptions of filmic (original or dubbed) dialogue and audio narrations. Over the last decade, however, we have witnessed the proliferation of **multimodal corpora** (Heiss and Soffritti 2008, Sotelo Dios 2011). Made up of both textual and audiovisual data, these tools aim to give empirical and systematic insights into the interplay between verbal and non-verbal semiotics, with particular emphasis on the extent to which the latter complement or constrain the translation of film dialogue.

One of such multimodal repositories is Forlixt 1 (Valentini 2006, 2008, 2009, 2013). Conceived as an electronic database of multimodal material, it holds a range of digitized films and TV series in five languages, in addition

> **Box 5.6**
>
> Categorization of tags used to annotate Forlixt 1 contents (Valentini 2013: 545):
>
> 1 **pragmatic categories**: communicative acts and situations;
> 2 **linguistic and cultural categories**: linguistic specificities, prosodic and paralinguistic means, specific cultural references, names of specific entities;
> 3 **sociolinguistic categories**: regional and social varieties, registers;
> 4 **encyclopedic and semiotic categories**: geographical, temporal and cultural settings, specificities of the AV support.

to the orthographic transcriptions of their respective original, dubbed and subtitled dialogues. As part of the compilation process, transcriptions are segmented into scenes and aligned with the corresponding fragment of audiovisual material. Each of these scenes is then tagged using a range of attributes clustered around five 'descriptive categories' (Box 5.6). Annotating the database contents along these lines enables advanced techniques of corpus interrogation. Researchers interested in specific linguistic structures, for example, may want to examine how these are translated in different semiotic environments – defined in terms of co-occurrence of different sets of features pertaining to 'film editing, body language, facial expressions, cultural specificities relating to the geographical, temporal and cultural setting, etc.' (Valentini 2013: 545).

As illustrated by Valentini (2006), users of Forlixt 1 can choose among different types of queries to interrogate the platform contents:

- free-text searches allow scholars to search for individual or multi-word lexical items, whether through exact or fuzzy matches. Searches can be narrowed by opting to interrogate only transcriptions of dialogue, subtitles, or both. The list of hits returned by Forlixt 1 features a range of metadata for each occurrence of the search item, including the title of the film or TV series it has been retrieved from; the name of the character uttering the relevant line of dialogue, and whether this is taken from the original, dubbed or subtitled speech sections of the data base; and the tags used to annotate the wider scene in terms of its semiotic configuration. A clickable link placed in the vicinity of each occurrence launches a separate page showing the search structure within a wider linguistic context (both in the source and target languages) as well as the clip corresponding to the scene in question.

- guided searches allow for customized analyses, with researchers interrogating only those sections of the database that possess one or more of the attributes grouped under the four major types of descriptive categories featured in Box 5.6. For example, 'the category "names of specific entities" [under linguistic and cultural categories] comprises labels such as names of famous characters and people, titles and names of cultural or trade products' (Valentini 2006).

Valentini herself has shown how multimodal corpora can be exploited to sensitize students to the role that audiovisual semiotics play in contextualizing and guiding the interpretation of selected verbal components of the source text, including cultural and pragmatic references (2006). Valentini has also illustrated the affordances of guided searches as part of her study on the distribution of certain verb-particle constructions (e.g. 'lift up your head') in Italian original and dubbed films. A targeted analysis of the interplay between such structures and a set of non-verbal semiotic resources, including body language, facial expressions and prosody, suggests that body language has a relatively significant influence on translators' use of verb-particle constructions in dubbed texts, especially when the particle emphasizes the direction of a character's gesture. According to Valentini's (2013: 555) discussion of the example below (Box 5.7), the translator has opted to translate Chloé's order 'Lève la tête!' ('raise your head') using the verb-particle structure 'Tira su la testa' ('lift up your head') – instead of the more idiomatic Italian expression 'Alza la testa' – to accentuate the movement of Chloé's head as she gives that order.

Despite their relatively small sizes, currently available multimodal databases represent an important development in scholarly efforts to study the idiosyncratic features of translated audiovisual texts in their multimodal

---

Box 5.7

Example from *Chacun cherche son chat* (1996):

| CARLOS: | Baisse les yeux! | Carlos: | Abbassa gli occhi! |
| CHLOÉ: | Arrête! **Lève la tête!** | Chloé: | Djamel, **tira su la testa!** |

integrity. More significantly, they are likely to remain an important research tool for as long as non-verbal data continue to be less computationally tractable than their textual counterparts. As Salway notes, '[t]he state-of-the-art in computer vision technology is a long way from . . . being able to recognize large sets of objects and actions in relatively unconstrained video data such as films' (2007: 166). Consequently, the alignment between orthographic transcripts of speech and suitable tagged audiovisual material will still represent a productive option to assist with the retrieval and indexing of non-verbal research variables. With the digitization of audio-visual material continuing unabated, studies driven by multimodal corpora are envisaged to yield increasingly refined quantitative and qualitative insights into audiovisual translation research and the situated learning of foreign languages (Sotelo Dios 2011, Sotelo Dios and Gómez Guinovart 2012).

Further reading on corpus-based methods

- Baños, Bruti and Zanotti (2013)
- Freddi (2012)
- Freddi and Pavesi (2009)
- Jiménez Hurtado and Seibel (2012)

5.4 TRIANGULATION

This chapter has surveyed different types of research methods in audio-visual translation studies. Some of them, e.g. corpus-based methods, are used independently. As is also the case within the wider domain of translation and interpreting studies, analysts regard the quantitative dimension of corpus-based analyses as a legitimate determinant of the validity and objective significance of their findings. By contrast, most of the examples explored in Section 5.2 present us with research methods that are used in combination, following a multi-method research approach known as **triangulation**. Approaching the study of the same data set from two or more methodological perspectives is meant to facilitate validation of the findings derived from the application of each method and to account for the complexity of multimodal communication in a more meaningful manner. Featured research surveyed in this chapter has illustrated, for example, how findings emerging from archival work (Li 2014) can be cross-checked through the use of questionnaires asking participants about their translation work. Similarly, this survey has also shown how insights derived from the use of eye-tracking technology and the administration of questionnaires (Caffrey 2009) can be brought together, so that the two sets of data can reinforce and shed further light on each other.

Of note is the fact that triangulation can lead to the combined use of qualitative and quantitative methodologies. Both in Kruger's (2012) and Caffrey's (2009) studies, the findings generated by observational and experimental methods are corroborated by statistical analyses. From a broader perspective, the complementarity of different research methods also serves to illustrate how the deployment of a given research method can be informed by different research models (process-oriented, comparative or causal). Overall, this prevalence of triangulation in audiovisual translation studies is reflective of a wider methodological trend in translation and interpreting studies: the status of **case study** as 'an overarching research method which can include different sub-methods' (Susam-Sarajeva 2009: 40).[7]

One of the most important points to come out of this overview is the emphasis that contemporary research is placing on the reception of audiovisual translations. As recently as 2003, Fuentes Luque noted that the existing literature had failed to meaningfully address 'the issue of how texts are received and perceived', adding that this was particularly the case with 'the reception of translated texts from an empirical perspective' (2003: 293–94). The critique of research methods delivered in this chapter indicates that audiovisual translation scholars have begun to redress this neglect. Significantly, these reception-oriented efforts are being championed by specialists working on emergent areas of audiovisual translation such as audio description and amateur translation. Indeed, recent work on the innovative paradigms of mediation that these assistive and participatory forms of audiovisual translation engender, and the concomitant emphasis on the study of audience reception, is stimulating methodological diversification. As technological developments continue to re-shape the media landscape, encouraging further fragmentation of audiences and a growing customization of media consumption habits, reception-driven research methods are bound to gain more prominence in our field.

FOLLOW-UP QUESTIONS FOR DISCUSSION

- According to the literature, there are a number of features pertaining to research design and execution that cut across individual methodologies. These include: *sensitivity* (research should aim to reveal subtle differences through the analysis of data), *objectivity* (the chosen methods should ensure that researchers' biases are minimized), *validity* (research undertaken should be credible to participants in the situation under scrutiny), *falsifiability* (research should aim to test and challenge established theories), *replicability* (research conditions should be accurately reported and allow for the repetition of previous research), *generalizability* (findings should be useful to scholars and participants investigating or operating in similar situations) and *reliability* (research design should be such that participants give the same answer given the same thing to measure or describe).

  Take one or more of the studies surveyed earlier in this chapter and try to evaluate the extent to which it/they address(es) this set of features. Do researchers discuss some or all of these features explicitly or implicitly? In your opinion, are there specific features that would appear to be more suited to each kind of research? If you are about to embark on your own project, what steps will you take to ensure that you show awareness of these research features?

- Although my overview of observational research methods in this chapter has focused on the use of eye-tracking technology, observation can be done in simpler ways. Fuentes Luque's (2003) study of the reception of verbal and allusive humour in dubbed and subtitled films is a case in point. Drawing on a number of hypotheses pertaining to the likely reception of these forms of humour by Spanish viewers, he observed viewers' reactions while watching selected film fragments. Sitting outside the participants' field of vision to avoid conditioning their reception of the film, he encoded their reactions as 'no reaction', 'smile', 'laughter', 'puzzlement'.

  After reading Fuentes Luque's detailed account of his experiment, consider the extent to which his observation addresses the research features listed in the previous question. How necessary is it to triangulate these observational findings with the participants' declared perception of these instances of humour, as expressed in their responses to questionnaires and interviews? How useful is it to cross-check input elicited through questionnaires with participants' responses to interviews? What other aspects of viewers' reception could be usefully investigated using a systematic observation scheme?

• Section 5.3.4 has critiqued Salway's (2007) claim that insights derived from the analysis of corpora of audio description scripts could facilitate the semi-automated production of new narrations. Consider this view against Kruger's (2012) claim that we do not yet fully understand how visually impaired viewers make sense of narrative content in audiovisual texts. Given that audio descriptions are conveyed exclusively through the spoken word, how likely are semi-automated narrations to succeed in providing a satisfactory and meaningful viewing experience? To what extent is it possible to reconcile these two authors' outlooks on the future development of audio description as a field of professional activity? How could multimodal corpora help to enhance awareness of the interplay between visual/narrative salience and the wording of audio narration scripts?

NOTES

1   The extent to which the interplay between different meaning-making resources contributes to the creative role of subtitling in Bekmambetov's film is further explored in Section 6.3.

2   See Chapter 6 for an extended account of the multimodal semiotic processes at the heart of audiovisual translation.

3   Ideographic and nomothetic interpretations are two complementary approaches to the study of social life. While the former focus on individual cases or events, the latter aim to account for the wider contextual patterns where individual experiences are inscribed.

4   The *Pear Stories* film is part of an experiment designed in the 1970s by Wallace Chafe (2002) to test how the same story was received and interpreted by different cultures. It is currently available online via Dr Mary S. Erbaugh's site – *The Chinese Pear Stories – Narratives Across Seven Chinese Dialects* – at www.pearstories.org/docu/research.htm (last accessed on 15 September 2013). The film is central to the *Pear Tree Project*, a collective research initiative in the field of audiovisual translation that aims to establish how different cultures interpret audiovisual input. Identifying the 'universals of A[udio] D[escription]', it is claimed, is the starting point for the development of rigorous guidelines to produce audio described narratives (Orero 2012: 198).

5   See Box 4.7 for definitions of the different types of corpora mentioned in this paragraph.

6   Information on these corpora, or the corpora themselves, can be assessed as follows: (i) spoken component of the *British National Corpus*: www.natcorp.ox.ac.uk; (ii) the *Corpus of Contemporary American English*: http://corpus.byu.edu/coca/; and (iii) the *LIP* corpus of spoken Italian (part of *BADIT*, i.e. *Banca Dati dell'Italiano Parlato*): http://badip.uni-graz.at/en/description (all URLs were last accessed on 15 September 2013).

7   See Section 8.2.1 for further discussion of the prominence of case studies in audiovisual translation studies.

8   Specific suggestions for further reading on the different methods are provided at the end of each sub-section.

CORE REFERENCES[8]

Tymoczko, Maria (2007) *Enlarging Translations, Empowering Translators*, Manchester: St Jerome. Chapter 4: 'Research Methods in Translation Studies'.

Saldanha, Gabriela and Sharon O'Brien (2013) *Research Methodologies in Translation Studies*, Manchester: St Jerome.

Part III

NEW DIRECTIONS

6

MULTIMODALITY

Audiovisual translation is one concrete example of an area of research that has to find its rightful place in Translation Studies. It is the responsibility of teachers and researchers to draw our attention precisely to those aspects which mark it out as different from other modalities [of translation] . . . Apart from descriptive studies on dubbing and subtitling, few authors have made a profound study on *the peculiarities of the construction of audio-visual texts, of the semiotic interaction that is produced in the simultaneous emissions of text and image, and the repercussions that this has in the process of translation.*

(Chaume Varela 2002: 1–3; *emphasis added*)

There is a strong paradox: we are ready to acknowledge the interrelations between the verbal and the visual, between language and non-verbal, but the dominant research perspective remains largely linguistic. The multi-semiotic blends of many different signs are not ignored but they are usually neglected or not integrated into a framework. Is it not a contradiction to set up a database or a corpus of film dialogues and their subtitles, with no pictures, and still pretend to study screen translation?

(Gambier 2006a)

In this chapter

Multimodality is fast becoming one of the theoretical frameworks that most informs research in audiovisual translation. The study of multimodal semiotics redresses some of the fundamental criticisms that have been traditionally raised against current audiovisual translation research: unlike other theoretical frameworks, multimodality does not prioritize language at the expense of other meaning-making modes.

This chapter surveys the theoretical apparatus of multimodality by focusing on a set of key notions, including **medium, mode, core mode, medial variant** and **sub-mode**. A number of examples will be drawn upon to explore the semiotic properties of those modes and sub-modes which are particularly productive in the context of audiovisual semiotics, as well as the different principles that inform the integration of individual modes into the overall semiotic ensemble of multimodal texts. The chapter finishes with an overview of research methods that have emerged to facilitate multimodal research, particularly **multimodal transcriptions** and **multimodal corpora**.

▶ WATCH THE INTRODUCTION VIDEO

6.1 MULTIMODALITY AND AUDIOVISUAL TRANSLATION

The emergence of cinematography as a revolutionary form of representational technology in the late nineteenth century ended the monopoly that the printing press had held on the mass production and consumption of culture since the Middle Ages. As the cultural historian Karin Littau (2006) explains, the materiality and semiotic fabric of film redefined our understanding of writing and reading practices. The medium of film was 'able to translate, by technologically reproducing, hallucinatory images onto the screen' (2006: 7) through a unique synthesis of content, form and matter. The extent to which the representational idiosyncrasy of films conditioned viewers' readings of and affective responses to these new texts was soon noted by literary critics and authors, concerned by the rapid rise of film as a rival form of entertainment to the novel. 'As a medium which bombards viewers with the quick succession of moving pictures', they feared, 'film so entrances spectators that they react to, rather than reflect on, what they see' (Littau 2006: 8).

The affordances of the new representational technology were seized upon by pioneering film directors to articulate and establish the aesthetic credentials of cinematic texts vis-à-vis those of traditional written texts (Izard Martínez 1992, Chaves García 2000). According to the media studies scholar

Kay Richardson (2010), the 'videocentrism' and 'logophobia' of early films helped cinema secure its status as a form of art, as both features underpin the performative ability of cinema to perceptually manipulate viewers in complex ways. The recognition of the new medium as the most universal and independent art form was therefore predicated on its capacity to '**remediate**' actions and emotions without recourse to language. The following review of Sergei Eisenstein's *Battleship Potemkin* (1925) – one of the most influential Soviet films in the era of the silent cinema – suggests that this perception still holds sway among contemporary audiences:

> Because of the strength of the images in both composition and montage, we are drawn into [this film's] beauty. Our eyes are free to wander the frame, searching for information that would be filled in by a talking soundtrack. At the very least, the film demonstrates the importance of the visual information we gather from a film. If a vast majority of human communication is non-verbal, then the same is true for film. The images speak volumes louder than words and *Battleship Potemkin* is the perfect reminder that silent cinema is not a dead genre that should be overlooked because of technological shortcomings. *Potemkin* comes from a time where films communicated primarily through images, even if its themes fade into historical irrelevance.
>
> (Morgan 2007)

Before these efforts to facilitate the emancipation of cinema as a visual medium could gain momentum, however, individual film makers had already begun exploring how language could enhance the aesthetic effectiveness of cinematic texts. As outlined in Section 2.2, the growing complexity of cinematic narratives prompted the incorporation of intertitles into the

---

Box 6.1

Resources to investigate this example further . . .

- Taylor, Richard (2000) *Battleship Potemkin*, London and New York: I.B. Tauris.
- Wood, Michael (2011) 'At the Movies', *London Review of Books*, 28 April, p. 25. Available online: www.lrb.co.uk/v33/n09/michael-wood/at-the-movies
- Eisenstein, Sergei (1925) *Battleship Potemkin*. Available online at: www.youtube.com/watch?v=Bh2SuJrEjwM

conglomerate of film semiotics as early as the turn of the twentieth century (Ivarsson 2002). However, it was the advent of sound two decades later that would ultimately throw these programmatic contradictions into sharp relief. The introduction of acoustically transmitted linguistic and paralinguistic signs into a medium that had so far relied primarily on visual expression further cemented the perception among film purists that 'dialogue was a distraction from the camera's ability to capture the natural world ... and encouraged too much attention to character psychology' (Kozloff 2000: 7), thus 'detracting from the viewers' enjoyment of cinema as a **gestalt** of stimuli' (Pérez-González 2007a: 3). But commercially minded industry players saw speech as the basis for new business opportunities, rather than the ultimate threat to the status of film as an art form. From the perspective of audiovisual translation professionals and scholars, the evolution of film into a compound medium (see Box 6.2) involving the (re)production of sound as well as of moving images would ultimately lead to the conception and generalization of subtitling and dubbing as widespread forms of audiovisual translation during the late 1920s (Díaz Cintas 2001, Whitman-Linsen 1992).

Although the popularization of spoken films predates the emergence of translation studies as an academic discipline in the middle of the twentieth

---

Box 6.2

The extent to which the aesthetic effectiveness and commercial performance of a translated audiovisual text is determined by the co-ordinated mediation of language, visuals and music can be illustrated by the Japanese series *Kagaku Ninjatai Gatchaman* (1972–74), which was distributed commercially in the USA as *Battle of the Planets* (1978). As Ruh (2010) explains, the 'translation' of this audiovisual text went beyond re-writing the Japanese dialogue in English and involved commissioning new animation, editing, dubbing and 'rescoring' (i.e. composing a new soundtrack) for the American version:

> Some of the people credited as 'writers' on the show were people who watched the Japanese originals and noted the action that occurred and the length of each speech utterance, which provided a template for rescripting. It does not seem that the *Battle of the Planets* staff worked on their episode scripts using a translation of the original Japanese scripts. Rather, they made up the story and dialogue based on what they saw (and created) onscreen. Additionally, a new score was created not only to make the show more familiar for a US audience but to supplement 'dead spots': silence in the original production.
>
> (2010: 35)

century (Baker and Pérez-González 2011: 40), much theorizing on translation between the 1950s and 1980s marginalized or ignored the mediation of audiovisual texts (see Section 1.3). During a period where the development of translation studies was steered mainly by linguistics, films sat uncomfortably with the 'text-type classifications or language-function categories which dominated the Translation Studies scene' (Zabalbeascoa 2008: 24). The effects are still felt in the field of audiovisual translation studies today. The self-sufficiency of spoken language as the basis of filmic meaning may have long been questioned by most scholars with an interest in cinematic texts, whatever their disciplinary affiliations (Richardson 2010). However, a large proportion of research efforts in audiovisual translation still revolve around elaborating taxonomies of different types of equivalence between short, decontextualized stretches of dialogue in the source and target languages, with little or no attention to the interplay between dialogue and visual semiotic resources. For Nornes (2007: 4), this emphasis on linguistic analysis is the main reason why, 'despite the rich complexity of the film translators' task and their singular role in mediating the foreign in cinema, they have been virtually ignored in film studies'. Recent publications by audiovisual translation scholars calling for a systematic theorization of 'meaning constructed from the conjunction of images and words' in audiovisual texts (Chaume Varela 2002: 3) and of 'the extent to which the different components of the audio-visual message influence' translation (Pettit 2004: 25) have begun to shift the focus away from dialogue towards the concerted action of language and visuals, in what is set to bring about 'yet another expansion of the concept of translation' (Tymoczko 2005: 1090).

Although **multimodality** – understood as the combination of speaking, writing, visualization and music – has been omnipresent throughout the history of film, the need to gain a better understanding of the interdependence of semiotic resources in audiovisual texts has become increasingly necessary against a background of accelerating changes in audiovisual textualities. The film industry's surveillance of professional audiovisual translation continues to impose the **excision** of language from other forms of meaning-making (forcing translators to restrict their involvement to the mediation of language), but audiovisual translation practices in other areas of the media marketplace pay increasing attention to the interaction between language and other communication modes within the text. This enhanced awareness of multimodality is gaining pace with the digitization of audiovisual texts and the growing prominence of amateur translating agencies.

Box 6.3

New discourse communities lobbying for multimodal intervention:

> Many films have been given a strong presence on the Internet to build anticipation, but *Snakes on a Plane*, a relatively low-budget movie at $32 million with a decidedly B-level vibe, took the practice to a new level. . . . New Line [the distribution company] incorporated ideas from bloggers, who began writing about the movie months ago, excited at the prospect of Mr. [Samuel L.] Jackson, with his ultracool image, facing down a plane full of snakes. The filmmakers even reshot some scenes at the bloggers' suggestion to make the movie harder-edged, with more rough language and violence to give it an R rating. They also added a signature line for Mr. Jackson, who shouts an unprintable epithet about the snakes that originated from Web chatter.
>
> (Waxman 2006)

Audiovisual translations are proliferating and being shared in ways that depart from traditional models of commissioning and distribution (see Section 3.2). Similarly, the production (including the translation) of audiovisual content is becoming ever more influenced by the participatory involvement of audiences, often in the form of co-creational, networked discourse communities, whose preferences shape decisively the range and scope of mediation strategies to be used in each case (Box 6.3). Ultimately, this shift from textual towards multimodal literacy is stretching the ability of audiovisual scholars to describe and theorize audiovisual translation, as most research conducted so far has tended to rely on linguistic means of analysis and critique.[1] This chapter sets out to redress this situation, examining how recent developments in multimodal theory can shape future research on audiovisual translation.

6.2 MULTIMODAL THEORY

Audiovisual texts 'are composite products of the combined effect of all the resources used to create and interpret them' (Baldry and Thibault 2006: 18). The terms **mode** and **modality** designate each type of acoustic and optic meaning-making resources or signs involved in the creation of such composite texts (Chandler 2002). As audiovisual texts involve the simultaneous deployment of several sign repertoires (including but not limited to speech or the written language of subtitles, film editing, image, music,

> Box 6.4
>
> Are multimodal texts always multimedial?
>
> No. Multimodal texts such as printed magazines (combining, for instance, written language, photographs, and a creative use of colours or fonts) or radio broadcasts (consisting normally of modes such as speech and music) are monomedial: they can only be seen or heard, respectively.

colour or perspective), audiovisual texts are often referred to as **multimodal**. For this panoply of semiotic resources to reach the viewers' senses, a range of material means or **media**, including screens and speakers, are required (Kress and van Leeuwen 2001: 67). Audiovisual texts – whose visual and acoustic modes need to be presented in a synchronized manner via 'a screen, with multimedia technology as the coordinating instance' – are therefore not only multimodal, but also **multimedial** (Negroponte 1991: 68) (Box 6.4). Audiovisual communication therefore consists in the production and interpretation of an ensemble of semiotic modalities that are made available via the synchronized use of multiple media.[2]

This section sets out to chart the complex territory of multimodality and deliver a systematic account of the range of modes that are woven into the semiotic fabric of audiovisual texts. I start from the premise that audiovisual translation, understood both as a professional activity and a field of academic research, should be informed by an enhanced, more conscious awareness of what is being communicated through each mode. The translation of audiovisual texts and the scholarly study thereof require critical reflection on the impact that different mediation strategies – whether they are restricted to the translation of written/spoken language or they extend to the manipulation of other meaning-making modes – may have on the viewer's holistic perception of the target language text as a semiotic unit. As Stöckl (2004: 16) notes:

> [w]hen 'reading' a multimodal text, average recipients will normally become only dimly aware of the fact that they are processing information encoded in different modes. The manifold inter-modal connections that need to be made in order to understand a complex message distributed across various semiotics will go largely unnoticed. All modes, then, have become a single unified gestalt in perception, and it is our neurological and

cognitive disposition for multimodal information processing that is responsible for this kind of ease in our handling of multimodal artefacts. A theory of multimodal communication, however, has to meticulously dissect an apparently homogeneous and holistic impression. It has to sensitise us for the essential differences of the modes involved ... Multimodal theory also needs to ask in how far are systematic similarities and ties between the modes involved.

Viewers of commercial films are normally able to make **inter-modal connections** and process the information realized through different modes in a routinized, often subconscious, manner. A less conventional distribution of meaning across the range of modes available to filmmakers, however, requires a more active involvement on the part of viewers to understand the multimodal artefact. Featured example 6.1, based on the Dutch film *Alles is Liefde* (*Love is All*, 2007) is an interesting case in point.[3]

Featured example 6.1: *Alles is Liefde*

The plot of *Alles is Liefde* revolves around Jan, a wanderer who has hitch-hiked his way from Spain to Amsterdam in the run-up to St Nicholas' day. As he approaches his final destination, the truck he has been travelling in crashes into a minivan and blocks the road by accidentally spilling its cargo of oranges (Figure 6.1). Unbeknownst to him, this accident could seriously disrupt St Nicholas' day celebrations. The occupants of the minivan – a group of short men with black-painted faces and colourful Moorish dresses – were on their way to join *Sinterklaas'* (as St Nicholas is known in Dutch) cortege, which every year arrives in the port of Amsterdam to the tune of thousands of screaming children eager for candy and toys. In a bizarre turn of events, the local stage actor hired to dress up as *Sinterklaas* during the festivities suffers a fatal heart attack at the very last moment and Jan finds himself stepping into his shoes.

The multimodal configuration of meaning in *Alles is Liefde* amounts to a unique **dischrony** between the information expressed through the verbal mode and the message conveyed through images: culture-specific symbolic information is encoded exclusively in the visuals. Viewers acquainted with the *Sinterklaas* tradition are therefore able to effortlessly interpret the visual semiotics and make the relevant inter-modal connections with the message communicated through diegetic speech. Take, for instance, the contribution of the following visual stimuli. Although there is no spoken reference to the point of origin of Jan's journey, the truck carrying him to Amsterdam is painted with the colours of the Spanish national flag and displays the words 'Naranjas Valencianas' [Spanish for 'Oranges from Valencia']. In the Netherlands, tradition dictates that St Nicholas travels from Spain every year to deliver goodies to the children. The visual presence of oranges is another important cue for the viewers' interpretation of these

Figure 6.1 Screen shot from *Alles is Liefde*: the accident scene

establishing scenes, as oranges – mentioned in many *Sinterklaas* folk songs – have been traditionally presented as gifts on this holiday. As visual stimuli accrue, Dutch viewers gradually construct a multimodally informed interpretation of the role that Jan is called to play in the unfolding narrative. By the time the wanderer steps out of the truck and starts walking listlessly among oranges and hysterical black *Piets*, *Sinterklaas*' black helpers, Dutch viewers know this is the story of Jan, a modern-day St Nicholas.

For non-Dutch viewers altogether unacquainted with the culture-specific connotations of the visuals, the dischrony between image and dialogue severely hampers their appreciation of the film. Subtitles conveying only a translated version of the Dutch dialogue would not help foreign viewers overcome their inability to grasp the contribution of visual semiotics to the overall meaning of this film. Their failure to gauge the subtlety and sophistication invested in the multimodal construction of Jan's symbolic identity as the new *Sinterklaas* would thus inhibit their capacity to understand the film's core narrative premise: 'both *Sinterklaas* and love require belief to survive. Without children who believe in him, *Sinterklaas* would cease to exist. Likewise without adults to believe in it, love would also disappear.'[4] In sum, a subtitled account of the film's dialogue would not allow foreign viewers to fully appreciate the implications of Jan's arrival. The connections between the events leading him to dress up as St Nicholas and his dramatic role as unifier piecing broken relationships back together across the multiple and interwoven storylines traced in this ensemble film would be poorly, if at all, understood (see Box 6.5).

Box 6.5

Inter-modal transfers of meaning in audiovisual translation

Just as literary or technical translators familiarize themselves with widely accepted textual and generic conventions in their fields of specialization, audiovisual trans- lators (and audiovisual translation scholars) should enhance their proficiency in reading and interpreting the complex semiotic mechanisms and resources that underpin the composition of multimodal texts.

Alles is Liefde represents a significant challenge for translators whose capacity to intervene is restricted to the mediation of dialogue. To overcome the multi- modal dischrony outlined above, the meaning encoded in the visual mode of the original film would have to be, to some extent, inter-modally transferred to the characters' speech in the subtitled or dubbed versions – whether in the form of subtitles explicitating the culture-specific dimension of the film visuals or the addition of an extra-diegetic narratorial voice-over track in the target language spelling out what is visually communicated, respectively.

The next section examines in detail the relevance of multimodal informa- tion to the work of audiovisual translators, modelling part of the sophisti- cated conceptual network that has assisted scholars in other disciplines with the interrogation of audiovisual data. Although multimodality is still a new discipline in the making, it already encompasses various strands (Ventola *et al.* 2004). The work of Stöckl (2004) has been chosen here as a signpost to guide the reader through the tangled paths of multimodal research.

For Stöckl, multimodality can be modelled as a **networked system of choices**. Creating an audiovisual text involves choosing those specific modes (among the total number of existing semiotic resource types) whose meaning potential will help communicators best realize their communicative intentions along the visual and the auditory sensory channels. The advent of sound in the late 1920s, for example, allowed film creators to incorporate spoken language to the mix of modes that had previously been used to convey meaning through films. For almost twenty years after the invention of sound, the use of spoken dialogue as part of the filmic text would remain a matter of authorial discretion.

Organized as repertoires of signs, each of the chosen modes opens up a new system of choices. In other words, each of these subsystems prompts communicators to make more delicate selections among the sets of additional semiotic resources associated with each mode. Going back to our earlier example, the first film directors using spoken dialogue were faced, for the first time, with the need to make additional decisions pertaining to dramatic characterization – involving, for example, the pitch of their characters' voices or the speed at which their lines would be delivered – to articulate the film's overall aesthetic message. An example of this decision-making process is illustrated in Box 6.6.

Box 6.6

Vicente Molina Foix (Spanish author and film maker) reflecting on how voice casting choices for the Spanish dubbed version of Stanley Kubrick's *The Shining* led to a box-office flop . . .

> All aspects of Stanley Kubrick's films were personally and painstakingly overseen by the director, even minor linguistic details and decisions on voice casting for the dubbed versions of his films. Kubrick would arrange to have recorded samples of actors' voices sent for his consideration; he would personally choose a specific voice for each part; this is why the voice of [Spanish actress] Verónica Forqué features, much to the consternation of Spanish viewers, in the Spanish dubbed version of *The Shining*. Kubrick clearly thought Forqué's voice was a perfect match for the distinctive timbre of Shelley Duvall's.
>
> (Molina Foix 2005; author's translation)

6.3 CORE MODES

According to Stöckl's framework, the visual and auditory semiotic resources required to create and interpret audiovisual texts can be grouped under four **core modes**: SOUND, MUSIC, IMAGE and LANGUAGE. Unlike the rest of the modes examined later in this section, core modes 'contain sign-repertoires that are deeply entrenched in people's popular perception of codes and communication' (2004: 14). Core modes are those sets of meaning-making resources that we intuitively fall back on to articulate our opinions on the audiovisual texts that we consume or produce. Unsurprisingly, the semiotic contribution of core modes to the overall message conveyed by films tends to feature prominently in most reviews. This is indeed the case in Morgan's critical piece on *Battleship Potemkin* reproduced in Section 6.1 above, or in the following selection of reviews:

> Sound in the review of James Watkins' *The Woman in Black*
> *The Woman in Black* is a doggedly old-fashioned Gothic chiller, filled with dank rooms, creepy old toys, flickering candles, and miles of gray mist. There are strange sounds in the night, glimpses of shadowy figures in mirrors and windows, and furniture that moves on its own [. . .] Watkins and his sound designers are attentive to the importance of the horror film's aural dimension, giving us sharp distinctions between the cadences of wet stone and hollow wood and at times presenting us with sounds that we think might be one thing, but are later revealed to be something entirely different.
>
> (Kendrick 2012)

> Music in the review of Martin Scorsese's *Taxi Driver*
> Martin Scorsese knew his music. From *Mean Streets* to *GoodFellas*, his films are anthologies of contemporary music. Yet Scorsese believed his film [*Taxi Driver*] had a rare soul that the music might indicate. Look at *Taxi Driver* without the sound. You know the story, you know the talk. Feel the paranoia, the violence, the jittery dread. Then turn on the sound track and sink into the deep, wounded romanticism of that saxophone score. In the turn of the dial, Travis Bickle has changed – he is a damaged man trying to save the city. With music, the film has gone from a bloody slice of life in 1970s New York to an opera with libretto by Dostoyevsky.
>
> (Thomson 2006: 17)

Image in the review of Pedro Almodóvar's *The Skin I Live In*

A second viewing . . . allows you just to savour the extraordinary texture of this film: the colours and surfaces contrived by Almodóvar . . . are delectable. The most casual scene or establishing shot looks as if it has been hand-painted in the subtlest detail. This is epitomised by Vera's remarkable ersatz skin, or super-skin. Did Almodóvar varnish it digitally? It is rich, creamy, without the pink quality of normal flesh, more pale ochre; it bears the same relationship to skin as AstroTurf does to grass.

(Bradshaw 2011)

Language in the review of Woody Allen's *Annie Hall*

Allen . . . really has a natural talent for dialogue. In a film like this, people don't just recite lines from the script. More often than not, scenes feel like they're filmed from real life. The thing about realistic dialogue is that it's got to be imperfect. In life, you cut sentences, you jump from a thought to another, you interrupt . . . And most of Allen's films are dialogue, and it always remains enjoyable, and often hilarious.

(*Montreal Film Journal* 1998)

Core modes are abstract types of semiotic resources that 'need to be instantiated in a specific **medial variant**' (Stöckl 2004: 14). The medial variants associated with each of the four core modes are schematically represented in Figure 6.2 and discussed in the remainder of this subsection.

To begin with, SOUND and MUSIC can be realized through auditory and visual media. In audiovisual texts, SOUND normally takes the form of recorded speech or effects, but forensic experts featuring in crime scene investigation dramas can often be seen poring over printed or electronic spectrograms – i.e. two-dimensional representations of sound based on actual measurements of the changing frequency content of a sound over time – to identify elusive suspects. Similarly, MUSIC is conventionally performed as part of a soundtrack accompanying and synchronized to the images, although printed score or sheet music occasionally finds its way into the visual texture of the film when relevant to the plot.

IMAGE and LANGUAGE can also be instantiated in more than one medial variant. While moving pictures are essential to the make-up of audiovisual texts, some directors make occasional use of 'freeze-frames, [or] elaborate tableau-like visual inserts' for a range of creative purposes (see, for example Romney's (2006) review[5] of Reitman's *Thank You for Smoking*). As far as the core

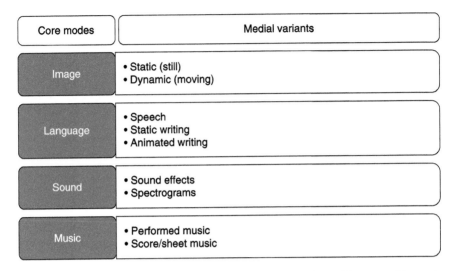

Core modes	Medial variants
Image	• Static (still) • Dynamic (moving)
Language	• Speech • Static writing • Animated writing
Sound	• Sound effects • Spectrograms
Music	• Performed music • Score/sheet music

Figure 6.2 Network of core modes and medial variants (adapted from Stöckl 2004)

mode of LANGUAGE is concerned, audiovisual texts have long relied on static writing, i.e. traditional intertitles and subtitles, to comment on the filmic action or to translate dialogue into another language, among other purposes. More recently, however, technological developments and other changes in the media marketplace (see Section 3.3) have led to the incorporation of animated writing in the overall semiotics of audiovisual texts. An interesting example that I have discussed elsewhere (Pérez-González 2007b) involves the use of animated writing in the opening and closing credit sequences of fansubbed productions of Japanese animated cinema or *anime*, where the viewer is faced with a wealth of information in Japanese and the target language (Figure 6.3). Intermingled with the names and roles of the original film creators (displayed in conventional Japanese characters), we find other strings of text in rōmanji (Romanized) script added by the fansubbing network translating the film. The inserted text features the pseudonyms used by individual network members and the roles that the latter play in the translation process, including but not limited to those of translator, timer or typesetter. Amid this profusion of static writing, karaoke-style titles located at the top of the frame are used to transcribe the soundtrack lyrics both in Japanese characters and Romanized script. Their use of animated titles demonstrates the fansubbers' awareness that their audiences, fellow fans and active consumers of *anime*, value performative and immersive viewing experiences. Much in the same way as video gamers expect to actively participate in the

Figure 6.3 Screen shot from *Naruto* (2006, episode 178): dynamic realization of the language mode

fantasy stories created by the game, *anime* fans demand an enhanced and comprehensive experience of the diegetic world they are about to enter. Karaoke-style titles pander to the audience's desire to wring every drop of meaning out of their favourite dramas, including interstitial elements such as the opening and closing songs. Whether it is through singing or closely scrutinizing the lyrics to develop their proficiency in Japanese, the forms of participation fostered by dynamic writing in fansubbed *anime* are central to the construction and maintenance of fans' collective identities.

But animated writing, in the form of moving subtitles, is also becoming increasingly used to professionally translate diegetic speech in commercial films. Timur Bekmambetov's *Nochnoi Dozor* (2004), which was released internationally as *Night Watch* in 2005 to widespread critical acclaim, is a good case in point. Based on a novel by Sergey Lukyanenko, it tells the complex tale of opposing groups of vampires, witches and shapeshifters, working for both evil and good purposes, in contemporary Moscow. The stills presented in Figure 6.4 correspond to a well-known scene: Yegor's swimming session is brought to a sudden halt when a voice in his head causes his nose to start

Figure 6.4a–d Screen shots from *Night Watch*: dynamic realization of the language mode

(c)

(d)

bleeding. In the subtitled version, the words 'Come to me . . .' appear in red letters that linger and float in the water, mirroring the distant calling of the distant voice, before dissolving away as blood would in the pool. Even after Yegor has stepped out of the water, the same inventive presentation is used again to translate the voice's repeated exhortations ('Come . . . I'm waiting . . .'). In this case, Bekmambetov's use of dynamic writing – a relatively uncommon semiotic resource in film – turns subtitles into 'another character in the film, another way to tell the story' (Rosenberg 2007) where written language interacts with his film and adds to the visuals. In terms of professional practices, the production and consumption of 3D subtitles (see Section 1.2.1) is emerging as another increasingly popular variety of subtitling that exploits the semiotic affordances of dynamic written language.

6.4 SUB-MODES

Each core mode commands a set of **sub-modes.** The modelling of multimodality as a networked system of choices entails that, once communicators have chosen to deploy or activate a given core mode, a range of sub-modes becomes available to further advance the realization of the said mode in a specific audiovisual text. In other words, the systems of sub-mode choices provide communicators with the opportunity to make more delicate selections among the specialized semiotic resources associated with each core mode. As each core mode often entails more than one system of sub-mode choices, its overall semiotic value and realization in a given communicative event is determined by the interplay between its constitutive sub-modes. As Stöckl himself notes, '[a]s a gestalt in perception, the concrete materialisation of a mode in text and discourse is always more than the sum of its parts' (2004: 15). Figures 6.5, 6.7, 6.8 and 6.10 provide schematic representations of the systems of sub-mode choices that become available for the realization of each of the four core modes examined above.[6] For reasons of space, this chapter will not attempt to define or discuss each sub-mode individually. The combined effect of different sets of interrelating sub-modes will be addressed below through various examples.

6.4.1 Language sub-modes

Figure 6.5 represents the networks of sub-modes that make up the core mode of LANGUAGE. Primarily, LANGUAGE is realized through choices among the systems of **verbal signifiers** available at different levels of linguistic

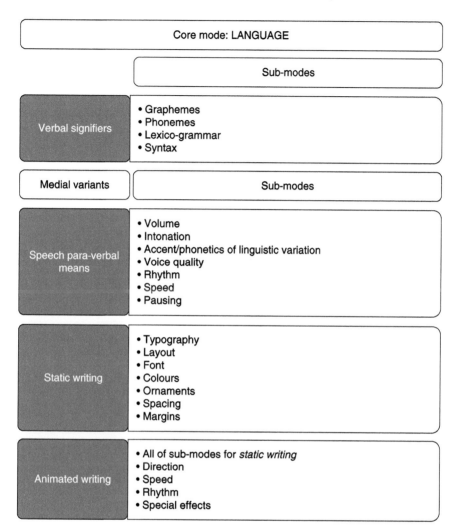

Figure 6.5 Network of sub-modes for core mode LANGUAGE (adapted from Stöckl 2004)

organization. GRAPHEMES (letters), PHONEMES (sounds), LEXICAL ITEMS, GRAMMAT-ICAL STRUCTURES and SYNTACTICAL PATTERNS are, according to Stöckl (2004), the sub-modes contributing to the realization of LANGUAGE across its different medial variants, i.e. speech and written language. As translators' choices from the semiotic resources available within these sub-modes have received considerable and sustained attention from audiovisual translation scholars (see Chapter 4), they will not be examined in detail in this overview. Figure 6.5, however, also represents the sub-modes that make up the core-mode of LANGUAGE but are specific to one of its medial variants. Acoustically,

LANGUAGE is realized through para-verbal means of speech. Visually, it is instantiated in the form of static and animated or dynamic writing.

Para-verbal means of speech

While language has always been uppermost in the minds of audiovisual translators and professionals, the semiotic potential of the **para-verbal** manifestations of speech remains relatively under-researched. The sum of the sub-modes that, according to my formalization of para-verbal means, underpin the materialization of dialogue in audiovisual texts delineates a 'site of intersection and negotiation between the body and language' that film studies specialists have traditionally conceptualized in terms of filmic 'voice' (Smith 2007: 205). A number of approaches informed by psycho-analysis and structuralism have acknowledged that voice, understood as a combination of prosodic features and phonetic markers of linguistic varia-tion, is central to perceptions of filmic performance and dramatic charac-terization (Bosseaux 2008). However, film scholars have been largely unable to systematize the contribution of voice to the semiotic fabric of films, often discussing the impact of vocal parameters on cinematic performance and characterization in impressionistic terms (ibid.: 350). Bosseaux's own research on the role of multimodality in the construction of diegetic personas seeks to redress this neglect from within the field of audiovisual translation studies. Her contrastive analysis of the original and French dubbed versions of an episode of the American TV series *Buffy the Vampire Slayer* examines how the manipulation of what I present here as para-verbal means of speech results in shifts in characterization and differences in the way fictional personas are perceived by American and French audiences:

> English-speaking Buffy has a nasal voice, somewhat flat with very few modulations, i.e. limited rise and fall in the voice pitch. Her speech pattern is characterized by a very fast pace with hardly any variations. Her voice has a childlike tone to it. French-speaking Buffy, on the other hand, has a more mature voice, with more depth and variation. Her voice does not seem to fit her body, nor the images and stereotypes she represents [. . .] [T]here are other issues that are worth considering. One is the play on the (character) type that Buffy represents: she is the stereotypical blonde cast in American horror movies who gets killed at the beginning of the film. She talks about fashion when she is supposed to be saving the world, and

recognizes the vampires simply because of their dress style. Her nasal, fast-paced voice and childlike tone match this representation. As for her singing voice, it often saturates: in other words, it reaches its limits – English-speaking Buffy's tessitura, or vocal range, is rather limited. This saturation, however, is in line with the character's feelings of frustration and depression. As the song unfolds, the English-speaking Buffy expresses stronger and stronger feelings, while paradoxically maintaining a 'bored' tone. At some point she is about to explode because of the spell, but she still maintains the same tone. The French-speaking Buffy's singing voice, on the other hand, sounds more trained, with wider tonal range. She does not use the full power of her voice all of the time and has more control over her vocal delivery, which does not quite reflect the situation she is in. When she sings the rhymes, she lingers on the diphthongs and shows more vocal mastery. Through her vocal delivery she thus appears to be more sophisticated and in control of the situation.

(2008: 56–57)

Bosseaux's account of the impact that choices in performance – as instantiated in the selection of voices for the dubbed version of an audiovisual text – have on filmic characterization addresses the contribution of most of the sub-modes that I have formalized under the category of para-verbal means of speech, including VOICE QUALITY, RHYTHM, and SPEED.[7] The idiosyncratic characterization of English-speaking Buffy – based on the mismatch between her clichéd looks and the bland prosody of her speech, on the one hand, and her key role in the progression of the plot, on the other – is not mirrored in the French dubbed version, which constructs a more 'nuanced' and assertive persona through a series of shifts in the use of para-verbal sub-modes. Admittedly, translators are not normally involved in making voice casting decisions in the dubbing industry. Interestingly, however, Bosseaux's multi-dimensional study shows that changes in cinematic characterization arising from the multimodal representation of a more mature French-speaking Buffy are reinforced through translation. In this respect, the fact that the 'vocabulary of French-speaking Buffy in the subtitled and dubbed versions is often selected from a higher register and can come across as more affected, pompous and archaic' (ibid.: 366) suggests that the implications of the semiotic dischrony between Buffy's physical/verbal representation and her narrative role in the original version have gone largely unnoticed by the translators.

Other important sub-modes associated with the para-verbal dimension of speech pertain to INTONATION, ACCENT and other aural aspects of linguistic variation with a bearing on cinematic characterization. Even when the VOICE QUALITY, the VOLUME or the PACE OF DELIVERY play a marginal role in the construction of a diegetic persona, the meaning encoded in the phonetic realization of a character's sociolect or dialect may be significant in terms of plot development. Ultimately, the translator's mediation of a character's accent or dialectal idiosyncrasy can either preserve or undermine the congruence of the fictional dialogue and the diegetic setting(s) within the wider semiotic configuration of the audiovisual text. Although her study is not theoretically framed by the conceptual framework of multimodality, Queen's (2004) study of the recreation of African American English (AAE) in German dubbed films provides interesting insight into the impact of translation on the mediation of this sub-mode. Queen draws on a corpus consisting of 32 films involving one or more speakers of AAE and identifies a number of distinctive features of this sociolect, including the use of a word-final glottal stop, initial stress shifts, level or falling tones in yes-no questions, or a rising-falling contour that extends over a full phrase and lengthened vowels. Queen's findings indicate that the dubbed versions of the films included in her corpus favour the use of an urban German sociolect that is normally associated with large sections of the working class, interspersed with features of informality characteristic of Jugendsprache ('youth language'). Queen's study thus corroborates Berthele's earlier claims that translators mediating films that feature AAE-speaking characters seem 'to give a light preference to the choice of a colloquial, slangy German which can be located in the "Ruhrgebiet", the important center of heavy industry in Germany', a solution that 'gives the German parallel to [AAE] a clear proletarian overtone' (2000: 607, quoted in Queen, ibid.: 523). Interestingly, when AAE-speaking characters are not young, male, urban or involved with street culture, the dubbed German versions tend to erase the para-verbal markers of sociolinguistic variation. 'Although the visual effects, gestures and general plotline no doubt maintain a clear ethnic distinction for the German-speaking audience', Queen argues, 'the loss of linguistic distinctiveness in the dubbed version nonetheless shifts the social meanings of those distinctions' (ibid.: 531).

Unlike dubbing, subtitling does not allow for a perspectival presentation of para-verbal meaning (Box 6.7). Commercial subtitling conventions do not allow mediators to spatialize, localize or give depth to diegetic voice. Speech is subtitled uniformly throughout a whole film or television drama,

Box 6.7

French film maker Claire Dennis discussing with Atom Egoyan the unwilling-ness of professional subtitlers to find new conventions for the mediation of scenes with partially inaudible dialogue . . .

In that scene you can barely hear the dialogue in French. But last night as I watched the film, the subtitles made it absolutely clear what was being said.

I was actually against that. I asked the guy who did the subtitles if we could perhaps print them with one letter missing or one word missing – as artists, you know [. . .] And he said that doesn't exist in subtitles. Either we have subtitles or we won't have subtitles.

So why did we need to subtitle that scene?

I don't know. I was too weak to say.

(Denis 2004: 72–75)

with translators making no attempt to recreate in their subtitles the occa-sional changes in the volume of utterances or in the physical distance between the speaking character and fellow diegetic characters or viewers – as realized through the use of close-up or long shots. Although '[s]ound-based prosodic features such as variations in tone of voice, pitch (intonation), loudness (stress), rhythm and speed, will modulate words and in certain cases even change their meaning to degrees that might imply irony and contradiction' (Neves 2005: 221), they are routinely ignored by commercial subtitlers, on the grounds that viewers have direct access to the relevant prosodic features in the original soundtrack (Díaz Cintas and Remael 2007). By contrast, when subtitling for Deaf viewers, mediating these para-verbal means of speech is crucial. The semiotic contribution of prosodic features, conveyed exclu-sively along the acoustic channel, must then be acknowledged through the insertion of bracketed annotations in the subtitles – which amounts to an inter-modal transfer of acoustic information into visual cues assisting Deaf viewers to successfully interpret audiovisual texts.

Static and dynamic writing

The examples provided in Section 6.3 to illustrate the differences between the static and dynamic realizations of written language (see Figures 6.3 and 6.4) exploit the semiotic potential of and interplay between different sub-modes, including LAY OUT, FONT, COLOUR, RHYTHM or SPEED. As Figure 6.5

indicates, the first three of these sub-modes are among those shared by both medial variants of written language. i.e. static and dynamic writing. The latter, however, strategically employs an additional range of sub-modes – including RHYTHM or SPEED, but also DIRECTION and SPECIAL EFFECTS – to unfold the full semiotic potential of the core mode LANGUAGE. Again, the innovative approach to subtitling adopted by Lukyanenko in *Nochnoi Dozor* shows how the sub-modes contributing to the materialization of dynamic writing can influence the audience's engagement with and immersion in the multimodal text.

The stills shown in Figure 6.6 feature one member of the Night Watch team talking and typing whilst delivering a briefing on the background of Svetlana Nazarova. As the briefing is given, the cinematic frame transmutes into a computer screen, with the subtitles taking the form of a word processor complete with cursor. This instance of animated writing derived from the deployment the sub-modes RHYTHM and SPECIAL EFFECTS is aesthetically very effective: the English translation of the Russian dialogue appears to be typed by the character himself. These animated subtitles break down the willing suspension of disbelief that occurs when watching a film and become a living part of it. Ultimately, this strategic realization of two sub-modes of LANGUAGE facilitates the integration of the act of reading into the film's diegetic space, thus capturing viewers' attention.

6.4.2 Sound sub-modes

Figure 6.7 represents the sub-modes that make up the core mode of sound through its two medial variants. Acoustically, sound is realized through sound effects; visually, it is instantiated in the form of spectrograms. The second of the parameters specified here, i.e. the visual representations of sound, is rarely used in audiovisual texts and will therefore not be explored in this chapter.

Sound effects – in particular natural noises presented in synchronization with the visuals – are the main medial variant through which the core mode of sound is realized in audiovisual texts. The range of sub-modes that underpin the materialization of noise in audiovisual texts – including INTENSITY, VALUE and QUALITY – are physiological semiotic resources influencing the viewers' multimodal perception of emotion (Planalp 1999: 44–48; Shackman and Pollac 2005). In his highly acclaimed silent film *The Artist* (2011), Michel Hazanavicius exploits the emotion-building role of the interplay between silence and sound to maximum effect. *The Artist* is the story of the decline of

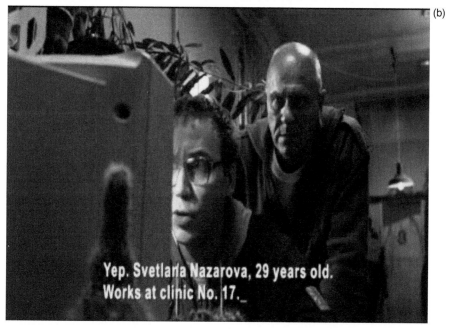

Figure 6.6a–b Screen shots from *Night Watch*: sub-modes of the animated writing

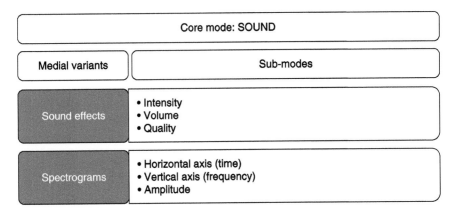

Figure 6.7 Network of sub-modes for core mode SOUND (adapted from Stöckl 2004)

George Valentin, a silent movie star whose world has been turned upside-down by the introduction of talking pictures. As reviewers have pointed out, the character's stubborn opposition towards *talkies* is also a reflection of the role that silence plays in his personal life – with his marriage under increasing strain due to his incapacity to communicate with his wife other than during their comical sideshows. Against this backdrop of oppressive silence, sound is occasionally introduced to bring into sharp relief George's 'slow descent into nothingness, circling through denial and bullheadedness along the way. He experiences sound in his own dream, as he hears the clank of a glass and the sliding of a chair, both to his horror, marking the transition into an era where he'll no longer be relevant'.[8]

Diegetic sub-modes deployed in the realization of sound effects are normally left unchanged when audiovisual texts are translated into other languages. As a constitutive component of the soundtrack, they seldom feature among the meaning-making resources that the audiovisual industry expects/allows audiovisual translators to mediate. In most cases, the role of noises will be one of complementing or accentuating the semiotic contribution of other signifiers.[9] As active specialized readers, audiovisual translators will need to be aware of their specific semiotic contribution and make the relevant inter-modal connections to ensure that an effective interplay between noises and translated speech or subtitles is in place in the target language version. In other cases, however, the presence of specific noises – with their distinctive quality and volume – may place stringent constraints on the translator's latitude. Chaume Varela (2004) examines the impact that sound effects can have on translational decisions, illustrating the discussion with an example pertaining to the animation series *The Real Ghostbusters* (1986–91). In the example below, corresponding to the episode entitled 'The Copycat', the Ghostbusters have completed their inspection of an allegedly haunted property and report their findings to the house owner (Chaume Varela ibid.: 207):

MRS CAMPELL: You are completely sure there's no ghost?
RAY: We checked the entire house. No ghost.
PETER: It's clean as a whistle.
RAY: Have you ever wondered how clean whistles really are?
EGON: Well, absolutely.
PETER: Frequently, why?

Just as Peter finishes delivering the sentence 'It's clean as a whistle', a whistling sound can be heard accompanying and synchronized to an image of the ghost slickly fleeing the property – unbeknownst to the other characters. As Chaume Varela (ibid.) notes, this represents an important translation difficulty, as the Spanish equivalent of the English idiomatic expression 'It's clean as a whistle' contains no reference to whistling:

> The translator, unable to find a Spanish equivalent expression that manages to connect cleanliness with whistling, . . . may opt for translations featuring alternative metaphors or comparisons. The recording studio [responsible for producing the Spanish dubbed version of this episode] may choose to remove the whistling sound from the original soundtrack and replace it with another sound that is coherent with the target language text. Compensating [for the loss of meaning resulting from the removal of the sound from the original soundtrack] elsewhere in the episode is another possible scenario: these animation cartoon series often rely on verbal, acoustic and visual puns and double entendres to please child audiences. If the metaphor chosen in the target language requires so, the translator may suggest to the studio that the original sound be removed and a suitable sound be incorporated when the dubbing actor delivers the utterance in question.

6.4.3 Music sub-modes

Figure 6.8 represents the sub-modes that make up the core mode of MUSIC through its two medial variants. Acoustically, music is realized through

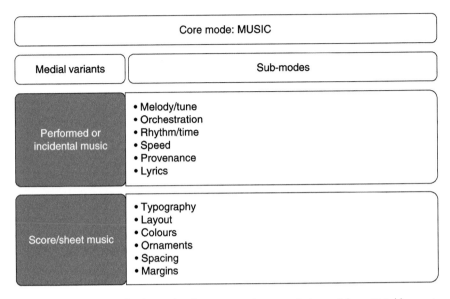

Figure 6.8 Network of sub-modes for core mode MUSIC (adapted from Stöckl 2004)

PERFORMED or INCIDENTAL MUSIC; visually, it is instantiated in the form of SCORE or SHEET MUSIC. The visual representations of music are rarely used in audiovisual texts and will therefore not feature in this chapter.

Most users or viewers are only dimly aware of the contribution that music makes to the semiotic fabric of audiovisual texts (Karlin and Wright 2004). As illustrated in Box 6.8, music can be used as a staged dramatic device (PERFORMED) or as a complement to the semiotic contribution of speech (INCIDENTAL). It can be produced diegetically – in which case it will be accessible to the characters themselves – or come from outside the narrative sphere of the audiovisual text – thus aimed solely at the recipients of audiovisual texts. The fact that the meaning of music is conveyed both through the tune itself and any accompanying text (both in terms of its linguistic and para-linguistic dimensions, i.e. lyrics and voice, respectively) makes it possible for audiovisual text recipients to enjoy **music-based signifiers** as a single unified gestalt in perception, without necessarily understanding, for example, the meaning of the lyrics. As Blacking (2004:10) notes,

> [i]n music, satisfaction may be derived without absolute agreement about the meaning of the code; that is, the creator's intention to mean can be offset by a performer's or listener's intention to make sense, without any of the absence of communication that would occur if a listener misunder-

Box 6.8

Film critic David Thomson (2006: 17) writes on the incommensurability of music as a multimodal resource in one of his reviews . . .

It was Hollywood wisdom that [American Film Composer] Bernard Herrmann was 'difficult'. He was immensely knowledgeable, talented and he had an innate sense that the music at the movies was not so much a series of themes for different characters, or changing tempi for degrees of action. No, Herrmann believed that in ideal situations there was an exact equivalence between the content of a movie and the melodramatic nature of the medium itself. In other words, music in the dark, music in the air, music apparently played by the screen, or music generated by the same mysterious and sublime force that is making the imagery move – as if it were alive! – on the screen. See how it writhes and reaches out tentacles that will draw us into the screen. The music is a beast from within the depth of the screen. It is the soul of the movie.

stood a speaker's intention to mean. In music, it is not essential for listeners or performers to understand the creator's intended syntax or even the intended meaning, as long as they can find a syntax and their own meanings in the music.

Traditionally, audiovisual translators' most common form of involvement in the mediation of music and music-based semiotics has pertained to the translation of song LYRICS. The interplay between musical and verbal signifiers allows for a range of translation strategies premised on the priorities at stake in each audiovisual text, as outlined by Franzon (2008). When conveying the content of the LYRICS into the target language is paramount, the translation can be done without taking into account the 'musico-poetic' requirements of the original tune. In this scenario, the semantically close prose renderings of the original LYRICS are not meant to be sung, but used, for example, in concert programmes or album inserts as supplements to the original lyrics. If the tune is the most important component of the music-based ensemble, on the other hand, the LYRICS will normally be rewritten to suit the tune's structural constraints. As Franzon notes, '[a] totally rewritten set of lyrics in a target language may contain only a single word, phrase, image or dramatic element taken from the source lyrics'. Indeed, the 'original lyrics (and singing performance) may influence the translator's impression of the melody, and thus the production of the new lyrics' (ibid.: 380) but, broadly speaking, the outcome of the translation process amounts to a radical reconfiguration of the musico-verbal artefact. Finally, on those rare occasions when 'singability' or 'performability' are as important as the content of the LYRICS, the original melody might be slightly modified to better fit the words.

As songs constitute an important 'narrational device' (Garwood 2006: 93), deciding when they need to be translated represents an important decision by itself. In most 'dubbing countries' (see Section 2.4), songs from the soundtrack of television dramas and feature films are often left untranslated. Even in 'subtitling countries', the semiotic contribution of music, as instantiated in songs, is not always acknowledged in the form of subtitles. In her attempt to gain a better understanding of the contribution that **nonverbal cinematic signifiers** (including songs) make to the overall semiotics of audiovisual texts, Desilla (2009) compares whether/how implied meaning is understood by British and Greek viewers of *Bridget Jones's Diary* (2001) original and Greek subtitled versions, respectively. Drawing on experimental methods, Desilla examines whether the unavailability of subtitles for the soundtrack songs is detrimental to Greek viewers' comprehension of the overall filmic meaning – as articulated by the director through the co-deployment of verbal and nonverbal cinematic signifiers. The example below corresponds to one of those scenes where a song strongly punctuates the unfolding of the plot:

> Bridget announces to Daniel her decision to resign. In an attempt to persuade her to stay, Daniel offers her lots of prospects, but to no avail; determined to leave her current job, Bridget says: 'If staying here means working within ten yards of you, frankly I'd rather have a job wiping Saddam Hussein's arse' . . . Immediately after Bridget's utterance Aretha Franklin's *Respect* starts playing and figures in the soundtrack until the very end of the scene. As evident by their exclamations, laughter and body language, Bridget's colleagues are shocked, while simultaneously relishing her remark. What Bridget intends to convey with such an exaggeration is, obviously, her detestation towards Daniel. At the same time, the latter's comparison to one of the world's most hated leaders, evokes how disrespectful Daniel has been to Bridget. Apart from setting a triumphant tone . . ., Franklin's song resonates with Bridget, reverberating the respect that she demands from Daniel. The overwhelming majority of the British viewers recognised the song and were perfectly conscious of its function . . . As anticipated, the tune proved much more difficult to identify for the

Greek audience. Only [one viewer] could provide the title of the song and a relevant explanation for its use.

(Desilla 2009: 301)

As Desilla's example shows, failure to address the interplay between verbal signifiers and MUSIC may result in 'an inevitably superficial and incomplete appreciation' of the audiovisual text (Di Giovanni 2008: 310). Professionals working to the requirements of the audiovisual industry, however, are often prompted to neglect this semiotic dimension of the multimodal text. This is particularly problematic when the rationale for the translation of a song is not obvious. Even when 'a song does not actually provide any insight into a character's thoughts or story, but merely suggests somebody's mood', translating it would be desirable (Díaz Cintas and Remael 2007: 209).

Meaning is also invoked when verbal signs play no role in the soundtrack. MUSIC and other meaning-making resources encoded in closely associated sub-modes – including VOICE QUALITY – often influence the viewer's (and hence the translator's) perception of characters and settings, shaping their engagement with and immersion in the multimodal artefact in more or less subtle ways. In his essay entitled 'Sound and Films' (1939), film director and producer Alberto Cavalcanti provides an interesting example of the impact that a subtle use of music can have on the unfolding of the narrative:

You remember in Fritz Lang's *M* the murderer has the habit of whistling a few bars of Grieg's 'Troll Dance'. Lang, with his usual brilliance, built this up to the climax of his film, at which the murderer was recognized by a blind man. Now, quite apart from the fact that Lang made the tune part of the plot, do you remember anything noteworthy about the effect of the sound on the dramatic intensity of the film? I do. I seem to recollect quite clearly that this harmless little tune became terrifying. It was the symbol of Peter Lorre's [starring as a serial killer who preys on children] madness and blood-lust. Just a bar or two of music. And do you remember at what points (toward the end) the music was most baleful and threatening? I do. It was when you could hear the noise, but could not see the murderer. In other words, when the tune was used 'nonsync', as film people say.

The contribution of music to audiovisual texts, understood as unified perceptual gestalts, is not an issue that most professional translators are sensitized to. After all, music can seldom be edited or adapted during the translation process. More importantly, as target language viewers can access the music of the original soundtrack, their disposition for multimodal information processing would remain unaffected by the fact that only speech is translated. Subtitlers working for the Deaf, however, must dissect the multimodal artefact and gauge the specific contribution of music to the viewer's holistic impression of the audiovisual text, as illustrated in Featured example 6.2.

Featured example 6.2: *A Clockwork Orange* (Wurm 2007)

Figure 6.9 Screen shot from *A Clockwork Orange*: the rape scene

In *A Clockwork Orange* Kubrick plays precisely with the concreteness of the image and the abstractness of the music. While the viewer is confronted with the explicit actions of fighting, rape and murder through the images, the music communicates a conflicting mood. For example, we hear Rossini's playful overture of *The Thieving Magpie* while watching a gang fight (scene 4), and in scene 6 Alex sings Gene Kelly's happy *Singin' in the rain* while raping a woman. The interaction between the image and music detaches the action from reality and makes it seemingly harmless. Beethoven's *Symphony No. 9*, coming out of a window of a passing car inspires Alex (scene 12) to beat up his friends after they try to rebel against him. In order to increase the 'metaphysic' effect that music has on Alex in this scene, the images go into slow motion as soon as we hear the music. What we receive is, as in the other scenes, a performance where the movements of the fighting are carefully choreographed to match the rhythm and elements of the music [. . .] Music is at the centre of these scenes, directing the images to follow it, rather than the other way around. At the same time, we cannot imagine any more contradictory pieces of music to accompany the action shown. Rather than amplifying expected emotions, music is used to divert our feelings to match Alex's and serves as a representation and 'translation' of his feelings during these scenes.

(Wurm 2007: 134)

In *A Clockwork Orange*, the incongruent combination of visual violence and musical sophistication 'stylizes' Alex's depravity and evil actions, articulating a 'euphemized' representation of violence. Faced with this unconventional distribution of meaning across visual and acoustic semiotics, Wurm aptly explains, the 'viewer is left in limbo in the attempt to judge whether Alex is simply naïve or instead immensely calculating' (ibid.: 133). In Kubrick's film, music not only punctuates the filmic plot; it actively prompts viewers to question their perception of what is unfolding before their eyes. To appreciate the sophisticated implications of the re-narrating role allocated to music within the overall semiotic ensemble, Wurm argues, the viewer must experience 'the emotion that is evoked by the act of listening to music' (ibid.: 134). The question then arises as to whether Deaf viewers could possibly grasp the complexity of Alex's inner world, particularly when the audible signifiers of the film are so central to the representation of the latter. Standard conventions for the mediation of music in intralingual subtitling would dictate that Deaf viewers be provided at least with the title of the piece of music, but that would not suffice to compensate for their inability to share in the aesthetic enjoyment of the soundtrack. Attempting to translate this experience for Deaf viewers, Wurm argues, involves 'leaving the sphere of traditional Translation Studies and entering the realm of semiology and psychology. A significant area for future research is thus the "translation" from music into a visual medium for a film' (ibid.).

6.4.4 Image sub-modes

Figure 6.10 represents the networks of sub-modes that make up the core mode of IMAGE through its two medial variants: static and dynamic or moving images. The range of sub-modes contributing to the realization of image along its two medial variants is remarkably large, thus allowing only for a partial discussion and illustration of visual meaning-making practices in this section.

ELEMENTS, be it in the form of animate beings, inanimate objects or other distinct figurative/abstract visual representations, are the smallest building blocks of the core mode of IMAGE. Whether ELEMENTS are realized statically or dynamically, these sub-modes are instrumental to the materialization of visual semiotics. In audiovisual texts, visual and verbal elements are bound together by what Stöckl refers to as the 'language-image-link' (2004: 21). Conflations of verbal and visual elements cohere by building inter-modal

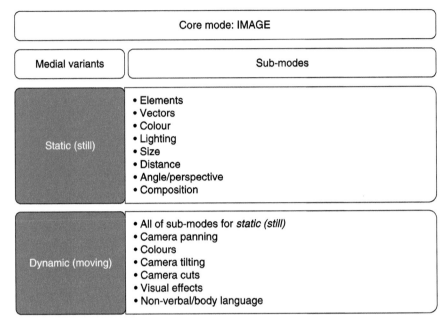

Figure 6.10 Network of sub-modes for core mode IMAGE (adapted from Stöckl 2004)

sense relations and adding to a common mental image that facilitates the viewer's comprehension of the multimodal artefact.

But inter-modal correlations of visual and verbal elements do not always hold across languages. When mediating audiovisual texts, professionals need to articulate new inter-modal synergies between the visual and verbal elements that can go unnoticed by the recipients of the translated text. As the production and representation of visual elements can be very expensive, visual ELEMENTS cannot normally be replaced during the process of translation. Effectively, their contribution to the overall communicative gestalt in the target language remains unchanged. Translational decisions aiming to restore the language-image-link in the target language thus become severely restricted, as the intended message must be conveyed exclusively through verbal semiotics. The pivotal and complementary roles of visual elements and verbal signifiers, respectively, in the production of inter-modal sense relations may today be widely taken for granted by audiovisual translation professionals. In the pre-history of audiovisual translation, however, the manipulation of the visual sub-mode ELEMENTS – for example, by replacing actors, objects or landscapes – was a common practice during the process of translation (see Box 6.2).

With the advent of the sound era (and the concomitant need to incorporate spoken language in the semiotic fabric of motion pictures), the American film industry began a struggle to maintain its foreign market which, in the early 1930s, brought up to 40 per cent of its gross income (O'Brien 2005). The multi-track sound recording systems that would subsequently allow the industry to dub films by replacing the original characters' speech – while preserving the ambient sound of the original shooting – had yet to be invented. Against this backdrop, multilingual versions, i.e. films structured around the same plots and featuring the same scenarios and sets but with different teams of actors speaking different languages, became the most important form of audiovisual transfer (see Box 6.9). The production of multilingual versions, the predecessors of contemporary 'remakes', involved a wholesale re-shooting of the film. By re-encoding the information conveyed through the sub-mode of visual elements (in this case, instantiated in the form of the actors and actresses), film makers were able to switch the narrative locale, bringing about a new geographical mapping of the diegetic universe and changing the language of those inhabiting it. Featured example 6.3 illustrates the scope of these changes.

Box 6.9

[Multilingual language versions] were essentially carbon copies of the same film, only in different languages. For example, after director Tod Browning finished up a day of shooting for *Dracula* (1931) with Bela Lugosi and Helen Chandler, the cast and crew all evacuated the set; then a new director, George Melford, entered with actors Carlos Villarias and Lupita Tovar to shoot the same scenes in Spanish ... They worked through the night, finishing in time for the English cast to take the stage in the morning. Both movies sprang from the same script, but demonstrate how the [multilingual language versions] ended up relatively autonomous texts. Most people familiar with the Spanish *Dracula* prefer its luscious photography and racy atmosphere to the 'standard' Lugosi version.

(Nornes 2007: 137)

Featured example 6.3: *Blotto* (1930)

Blotto (1930), a comedy film starring Stan Laurel and Oliver Hardy, is an interesting case in point. During the Prohibition era, the characters played by Stan Laurel and Oliver (Ollie) Hardy are eager to spend a wild night out at the Rainbow Club. Ollie phones Stan at home, and suggests a plan for the latter to trick his domineering

Figure 6.11 Stan Laurel and his three wives in *Blotto*, *La Vida Nocturna* and *Une Nuit Extravagante*

wife into thinking that he has been called away on business. As part of the plan, Stan is to swipe his wife's treasured bottle of liquor to drink it up during their night out. The film was shot in English (with Anita Garvin playing the role of Mrs Laurel), Spanish (*La Vida Nocturna*, where Linda Loredo played the wife's role) and French (*Une Nuit Extravagante*, featuring Georgette Rhodes as Stan's wife) (Figure 6.11).

On the surface, the French and Spanish versions could be regarded as scene-for-scene re-enactment[s] of the original film. Stan and Ollie 'read their lines and pronounced them phonetically from cue cards viewed just off screen', while most 'labels and signs seen throughout the film', including 'the "Reserved" sign on their [club] table, and the packets of food in Mrs. Laurel's kitchen [were] in English'.[10] *Blotto*, however, contained a number of scenes – particularly the cabaret acts at the Rainbow Club – that were too risqué for the American audience. Shot during the pre-Code years, i.e. shortly before the production and enforcement of the Motion Picture Production Code censorship guidelines, the film's take on marital relationships, alcohol and public morality was not strictly in line with the values that the major American studios were expected to promote. So while the spoken dialogue was being literally translated, the range of visual sub-modes (not least the ELEMENTS one) was being strategically employed in the Spanish and French versions to increase box-office revenues in Spanish- and French-speaking countries. As Skretvedt (1987) explains, the Spanish version was lengthened from three to four reels. 'Longer pictures', Skretvedt notes, 'meant higher rental fees, and the team's popularity was such in Spanish-speaking countries that their short films were often billed over the feature attraction'.[11] Of note is the fact that 'most of the new scenes take place during the nightclub floor show'. For example, 'the Latin girl dancer has a much longer routine here (accompanied by different music)' than the entertainer in the original version. As Skretvedt explains, '[t]he floor show concludes with a hoochy-coochy dancer whose gyrations, one suspects, might not have passed the American censors even during this Pre-Code era' (ibid.). The original running time is also extended by a full reel in the French version. 'Besides some new gags, the extra footage allows more time for the floor show (with a live orchestra) featuring a scantily-clad dancer . . . which is intended exclusively for French audiences'.[12]

The semiotic potential of the sub-mode VISUAL ELEMENTS has been exploited differently in *Blotto*, *La Vida Nocturna* and *Une Nuit Extravagante*. Although the information encoded in the core mode LANGUAGE was translated in a literal and straightforward manner, additional footage and a strategic redeployment of visual ELEMENTS have allowed the Spanish and French versions, in the absence of censorship constraints, to enhance their profit-making potential.

COLOUR, LIGHTING and CAMERA MOVEMENT (e.g. panning, tilting, cuts) are other productive visual sub-modes in multimodal artefacts. The manifold connections between colour and camera movement – and, indeed, the interplay with other sub-modes commanded by the core modes SOUND and MUSIC – communicate emotional information. So while the manipulation of such sub-modes and their semiotic potential is not an option normally available to audiovisual translators, they should still inform their choice of verbal signifiers when mediating audiovisual texts (Chaume Varela 2004).

A good example of how COLOUR and CAMERA MOVEMENT can mutually determine the realization of their respective semiotic potential can be found in *Lost in Translation* (2003), the story of two people drawn together during their stay in the megacity because of their loneliness and boredom. The sub-modes COLOUR, LIGHTING and CAMERA MOVEMENT are employed by the director to construct and represent multi-modally the emotions of the characters. As Bob Harris, an aging actor going through a rough patch and experiencing a growing sense of emptiness, arrives in Tokyo, a **point-of-view shot** is used to show the scene from the character's perspective to the viewer. The profusion of colour flashing signs in Japanese, the crowded vertical buildings towering over Bob and an overwhelming sense of motion imbue the scene with emotional overtones, expressing Bob's alienation and confusion across various visual sub-modes. A similar sense of loneliness and culture shock is experienced by Charlotte, a newlywed who voluntarily finds herself confined in her hotel room. Charlotte is shown to the viewer in the foreground of the shot, sitting in half-light on the window sill of her dark room. A colourful and noisy Tokyo cityscape threatening to intrude in her room provides a dramatic background to the shot. The contrast between the dark shading and the chromatic chaos that saturate, respectively, Charlotte's inner and outer world brings into sharp relief her feeling of alienation from her surroundings. This emotion is further accentuated through the use of a **rack focus** technique, which renders only part of the action field in sharp focus. As the scene unfolds, the focus shifts from the background (with Charlotte featuring as a blurred, anonymous bulk) to the foreground (throwing the composition of the night skyline out of focus). The director's sustained attempts to make viewers aware of the characters' existential *angst* should not go unnoticed by translators. Further visual manifestations of Charlotte's alienation are discussed in Box 6.12.

Based on his analysis of translated films where the semiotic contribution of visual sub-modes is particularly salient, Chaume Varela (2004: 253) advocates the centrality of inter-modal connections between visual and verbal semiotics to the audiovisual translation process. Lexical or registerial choices made by translators mediating speech, Chaume Varela contends, should contribute to further articulating the nuances and connotations that the use of specific COLOURS, LIGHTING arrangements or CAMERA MOVEMENTS are intended to evoke.

The semiotic potential of other sub-modes such as VISUAL EFFECTS, BODY LANGUAGE and COMPOSITION (the way in which the elements of an image are arranged) also require the translators' attention – as illustrated in Boxes 6.10, 6.11 and 6.12, respectively.

Box 6.10

Visual effects

In *28 Days Later* (2002), a chimpanzee virus has wiped out much of the human population. The few uninfected individuals wander around the empty streets of London fighting for survival against ever growing hoards of zombies. At some point in the film, director Danny Boyle substitutes what looks like an impressionist painting of a field for an actual field, complete with a real vehicle driving along the horizon line. Of particular importance is the fact that the rest of the shot is left unchanged. This use of painted effects in this scene is particularly effective: the graininess that pervades the film's photography is enhanced to generate maximum aesthetic and emotive effect. Boyle thus manages to capture and present to the viewer a fleeting impression of emotion against the background of post-apocalyptic Britain. In *28 Days Later*, translational choices can therefore either reinforce or undermine the contrast between the prevailing 'lo-fi' visual representation of destruction and the occasional token of visual sensibility that may pull humanity back from the edge of collapse.

Box 6.11

Non-verbal/body language

After the death of her lover, the character that Ingrid Bergman plays in *The Arch of Triumph* (1948) is on the brink of collapse. Things then take a turn for the better when she starts a relationship with the refugee physician who saves her from committing suicide. But disaster strikes again. Amid a number of tumultuous events in the run up to the Second World War, the authorities decide to deport her partner from France. Bergman, a singer by profession, becomes a courtesan dragging out a disillusioned existence. The loose moral standards that Bergman's character shows in this film represented an affront to the natural moral order and Catholic values at the time. It is therefore no surprise that the original Spanish dubbed version, carefully scrutinized by the censors, tried to tone down Bergman's licentious behaviour. At some point in the film, when asked whether she is married to a wealthy young playboy who has been courting her, Bergman vehemently shakes her head. Despite the visual salience of the sub-mode BODY LANGUAGE delivering a negative response in the original version, Ingrid Bergman can be heard answering 'Sí' ('Yes') in the Spanish dubbed version (Gubern and Font 1975).

Box 6.12

Composition

The well-known swimming pool scene in *Lost in Translation* clearly illustrates the extent to which the semiotic potential of the sub-mode COMPOSITION can set the mood of a film – and hence the impact of visual semiotics on the translator's linguistic choices for the purposes of characterization. The scene in question shows Charlotte's lonely figure against a massive glass wall overlooking the Tokyo skyline. From the viewer's perspective, the sides of the triangular pattern on the glass wall and the lateral borders of the swimming pool converge to one point somewhere above the upper limits of the frame, thus directing viewers' eyes toward Charlotte and emphasizing her loneliness. The grid of crossing lines projected across the glass wall bears some resemblance to the metal bars of a prison window, thus adding a sense of entrapment.

6.5 MODE INTEGRATION AND PROCESSING

The previous section has provided a detailed overview of the network of core modes, medial variants and sub-modes that make up multimodal texts. A conceptual framework facilitating the meticulous dissection of the holistic ways in which audiovisual text users (including translators) process multi-modal texts has been articulated, making it possible for translators and audiovisual translation scholars to **operationalize** their processing of information encoded in different modes. In turn, the **materialization** of each of the core modes has been conceptualized as the result of communicators' choices among the different systems of semiotic resources available at different levels of textual organization (i.e. selections at the sub-mode level across specific medial variants). This section focuses on a complementary aspect of multimodal communication, i.e. the ways in which inter-modal connections are made to afford the homogeneous gestalt-perception that we normally experience as users of audiovisual text.

According to Baldry and Thibault (2006), the '**resource integration principle**' is central to multimodal communication. Multimodal texts, they argue, are not only about juxtaposing resources as separate modes of meaning-making. The communicators' selections must be integrated 'to form a complex whole which cannot be reduced to or explained in terms of the mere sum of its separate parts' (ibid.: 18). The integration of different modes is not a smooth process as each mode has its own **semantic properties**. For example, as Stöckl explains,

> [l]anguage has what linguists call double articulation, i.e. discrete signs on two levels of organisation, phonemes and morphemes, which combine to form words and utterances ... Images, in contrast, have no distinct signing units. There are no rules that would explain how pixels yield higher-level units when combined.
>
> (2004: 16)

Each mode, on the other hand, requires a different form of **cognitive orientation**. Unlike language, which is a linear mode based on the 'successive integration of signs into phrases' (ibid.) and requires parsing to be processed, images 'directly tap into the emotions and provide immediate sensory input' (ibid.: 17) – thus allowing for much faster processing. The integration of linguistic, aural, and visual signifiers is thus best described in terms of a '**multidirectional investment' of meaning** (Yin Yuen 2004) between the different modes deployed in the text. Although the term 'multidirectional' evokes the perception of a level playing field between individual modes, this is rarely the case. As Stöckl notes, images 'are seen to be inherently vague and ambiguous and can only be made to mean and communicate specific contents by a combination with other modes' (2004: 18), such as language. In some cases, this means that language will play a dominant role within the communicative encounter, thus paving the way for something closer to a unidirectional investment of meaning. The fact that one mode may be dominant enough to contextualize the meaning of others determines the '**contextual propensity**' (Yin Yuen 2004) of the multimodal artefact at any given point.

An interesting example where the image plays a dominant role in shaping contextual propensity can be found in *Bridget Jones: The Edge of Reason* (2004).[13] At the beginning of this sequel, Bridget crosses paths again with her former boss. Womanizing heartthrob Daniel Cleaver has just started a career as a broadcaster and presenter of the travel show 'The Smooth Guide: Making Culture Bearable'. Standing against a magnificent backdrop of Roman architecture, Cleaver addresses the viewer in a teasing, facetious tone. The Colosseum, he says, is boring as Romans 'are not allowed to slaughter Christians any more'; the Sistine Chapel, on the other hand, is presented as the 'first example in history of a poof designer gone bonkers'. Daniel proceeds to announce that he is being joined 'by the equally serene and equally beautiful Professore Giovanna Debrace who, I believe, is about to show me . . . her diptych' (Figure 6.12).

As Daniels delivers the last word of his line, his gaze shifts to Professore Debrace's salient cleavage – thus forging an unexpected tie between language and image. The result of this kind of visual-verbal metaphorical play establishes a well definable inter-modal relationship. Ultimately, the mental mapping of the linguistic signifier ('diptych') onto its visual counterpart (cleavage)

Figure 6.12 Screen shot from *Bridget Jones: The Edge of Reason*: the diptych scene

significantly increases the contextual propensity in this frame and, concomitantly, lowers the viewer's **'interpretative space'** (Yin Yuen 2004). In other words, the more explicit the film director's communicative intentions are, the more limited is viewers' capacity to construct their own interpretation.

Although the study of semiotic resources used in visual and aural meaning-making signs is receiving increasing attention, there is still a tendency among scholars of audiovisual communication to conceptualize the semiotic potential of images and sound in terms of linguistic properties. The fact that, as Kress and van Leeuwen (2006) note, 'most accounts of visual semiotics have concentrated on what might be regarded as the equivalent of 'words' – what linguists call 'lexis' (2006: 1) attests to the dominance of language over other core modes. Their own 'grammar' of visual design – envisaged as an attempt to 'describe the way in which depicted elements . . . combine in visual "statements" of greater or lesser complexity or extension' (ibid.) – provides further corroboration of the extent to which 'the metaphoric stance of a pictorial language is engrained in our naturally logo-centric take of communication' (Stöckl 2004: 17).

The growing **grammaticization** of meaning-making resources involves the systematization of their semiotic potential, i.e. mapping how those resources can be used for the purposes of communication in different audiovisual texts. As the meaning potential of both verbal and non-verbal semiotics can be ultimately reduced to system networks of choices, recurrent associations between certain semiotic selections and specific communicative intentions are likely to obtain.

Take, for instance, the sub-mode ANGLE/PERSPECTIVE – one of the sub-modes shared by both the static and dynamic realizations of the core mode IMAGE. The sub-mode PERSPECTIVE can be modelled into two different angles: horizontal and vertical, each of which has a relatively stable semiotic potential. While the horizontal angle is used to visually represent the communicator's 'degree of involvement in, or empathy with' the depicted world and its participants (Kress and van Leeuwen 2006: 140–48), the vertical angle signifies 'power, status, and solidarity relations' between the depicted world and the viewer (ibid.). There are three possible realizations of the vertical angle. In an audiovisual text, the use of a high angle – where the viewer looks down on the depicted world – positions the viewer as 'superior' to the depicted world. Instead, opting for a medium angle – where the viewer looks at the depicted world from the same level – places the viewer as equal to the represented participants. Finally, choosing a low angle – where the viewer looks at the depicted world from below – articulates a visual representation of inferiority on the part of the viewer.

Elsewhere (Pérez-González 2007a), I have demonstrated how the arrangement of visual perspectives on the unfolding of the diegetic narrative shapes the translation of dialogue in Sidney Lumet's 12 *Angry Men* (1957). As I explain in that paper (ibid.: 13–14), the choice of angles underscores the character-building role throughout the jurors' deliberations':

> the deliberations aim to question the alleged infallibility of the American judicial system and challenge the jurors' capacity to make an informed and objective decision on the issues they are asked to assess ... As the film advances, the characters' individual stances on the case under scrutiny sway between the two possible verdicts. Their 'heated discussions, the formation of alliances, the frequent re-evaluation and changing of opinions, votes and certainties, and the revelation of personal experiences, insults and outbursts' (Dirks 1996) help to flesh out their personalities and backgrounds for the benefit of the viewer ...
>
> The opening of the discussions is shot with a wide-angled perspective of the room. Viewers are thus placed in the position of 'objective onlookers': they are free to monitor how individual jurors 'are reacting while listening to the speaker and sometimes watching him to see if he's ready to fold or explode' (Lorefice 2001). As deliberations unfold, the cameras start narrowing down their focus, accentuating the throbbing pulse of the ceiling fan and even 'picking out individual beads of sweat' (Cannon 1997). Smith (2006:47) describes this technique as follows: If you feel that the jury room is getting more and more confining as the movie progresses, that's testimony to the success of what Lumet called his 'lens plot'. By shifting the camera angle and varying the focal length of the lenses, he subtly creates the impression that the walls and ceiling are actually closing in on his characters.

In 12 *Angry Men*, jurors are not individuals but fictional characters embodying (in the eyes of the viewer) conflicting systems of values and attitudes in life that spark successive clashes and allow for renewed empathy, all of which is punctuated by shifts in visual perspective. As my analysis shows, the Spanish dubbed version of this film, however, neglects the character-building role of dialogue as the major narrative force in the film, opting instead for a sentence-by-sentence translation that overlooks the full interactive potential of each contribution.

In this chapter, I have contended that an enhanced awareness of multimodality is crucial to better understand the scope and impact of translational decisions in the context of audiovisual texts. In the next chapter, I argue that multimodality is bound to become even more central to audiovisual translation scholarship in the future, as new forms of amateur and participatory audiovisual translation in the era of digital culture come to play a more important role in the media industries, often proposing new and sophisticated ways to encode meaning across various semiotics. Although Tymoczko's statement that 'future media developments will present additional research questions that we cannot yet even foresee' predates the emergence of some of these participatory agencies of translation, her claim that such advances may 'necessitate the retheorization of various aspects of the entire field of translation studies' (2005: 1090) may be more relevant than ever.

FOLLOW-UP QUESTIONS FOR DISCUSSION

- Ortabasi (2006) examines the English subtitled version of the Japanese anime feature film *Millennium Actress/Sennen joyû* (Kon Satoshi 2001) where 'cinematic imagery becomes the primary medium of communication' and 'narrative action and dialogue, considered the main components of cinema by many viewers, take a back seat' (2006: 278). According to Ortabasi's analysis of her examples, the subtitler responsible for the English version of the film focused almost exclusively on translating textual information, leaving most of the visual richness and the intertextual meaning conveyed through the visual channel 'mostly "untranslated" and therefore misunderstood' (ibid.: 280). Consider Ortabasi's examples critically in the light of this chapter's overview of multimodal resources. To what extent did the translator show awareness of the basic mechanisms of mode integration and processing examined in Section 6.5 above?

- French historical drama *Jean de Florette* (1986) revolves around a bizarre battle to control access to a valuable natural spring in a remote French farming community shortly after the First World War. At one point in the film, one of the protagonists (Ugolin) announces that he has stopped the clock pendulum ('je vient d'arrêter le pendule') at somebody else's house. The subtitler's decision to translate Ugolin's announcement as 'I've just come from . . . He's dead' assumes his/her

English-speaking viewers will be unfamiliar with the old French custom of reaching into the household clock and respectfully stopping the pendulum to mark the stopping of time in the life of a loved one when they die. Could the subtitler have opted for an alternative strategy that would convey the culture-specific connotations of this ritual? Consider the use of 'headnotes' by fansubbers, as described by Pérez-González (2006: 271, 2007b: 76)? Could a similar strategy have been used here? How could any of these two strategies be accounted for and appraised from a multimodal perspective?

- *Goodbye Lenin* (2003) is a German tragicomedy film set mainly in East Berlin. There is a scene in the film where images of newspapers flash across the screen with headlines detailing the collapse of the Berlin Wall, with an off-screen voice announcing that 'Der Mauer is offen' ('The Berlin wall is open'). As this is coupled with images of the wall being destroyed, it could be argued that there is no apparent need for a subtitle: it would intrude in the viewer's enjoyment of this unique event in German history. Similarly, the welcome Helmut Kohl (former Chancellor of West Germany) receives upon arriving in Berlin in another scene is not subtitled either. The chanting of 'Helmut, heb auf!' from the crowds could have been easily translated, for example, as 'Rise up, Helmut'. The translator deems instead that subtitling the shouts (even though the German is clearly heard) would be unnecessary. How do the concepts of intersemiotic cohesion and inter-modal connections help you make sense of this decision?

- Desjardins (2008: 51) theorizes the production of newscasts or television news programmes as a translation process. According to Desjardins, television news programmes originally draw on public discourse – whether this is circulating in a given community in the form of government policies, written/broadcast journalistic reportage, legislation, electoral manifestos, or virtual debate on social networking platforms – as their source texts. To construct their televised news stories (target texts), the verbal narration must incorporate a multimodal dimension. For example, footage of veiled Muslim women would appear to be routinely used to 'illustrate' news reports on multicultural models of social organization:

> What is particularly interesting with the newscast format is that it appropriates discourses occurring in the public and political spheres

and represents them on a multimodal, multisemiotic interface. When the nightly news appears on the TV screen, the viewer is not just confronted with a verbal discourse pertaining to current affairs [the source text], but also a visual discourse that fuels the overall message [the target text].

The process whereby visual semiotics are deployed contemporaneously with the verbal narrative of the newscaster or journalist is, in Desjardins' view, a form of 'inter-semiotic translation'. Drawing on a small corpus of televised news narrations: (i) examine the relevance of Desjardins' argument to your own data set; (ii) reflect on the extent to which the conceptual framework presented in this chapter can inform your critique of the selection and deployment of visual and aural sub-modes in your chosen audiovisual narratives.

NOTES

1 The increasing attention towards the multimodal nature of texts is not restricted to the domain of audiovisual translation (Baker 2014: 15).
2 Audiovisual translation scholars have so far failed to agree on a common set of terms to signal the semiotic complexity of audiovisual texts. Wurm (2007), for example, reports on Gottlieb's (1997: 95) use of the term 'polysemiotic' to refer to audiovisual texts, on the grounds that they communicate through more than one medium (i.e. the visual and the audible). Subtitled texts, according to Gottlieb, are instances of 'diasemiotic' or 'intermodal' trans-lation, as they prompt 'a change of the mode from the spoken dialogue of the source film to the written subtitles of the target film' (Wurm 2007: 116). 'Intersemiotic translation', on the other hand, designates the transfer of meaning across different media (Remael 2001: 13–14, Gottlieb 1997: 111), as in the filmic adaptation of a literary text. While, under this framework, subtitling would be accounted for in terms of a shift between two different 'sign systems' (speech in the source text vs writing in the target text), other authors 'define any movement of speech into writing, or vice versa, as an intersemiotic translation' (Fine 1984: 96, quoted in Wurm 2007: 116–17, footnote 3). The specialized terms that I will be drawing upon in examining the relevance of multimodality to the translation of audiovisual texts are in line with disciplinary conventions on terminological usage within multimodal theory.
3 I am grateful to Nienke Brandsma for introducing me to this example.

4   See http://movielistmania.blogspot.co.uk/2010/11/alles-is-liefde-movie-review-love-is.html (last accessed on 15 September 2013).

5   Romney, Jonathan (2006) 'Filtered for Extra Smoothness', *ABC: The Arts, Books and Culture Magazine from The Independent*, 16 June, 10.

6   It should be emphasized at this stage that the systematization of semiotic resources proposed here in the form of sub-mode repertoires is only tentative, as it is just beginning to be unravelled by multimodality scholars themselves. Systems of sub-mode choices represent, at this stage of multimodality research, preliminary mappings of resource-types available for the materialization of communicative intentions in audiovisual texts, and no claim to completeness is to be inferred.

7   Bosseaux refers to these para-verbal means as 'modalities' – a term that, as explained in the introduction to Section 6.2, I use as a synonym of 'mode'.

8   Bean, Travis (2012) '*The Artist* or the Failed Use of Sound and Silence', 24 January. Available online at: http://cinemabeans.blogspot.co.uk/2012/01/artist-2011.html (last accessed 15 September 2013).

9   As was also the case with para-verbal means of speech, noises can play an important diegetic role. By slamming a door when they leave a room, for example, characters are able to signal their emotions. More generally, noises serve to propel the narrative forward or enhance dramatic characterization. Consider, for example, the role of the typewriter sound in Joe Wright's adaptation of Ian McEwan's *Atonement* (2007). Briony, the central character, is multimodally constructed as an obsessive teenager. Her 'intense need of control', for example, 'is suggested in the way all the toy animals in her immaculate bedroom are arranged facing in exactly the same direction' (McFarlane 2008: 12). In one of the initial scenes of the film, Briony can be seen typing the final words of her play, *The Trials of Arabella*. As she walks in search of her mother to elicit her opinion on the play, the sound of a typewriter at work appears to punctuate the pace of Briony's confident stride. In the filmic adaptation of *Atonement*, this use of the typewriter sound therefore brings to the fore Briony's obsession with her writing and draws attention to the central role that epistolarity plays as a narrative force in the film. When subtitling for Deaf viewers, the presence of diegetic and extra-diegetic noises performing similar functions have to be signalled in the text of the subtitles, in the form of an inserted annotation – often between brackets.

10 See www.lordheath.com/index.php?p=1_365_La%20Vida%20Nocturna (last accessed 15 September 2013).

11 www.cinema.ucla.edu/support/laurel-hardy-spanish (last accessed 15 September 2013).

12 www.laurel-and-hardy.com/films/refilmings/fr-nuit.html (last accessed 15 September 2013).

13 Credit is due to Louisa Desilla for drawing my attention to this example.

CORE REFERENCES

On multimodality:

Baldry, Anthony and Paul. J. Thibault (2006) *Multimodal Transcription and Text Analysis*, London/Oakville: Equinox.

Kress, Gunther and Theo van Leeuwen (2006) *Reading Images: The Grammar of Visual Design*, 2nd edition, London and New York: Routledge.

Van Leeuwen, Theo (2011) *The Language of Colour*, London and New York: Routledge.

On multimodality and audiovisual translation:

Desilla, Louisa (2012) 'Implicatures in Film: Construal and Functions in Bridget Jones Romantic Comedies', *Journal of Pragmatics* 44: 30–53.

Pérez-González, Luis (2007b) 'Intervention in New Amateur Subtitling Cultures: A Multimodal Account', *Linguistica Antverpiensia* 6: 67–80.

Pérez-González, Luis (2014a) 'Multimodality in Translation Studies: Theoretical and Methodological Perspectives', in Sandra Bermann and Catherine Porter (eds) *A Companion to Translation Studies*, Wiley-Blackwell, 119–31.

7

SELF-MEDIATION

Scholars of digital culture and – as their work essentially pertains to Internet or the World Wide Web – cyberculture point at the same phenomenon: Something is going on in the daily lives of media users worldwide that makes them (us) accept the fact that reality is constructed, assembled, and manipulated by media, and that the only way to make sense of that mediated world is to intervene and thus adjust our worldview accordingly – which in turn shapes and renews the properties of media, more closely reflecting the identity of the remediating bricoleur instead of the proverbial couch potato.

(Deuze 2006: 66)

As audiences themselves are becoming more involved in steering the processes of aesthetic and political expression in the media industries, pre-existing discursive or ecological backgrounds are beginning to influence the way in which heteronomy is represented. Amateur subtitling is therefore non-referential to the extent that it uncovers the differences that commercial subtitling tries to gloss over, bringing to the fore the expression of competing desires by individuals and collectivities.

(Pérez-González 2012: 349)

> **In this chapter**
>
> The shift from an electronic to a digital culture is responsible for the proliferation of **self-mediated textualities**, as citizen networks engage in playful or 'monitorial' participatory practices to produce and share media experiences – translation being one more aspect of this process. Amateur **prosumers** – either on an individual basis or as members of organized networks or transient '**ad-hocracies**' – are responsible for **transformational** translation practices that increasingly fall beyond existing means of analysis and critique. Given the importance that affectivity plays in self-mediated textualities, audiovisual translation practices appear to be increasingly assuming a **non-representational** function. Rather than seeking to convey pre-encoded linguistic messages or communicative intentions, non-representational translation is a platform for the expression of subjective spectatorial experiences. Self-mediation practices, which are already influencing the production and translation of commercial media content represent a unique opportunity to learn more about how audiovisual translation can be done, rather than simply document how the industry wants it done.

▶ WATCH THE INTRODUCTION VIDEO

7.1 THE DEMOTIC TURN IN AUDIOVISUAL TRANSLATION

After much shuffling and secrecy, in June 2012 the leading Japanese video game developer Square Enix – known for its role-playing video game franchises, including *Final Fantasy* and *Dragon Quest* – confirmed rumours that had been swirling around in Southern Europe and Latin America for months. *Kingdom Hearts 3D: Dream Drop Distance*, the seventh instalment in the best-selling *Kingdom Hearts* series, would not be translated into Spanish and Italian. This decision was bound to cause disillusionment among large sections of the company's European fandom, not least because the game had been developed exclusively for Nintendo 3DS and incorporated spectacular action elements to capitalize on the console's sophisticated functions. As it became increasingly evident that postponing the announcement would ultimately cause fans more dismay, the company published the relevant confirmation via its website (see Box 7.1).

In today's market, most major video game releases contain a growing amount of spoken dialogue, often limited to 'cutscenes'. These sequences, over which players have no or very restricted control, 'break up the gameplay and are used to advance the plot, strengthen the main character's

---

Box 7.1

Square Enix's statement:

Kingdom Hearts 3D [Dream Drop Distance] will be localised into English, French and German. The VO [voice-over] will be in English only, with English, French and German subtitles. In Spain and Italy the game will be available in Spanish and Italian boxes with accompanying documents, but the game itself will be playable in English only.

We understand that there has been huge disappointment from fans in Spain, as well as other European countries. We completely understand this and we are sorry that we have not been able to fully satisfy all the fans' needs for this version of the game.

---

development, introduce enemy characters, and provide background infor-mation, atmosphere, dialogue, and clues' (Rodgers 2010: 183). Developers, however, continue to seek ways of enhancing interactivity and creating ever more immersive experiences for fans, so it is now increasingly frequent for even minor characters in the game to have at least a line or two of incidental voice-over in fully interactive scenes.

Over the last two decades, subtitling and dubbing have become instru-mental in facilitating users' deep involvement in the gaming experience, with consensus growing among developers and translators alike that 'the main priority of game localization is to preserve the gameplay experience for the target players, keeping the "look and feel" of the original' (Mangirón and O'Hagan 2006). Against this background of growing scholarly and creative interest in immersive gaming (Jennett *et al.* 2008), Square Enix's decision to do without any of the standard forms of game localization in this much anticipated release proved difficult to accept.

But fans were not going to take it lying down. True to the interventionist spirit that drives digital media **audienceships** (Section 3.2.2), Spanish gamers used Square Enix's own website to create a virtual community of interest and set out an agreed course of action to reverse the company's decision. Through the publication of posts in response to the game developer's announcement, fans sought to pile pressure on Square Enix on a range of fronts. Online petitions 'clamoring for a translation of the expected masterpiece' were set up;[1] wiki-based collaborative manifestos were agreed and circulated;[2] a Twitter hashtag to capture followers

(@KH3Dencastellan) was created; and some fans went as far as to research and publish a short feature alleging that Square Enix was gradually developing a track record in snubbing its Spanish-speaking fans, primarily driven by its determination to stall the growth of Spanish into an international language capable of threatening the dominance of English in the cultural industries.[3]

Three months after *Kingdom Hearts 3D: Dream Drop Distance* was commercially released, specialized media reported that All Destiny Dubbing would be localizing the game into Spanish.[4] Like other **fandubbing** groups, All Destiny Dubbing comprises a pool of 'talented' translators and dubbing 'artists' who become involved in the revoicing of audiovisual media content on a volunteer basis – irrespective of their amateur or professional status.[5] Translation and voice talent is drawn to the group through tests and cyber-auditions, respectively. As far as the voice castings are concerned, dedicated areas in the group's website are developed to facilitate the prospective actors' preparation: volunteers can access these spaces to view sample clips of the group's next project, identify the character they feel best suited to dub, and rehearse until they become familiar with the prosodic idiosyncrasies of their *alter ego* on screen. Selected clips are then used as the basis for the audition, during which the voices of volunteers are digitally recorded and sent to the group for their consideration.

In the course of an interview with an online cultural magazine,[6] All Destiny Dubbing's co-ordinator Rubén Armadà Vega confirmed the group's commitment to standard fandubbing codes of practice. In taking on this project, they were not seeking to undermine Square Enix's commercial interests, neither by circulating a dubbed 'playable' game, nor by releasing a downloadable patch to fix the 'language glitch' of the commercial version. Instead, their work would be shared in the form of 25-minute 'watchable-only' clips posted on the group's YouTube channel. And while All Destiny Dubbing would not actively approach the game developer to seek legitimation of their immersive localization activities, Armadà Vega hoped that the ripple effect of fans' enthusiastic reception across social networking sites would lead Square Enix executives to reconsider their decision.

The voluntary involvement of All Destiny Dubbing in the localization of *Kingdom Hearts 3D: Dream Drop Distance* is yet another example of the interventionist potential of audiovisual translation. As the production and consumption processes become increasingly collaborative, fans challenge traditional discourses around media content ownership, while demanding recognition of the capital they have accrued as 'subcultural' arbiters of fans' taste through competitive, even combative, means (Napier 2007).

The emancipation of audiences from the control of the media industry, as illustrated by the *Kingdom Hearts* example, is no mean feat. In this chapter, I will argue that the involvement of ordinary citizens in the production and circulation of media content and experiences represents the most significant development in the history of audiovisual translation, and a very recent one at that. This is not a hyperbolic statement simply used for effect. Audiovisual translation emerged, developed and remained under the tight regulatory grip of media companies until the mid-2000s, when the spread of networked digital technologies brought the hegemony of industrial practices to an end. Throughout the twentieth century, audiovisual translators worked under close surveillance of the film and television industries, which held in monopoly the technology required to produce subtitled and dubbed content, but also to distribute it and exploit it commercially. During this period, audiovisual translators were bound by highly constraining conventions, as subtitled and dubbed films had to be recorded in ways that allowed 'for a certain kind of post-production manipulation and eventual playback' (Mowitt 2004). The **demotic turn** in audiovisual translation – enabled by the democratization of access to digital technologies and the proliferation of collaborative mediation processes – marks the end of this monopoly.

'Consumers-turned-producers' or 'prosumers' (Denison 2011) are now resisting the 'commodification' of media content and the 'cultural politics of standardization' (Mowitt 2004: 397) that it promotes, whether through the enforcement of assimilationist translation practices or even the occasional decision not to translate certain texts. The shift towards **participatory audiovisual translation** crucially undermines some long-standing tenets of the discipline, including the generalized perception of translators as politically disengaged mediators without agendas of their own; prevalent critiques of subtitling and dubbing as exclusively patron-driven activities, and hence restricted to the mediation of commercially viable genres; and the unquestioning acceptance of the narrative that translatorial creativity is subordinated to medial constraints and the 'self-effacing' presentational style that they demand on the part of the translator (Nichols 1991: 165).[7] The involvement of ordinary citizens in participatory mediation is, in sum, opening up a new window into uncharted territory. For the first time, scholars can access sites of negotiation where audiovisual translators are able to inscribe their own narratives and exert their discretion to the full. Ultimately, these new domains represent an opportunity to learn more about how audiovisual translation *can be done*, rather than to simply document how the industry *wants it done*.

7.2 AUDIOVISUAL TRANSLATION AS A FORM OF SELF-MEDIATION

Within the growing body of scholarship on new forms of media production and consumption fostered by networked technologies, the term **self-mediation** (Chouliaraki 2010, 2012) designates the participation of ordinary people in public culture by assembling and distributing audiovisual representations of their experiences (Box 7.2). More widely, the term is also used to refer to the engagement of ordinary people in the manipulation and propagation of media content that circulates in their environment. Individuals involved in self-mediation practices produce and edit amateur clips; capture and tamper with commercial footage; and make the output of these processes available to other individuals via social networking sites and self-broadcasting platforms.

Box 7.2

Chouliaraki on self-mediation:

> Blogs, online tutorials, citizen journalism and interactive services across institutions are but a few of the new technological platforms available for people to express themselves in public. This mediated participation of ordinary people in public culture is being hailed as blurring traditional boundaries between media producers and consumers, and leading to new forms of playful citizenship, critical discourse and cosmopolitan solidarity.
>
> Self-mediation is a textual process par excellence. In re-presenting ordinary voice through media technologies, it inevitably employs configurations of semiotic systems, from language to image (still or moving) to sound, in new technologised or hypermediated textualities that change both the genres of public communication and our modes of engagement with them.
>
> (2010: 227; 229)

This section focuses on the role that audiovisual translation plays within the burgeoning phenomenon of self-mediation. For the practices of reflective prosumers are not limited to the creation, appropriation or recirculation of audiovisual content. Ordinary people involved in self-mediation activities also 'annotate' media texts, whether by incorporating subtitles or, as in the case of All Destiny Dubbing, by replacing the original voice track with a re-recorded version in a different language. As this chapter will reveal, audiovisual translators working outside professional circles are developing non-standard practices of mediation, where referential accuracy is often subordinated to the expression of affinity with their audience. The central role that affectivity plays in self-mediation, including amateur audiovisual translation, is crucial for the articulation of subjective 'spectatorial experiences' (Pérez-González 2012) and the clustering of virtual communities of interest within which such experiences are shared and consumed.

From the perspective of audiovisual translation scholars, self-mediation practices and the communities that are built around non-commercial media flows are of particular interest. Unlike their professional counterparts, amateur prosumers do not operate on the assumption that translation should be limited to the manipulation of language. As this chapter will illustrate, the co-creational nature (Section 3.2.1) of self-mediation empowers translators to adapt or modify any component of existing media content, including its visual or acoustic realizations. By extending their domain of influence beyond the manipulation of written and/or spoken language, amateur audiovisual translators are able to induce changes in the way meaning was distributed across the different constitutive modes of the source text. Such inter-modal shifts of meaning may be required, for example, when certain culture-specific connotations of non-verbal modes — whether these have to do with people's attire or the dominant colour in a given film scene — need to be accentuated or neutralized through translation, in order to influence the reception of the text by the target locale.

But the prevalence of co-creational dynamics in participatory contexts of media production has further implications for audiovisual translation. Subtitling or dubbing are no longer necessarily excised from other creative decisions behind the construction of media content — not least because, in citizen-driven production environments, the same individuals are often involved in different stages of the production process. With subtitled and dubbed material becoming an integral part of original media artefacts, the use of audiovisual translation in self-mediated textualities is moving beyond existing conceptual frameworks and methods of critique available in the discipline.

Featured example 7.1: *Avatar September 2011*

2010 and 2011 will be remembered as the years of the 'Arab Spring',[8] a series of revolutionary events – including demonstrations, protests and even wars – that shook several countries in the Arab world. The Egyptian Revolution, which began as a popular uprising with the first occupation of Tahrir Square on 25 January 2011, to demonstrate against President Hosni Mubarak, is one of its best-known episodes. That occupation marked the beginning of a long campaign of non-violent civil resistance, which included a number of important demonstrations and marches, even after the overthrow of Mubarak's regime. To a large extent, social unrest in the post-Mubarak era was motivated by two main factors: the revolutionaries' perception that the ruling Supreme Council of the Armed Forces (SCAF) was not following through on their demands, and the growing belief among secular Egyptians that the Muslim Brotherhood was acquiring a worryingly sizeable institutional power base.

In the run-up to the uprising, Mubarak tried to prevent the explosion of social unrest by launching a crackdown on independent satellite channels and putting restrictions on the mass sending of mobile text messages (a practice widely used for campaigning by opposition movements in Egypt). However, it was social networking media that played the most decisive role in channelling popular discontent against the regime and cementing what has been labelled as 'a Facebook revolution' (Diab 2010). Islam Ahmed El-saeed (a.k.a. Sony Islam) is an Egyptian activist who contributed very actively to the revolution by building a strong presence on different social networking media.[9] Specifically, Sony Islam specialized in the production of political video montages made out of clips appropriated from different sources. In these assemblages, different bits of footage are interspersed with textual elements conceived as prompts for the political mobilization of fellow Egyptians.

On 5 September 2011, Sony Islam published أفاتار ٩ سبتمبر (*Avatar September 2011*),[10] a video montage intended to encourage mass participation in a rally to be held on the 9 September in order to press Egypt's military rulers to keep their promises of reform after Mubarak's ousting. The opening part of the clip presents viewers with snippets of Arabic text where an initial question ('Remember what we did after the revolution?') is followed by a series of responses showcasing the achievements of the revolutionary movement since January 2011. This is followed by a clip from a popular Egyptian comedy series, where members of a local football team and their supporters (many of whom bear the hairstyles and headwear of poor peasants) celebrate wildly after beating what the characters refer to as the 'American' team. Snippets of Arabic text take centre stage again at this point, exhorting viewers to take part in the 9 September demonstrations 'to correct the path' of the revolution and reminding them of their original demands.

Approximately five minutes and 20 seconds into the video montage, Sony Islam incorporates a one-minute clip of James Cameron's feature film *Avatar* (2009) – a futuristic fable about a mining colony set in the alien world of Pandora and the complex relationships between humans and the local Na'vi population. The chosen fragment features wheelchair-bound marine Jake Sully, who agrees to inhabit an avatar – i.e. an artificially grown Na'vi body into which human consciousnesses can be implanted – to infiltrate the indigenous population of Pandora and persuade them to facilitate the mining of their unobtanium reserves. But seduced by a Na'vi female and the eco-wisdom of the Pandora aboriginals, Sully switches sides and ends up exhorting the Na'vi to rally around and prepare for battle against the human army in defence of their land. As he delivers his speech, Sully's words are interpreted into the local language by an English-speaking Na'vi:

SULLY: The Sky people [as humans are referred to by the Na'vi] have sent us a message: That they can take whatever they want, and no one can stop them. But we will send them a message. You ride out as fast as the wind can carry you, you tell the other clans to come. You tell them Toruk Makto [in reference to himself, using the term designating Na'vi individuals who successfully manage to ride a great dragon-like creature] calls to them. You fly now, with me, brothers and sisters! And we will show the Sky people that they cannot take whatever they want, and that this . . . This is our land!

Sony Islam's subtitled version of Sully's words in Arabic is presented in Box 7.3, together with a back-translation into English.

Box 7.3

SULLY: لقد أرسل لنا المجلس العسكري رسالة
The Military Council (SCAF) has sent us a message

بأنَّ استطاعتهم فرض ما يشاءون [sic]
that they can impose whatever they want,

ولا يمكن لأحد أن يوقفهم
and no one can stop them

ولكن سنرسل لهم رسالة
But we will send them a message

تجمّعوا بكل سلمية لتعبّروا عن رأيكم
في إدارة ثورتكم
Assemble peacefully to express your opinion
about how your revolution is being run

وأخبروا أصحابكم وجيرانكم أن يأتوا

Tell your friends and neighbours to come

أخبروهم أن الحق والحرية والعدالة

لا يحتاجوا [sic] لانتخابات

Tell them that truth and freedom and justice
don't need elections

أنزلوا وتجمعوا الآن

معي

Come down [into the streets] and gather
with me

أخوتي [sic]

My brothers,

أخواتي

my sisters

علينا أن نظهر لهم ما الذي

استشهد شهداؤنا [sic] من أجله

We must show them what it was
that our martyrs died for

أنه لا يمكنهم فرض ما يشاؤون

من محاكمات عسكرية وقوانين انتخابية

That they can't impose whatever they want.
Things like military trials [for civilians] and [unfair] electoral laws

وأنّ هذا

And that this [. . .]

هذا ميداننا

that this is our square [i.e. Tahrir Square]!

This is followed by another clip from the same comedy series that Sony Islam used earlier in this video montage. The coach of the Egyptian team is shown here addressing his players and warning them that the 'other side' will attempt to provoke them and spoil the match. The montage closes with yet more snippets of Arabic text inviting viewers to express their opinions on Sony Islam's Facebook page and share the video montage via their social network accounts.

This particular assemblage of footage – clearly conceived as an attack against the ruling Supreme Council of the Armed Forces – mobilizes narratives that are expected to resonate with frustrated revolutionaries and protesters. In particular, Sony Islam sets out to exploit James Cameron's 'heavy-handed attempts to implant contemporary references' (Pulver 2009) in *Avatar* to maximum effect. This is particularly so with *Avatar*'s references to past and present military conflicts, which Cameron introduces to criticize the deployment of troops 'under false pretences' and contribute to 'opening our eyes' (Lang 2010). Sony Islam's politically engaged approach to subtitling facilitates the localization of *Avatar*'s anti-militarist subtext. By prioritizing his political agenda over translational accuracy, this activist effectively transforms the original clip. Instead of urging viewers 'to root for the defeat of American soldiers at the hands of an insurgency' (Podhoretz 2009), the clip now aims to stir up Egyptian public opinion against the military and prompt people to support the symbolic role of Tahrir Square in the revolutionary process.

Sony Islam and his work will serve as a *leitmotif* throughout the first half of this chapter. Drawing on examples of his work and the relationships that he develops with his followers, the remainder of this section will explore three main aspects of the dialectic between audiovisual translation and the phenomenon of self-mediation. First, the rationale for the involvement of ordinary people in self-mediation networks (participation); second, the values and narratives that self-mediators inscribe and privilege in their translated work vis-à-vis those that prevail in commercial media output (remediation); and finally, the very processes through which self-mediated content is assembled and distributed (*bricolage*). The study of audiovisual translation practices in terms of participation, remediation and *bricolage* adopted here reflects the centrality of these dimensions to other manifestations of self-mediation in the digital culture (Deuze 2006).

7.2.1 Participation

The involvement of ordinary people in self-mediation practices, including amateur audiovisual translation, is primarily motivated by processes of **individual** or **collective reconstitution** (Deuze 2006: 66). By producing, annotating and distributing media content themselves, individuals make sense of 'the manifold scrambled, manipulated and converged ways in which we produce and consume information worldwide' (ibid.) in the era of digital culture. Self-mediation practices, however, are not simply about computerizing the production and circulation of media content. Ordinary people who, whether individually or as part of networks of like-minded individuals, take on the role of prosumers are normally driven by 'an emerging value system and set of expectations' (ibid.). For scholars in digital media studies, the **participation** of these agents in processes of reconstitution represents 'an expression of individualization, postnationalism and globalization' (ibid.: 63–64).

The video montage described in Featured example 7.1 illustrates the extent to which our perception of and participation in public life is influenced by the media. Whatever agendas they were originally meant to promote, the clips collated in this video montage have been chosen because they resonate with Sony Islam's anti-SCAF stance. From the perspective of audiovisual translation studies, however, the importance of these emergent media textualities lies elsewhere. Through the use of abundant screen writings and subtitles, Sony Islam is able to repurpose those clips and, in so doing, frame other people's interpretation of events and their perception of reality in post-Mubarak Egypt. Ultimately, this instance of self-mediation brings into sharp relief how, in the era of digital communication technology, ordinary people can become active agents in the process of meaning-making through media.

Understanding the affordances of digital technologies allows us to appreciate the impact of self-mediation on public life. During the last two decades of the twentieth century, also known as the electronic or pre-digital era, participation in the media industry was conceptualized primarily in terms of **reproducibility**. By enabling the serial reproduction of screen-based commodities, computerization invested media flows with a 'simulacral quality' (Venuti 2008: 18–19). In other words, the possibility of perfectly replicating reality on a screen and, more importantly, being able to share and store those representations for personal use generated the illusion of total identity between the original and its virtual reproduction. According to Baudrillard (1983), enhancements in the reproducibility of media content during the early stages of computerization subordinated the message itself to the collective fascination for the medium. Capitalizing on these developments, the media industry favoured certain forms of mass media consumption that, in Baudrillard's view, imposed a cultural politics of uniformity and standardization, often resulting in the minoritization of critical social groups. Media corporations were thus able to keep a tight grip on the receiving situations, saturating people's lives with commercial media content that only lent itself to passive consumption.

In the digital era, however, participation is conceptualized around the notions of **individualization** and **hypersociability**. Through their involvement in self-mediating activities, networked individuals are able to serially reproduce media content, but also to manipulate it. This newfound capacity to refashion audiovisual texts opens up new opportunities for hypersociable prosumers to renegotiate and 'rebuild structures of sociability from the bottom up' (Deuze 2006: 12). Again, Sony Islam's montage is a good example of this process. Amid the 'proliferation and saturation of screen-based, networked, and digital media' (ibid.: 66), Islam articulates his own aspirations and personal values in the public sphere, effectively constructing a collective platform for political action. Social media networks are essential in the process of hypersocialization: the comments posted by Sony Islam's friends on Facebook allow him to gauge the efficacy of his montage, as well as appraising the cohesion of the audienceship clustered around his work.

Following the publication of the أقاتار ٩ سبتمبر (*Avatar September* 2011) clip published on Facebook, Sony Islam and his friends/audience discussed how to gain more exposure for his work and tried to determine which components of the montage are most effective in prompting social mobilization – e.g. debating whether the inclusion of the comedy series scene undermines the solemnity of the *Avatar* clip. A selection of the comments posted in relation to this montage, translated into English, is available in Box 7.4.

Box 7.4

Sony Islam @HichamAlmeldine What was the bit you liked best?

September 5, 2011 at 12:51am

Hicham Almeldine Avataaaaaaaaaaar is really awesome[.] I swear it's price-less[,] and the list of demands[.]

September 5, 2011 at 12:53

ŦŘɹrm MěŘo I just think that it's really not at the level of the last ones, like Sayed said [.] It doesn't give me the feeling of enthusiasm you always use[,] really y'know[,] rousing music[,] whereas here the tone isn't encouraging . . . But the Avatar scene is coool and the al-Kabir [the TV series] too especially the advice about bilinbaat . . . Thanks a lot but you could have done better . . .

September 5, 2011 at 12:57am

Abo Mawada [@SonyIslam] Sony my darling you've always been awesome but I have one comment[.] I don't think joking [Abo Mawada is referring to the use of the Egyptian comedy series as part of the video montage] is any use right now[.] I mean people who are all happy about bilinbaat[.] It's just not the time for it. Sorry Sony I really really liked the video from a technical point of view[,] especially Avatar[,] but it needs to be more rousing. . . But I still liked it and I always learn from you even if you just do a Sesame Street video[.]

September 5, 2011 at 1:49am

Abdelaal Shehta The video's great but[,] with all due respect to the designer[,] it would be very easy for anyone to ruin our revolution because of this video[.]

[T]hey could say these are foreign agendas [N.B. Allegations were made during the occupation of Tahrir Square that the revolution was driven by infiltrators with 'foreign' or 'external' agendas] [.] [L]ook they are even citing Avatar ... And instead of putting a verse from the Quran they are saying 'raise your voice in song' [line from pop song used as background] so you deal with the stuff that's going to get said because of all these comments[.]
[no one replies to this comment]

September 6, 2011 at 12:00pm

In taking over from reproducibility as the main drive behind self-mediation practices, hypersociability has prompted a 'shift in the identity of citizens [...] from a rather passive informational citizenry to a rights-based, monitorial and voluntarist citizenry' (Schudson 1995). These emerging forms of civil engagement are also being played out in the media landscape, as ordinary people increasingly turn to self-mediation when their personal interests are at stake in one way or another. Crucially, the realization of individual reconstitution through the production and circulation of media content often brings to the fore concerns that are shared by other individuals – not necessarily in close geographical proximity. Indeed, the developmental progression from passive to voluntarist citizen agencies is widely regarded as the main impetus for the clustering of prosumers around engaged communities of interest, whether these take the form of traditional organizations or virtual, geographically dispersed groupings.

Sony Islam's work clearly illustrates the extent to which the **monitorial and voluntarist paradigms of civil engagement** have penetrated amateur audiovisual translation in recent years. But this engaged form of self-mediation is not confined to the work of individuals working under their own steam; neither is it limited to the voicing of political concerns. Sustained online interaction within networks of like-minded individuals, for example, also provides the necessary and sufficient conditions for the emergence of monitorial communities of self-mediation. Take, for example, the case of fansubbing communities and their global movement of resistance against commercial translations of Japanese anime. As explained in Section 3.3, fansubbers' subversive refashioning of commercial media content aims to tamper with the industrial context of production that promotes 'culturally odorless' (Iwabuchi 2002: 27) translations of Japanese anime into

English – even when that means engaging in what the industry regards as copyright infringement. For these monitorist fansubbers, the search for reconstitution involves positioning themselves as outside and in opposition to the regulatory framework that underpins the dynamics of the media marketplace. As part of a geographically dispersed and linguistically diverse audience clustered around thousands of fan communities all over the world, fansubbers manipulate media texts and reform conventional representations of reality through transformative subtitling to effect aesthetic change. By capitalizing on the potential of self-mediation, fans and the prosumers who subtitle for them 'have learnt to articulate for themselves and for anime distributors their product specifications' (Cubbison 2005: 45) in terms of preferred subtitling conventions. From a self-mediation theoretic perspective, fansubbing networks can be said to amalgamate hypersociable individuals into monitorial communities, with their grassroots creativity increasingly being recognized as an engine of cultural transformation (Dwyer 2012, Pérez-González 2012).

Networked technologies endow amateur monitorial translators with the capacity to reach beyond their immediate personal environments and become members of transnational communities of affinity. But not all instances of unsolicited self-mediation are the work of stable networks of 'virtual communitarians' (Castells 2001: 54). The mediation of media content is increasingly being undertaken by 'ad-hocracies' of amateur translators, a notion proposed by Pérez-González (2010). Unlike their counterparts involved in stable networks, members of these ad-hocracies are 'brought together because their diverse skills and knowledge are needed to confront a specific challenge and then dispersed onto different clusters . . . when new needs arise' (Jenkins et al. 2006: 41). In Pérez-González's case study, the term 'ad-hocracy' designates a fluid virtual grouping formed in July 2006, when readers of a Spanish progressive blog decided to work together to subtitle (into Spanish) an interview that Spain's former Prime Minister, José María Aznar, gave to HARDtalk (BBC News) against the backdrop of the, at the time, ongoing military conflict between Lebanon and Israel. For a range of reasons (see Pérez-González 2010 for an in-depth account), this interview provided progressive constituencies in Spain with useful ammunition to continue fuelling the public backlash that had led to the electoral defeat of Aznar's conservative party in March 2004. In the interview, the former Prime Minister reasserted his unreserved commitment to the neoconservative narratives circulating during the Bush years and the practical implications of those policies – not least the invasion of Iraq in 2003 that much of the Spanish public regarded as the cause of the Madrid train bombings on 11 March 2004 (Govan 2009). As it became apparent that none of the main Spanish TV channels would broadcast the full translated interview, and in view of the Spanish conservative party's attempts to 'reframe' Aznar's interview statements, this spontaneously formed network of engaged individuals decided to produce and distribute a subtitled version in Spanish.

As was also the case with fans' reaction to Square Enix's decision, readers of the blog entry reporting on Aznar's BBC interview used the comment-posting facility to express their frustration with the patchy journalistic coverage that the interview received in the Spanish printed media. Overall, their posts – most of which were highly critical of the former prime minister – were used by blog readers to negotiate their **narrative location** relative to that of other members of this temporary online community; mutually reinforce their shared political affiliation against occasional challenges from Aznar's supporters; and jointly construct a cohesive **affinity space** leading to concerted action – i.e. the formation of a temporary subtitling community to distribute a subtitled version of the interview among like-minded individuals.

Processes of negotiation of narrative affinity – as defined by Baker (2006) – between members of ad-hocracies are central to the formation of these groupings of engaged citizens. As they normally lack organizational support and, in many cases, even an explicit set of programmatic objectives, exploring fellow members' affiliations and identifying narratives that most members of the community subscribe to is crucial to building a platform for collective intervention in the media marketplace. Studying ad-hocracies thus involves looking at the dynamic construction of a narrative community, placing particular emphasis on the role played by the Internet in the spontaneous process of network formation and, hence, paying less attention to the use of the Internet as a medium for the circulation of self-mediated messages. Ultimately, ad-hocracies represent 'extreme manifestations of dynamic identity generation' (Pérez-González 2010: 264), where individuals take on the role of audiovisual translators on a transient basis in the context of post-national media landscapes.

7.2.2 Remediation

Ordinary people involved in self-mediation practices, including audiovisual translation, are motivated by monitorial or voluntarist agendas. Whether it is in an individual capacity, through stable citizen networks or as part of engaged ad-hocracies, amateur translators participate in public life through the appropriation, manipulation and distribution of audiovisual content, orienting to the demands and expectations of the audienceships that gravitate around these individual or collective prosumers. In their capacity as 'self-appointed translation commissioners' (Pérez-González 2006: 265), Sony Islam, fansubbing network members and virtual communitarians affiliated to subtitling ad-hocracies set out to mediate audiovisual broadcasts that strengthen their narrative location, i.e. the agendas driving their participation in self-mediation activities. Such programmes are then mediated and recirculated for the benefit of their respective niche audiences, on the assumption that the translated output – whether it is subtitled or dubbed – will resonate strongly with viewers' own narrative location.

Insofar as these interventionist forms of self-mediation practices challenge the control that media corporations have traditionally exerted over the production, distribution and consumption of their broadcasts, the individual or collaborative translation work of prosumers can be constructed as an act of resistance against the dynamics of the media marketplace and the socio-economic structures that sustain it. As an increasingly co-creational, participatory activity, audiovisual translation can

> intervene into the postmodern situation by tampering with the simulacra that drive the global economy. A translator might use the images on which capital relies to short-circuit or jam its circulation by translating so as to question those images and the practices of consumption that they solicit.
>
> (Venuti 2008: 21)

Deuze's (2006: 66) notion of **remediation** precisely designates the engagement of ordinary people in the 'remix[ing] of old and new media' to resist or subvert discourses that circulate in their environment. Through remediation, prosumers taking on the role of translators refashion commercial audiovisual representations of reality in different ways, one of which is illustrated in Featured example 7.2.

Featured example 7.2: *Braveheart*

On 2 July 2011, Sony Islam published an untitled video montage via his Facebook page[11] and YouTube channel.[12] The chosen theme of this montage was '8th July: The Resolve of the Revolution Friday'. Having just won Egypt's presidential run-off against the last prime minister under deposed leader Hosni Mubarak, Islamist President Mohamed Morsi chose 8 July to issue a decree calling for new parliamentary elections and announcing the drafting of a new constitution for the country. Although these were, on paper, positive developments, many protesters were becoming increasingly concerned over the concentration of power in the hands of Morsi's Freedom and Justice Party (founded by the Muslim Brotherhood) and the ensuing marginalization of other democratic secular forces. This video montage urges Egyptians to take part in the 8 July demonstration to ensure that Morsi did not ignore the demands of non-Islamist parties (freedom, social justice and human dignity).

As in Featured example 7.1, Sony Islam's new video montage revolves around a subtitled extract from a film – in this case, Mel Gibson's *Braveheart* (1995). Written political slogans and lyrics of popular revolutionary chants are used, both before and after the chosen clip of Gibson's film, to frame the viewers' interpretation. The fragment under scrutiny here is set in the period following the death of Scottish King Alexander III in a famous equestrian mishap (1286). Although, for a few years, Scotland was governed by the premier nobles and bishops of the country, known collectively as the Guardians of Scotland, a number of claimants soon emerged for the vacant throne. Sony Islam's chosen scene takes place after Wallace, prompted by a number of personal circumstances, rebelled against and defeated the English at Stirling Bridge. Following this historical victory, different contenders to the Scottish throne try to secure William Wallace's support:

BALLIOL SUPPORTER:	Sir William! Sir William. Inasmuch as you and your captains hail from a region long known to support the Balliol clan, may we invite you to continue your support and uphold our rightful claim.
WALLACE:	Gentlemen! Gentlemen!
BALLIOL SUPPORTER:	Now is the time to declare a king.
MORNAY:	Wait! Then you are prepared to recognize our legitimate succession.
BALLIOL SUPPORTER:	You're the ones who won't support the rightful claim.
MORNAY:	Those were lies when you first wrote them.
BALLIOL SUPPORTER:	I demand recognition of these documents.
CRAIG:	Gentlemen! Please, gentlemen! Wait! Sir William, where are you going?
WALLACE:	We have beaten the English, but they'll come back because you won't stand together.
CRAIG:	Well what will you do?

WALLACE:	I will invade England and defeat the English on their own ground.
CRAIG:	Invade? That's impossible.
WALLACE:	Why? Why is that impossible? You're so concerned with squabbling for the scraps from Longshanks' table that you've missed your God-given right to something better. There is a difference between us. You think the people of this country exist to provide you with possession. I think your possession exists to provide those people with freedom. And I go to make sure that they have it.

Sony Islam's subtitled version of this fragment into Arabic is presented with the corresponding back-translation in Box 7.5.

Box 7.5

BALLIOL SUPPORTER: سيّد ويليام[!]
Sir William[!]

سيّد ويليام[!]
Sir William[!]

انت والثوّار من منطقة معروف عنها منذ زمن طويل
تأييدها للإخوان المسلمين
You and the revolutionaries hail from a region long known
to support the Muslim Brotherhood

ونحن ندعوك لأن يستمرّ هذا التأييد
وتبايعوننا [sic] على حكم مصر
We invite you to continue this support
and pledge allegiance to us in ruling Egypt[.]

CROWD: سحقاً للإخوان المسلمين[!]
Damn the Muslim Brotherhood[!]

إنّهم يستغلون الثورة[!]
They're exploiting the revolution[!]

WALLACE: أيّها السادة
Gentlemen[!]

أيّها السادة
Gentlemen[!]

BALLIOL SUPPORTER: لقد حان الوقت لكي نعلن حاكماً للبلاد
The time has come to announce a ruler for the country

MORNAY: لا بدّ من أن تعترفوا بأحقيتنا كي ننظم أنفسنا
You must recognize our prerogative to organize
ourselves

BALLIOL SUPPORTER: بل لا بدّ من أن تعترفوا أنتم
No, it is you who must recognize

MORNAY: هذا كذب فهذه الوثائق تؤكد أحقيتنا نحن
That's a lie, those documents confirm our precedence[.]

BALLIOL SUPPORTER: تبّاً لهذه الوثائق الكاذبة
To heck with those lying documents[!]

CRAIG: أيّها السيد ويليام
أين أنت ذاهب؟
Sir William,
where are you going?

WALLACE: لقد أسقطنا النظام ولكنه سيعود
لأنّكم لا تريدون أن تقفوا مع بعضكم البعض
We brought down the regime but it will come back
because you don't want to stand together

CRAIG: وماذا أنت فاعل؟
And what [will] you do?

WALLACE: سأعتصم في التحرير حتى تحقيق
أهداف ومطالب الثورة بالكامل
I will occupy/stage a sit-in in Tahrir Square until
the aims and demands of the revolution are fully
realized[.]

هذا هو الفرق بيننا
That's the difference between us[.]

CRAIG: اعتصام؟
هذا مستحيل
An occupation/sit-in?
That's impossible

WALLACE: لماذا؟
لماذا هذا مستحيل؟
Why?
Why is that impossible?

أنتم مهتمون بالسعي وراء فتات من
التغيير والحرية والعدالة
You're concerned with chasing after scraps
of change, freedom and justice[,]

وتنسون حقاً أعطاه الله لكم
في شيء أفضل
and you forget your God-given right
to something better

هذا هو الفرق بيننا
That's the difference between us

أنتم تعتقدون أن الشعب في هذا البلد
قد وجد ليمدكم بالمناصب
You think the people of this country
exist to provide you with positions

ولكني أعتقد بأن مناصبكم قد وجدت
لكي تمد الشعب بالحرية
But I think your positions exist
to provide the people with freedom

وأنا ذاهب الميدان لكي أتأكد
من أنهم سيحصلوان [sic] عليها
And I'm going to the Square to make sure
that they will get it.

The Arabic subtitled version reveals the rationale for the choice of this clip. The positioning of William Wallace with reference to the internal squabbles between Scots closely mirrors Sony Islam's own stance towards political 'bickering' among Egyptian secular parties in the run-up to the 2012 presidential election. Just as Wallace understood the detrimental impact that the claimants' quibbling was bound to have on Scotland's newly won freedom, Sony Islam's engaged approach to the subtitling of the dialogue is indicative of the translator's concerns and goals. Tensions among the claimants to the Scottish throne become, through Sony Islam's subtitling, effectively transposed to post-Mubarak's Egypt. Thus, in the Arabic subtitled version, Gibson urges the representatives of Egyptian political parties to stand together and prioritize the people's goals and welfare over their own. The subtitled clip ends with a call for participation in the 8 July demonstration.

The audienceship of the '8th July: The Resolve of the Revolution Friday' montage is very supportive of Sony Islam's approach to remediation. As the comments from his Facebook page show (Box 7.6), the parallelisms between late thirteenth-century Scotland and post-Mubarak's Egypt have not gone unnoticed by viewers. Sony Islam's subtitled version of *Braveheart* evokes a sense of frustration and pessimism about the unfolding of the Revolution that resonates with the individual stances of his viewers. Subtitling – and the wider process of remediation – thus facilitates the formation of a community of individuals who come to share and identify with it. It is the **refashioning** and **repurposing** of media content through remediation that makes this community grow and evolve, with members continuing to renegotiate their narrative location through the co-construction of new video montages. The perception of novelty inherent in any innovation, on the other hand, also features prominently in viewers' comments. Although remediation and other practices of self-mediation continue to move towards the core of the media marketplace, Sony Islam's interventionist subtitling has the appeal of the unconventional about it.

Box 7.6

Ahmed Abd Al Fattah I can't find words to say, I swear
I was watching that film a few days ago and when that scene came up
I thought of the situation of our revolution
Everyone wants to divide it up and take his own share and forget its [original] aims and the blood of the people who have died
Thanks so much boss
Seriously I swear the idea is inexpressibly good
July 2, 2011 at 1:33pm

Ahmed Fahmy Amaaaaaazing in the full sense of amaaaazing . . . great idea . . . new imagination and non-traditional creativity . . . words/ discourse and aims which are agreed upon . . . God bless you Islam, hope your skills increeeeease God willing
July 2, 2011 at 5:35pm

In self-mediated textualities, including Featured example 7.2, amateur translators make their presence felt within the subtitles, turned into sites of narrative negotiation to facilitate the co-construction of an affinity space with their online audienceships. The prosumers' alignment with viewers' expectations is then normally expressed through recourse to performative subtitles (see Section 7.3.2) that draw attention to their artifice and lack of concern over their perceived objectivity. Flaunting their disregard for 'accurate' representations of fictional dialogue allows amateur translators to maximize their own visibility as mediators and promote an alternative aesthetics of reception based on mutual recognition – with viewers being encouraged to reflect on their spectatorial experience through the range of channels that digital technologies make available to them.

7.2.3 Bricolage

The notion of remediation accounts for the way in which amateur transla-tors manipulate and 'reform consensual ways of understanding reality' (Deuze 2006: 66) simply by annotating (i.e. translating) the original media content. By contrast, the term **bricolage** designates the 'highly personalized, continuous, and more or less autonomous assembly, disassembly, and reassembly of mediated reality' (ibid.) by such translators.

The discussion around Featured examples 7.1 and 7.2 in previous sections has illustrated the importance of manipulated media content in the era of self-mediation. The organization of Sony Islam's video montages as assemblages of reused manipulated footage provides ample evidence that he has fully embraced his **bricoleur** identity. As Chandler (1998) notes, the 'bricoleur's strategies are constrained not only by pragmatic considerations such as suitability-to-purpose and readiness-to-hand but by the experience and competence of the individual in selecting and using "appropriate" materials'.

But Sony Islam's status as 'bricoleur-citizen' (Deuze 2006: 70) is also evident in the complex articulation of his digital persona. Indeed, his two different Facebook pages, YouTube channel and Daily Motion account[13] – that are closely aligned with his interests as a writer and lyricist, graphic designer and political activist – allow him to tap into different constituencies. By randomly posting content in one or more of his different online profiles and linking, often in a random manner, to video assemblages published in the others, Sony Islam effectively acts as a node around which different engaged groupings coalesce. His collection of videos, some of which incor-porate subtitles, reflects his frontal opposition to the Muslim Brotherhood and the Egyptian military, and articulate his highly critical views of the pre- and post-electoral strategies of other Egyptian secular forces. Given the fluid nature of social identities in the digital culture, members of the audi-enceships gravitating around Sony Islam's different self-mediation outlets appear to be drawn to the communities for different reasons, including their disapproval of Western meddling in the Middle East, the economic consequences of regional power politics or the perils of religious radicaliza-tion and Islamic fundamentalism, to give but some examples.

Through hyperlinks, whether internal (featuring within the media content itself) or external (displayed somewhere on the interface where media content is being played), bricoleurs provide their viewers with access to media archives, newspaper reportage or simply other assemblages of annotated content; but it is also through **hyperlinked navigation** that a *bricoleur*'s own output becomes available to other groupings. This 'repurposing or windowing of content across different sites, media, and thus (potential) audiences', known among digital culture scholars as **shovelwaring** (Deuze 2006: 70), creates hubs of narrative clustering where like-minded individuals and collectivities intersect. But there are other ways in which shovelwaring can accelerate the spread of self-mediation practices. By making video embedding codes, files and images available for download, *bricoleurs* encourage other media users to take on a *bricoleur* identity and engage in further manipulations of existing content.

Participatory self-mediation – whether it is driven by political, aesthetic or simply recreational concerns – results in disjunctive relationships between monitorial and voluntarist prosumers, on the one hand, and the media establishment, on the other. The active participation of engaged ordinary people as meaning-making agents through media; *bricoleurs*' creation of audiovisual artefacts through the manipulation of previously existing content to promote personal or collective values; and the interventionist remediation of content outside the circuitry of the audiovisual marketplace amount to 'a more or less deliberate social act – deconstructing and/or subverting symbols, images, and other mediated products of whatever is perceived as "mainstream"' (Deuze 2006: 60).

7.3 TRANSFORMATIVE PRACTICES: FROM REFERENTIALITY TO AFFECTIVITY

The conceptualization of subtitling and dubbing as approximate linguistic representations of the meanings that were verbally encoded in the source text is firmly rooted in audiovisual translation studies. Although it has been argued that audiovisual translators should be 'less concerned with the words of the speaker than with the intention of what the speaker wanted to say' (Luyken *et al.* 1991: 156), most scholarly studies in the field tend to 'automatically assume that the target of translation is the verbal soundtrack and, possibly, any text that appears onscreen', to the extent that 'actually addressing the non-linguistic realm is something of a taboo' (Ortabasi 2006: 280).

The shift from an electronic to a digital culture, however, is facilitating the active participation of ordinary people in public life through media-based representations of their experiences. Their self-mediation practices, involving either the production of new content or the refashioning of previously existing material, are often associated with interventionist forms of mediation that clash with scholarly and professional discourses on audiovisual translation. In keeping with their penchant for disassembling and reassembling mediated reality, prosumers use translation to re-narrate the message conveyed by the original text – which normally entails throwing aside traditional allegiances to translational accuracy and fidelity, as demonstrated by Featured examples 7.1 and 7.2. Unlike professional audiovisual translators, prosumers seek to promote their own agendas, as well as to capture the relationality of different networked constituencies. By capitalizing on the **intersectionality** and **fluidity** of cultural identities in post-industrial societies, prosumers are able to build audienceships that are bound together by **mutual affinity** between members.

As Pérez-González (2012) notes, this shift towards a conceptualization of translation as a non-referential expression of subjectivity and social engagement mirrors changes in the way that the notion of **representation** has been conceptualized in other disciplines. Cultural studies scholar Lauren Berlant (2011), for example, argues that the old relational dynamic of fidelity – whereby cultural artefacts were meant to deliver faithful representations of the reality they draw on – is in complete crisis. The ongoing neoliberal 'restructuring' of public life, she argues, is bringing about sweeping changes to our socio-economic environment and traditional welfare state models. Faced with precarity, contingency and crisis, individuals turn to affect and aesthetics as a way of coping with transformations taking place around them. Against this background, Berlant argues that new emergent aesthetic forms and cultural manifestations driven by affect are taking hold of our ordinary experience, which she labels as 'crisis-ordinariness'. By drawing on crisis-shaped subjectivity, we accept and adjust to new modes of living that are no longer rooted in mainstream 'good life' fantasies.

The widely held assumption among producers and consumers of commercial media content that each audiovisual text contains a single reality waiting to be deciphered or understood has also been challenged within film studies. The insight that '[w]e can no longer talk of film representing, or mimicking, reality, because we can no longer assume that there is a single, coherent reality waiting out there to be filmed' (Aitken and

Dixon 2006: 326), underlines the importance of socio-politically engaged and culturally diverse audiences in the consumption of media content. From the perspective of audiovisual translation studies, the growing importance of **expressivity** over **referentiality** and the representational dimension of life, as articulated by Berlant and Aitken and Dixon in their respective fields, provides a sound platform for the theorization of translation in the context of self-mediation.

As traditional, representation-centred approaches to audiovisual translation become increasingly less relevant, it is imperative to account for the transformations that are currently under way in the field from an alternative angle. The overview of emergent practices delivered in the remainder of this section examines and illustrates how prosumers depart from deep-rooted translation conventions that tended to privilege the source text. This deviation is presented here as a deliberate attempt to foster new forms of social engagement with media content – whether by projecting viewers immersively into the translated text (as in fandubbing) or by deploying subjective filters in the representation of narrated reality to effect socio-political change (as in activist subtitling). The impact of amateur audiovisual translation – and the wider phenomenon of self-mediation – on the construction of these new spectatorial experiences is gauged and illustrated in terms of four features that I have proposed elsewhere (Pérez-González 2012): **mutual recognition** between prosumers and their audiences; **performativity** in the delivery of translations; prominence of translation **materiality**; and **transformational effect** of the viewing experience.

7.3.1 Mutual recognition

Section 7.2.1 has illustrated how processes of narrative negotiation allow for the co-construction of affinity spaces populated by prosumers and their online audiences, and revealed the extent to which such processes shape the production and consumption of audiovisual texts in the era of self-mediation. Achieving the degree of playful or political affinity required to keep virtual audienceships together places high demands on prosumers and requires the active involvement of their audiences. To a large extent, interventionist translation practices favoured in the digital culture are based on a relational dynamic of **mutual recognition** between producers and users of audiovisual texts. By enhancing the translator's visibility and exploiting the affordances of new communication technologies to facilitate the expression of viewers' subjectivity, the perception and acknowledgement of mutual affectivity take centre stage in these emergent textualities.

One of the most explicit manifestations of prosumers' orientation towards mutual recognition involves the display of titles conveying extra-diegetic material in different regions of the frame. Unlike traditional subtitles, these textual elements do not convey translated versions of the original dialogue or any written element featured in the fictional or narrated world. Instead, non-diegetic titles provide prosumers with a space to inform, amuse, exhort or otherwise attend to the expectations of their viewers. As part of his study of an activist subtitling network specializing in media appearances by Spain's former Prime Minister José María Aznar López, Pérez-González (2013a: 169) discusses how extra-diegetic titles are used to enhance the mediator's visibility and deliver material that will resonate strongly with the audience's narrative location:

> Throughout the remediated version of Aznar's address to the World Jewish Congress (Jerusalem, 1 September 2010), [the activist network] *Ansarclub* subtitles draw the viewer's attention to the former Prime Minister's poor command of English ... [In certain subtitles,] the network members pick up on the fact that part of the audience is looking away from Aznar to note that 'Los pobres en primera fila ya no aguantan más' ('The poor sods in the front row can't cope any longer'). By bringing into sharp relief the occasional unintelligibility of Aznar's speech, it is assumed by these subtitlers that the pointlessness of both his speech and the wider event will become evident for the audience. A similar lack of concern over their perceived objectivity is exhibited by *Ansarclub*'s members [in other sub-titles]. The subtitling of Aznar's argument (i.e. the West needs to defend Israel to defend itself) is interjected with sarcastic remarks alluding to the potentially hostile reception that such views would receive in Spain: 'Por qué no dices eso en casa, Ansar?' ['Why don't you say that at home, Ansar'].

In the case of Ansarclub, recourse to non-diegetic titles interspersed between conventional subtitles facilitates associative relations among members of its geographically dispersed virtual audience and prompts recognition of their collective attempt to undermine Aznar's political standing in the eyes of Spanish-speaking progressive constituencies worldwide.

Figure 7.1 Interplay between diegetic subtitles and non-diegetic titles (*Naruto*, episode 178)

But the relationship between prosumers' non-diegetic titles and traditional subtitles is not always mutually exclusive. The fansubbing subculture, for example, often relies on combinations of diegetic subtitles conveying the meaning of the original spoken dialogue and unconventional titles incorporating a non-diegetic dimension into the subtitled text. In Figure 7.1, for example, the subtitle at the bottom of the frame ('You don't mean a dried plum, but a star from the sky') seeks to render into English the comic effect of the pun used in the original Japanese dialogue. Viewers interested in grasping the logic behind the pun can then follow the notional hyperlink to the non-diegetic 'headnote', where

> we come across an overt attempt on the part of the fansubbers to frame the viewer's interpretation and even impose their assessment of the comic effect arising from the narrated action ('In an unprecedented episode of bad hearing and even worse jokes, Naruto [the character] has misheard . . . God help us'). The fansubbers' assumption of this interventionist role

represents thus the ultimate statement against the effacement of the translator prevailing in commercial subtitling.

(Pérez-González 2006: 271)

The display of additional non-diegetic material to complement traditional subtitles positioned at the bottom of the frame promotes 'connective' forms of reading (Landow 1992), similar to those required to navigate the hyperlinked textual environments that continue to proliferate around us. As in other genres featuring notional or material hyperlinks, the simultaneous use of various self-standing texts in fansubbed material brings about a plurality of reading experiences. By undermining the seriality of the written text(s) displayed on screen, fansubbers 'pluralize' and rewrite the original content (Littau 1997) in what can be effectively regarded as an overt expression of subjectivity. The allegiance that professional audiovisual translators have traditionally professed to the voice-title synchronization principle – using subtitles only to deliver target language renditions of a spoken narration or the characters' speech – is often dispensed with in the context of fansubbing, as prosumers set out to gain maximum visibility and viewers attempt to engage in the construction of mutual affinity.

Hypertextual environments are central to the viewers' ability to express their subjectivity and participate in a relational dynamic of mutual recognition. For some years now, broadcasts and films translated by prosumers have been published and circulated via dedicated websites. Within these hypertextual domains, translated media content features alongside downloadable subtitle files containing different translation versions of the same text (Pérez-González 2012); downloadable transcripts; video embedding codes to facilitate data mash ups; and links to relevant freeware applications – all of which encourages viewers to engage in shovelwaring practices, as defined in Section 7.2.3, and to strengthen their collective identity as 'communities of imagination' that perform themselves for the benefit of other imagined audiences surfing the Internet (Hills 2002). Most crucially, however, these websites also incorporate message boards and online forums where viewers gather, communicate and become active community members. As Denison (2011: 456) aptly notes, '[t]he authority and power that the fan subtitling prosumer wields in relation to their audience is evidenced in the way anime fan viewers interact with their fansub providers' as part of the process of mutual recognition. Negotiating their collective identity, however, is not always a straightforward task, for 'the communities of imagination around anime fansubs are complex entities filled with (often divergent) hierarchical understandings of how fansubs should look, as well as what fansubs are for and how the groups and their users should behave' (ibid.: 458).

Recent advances in communication technology continue to pave the way for more radical forms of viewer intervention in the translation of media content, and to prompt new manifestations of mutual recognition between prosumers and their audiences. These emergent forms of intervention are not restricted to the strategies discussed in relation to anime-centred fansubbing – i.e. the reinforcement of translators' visibility through non-diegetic subtitles and the empowerment of audience members to express their views on the translators' work through online forums. New amateur subcultures gravitating around the subtitling of drama, for example, are deploying tools that allow audience members to express themselves within the actual frame. An example of these is the online subtitling platform developed by Global TV site Viki (Dwyer 2012). As illustrated by Figure 3.6, Viki's interface facilitates the expression of viewers' subjectivity and the playful exploration of shared affiliations through subtitles that other viewers of Asian drama can choose to read via a dedicated 'discussion band'.

The community-building strategies surveyed in this section are examples of the ongoing re-conceptualization of audiovisual translation against the background of ever more ubiquitous self-mediation practices. In this context of production, subtitles are no longer regarded as 'signifiers and representations of narratives which seemingly are pre-existent to or transcend [a] film itself' (Curti 2009: 202). Instead, they are conceived 'as spatially affective- and expressive-movement[s]' enabling the achievement of mutual recognition among members of the same community of interest (ibid.). The remainder of this section will therefore focus on the formal implications of this development, gauging the extent to which the growing importance of expressivity has led prosumers to exploit the affordances of semiotic resources normally deployed in audiovisual artefacts.

7.3.2 Performativity, spectacularization

Capitalizing on the expressive potential of semiotic resources is bound to involve formal experimentation. An ever expanding body of literature published over the last decade has identified and explored some of the main innovations pioneered by the fansubbing subculture – including but not limited to fans' creative use of fonts or preference for unconventional subtitle layouts (Section 3.3). As I have shown in earlier work (Pérez-González 2006), however, some forms of experimentation intended to create immersive spectatorial experiences go beyond the mere manipulation of written text and foster new kinds of interplay between the linguistic and visual modes. In 'pictorial subtitles', for example, snippets of text in the target language are styled to ensure that the chosen fonts and colours blend with the overall visual semiotics of the scene at hand (Figure 3.5). This effort to enhance the **performativity** of subtitles also involves displaying them in unconventional regions of the frame, in a playful attempt to create the impression that they are part of the original text.

To illustrate the performative dimension of subtitles, Pérez-González (2006, screen capture 4) compares how an American commercial distributor (FUNimation) and a fansubbing group (Lunar Anime) translated a specific frame of the Japanese anime series *Burst Angel* (2005).[14] The frame in question (scene two, episode one) delivers a long angle, point-of-view shot that grants viewers access to the protagonist's visual perspective as he motorcycles into Kabukichō, an entertainment and red-light district in Tokyo. Positioned as if it had become one and the same with the motorcyclist's eyes, the camera shows the Kabukichō iconic entrance sign – an arch-like structure straddling the road – and a plethora of other smaller signs and neon advertisements attached to buildings and a range of metallic structures erected on the sides of the road.

Pérez-González (ibid.) reports that the commercial subtitled version (frame 4a) exhibits the same distribution of meaning across linguistic and visual semiotic resources as the original text. As the Kabukichō entrance sign features the name of this Tokyo district only in Kanji characters (歌舞伎町), most foreign viewers will be unable to recognize the area that the main character is about to enter. They are also unlikely to be stirred by the sense of excitement and latent threat that the name of this district evokes among their Japanese counterparts. Unlike viewers of the original version, they will not sense the imminence of the shoot-up that the protagonist is about to be caught up in as he rides on under the Kabukichō entrance sign. By contrast, Lunar Anime prosumers preserve the Kanji characters, but a highly styled title conveying a transliteration of the district's name ('Kabuki-cho') is added within the entrance sign itself. True to fansubbers' penchant for visually harmonious intervention, the new subtitle looks as if it had always featured in the original film, both in terms of font and colour choices. By incorporating the transliterated name, Lunar Anime prosumers enhance the enjoyment that *otakus* (anime fans) dispersed all over the world derive from this exposure to material manifestations of the narrated culture.

But the **spectacularization** of subtitles through the foregrounding of formal experimentation is not restricted to animation films. Titles can also be creatively styled for and positioned within feature films, as illustrated in an amateur subtitled version of *Das Leben der Anderen* (*The Lives of Others*, 2006) into Chinese.[15] Throughout the picture, highly aestheticized titles become almost completely blended in the visuals, often making it difficult for viewers to spot their very presence in the frame. In one of the stills, for example, a close-up shot of a newspaper front page shows a Chinese text ('戈尔巴乔夫当选苏联共产党主席'; back-translation: 'Gorbachev elected Chairman of the Communist Party of the Soviet Union') filling the blank space around an article headline ('Michail Gorbatschow Generalsekretär des ZK KPdSU gewählt'; back-translation: 'Mikhail Gorbachev elected General Secretary of the CPSU Central Committee'), as if it had been printed at the same time as the rest of the newspaper's front page contents.

In other shots, Chinese titles appear interspersed with handwritten notes on blank pieces of paper – for example, the name of a famous actress in the film (Christa-Maria Sieland) is accompanied by its transliteration ('克莉丝塔西兰') in the Chinese version. Chinese titles also appear on the pages of open books, somewhere in the vicinity of their corresponding German words or sentences – as seen on the title page of the protagonist's novel *Die Sonate vom Guten Menschen* (Song for the Good People), translated as '献给好人的奏鸣曲' (Song Dedicated to the Good People). A set of Chinese characters ('卡尔马克思书店'; back-translation 'Karl Marx Bookstore') is even superimposed on the façade of the iconic 'Karl Marx Buchhandlung', as if composing a street sign that mimetically reproduces the proportions and colour of the letters of its German counterpart displayed right beneath.

Generally speaking, the aestheticized approach to the subtitling of this thriller about the surveillance of East Berlin's cultural scene by Stasi agents is entirely in keeping with the overall semiotic configuration of what has been described as a 'slightly stylized' (Elley 2006) film. The subtlety and sophistication of the titles, designed to look as if belonging to the original multimodal artefact, adequately complement 'a powerful but quiet film constructed of hidden thoughts and secret desires' (Ebert 2007), where even the 'tensest moments take place with the most minimal of action' (Schwarzbaum 2007).

The instrumental role and referential function of these titles becomes, to some extent, subordinated to the performative nature of amateur subtitles. Drawing on their genre expertise and familiarity with their audience preferences, amateur subtitlers choose to enhance the pictorial dimension of the overall semiotic gestalt, even when that means that some of the titles described above might be inadvertently missed by viewers watching the film in real time – thus diluting the ultimate *raison d'être* of subtitles as a form of mediation across languages. The deployment of colour, fonts, perspective and other multimodal aspects of composition (Section 6.4.4) that turns performative subtitles into affective spaces is a very important aspect of this trend towards spectacularization. In the case of the example under scrutiny here, neither the thematization of performance over functionality, nor the capacity of titles to boost affinity between amateur prosumers and their audience have gone unnoticed by viewers, as the selection of comments presented in Box 7.7 confirms.[16]

Box 7.7

富贵不能淫 [username]:

翻译字幕不稀奇，关键是大家仔细看翻译在原银幕上，且还得搭配字体，颜色，甚至透视效果，如上图报纸，字是近大远小

[Back-translation]: There's nothing new about translated subtitles, but the key for everyone to carefully note is that the translations are on the original screen, and what is more, match the script/typeface, colour, even the perspective, for example on the newspaper, the words are larger up close and smaller further away.

KeninChina:

That's not just adding translations, that is putting the translation into part of the production, which, i might add, is very very smart especially if you plan to increase international box office sales. *applaud*

Jordan:

This is old news.
Last year I saw a movie . . . forgot the title . . . it was an American film, but the DVD I saw was a Russian copy, anyway, the main character went to an ATM, and it displayed Russian on the ATM screen. Now the guy was in the US, and I was thinking what ATM in America would display Russian? Then I realized it was a subtitle!

Shanghairen:

> Of course the Chinese think it's great that the subtitles are aesthetically pleasing, but they won't care if the subtitles are an accurate reflection of the original German.

GuruConnector:

> i was watching a chinese movie the other day and i am not sure exactly why they even bother putting subtitles at all but it was a riot watch and read ... they were watching and kind of guessing what they were saying and writing what they were doing like ... he is arguing with this other man about something, they are shouting at each other, he told him to get out of there etc. etc.

7.3.3 Materiality, corporeality

Formal experimentation with the **materiality** or **corporeality** of titles is another distinctive feature of performative mediation, as undertaken by amateur subtitlers within their networks of self-mediation. Exploring the physicality of titles and exploiting the meaning-making potential of the semiotic resources or modes deployed in the production of these snippets of text are effective ways of favouring expressivity over referentiality, and promoting the aesthetics of mutual recognition between prosumers and their audiences. Unlike traditional titles, which could rely exclusively on 'the punctuation, typeface, type size, and layout of the text on the screen ... to suggest, symbolize, or emphasize' (Dick 1990: 47), their counterparts in the era of the digital culture capitalize on the affordances gained through technological developments to allow for an immersive subtitling experience. Movement is one of such affordances – as argued by Curti (2009: 205) in his analysis of similar instances of affective subtitling (Box 7.8).

Box 7.8

> As part of the creation of something different subtitles are not (or are no longer) signifying superimpositions of static representations, but intimate living components of a(n) (un)folding filmic assemblage(s)cape ... No longer simply about approximate or pre-existent meanings or representations statically superimposed onto pure or original territorial images, through animation subtitles become living and affective forces and

> performances univocally, yet heterogeneously, pushing the audience towards filmic content. The living subtitle moves the spectator by its own movement to what is present and immanent in and to the film itself.

I have elsewhere (Pérez-González 2012) examined the extent to which expressive salience can be achieved through the movement of titling elements across different regions of the frame, particularly in audiovisual material aiming to posit subjective or engaged spectatorial experiences. *Israeli Apartheid 5* (2010), an activist video montage consisting of a compilation of images provided by 'photographers on the ground who have documented the ongoing Palestinian Nakba (Catastrophe)' and submitted to the 2010 'Israel Apartheid Video Contest', will be used here as an example of the role that the materiality of titles plays in the reception of audiovisual texts.[17] Stills of the Israeli West Bank Barrier punctuated by the occasional use of intertitles – i.e. short texts flashed on the screen displaying, in this case, historical data – serve as the building blocks of a narrative of aggression and resistance, with 'the Wall' emerging as 'the most visible manifestation of Israel's apartheid regime'. A melancholic theme played on a solo flute, evoking a sense of despair or disillusionment, crucially contributes to the overall meaning of this montage, in the absence of dialogue or a spoken narration.

Unlike mainstream subtitled material, where static subtitles are superimposed on moving images, *Israeli Apartheid 5* features moving titles that hover over photographs of the Wall. But given that, as already noted, no diegetic or narratorial voices feature in this montage, what is it that these titles convey? Attention to the role that titles play in this material is indicative of the extent to which the study of translation has widened its scope in recent years, both by incorporating 'within its remit various types of non-verbal material' and coming to 'encompass a wide range of activities and products that do not necessarily involve an identifiable relationship with a discrete source text' (Baker 2014).

In *Israeli Apartheid 5*, subtitles travel horizontally, vertically or diagonally across the frame, affectively accentuating different aspects of visually encoded meaning in relation to the Wall. The stills in Figure 7.2 feature a title containing the text 'watchtowers' moving upwards against a picture of one such tower, as if to enhance its height in the eyes of the viewer. In a different shot, the viewer is presented with an aerial image of a curved

Figure 7.2 Screen shots from *Israeli Apartheid 5*: moving titles

section of the Wall at the foot of hill slopes, while a title containing the text 'Wall length/626–788 Km'[18] undulates along the contour of the Wall – subtly drawing attention to how well it conforms to the topography of the terrain. The expressive function of titles, which can be observed throughout the montage, suggests that amateur mediators do not always use them as 'signifiers and representations of narratives which seemingly are pre-existent to or transcend' an audiovisual text, but as 'spatially affective- and expressive-movement[s] intimately involved with and inseparable from the viewer's involvement in the co-creation and experience of the audio-visual text' (Curti 2009: 202).

As has been demonstrated throughout this section, translation in the era of self-mediation often intervenes in audiovisual material, not to 'represent pre-existing selves, individual or collective, but [to] constitute such selves in the very process' (Chouliaraki 2010: 229). Whether they are used by prosumers affiliated to fansubbing subcultures or by engaged citizens seeking to effect social or political change, titles are 'acts, events, happenings, and they should not be primarily evaluated according to their referentiality or degree of correspondence with pre-existent meaning or communicative intentions' (Pérez-González 2012: 348). Instead, their value resides in 'their affective contribution to the materiality of audiovisual texts' (ibid.) and their **transformational impact** on the viewers' spectatorial experience.

7.4 THE IMPACT OF SELF-MEDIATION ON COMMERCIAL PRACTICES

Earlier sections in this chapter have shown how amateur translators involved in self-mediation activities subscribe to a 'view of publicness that thematizes performance, voice and claims to recognition' (Chouliaraki 2010: 227). Fandubbing groups such as All Destiny Dubbing, prosumers such as Sony Islam or fansubbing communities such as Lunar Anime make their presence visible through their translations. Amateur subtitlers do not hold allegiance to the synchronous diegetic sound principle in the way their professional counterparts did during the best part of the twentieth century (Sinha 2004). Prosumers and engaged citizens undertaking translations in the digital era often criss-cross the boundaries between the diegetic and the extra-diegetic, thus delineating spaces for the expression of subjectivity and developing further affinity with their audienceships.

7.4.1 Towards an ontology of deconstruction

Translators' confinement to the mediation of the diegetic ceased with the transition from 'recording technologies' (e.g. analogue forms of media content production) towards 'synthesizing technologies' (e.g. digital communication), and the ontological shift from **referentiality** to **deconstruction** that this shift entails (Kress and van Leeuwen 2006). Cinematography, the creative and interpretive process that most informed the development of audiovisual translation practices during the best part of the twentieth century, has historically relied on recording technologies and thus contributed to developing and imposing an ontology of referentiality. The centrality of synchronous diegetic sound conventions in the classical cinematic apparatus seeks to hide the artifices and machinery of film-making (Minh-ha 2005) and promote 'a view of representation being founded on direct, referential relations between the representations and the world' (Kress and van Leeuwen 2006: 218). Against this background, the conceptualization of subtitles as gate-keepers of the diegetic, to be used only with the sole purpose of translating the original dialogue, reinforces a perception of media content as unified naturalistic representations and, more widely, favours an aesthetic of objectivity. By contrast, synthesizing technologies, including digital communication technologies, foster an ontology of deconstruction – exposing the cultural and semiotic resources deployed in the production of audiovisual material.

Kress and van Leeuwen's (ibid.) mapping of specific ontologies onto different technology types supports the argument I have tried to develop in this chapter. In the digital era, the prevailing ontology of deconstruction fosters experimental approaches to subtitling, articulating new 'rhetorical' practices that open the way for new forms of interaction between mediators and their audiences, and conjuring up new 'designs' based on unconventional arrangements of semiotic resources.

In this final section, I propose to consider the prospects for the consolidation of this ontological orientation developed by ordinary citizens clustered around networks of collective intelligence. If, as has been argued in this chapter, experimental subtitling practices are indicative of the growing ubiquity of synthesizing technologies and the shift from referentiality to constructedness that they entail, it would be reasonable to expect amateur subtitling to emerge as an ever stronger influence on the production and subtitling of commercial media content.

Ontological changes, both in terms of rhetoric and design, are increasingly evident in a small range of commercially (sub)titled media products where the aesthetics and delivery of the subtitles could be regarded as part of the overall artistic or pedagogical agenda at the heart of a given audiovisual product. This is the case with the BBC's *Human Planet*, an eight-part television documentary series first broadcast in 2011, that was widely acclaimed for turning 'its lens on the human race [instead of filming animals], treating it as any other curious species clinging to survival' (Radford 2011). To document the relationship between the human species and the natural world, the series brings to the fore the remarkable ways in which humans have adapted to life in every environment on Earth, often trying to develop a sense of affinity with viewers along the way. Enhancing affectivity is key to the reception and success of the series, hence the deliberate inclusion of emotionally upsetting material and the recourse to direct narrator-audience interaction – as when the former, for example, invites viewers to hold their breath for as long as they can, while a Bajau fisherman's dive is shown in real time.

With each episode of the series focusing on a different human-inhabited environment, subtitles are occasionally required to translate dialogue between people all over the world. And while the titles adopt a referential function, primarily conveying an English version of the original dialogue, subjectivity and expressivity are enhanced in other ways. The stills in Figure 7.3 (episode 4)[19] illustrate the series creators' attempt to extend to the English viewer the playfulness of the children's dialogue as they go about hunting tarantulas in the Venezuelan jungle. Through the use of capital letters, the transcription of interjections that don't normally find their way into commercial subtitles, or the use of multiple exclamation marks signalling the speakers' mood, the creators go some way towards evoking the children's fascination with the thrill of a potentially lethal adventure.

A similarly performative use of titles can be observed in the first episode of the series (Figure 7.4) about goose barnacle collection in Galicia, Northern Spain. These crustaceans grow attached to wave-battered rocks at the bottom of steep cliffs, so harvesting them is dangerous even when they become exposed at low tide. Braving the rough waves that could easily sweep them away, local collectors Javier and Ángel descend on to the lowest rocks, where the biggest barnacles grow. As they shout over the noise of the rock-battering waves, snippets of text appear somewhat randomly in different regions of the frame, revealing themselves one letter at a time before dissolving into the water, as if brought and carried away by the tides.

Figure 7.3 Screen shots from *Human Planet* (episode 4: 'Jungles: People of the Trees')

The insight that styled titles promote subjective spectatorial experiences, and hence increase affinity between media creators and their viewers, would seem to be at the centre of performative approaches to the translation of commercially sensitive media content, including film trailers. Well known for their dislike of subtitled films, US audiences have traditionally forced international distributors to develop ways of disguising the foreign origin of their films in their promotional materials. In practice, this has led to important

Figure 7.4 Screen shots from *Human Planet* (episode 1: 'Oceans: Into the Blue')

changes in the semiotic configuration of trailers over time. In this sense, film distributors have adopted 'a new form that [is] increasingly incompatible with all dialogue, whether in English or another language' (Rich 2004: 160), effectively leading to the widespread use of speechless trailers. However, in view of 'the alacrity with which people have taken up keyboard-based communication' (ibid.: 166) in recent years, some distributors have opted to win English-speaking viewers over to the enjoyment of cosmopolitan films by commissioning performative subtitles for their trailers.

This is the case, for example, with Swedish-French comedy-crime *Sound of Noise* (2010).[20] In this film, a tone-deaf cop attempts to track down a group of guerrilla percussionists who are terrorizing the city through anarchic public performances where music is made in unconventional ways, e.g. using high-tension power cables as if they were violin strings. As one of the stills in Figure 7.5 illustrates, titles conveying English versions of the original dialogue are playfully placed in the frame, normally in the vicinity of the character's mouth, evoking the semiotic contribution of speech balloons in comic books. For more effect, titles undergo further processes of spectacularization in places. For example, during the count-off leading to one of the percussionists' unique performances that will involve the shredding of bank notes, white-bordered transparent numbers appear in the centre of the frame. Through this contrivance, the trailer accentuates the transition from a standard filmic narrative, where music is deployed as part of the extra-diegetic dimension, towards a fragment of the trailer where music takes on a diegetic role. Unfortunately, audiences attracted to cinemas by the original interplay between music, speech and titles presented in the trailer will have been disappointed by the use of conventional subtitles in the film proper.

7.4.2 Cross-fertilization of amateur and professional practices

In this chapter I have argued that formal experimentation involving screen translation is more evident when mutual recognition between creators and recipients is deemed central to the reception and/or enjoyment of audio-visual material. But, as illustrated by O'Sullivan (2011: 149), formally innovative subtitles can perform a number of dramatic functions, in addition to simply delivering translations of the original dialogue. In the remainder of this chapter, I explore how these new manifestations of audiovisual translation, in the form of written titles, are becoming ever more prevalent in commercial films and dramas where no interlingual translation is required.

Pérez-González (2012) illustrates this emergent practice with examples from the British television series *Sherlock* (2010),[21] which showcases the centrality of Holmes' intellectual skills – in particular, his keen observation powers and ruthless logic – to the resolution of his cases:

> His [Holmes'] brilliance is shown by allowing him to tell us what is about to happen before it does . . . *Sherlock* [the series] takes this a stage further: one of its great joys is the way in which Moffat [one of the series creators]

Figure 7.5 a–b Screen shots from *Sound of Noise* (2010)

and his collaborators have devised ways of showing its protagonist's mind working. Labels are flashed onto people's clothing to reveal the methods by which Holmes deduces history and character; pin patterns are painted on the screen as he tried to break into a phone; numbers float across his face as he cracks a code.

(Crompton 2012)

As Featured example 7.3 demonstrates, the use of Holmes' cleverness as a rhetorical device to propel the narrative forward leads the series creators to transcend the boundaries of the diegetic space and address their viewers directly, as they struggle to represent the unfolding events while, simultaneously, providing the viewer with insights into Sherlock's powers of observation at work.

Featured example 7.3: *Sherlock* (Pérez-González 2013b: 16–17)

Featured example 7.3[22] begins with Holmes and Watson joining Detective Inspector Lestrade at the scene of the latest in a series of unexplained suicides. The sequence where Holmes silently inspects the scene, walking around the body of a woman lying in prone face-down position, is filmed using the shot-reverse-shot technique – with the camera switching between Holmes' face and different parts of the victim's body. His attention is first caught by the word 'RACHE', which appears to have been carved on the wooden floor by the victim's nails. As he scrutinizes the broken nails of the woman's left-hand, the title 'Left handed' appears between the tips of her middle and ring fingers. Sherlock's gaze shifts back to the wooden floor, where a kinetic title – composed in the style of a dictionary definition ('RACHE/German (n.) revenge') – is printed next to the carved word (Figure 7.6).

A point-of-view shot putting the viewer in the position of the dead woman then shows Sherlock looking down at the body, at which point an effective rhetorical device is used (Figure 7.7). The title containing the dictionary definition remains suspended half-way in the diegetic space between Sherlock and the victim/viewer, who can read it back to front for a few seconds – as if it was meant only for the detective – before it vanishes (indicating that the relevance of the German word has been discarded by Holmes). Holmes proceeds to examine the victim's clothes. As he slips his gloved hand behind the coat's collar or pockets, titles with the words 'dry' or 'wet' appear next to close-up shots of his fingers. His inspection of the victim's jewellery is also accentuated by variously placed titles indicating that her bracelet, earrings and necklace are 'clean', while her wedding ring is 'dirty'. Holmes' interpretation of the latter finding is delivered in the form of a kinetic title formed by the words 'married', 'unhappily' and '10+ years' appearing on the frame. Further titles serve to make the point that, while the outside of the victim's wedding ring is 'dirty', the inside is 'clean'. The titles

Figure 7.6 Screen shot from *Sherlock* (2010): definition of 'Rache' (1)

Figure 7.7 Screen shot from *Sherlock* (2010): definition of 'Rache' (2)

conveying the conclusions of this contrast are then superimposed on the victim's ring ('regularly removed') and face ('serial adulterer').

In Featured example 7.3, *Sherlock*'s creators have opted to transgress the conventions of narrative framing through 'narrative metalepsis' (Genette 1983 [1980], quoted in O'Sullivan 2011: 161). In other words, information that would have normally remained confined to the diegetic (Sherlock's reflections while inspecting the body) is made available to the audience through the use of what Pérez-González (2013b: 15–16) calls **authorial titling**:

> To represent Sherlock's brilliance, the creators thus exploit the 'double-layeredness' of filmic communication (Vanoye 1985), prioritizing the vertical level of interpersonal communication (between the filmmakers and the audience) at the expense of its horizontal counterpart (between the film characters). The upshot is that Watson remains oblivious to the working of Sherlock's logic, while viewers have been provided with the information required to appreciate Holmes' brilliance as both narrative planes unfolded.

This highly subjectivizing rhetorical strategy, combined with the lack of diegetic speech, articulates through visual semiotic resources the alienation that Lestrade and Watson feel as they are unable to keep up with Holmes's powers of deduction. Diegetic silence is used in combination with a narratological 'free indirect style' at the visual level. The ensuing 'interjection of the personal/direct discourse into the narratorial/indirect discourse' through '[p]oint-of-view shots, cut-aways, perception shots, even certain shot-reverse-shot configurations' (Naficy 2004: 136) enhances the dramatic function of authorial titling. *Sherlock* creators thus indulge in the use of narrative metalepsis to create a shared space of affinity between Holmes and the viewer, where subtitles act as a projection of the detective's actions and mental processes, complementing the semiotic value of the expressive camera movements and editing in this scene.

Drawing on Kress and van Leeuwen (2006: 264), it could be argued that the use of authorial titling creates 'an "alienation effect", to break with conventions meant to naturalize the fictional world of stage and screen, and so to make audiences more aware that they [are] watching a fiction and invite them to reflect on its content'. To foreground their affinity with viewers, the series creators incorporate titles that draw attention to the material apparatus of filmic production – much in the same way as the translation practices of ordinary people involved in self-mediation. Just as media content and experiences mediated by prosumers foreground a spectacularized and aestheticized approach to translation as a means to facilitate mutual recognition between producers and users, this thematization of performance is bound to shape rhetorical and design choices in commercial media content seeking to promote subjective spectatorial experiences – with the use of authorial titles becoming an ever more prominent one.

Rather than simply contributing to the representation of reality, experimental and authorial titling – as used by amateur prosumers and commercial media creators, respectively – promote 'parataxic' reading experiences (Grillo and Kawin 1981). They prompt viewers to experience 'the whole film in an additive way, by combining the various elements [images, dialogues, titles] consciously' (Naficy 2004: 147), for their function is often a playful or engaged one that can project viewers immersively into the narrated text. Only by positing spectatorial subjectivity through emergent subtitling and dubbing practices can producers of media content attend to the demands and expectations of their ever more dispersed constituencies and harness the process whereby their shifting identities are negotiated both within and outside the margins of the frame.

FOLLOW-UP QUESTIONS FOR DISCUSSION

- In recent years, the Palestinian village of Bil'in – located near Ramallah in the central West Bank – has felt increasingly threatened by Israel.[23] Of particular concern for villagers is the construction of Israel's Apartheid Wall, against which they demonstrate on a weekly basis. In 2010, one such demonstration involved a re-enactment of James Cameron's *Avatar*. As reported by CNN, '[i]n the James Cameron movie, ... the Na'vi defend themselves against a corporation that has occupied their land to mine it for resources. The Bil'in protesters say the Israelis are occupying their land in a similar manner by constructing the barrier'.[24] As part of this re-enactment, a number of Palestinian, Israeli and international activists dressed like Na'vi aboriginals and marched towards the Wall. A video montage of the demonstration is available on YouTube at (www.youtube.com/watch?v=KStnbXWfnuk&feature=player_embedded).

  After watching the clip, consider the extent to which the concept of self-mediation (including practices such as remediation and *bricolage*) can help you articulate the rationale for the assembly of audiovisual material included in this montage. Compare the ways in which Bil'in activists and Sony Islam (Featured example 7.1) appropriate and re-deploy fragments of *Avatar* and draw on its political subtexts. Finally, explain the differences between the ways in which both montages make use of subtitling for the purposes of collective reconstitution.

- Iranian film studies scholar Hamid Naficy (2004: 132) has theorized the idiosyncrasies of films produced by 'postcolonial, third world and displaced native filmmakers'. 'Accented' films, as Naficy calls them, 'signify and signify upon cinematic traditions by means of their artisanal and collective production modes, their aesthetics and politics of smallness and imperfection, and narrative strategies that cross generic boundaries and undermine cinematic realism' (ibid.: 134). One of the ways in which directors of accented cinema foster subjective spectatorial experiences is, according to Naficy, through the extensive use of titling: 'in some epistolary films, words are either superimposed over the images or the flow of images is interrupted to display intertitles ... These titles are treated in the tradition of the best silent-era films, as essential to the narrative' (ibid.: 134). Read Naficy's paper in full and consider the similarities that may exist between experimental subtitling (e.g. in fansubbing), authorial titling (as illustrated by Featured example 7.3) and the centrality of calligraphy in accented cinema. According to Naficy, accented films are 'interstitial' because they are produced by exilic and diasporic directors. To what extent is it necessary to re-theorize the concept of accented cinema in terms of the ongoing deterritorialization of media producers and audiences in the digital culture?
- Eric Cazdyn (2004) reflects on the impact of recent advances in subtitling technologies and focuses on the innovative ways in which running subtitles interplay with audiovisual broadcasts. Whereas traditional subtitles traditionally acknowledged the presumed ontological status of the original text, new forms of subtitling (including running subtitles) are in a dynamic relation with it. As a result, running subtitles disrupt the assimilation of subtitles into the visual mode, challenging their marginalization within conventional audiovisual texts. Consider Cazdyn's stance critically in the light of the self-mediation practices surveyed in this chapter. To what extent does the orientation of amateur prosumers towards mutual recognition and the performative dimension of their subtitles resemble the function and effects of running subtitles, as described by Cazdyn?
- On 14 January 2012, Nobel peace prize laureate Mohammad ElBaradei declared he would not run for the Presidency of Egypt. In post-Mubarak's Egypt, he claimed, a fair vote would be impossible during a muddled transition period dominated by the powerful Muslim

Brotherhood and the popular ultraconservative Salafi groups. His pull-out represented a blow to liberal and leftist groups behind the 2011 uprising, who regarded ElBaradei as a rallying figure in their struggle for democracy. Three months later, ElBaradei returned to public life to launch the Constitution Party, which aimed to unite Egyptians and save the country's revolution. Although the Constitution Party would be unable to field a candidate in the May 2012 presidential election, ElBaradei said its aim was 'to unite Egyptians behind democracy, and to take power in four years time'.[25]

Sony Islam's remediation of the Kung Fu Panda montage[26] – based on the homonymous Dreamworks blockbuster released in 2008 – relates to these events. After watching the clip, compare the source dialogue with its Arabic version (or its back-translation into English) provided in Box 7.9. Consider the reasons why this particular clip of Kung Fu Panda has been chosen as the basis for this instance of self-mediation. Can you find similar examples in other languages and/or political contexts?

Box 7.9

MASTER SHIFU:	معلّمي, معلّمي
	Master[!] Master[!]
	لدي أخبار سيئة
	I have bad news.
MASTER OOGWAY:	إنها مجرّد أخبار
	لا يوجد أخبار سيّئة وجيّدة
	It's just news[.]
	There is no bad or good news
MASTER SHIFU:	معلّمي
	رؤيتك كانت صحيحة
	Master[,]
	your vision was right
	السيطرة على مصر من تيّار واحد
	وهو في طريقة [طريقه؟] لذلك
	Control over Egypt by a single faction[,]
	and it's on [its] way to that
MASTER OOGWAY:	هذه أخبار سيّئة
	This is bad news[,]

لو لم تؤمن

أنّ حزب الدستور بإمكانه المشاركة

Unless you believe

that the Constitution Party is capable of participating

MASTER SHIFU: حزب الدستور[؟!]

The Constitution Party[?!]

حزب الدستور هذا

لا يزال حديث التأسيس

That Constitution Party

is still only newly formed[,]

والتفاف الشباب حوله

كان مصادفة

and the fact young people have rallied around it

was a coincidence

MASTER OOGWAY: لا يوجد مصادفات

There are no coincidences

MASTER SHIFU: نعم أعرف

قلتَ ذلك من قبل

Yes, I know.

You've said that already [. . .]

مرّتين

twice[.]

MASTER OOGWAY: حسناً

هذه لم تكن مصادفة أيضاً

Well[,]

that was no coincidence either

MASTER SHIFU: ثلاثة

Thrice

MASTER OOGWAY: يا صديقي

My friend[,]

حزب الدستور لن يحقق مصيره

في تحقيق أهداف الثورة

the Constitution Party will not realize its destiny/path

of realizing the aims of the revolution

لو لم تتخل عن وهم السيطرة

unless it gives up the delusion of control

MASTER SHIFU: وهم

Delusion[?]

MASTER OOGWAY: نعم

أنظر لهذه الشجرة

Yes[,]
look at this tree

لا يمكنني أن أجعلها تكبر
حين يناسبني الأمر
I cannot make it grow
when it suits me

ولا يمكن أن أجعلها تنضج فاكهتها
قبل أن يحين الوقت
And I can't make it bear its fruit
before the time comes

MASTER SHIFU: ولكن هناك أشياء
يمكننا السيطرة عليها
But there are things
we can control

يمكنني التحكم بوقت سقوط الفاكهة
I can control when the fruit will fall[,]

ويمكنني التحكم
and I can control

أين أزرع البذرة
where to plant the seed

هذا ليس وهماً معلمي
That is no delusion, master

MASTER OOGWAY: نعم
ولكن مهما تفعل
Yes,
But no matter what you do [. . .]

تلك البذرة ستكبر
وستصبح شجرة خوخ
that seed will grow
and become a peach tree

ربّما تريد تفاح أو برتقال [sic]
You may want an apple or an orange[,]

ولكنك ستحصل على خوخ
but you will get a peach

MASTER SHIFU: ولكن الخوخ
لا يمكنه الفوز في الانتخابات
But the peach
can't win the elections

MASTER OOGWAY: ربّما يمكنه
اذا كنت مستعدّاً لإرشاده وتنميته

Maybe it can[,]
if you are prepared to guide it and nurture it[,]

والإيمان به
and believe in it

MASTER SHIFU: ولكن كيف[؟]
كيـــــف[؟]
But how[?]
How[?]

أحتاج مساعدتك معلمي
I need your help master

MASTER OOGWAY: لا
أنت فقط تحتاج أن تؤمن
No[,]
you just need to believe

عدني صديقي
Promise me friend[,]

عدني
أنّك ستؤمن
promise me
you will believe

MASTER SHIFU: سوف أحاول
I will try

MASTER OOGWAY: جيّد
Good

ربّما حان الوقت
Perhaps the time has come

يجب أن تستمرّ في رحلتك بدوني
You must continue your journey without me

MASTER SHIFU: معلمي
لا يمكنك أن تتركني
Master,
you can't leave me[.]

MASTER OOGWAY: يجـــب أن تؤمـــن
You must believe

The Constitution
is a dream not a political party[.]

Bread Freedom Human Dignity [Slogan of Constitution
Party]

NOTES

1   The petition can be accessed at www.gopetition.com/petitions/kingdom-hearts-3d-localization-for-spanish-and-italian.html (last accessed 15 September 2013).

2   The manifesto (in Spanish) is available at www.nextn.es/2012/07/la-plataforma-kingdom-hearts-en-castellano-se-comunica-hoy-con-square-enix-revisa-el-texto/ (last accessed 15 September 2013).

3   The feature (in Spanish) in question can be accessed at http://blogocio.net/crimen-perfecto-op-875/ (last accessed 15 September 2013).

4   One of the many announcements published at the time is available at www.meristation.com/es/nintendo-3ds/noticias/un-equipo-de-doblaje-de-fans-pondra-voces-en-castellano-a-kingdom-hearts-dream-drop-distance-para-3ds/1533592/1802522 (last accessed 15 September 2013).

5   All Destiny Dubbing's website is available at www.dubbing.alldestinyproductions.es/ (last accessed 15 September 2013).

6   The interview can be read at http://frikarte.com/2012/09/entrevista-all-destiny-productions-nos-habla-sobre-el-doblaje-de-kingdom-hearts-dream-drop-distance/ (last accessed 15 September 2013).

7   See Nornes (2007) for a detailed overview of what this 'self-effacing' style involves and how it developed over the twentieth century.

8   This term, created by Western media, has been often contested by Arab activists and scholars.

9   www.facebook.com/ILOVERS (last accessed 15 September 2013).

10   The video montage can be accessed at www.facebook.com/photo.php?v=236065976440267&set=vb.130477763649480&type=3&theater (last accessed 15 September 2013).

11   The video montage can be accessed at www.facebook.com/photo.php?v=205855889461276&set=vb.130477763649480&type=3&theater (last accessed 15 September 2013).

12   The YouTube copy (www.youtube.com/watch?v=1PcHmToW7SQ) has since been blocked on copyright grounds.

13   www.dailymotion.com/mrsooooony#video=xkvnjd (last accessed 15 September 2013).

14   The work of Lunar Anime can be accessed via www.lunaranime.org (last accessed 15 September 2013).

15   A range of screenshots of this Chinese version are published online ('Incredible Chinese Subtitles for *Das Leben der Anderen*') at www.chinasmack.com/2010/pictures/incredible-chinese-subtitles-for-the-lives-of-others.html (last accessed 15 September 2013). ChinaSMACK, the website hosting this article, seeks to provide 'non-Chinese language readers a glimpse into modern China and Chinese society by translating into English popular and trending Chinese Internet content and netizen discussions from China's largest and most influential websites, discussion forums, and social networks' (www.chinasmack.com/about, last accessed 15 September 2013). The blog entry in question features the screenshots containing the Chinese subtitles but does not identify

their individual or collective author(s). Most of the blog readers posting comments on these subtitles, however, assume that they are the work of fansubbers or 'hobbyists'. I would like to thank Dr Carol O'Sullivan (Bristol University, UK) for having drawn my attention to the existence of these titles.

16   The comments quoted here are available via the Chinasmack URL provided in note 15.

17   *Israeli Apartheid 5* was a finalist entry in the 2010 Israeli Apartheid Video Contest, sponsored by 'Stop The Wall' and the itisapartheid.org collective. The video is available at www.youtube.com/watch?v=ol-wFyQg32Y (last accessed 15 September 2013).

18   The forward slash in the middle of the title indicates that the text preceding and following this character is displayed on separate lines on screen.

19   I would like to thank Dr Marie Noelle Guillot (University of East Anglia, UK) for having drawn my attention to this example.

20   The trailer is available at www.youtube.com/watch?feature=player_embedded&v = ZSYQolbNsBw (last accessed 15 September 2013).

21   See www.bbc.co.uk/programmes/b00t4pgh (last accessed 15 September 2013).

22   This fragment described here, taken from episode 1 (season 1), starts at 22':40".

23   For background information on Bil'in, see www.bilin-village.org/english/discover-bilin/ (last accessed 15 September 2013).

24   http://ireport.cnn.com/docs/DOC-408462 (last accessed 15 September 2013).

25   www.bbc.co.uk/news/world-middle-east-17880367 (last accessed 15 September 2013).

26   www.youtube.com/watch?v=ui-MEbfJuiM&feature=plcp (last accessed 15 September 2013).

CORE REFERENCES

On self-mediation in the digital culture:

Chouliaraki, Lilie (2012) 'Re-mediation, Inter-mediation, Trans-mediation', *Journalism Studies*, 14 (2): 267–83.

Deuze, Mark (2006) 'Participation, Remediation, Bricolage: Considering Principal Components of a Digital Culture', *The Information Society* 22: 63–75.

On emergent audiovisual translation practices:

Cazdyn, Eric (2004) 'A New Line in the Geometry', in Atom Egoyan and Ian Balfour (eds) *Subtitles: On the Foreignness of Film*, Cambridge, MA and London: The MIT Press, 403–19.

Curti, Giorgio Hadi (2009) 'Beating Words to Life: Subtitles, Assemblage(s) capes, Expression', *GeoJournal* 74: 201–8.

O'Sullivan, Carol (2011) *Translating Popular Film*, Basingstoke: Palgrave Macmillan. Chapter 5: 'Where Are the Subtitles? Metalepsis, Subtitling and Narration', 143–75.

Pérez-González, Luis (2012) 'Amateur Subtitling and the Pragmatics of Spectatorial Subjectivity', *Language and Intercultural Communication* 12 (4): 335–53.

Pérez-González, Luis (2014b) 'Translation and New(s) Media: Participatory Subtitling Practices in Networked Mediascapes', in Juliane House (ed.) *Translation: A Multidisciplinary Approach*, Basingstoke: Palgrave Macmillan.

8

LEAD THE WAY

In this chapter

This chapter offers guidance for students, reflective professionals and early career scholars aiming to work on audiovisual translation research projects. Orientation is first provided for readers embarking on **theory-driven projects** at postgraduate level (whether at MA or PhD level). In addition to general aspects of research design, the chapter places particular emphasis on the ubiquity of the case study methodology in audiovisual translation scholarship, the formulation of research questions and hypotheses, and other AVT-specific methodological considerations – identifying useful analytical tools, obtaining copyright permissions and securing ethical approval for one's project. The chapter then offers specific guidance to students working on **practical dissertations** consisting of an extended translation project and a critical analysis or commentary; the importance of presenting a rigorous and plausible translation brief is highlighted and a suggested structure for the student's commentary is outlined.

▶ **WATCH THE INTRODUCTION VIDEO**

8.1 FORMALIZING REFLECTION, GENERATING RESEARCH

This chapter aims to assist budding audiovisual translation researchers – whether they are students registered in a specialized training programme or reflective professionals with an inquiring attitude towards their own

practices – in finding their bearings and developing a research consciousness through the execution of their research projects. In taking their first
steps towards the design and operationalization of their studies, they will
need to make a series of informed choices pertaining to a range of research
parameters – regardless of how their research ideas originate. For example,
a given proportion of new scholars to the field of audiovisual translation
studies may follow a 'theory/methodology first' approach, seeking to test
out, (re)interpret or refine theoretical insights and methodological instruments that they have become acquainted with as part of their programme
of study. Other scholars and audiovisual translation professionals grounded
in the context of their everyday practice, however, may intuitively favour
a 'data first' approach. In these cases, their study will be driven by a
desire to reflect critically on translation assumptions, practices and
phenomena; in this second approach, theoretical and methodological
aspects will still play a significant role, although they will initially adopt the
form of intuitive or impressionistic beliefs and constructs shaped by
personal experience.

Conceptualizing, designing and implementing a project for the generation
of new knowledge or, at least, the development of new angles on previously
existing knowledge, involves making decisions on a number of aspects:

- **Data**: to a large extent, the scope of a research project will be determined by the researcher's decision to focus on one or more of the
  audiovisual translation modalities surveyed in Chapter 1; and by the
  body of literature available on the chosen modality of audiovisual
  transfer. It is always possible to shed new light on the study of subtitling
  or dubbing by focusing the research lens on what may have so far been
  peripheral areas of interest – such as the technologization of subtitling,
  or the amateurization of subtitling and dubbing, to give but two
  examples. However, the potential to create new knowledge is greater
  when studying less established forms of intersemiotic mediation, such
  as subtitling for the hard of hearing or audio description, where the
  researcher is bound to find relatively bigger patches of unbroken
  ground. The prevalence of the chosen modality(-ies) of audiovisual
  translation in the source and target contexts is another important data-
  related consideration. Data sets often need to be enlarged or discarded
  during the lifetime of a project, hence the importance of being able to
  tap into alternative data samples if and when required.

- **Researcher's outlook**: after familiarizing themselves with the key issues, debates and new directions in their field, examined in Chapters 2 and 3, scholars and reflective practitioners will need to articulate and ground their research perspective. The interplay between their background as academics or practitioners; their engagement with the dynamics of the media industry beyond the confines of audiovisual translation; and their approach to the study of audiovisual material as an end in itself or a means to interrogate the values inscribed and represented in it will largely determine students' and scholars' areas of interest. For example, they may choose to explore issues of particular relevance to the audiovisual marketplace and the commercial circuitry of audiovisual translation. Alternatively, they may favour a more critical standpoint, questioning dogmatic discourses on best practice that circulate in professional circles and querying the rationale for the standardization of audiovisual mediation practices. Placing themselves in a specific position along the spectrum from corroborative to speculative research, from language-based to more-encompassing multimodal description, from pure to applied inquiry will prompt scholars to align themselves with compatible theoretical frameworks and relevant research methodologies.
- **Research models and methods**: the project's topic and the researcher's position within the field may demand the adoption of comparative, causal or process-based models, as examined in Chapter 4. In turn, the choice of a particular translation model and a specific theoretical framework(s) to structure the research project will normally favour the deployment of one or more research methods, as surveyed in Chapter 5.
- **Practical constraints**: the timescale available for the completion of the study, the word count, expectations and requirements of sponsoring organizations, access to bibliographic and technological resources, and the idiosyncratic research culture of the institution in which the project is embedded are other significant parameters shaping the design and execution of the research.

This chapter is organized in two sections. Section 8.2 provides orientation for those readers embarking on a **theory-driven research project** at postgraduate level. Section 8.3, on the other hand, is aimed at students undertaking **practical dissertations**, i.e. studies typically consisting of an extended translation assignment accompanied by a critical analysis or commentary where reflective translators report on their translation strategy and key micro-textual decisions.

8.2 ORIENTATION FOR THEORY-DRIVEN PROJECTS

Broadly speaking, **theory-driven research projects** aim to tackle an existing gap in knowledge. To demonstrate the viability of their proposed study, scholars will normally put together a research proposal addressing the following aspects:

- Rationale outlining the aims and objectives of the project. The rationale should articulate effectively the reasons why the proposed project has to be carried out, as well as identify who would benefit and how.
- Set of research questions or hypotheses articulating the main focus of the project (e.g. delivering an in-depth description of data, extending a given methodological framework or refining an existing theoretical model). Research questions and hypotheses are crucial in turning he proposed topic into a clearly delimited, worthwhile research proposition.
- Theoretical framework selected to shed light on the translation phenomenon under study. By choosing a theory that is compatible with the process-oriented, comparative or causal focus of the project, scholars are able to tap into a range of conceptual and logical tools to interrogate the primary object of investigation. Justifying the choice of a specific theoretical framework normally involves three steps: delivering an overview of relevant literature to show awareness of the research area; presenting the conceptual framework and main arguments underpinning the theory; critiquing the applicability of the chosen theoretical framework to the study of one's data — thus opening up potential avenues for refinement.
- Research methodology chosen to operationalize and respond to the research questions and engage with the analysis of the data set, the primary material of the project. As shown in Chapter 5, scholars often draw on more than one methodology to address their research questions or test their hypotheses. Apart from general methodological considerations, pertaining to whether a given research topic would benefit from a quantitative or qualitative approach, audiovisual translation projects need to include additional considerations regarding (i) the reproducibility of the data set (is there any potential copyright infringement arising from the amassing or copying of audiovisual

data?); (ii) the manipulability of the data samples (what tools can be used to enhance the editing and analysis of audiovisual data?); (iii) the ethical implications of undertaking the proposed research.
- Statement of data outlining the nature of the material to be examined in the project and the criteria informing the compilation of the data set in some principled way – e.g. in terms of sources, genre, volume, language combination, type period, etc.

The range of theoretical frameworks and research methods available to audiovisual translation scholars has been explored in some depth in Chapters 4 and 5, respectively. Consequently, the remainder of this section focuses on three other areas of research project design: the scope of the project (subsection 8.2.1), the formulation of research questions and hypotheses (subsection 8.2.2), and other AVT-specific methodological considerations (subsection 8.2.3).

8.2.1 The case study method in audiovisual translation research

Although 'other areas of the humanities – perhaps philosophy or theology, for example – may often favour debating conceptual arguments' (Olohan and Baker 2009: 148), data analysis is central to most theoretical research projects on audiovisual translation.

The centrality of data analysis is inextricably intertwined with the popularity of **case study** within audiovisual translation studies. Whether the 'unit of translation activity' at the heart of the research project is the translation strategy behind the production of a given language version of a film, or extends to cover wider socio-economic and political aspects of the receiving culture, case studies assist scholars in determining the scope of and the amount of data required in each research project. Case studies are, in sum, 'the preferred [research] strategy when "how" and "why" questions are being posed, when the investigator has little control over events, and when the focus is on a contemporary phenomenon within some real-life context' (Yin 1994: 1). There are four main approaches to case study research in audiovisual translation studies:

- **Single-case-studies** (Box 8.1) revolve around 'the global aspects of the unit of analysis' and use a 'holistic design' (Susam-Sarajeva 2009: 41).

> **Box 8.1**
>
> *Example of single case study: Ballester (2001)*
>
> - Context of the study: This study examines the reception of American cinema during the formative years of dubbing in Spain (1928–48). During this period, Franco's fascist regime regarded the translation of imported films as a matter of national interest. Censorship boards were set up to shield and protect Spain from 'foreign values': for decades, they interfered in the translation of what they regarded as sensitive films.
> - Case (main unit of analysis): Spanish dubbed version of Rouben Mamoulian's *Blood and Sand* (1941).

- **Embedded case studies** (Box 8.2) do not focus on the unit as a whole but on one or more 'sub-units of analysis' (Susam-Sarajeva 2009).
- **Multiple-case studies** (Box 8.3) scrutinize more than one unit of translation; in other words, they draw on 'multiple holistic cases' (Susam-Sarajeva 2009: 43).
- **Multiple embedded case studies** (Box 8.4) explore several sub-units for each of the units of translation included in the project.

Embedded case studies often call for the deployment of different research methodologies to study the various sub-units under scrutiny. But while a number of advantages can be derived from the use of a multi-method approach (Yin 1994: 41–42), insights yielded by the different strands of data must be always brought to bear on the study of the main case(s).

> **Box 8.2**
>
> *Example of embedded case study: Fuentes Luque (2000)*
>
> - Context of the study: This project focuses on the reception of humour in the context of translated films, placing particular emphasis on the intercultural dimension of the humour production-reception process.
> - Case (main unit of analysis): Marx brothers' *Duck Soup* (1933).
> - Embedded sub-units: Spanish dubbed and subtitled versions of the Marx brothers' film.

Box 8.3

Example of multiple case study: Asimakoulas (2004)

- Context of the study: Drawing on Attardo's script theory of humour, this study examines how humorous sequences and inventive puns used in American films are subtitled into Greek. Asimakoulas aims to gain a better understanding of how humour, a culture- and language-specific communicative phenomenon, is transferred across linguacultures.
- Case 1 (unit of analysis): Greek subtitled version of David Zucker's and Jim Abrahams' *Airplane!* (1980).
- Case 2 (unit of analysis): Greek subtitled version of David Zucker's *The Naked Gun: From the Files of the Police Squad* (1988).

Box 8.4

Example of multiple embedded case study: Morris (2009)

- Context of the study: Morris explores how subtitlers overcome the multiple cultural barriers they find when translating 'heritage films'. Morris hypothesizes that the abundant cultural and historical references featuring in these films will have to be explained to the target language viewer. To establish whether these 'inherently cultural texts' call for genre-specific mediation strategies, the author looks at the subtitled versions of both Spanish and French Heritage films.
- Case 1 (unit of analysis): The subtitling of Spanish Heritage cinema
- Case 2 (unit of analysis): The subtitling of French Heritage cinema
- Embedded sub-units: Subtitled versions of *Ay, Carmela!* (1990), *Cyrano de Bergerac* (1990), *Belle Époque* (1992), *La Reine Margot* (1994), *Ridicule* (1996), *La Lengua de las Mariposas (1999)*.

Ultimately, it is through the formulation of precise research questions that a successful 'delimitation of the main unit of analysis, i.e. the case, the content and the sub-units' can be achieved (Susam-Sarajeva 2009: 42).

8.2.2 Research questions and hypotheses in audiovisual translation research

Research questions provide the impetus for scholars to explore and analyse their data in a systematic and focused manner. Generally speaking, the set of research questions at the centre of a given study – often consisting of a broad research question and a number of specific sub-questions – should provide a good indication of 'what' students or scholars are investigating, 'why' it is worth doing so and 'how' they intend to go about it. In practice, however, research projects tend to prioritize one of these aspects over the others. As Olohan and Baker (2009) explain, refining a previously existing methodology may take precedence over the elaboration of a 'novel' theoretical model, or vice versa:

> by 'novel' here we do not mean a completely new theoretical model . . . Rather, what we mean is that some doctoral students specifically set out to modify an existing theoretical model, for example by addressing a perceived lack of coherence in some part of the model, by extending the model to accommodate new and/or more challenging types of data, or by enriching it in more detail. The latter might include replacing broad or crude categories with more nuanced ones.
>
> (ibid.: 149)

For example, the set of research questions listed in Box 8.5 (Al-Adwan 2009) elaborates core aspects of Brown and Levinson's (1987) politeness theory, a framework originally built around the key notion of face management. Brown and Levinson's concept of euphemization, theorized as a 'negative politeness' and 'off-record' face management strategy, is modified and extended here to elucidate whether it can be productively applied to the study of subtitled sitcoms. Drawing on the Arabic subtitled version of selected episodes of *Friends* (1994–2004), Al-Adwan examines how the subtitler mediates scenes that are potentially face-threatening (offensive) to an Arab audience. His enhanced theoretical model allows Al-Adwan to identify those issues and themes that are most commonly euphemized in the Arabic version of *Friends* (including, but not limited to, sex, death, disease and bodily functions), and to put forward a systematic classification of euphemization strategies used in his data set. In Al-Adwan's study, the choice of a highly successful sitcom is secondary to the main theory-driven focus. But while the actual analysis of the chosen data is not meant to be the main contribution of this study, it provides a productive testing ground for the theoretical enhancements that Al-Adwan proposes. As Box 8.5 shows, the extension of the concept of euphemization and its scope of application to account for audiovisual transfers across two specific *linguacultures* is signalled in the wording of the research questions.

Box 8.5

Research questions focusing on the elaboration of a theoretical model (Al-Adwan 2009: 27–28)

To what extent can Brown and Levinson's theory of politeness explain the use of euphemization as a translation strategy in the Arabic subtitles of *Friends*?

- How adequately does Brown and Levinson's theory treat euphemism as a politeness strategy?
- Can a robust model of euphemization as a politeness strategy be elaborated within the overall context of politeness theory?
- What topics tend to trigger instances of euphemization in the Arabic subtitles?
- What strategies of euphemization can be identified in the Arabic version of *Friends*?

In other cases, however, the research questions reflect the researcher's attempt to develop a novel methodological approach. Take, for instance, Li's (2014) study of the role that a specific fansubbing community plays in developing participatory subtitling practices in China (Box 8.6). In this

Box 8.6

Research questions focusing on the elaboration of a methodological approach (Li 2014)

What is the role played by amateur translation, as exemplified by fansubbing online communities organized by Chinese media fans, in the development of a participatory culture in China?

- How does the fansubbing group in this study apply digital networked technologies to set up its online platform to facilitate group activities towards its goals?
- What are the social dynamics operating within the fansubbing group?
- How do members in the fansubbing group make use of technologies to create media texts to express themselves and communicate with each other?
- Does the use of digital networked technologies to realize members' shared interests and goals towards creative media consumption facilitate a sense of collectiveness, if so, what does it mean for them within the social context of China?

project, the overarching research question is operationalized as follows: different research methods are used to investigate each organizational dimension of Li's chosen fansubbing community, as reflected in the wording of the research sub-questions. To investigate how the community's online platform facilitates the group's activities, Li draws on a netnographic approach (see Section 5.3.3). Through her participation in the work of the community, Li examines whether and how the structure of the group's platform favours participation, allows for (a)synchronous communication between group members, or facilitates the appraisal of fans' competence to undertake certain roles (sub-question 1). A qualitative analysis of the roles adopted by group members, involving the coding of their contributions to the group's online forums, is the basis for Li's study of the social dynamics at play in this instance of computer-mediated communication (sub-question 2). Li's insight that fans engage in subtitling activities to negotiate a sense of collective affectivity is explored by encoding and analysing the interpretative modes that members adopt when consuming subtitled media content (sub-question 3). Finally, a questionnaire is used to establish whether and how fans align themselves with the group's collective identity and values against the backdrop of the wider media landscape in China (sub-question 4). Overall, methodological considerations are foregrounded as the main contribution of Li's thesis.

Although both Al-Adwan's (2009) and Li's (2014) projects rely on open research questions, there are other options available to researchers. Of particular note are **hypotheses**, i.e. 'testable assertions about a relationship or relationships between two or more concepts' (Matthews and Ross 2010: 58, emphasis in the original). Hypotheses have been used in a range of experimental studies on audiovisual translation, e.g. Caffrey (2009). As discussed in Section 5.3.2, Caffrey investigated whether and how the use of pop-up glosses relating to culturally marked visual nonverbal cues (CVNCs) found in selected excerpts of anime material interfered with viewers' comprehension of the material. That interference was measured by the number of participants' correct responses to a series of questions about the meaning of the CVNCs and the subtitles featuring in the selected excerpts. The set of hypotheses tested by Caffrey are listed and glossed in Box 8.7.

To formulate sound research hypotheses, it is important to identify appropriate variables of analysis and rigorous measurement tools, including statistical tests – hence the prevalence of hypotheses in experimental

---

Box 8.7

Caffrey's (2009) hypotheses

H1: Mean correct answers to CVNC question$_{abusive}$ > Mean correct answers to CVNC question$_{corrupt}$

Subjects watching CVNCs with pop-up glosses ('abusive version', see Box 3.4) will understand the excerpts better that those watching the excerpt without glosses ('corrupt version'). When asked to complete a questionnaire on their understanding of CVNCs, the former group will obtain more correct answers.

H2: Mean declared understanding of CVNC$_{abusive}$ > Mean declared understanding of CVNC$_{corrupt}$

Subjects watching clips with pop-up glosses (abusive version) will be more confident about the accuracy of the information they gather from the excerpt. Consequently, a higher number of subjects watching the abusive version will 'declare' that they have understood the CVNCs.

H3: Mean correct answers to subtitle question$_{abusive}$ > Mean correct answers to subtitle question$_{corrupt}$

The use of pop-up gloss will distract attention from the subtitles. As a result, subjects watching clips without pop-up glosses (corrupt version) will obtain more correct answers to questions about the content of subtitles.

H4: Mean declared fast$_{abusive}$ > Mean declared fast$_{corrupt}$

Viewing watching excerpts without glosses (corrupt version) requires more processing effort. As a result, more of these subjects will experience the subtitle speed as being fast or too fast to read.

---

quantitative research (Kalaian and Kasim 2008). Open research questions, on the other hand, are preferred in qualitative studies, as they allow students 'scope for interrogating the data from several perspectives and engaging with a range of potentially complex findings that cannot be reduced to the terms of a tightly worded hypothesis' (Olohan and Baker 2009: 152).

8.2.3 Other AVT-specific methodological considerations

Chapter 6 has explored in depth the difficulty inherent in studying meaning-making elements that are encoded in different modes. Indeed, conducting audiovisual translation research often involves scrutinizing *some* of the semiotic resources at play in a given multimodal text (e.g. music and language), rather than the *whole* filmic assemblage. For this reason, it is important for students and scholars to be familiar with the use of tools that may assist with the dissection of the processes enabling the 'holistic gestalt-perception' of audiovisual texts (Stöckl 2004: 17).

Multimodal transcriptions were first developed by Paul Thibault (2000) as a means to gauge the specific contribution of each mode to those multi-modal constellations that we refer to as audiovisual texts, and to gain a better understanding of the inter-modal relations within the texts in question. Conventionally presented in tabular form, multimodal transcriptions entail the segmentation of audiovisual texts into their smallest syntactical units, i.e. visual frames (Table 8.1). The selection of the frames included in the left-most column of the transcription is informed by the organization of the film into shots, phases and sub-phases 'within which various semi-otic modalities are seen to function together as a set before giving way to a new set of modalities' (Taylor 2003: 192). If the issues under scrutiny straddle the boundaries between phases, visual frames from each of these phases will need to be included in the multimodal transcription. Ordered chronologically from top to bottom, this series of visual frames effectively provides an abridged visual synopsis of the action.

Each column of the transcription delivers a coded analysis of the film director's semiotic choices in each of the selected frames. The third column from the right describes different elements of the visual image, including the camera position (CP), the visual distance of the shot (D), the visual focus (VF), or instances of visual collocation (VC) – all of which convey meaning from a multimodal theoretic perspective. In successive columns, we find descriptions of the actors' kinesic action (second column from the right), and a record of the complete soundtrack of the film – including speech, music and other sounds (right-most column). The number and ordering of the columns included in the transcription, the range of modes and sub-modes covered in the analysis, and the set of notation conventions used for coding purposes depend on the specific needs of the individual project.

Although they were originally created to investigate multimodal texts (Baldry and Thibault 2006), multimodal transcriptions are becoming increasingly used to study the translation of such texts. Chris Taylor (2003), for example, has relied on this type of transcription to sensitize translation students to the particular demands of multimodal translation. He envisages that, by exposing students to multimodal transcriptions, they will be able to grasp the contribution of each mode to the overall

Table 8.1 Multimodal transcription sample (Desilla 2012: 37)

Frame No.	Time	Frame	Visual image	Kinesic action	Soundtrack
1	00:01:03		CP: stationary D: MCS VC: coffee bar VF: Pam looks at Bridget, Bridget's gaze is disengaged, Colin looks towards the counter	[Colin turns towards the bar, Pam turns to Bridget]	FIELD SI chatter, ☼ coffee bar noise FIGURE: Pam: *Ridiculous! Your motto must be: 'Don't let him pop it in . . .'* f, smooth, tense, high pitch
2	00:01:06		CP: zooming in D: MCS VC: as above VF: Pam looks at her finger, Bridget's gaze is disengaged	[Pam makes as if she puts a ring on her finger, Bridget presses her lips tight together]	FIELD SI chatter, ☼ coffee bar noise FIGURE: Pam: *'. . . until he's popped it on.'* n, smooth, tense, high pitch, unwavering, M

semiotic ensemble on a case-by-case basis. The **intersemiotic cohesion** (Chaume Varela 2004, Díaz Cintas and Remael 2007) that holds between subtitles and other non-verbal modes dictates that subtitlers need not include in the subtitle semiotic information that is already conveyed through the visuals; consequently, novice subtitlers should learn to make 'reasoned choices in translating the verbal element of the text' (ibid.: 192). The intersemiotic cohesion principle is also at the heart of other pedagogical initiatives based on the use of multimodal concordances. Lúcia Santiago Araújo and Magalhães (2009), for example, have drawn on the affordances of Adobe Creative Suite 4 (a software application that automatically divides footage into frames) to create multimodal concordances of selected video excerpts. Concordances are then analysed and used by trainee translators as blueprints for the development of audio descriptions.

Beyond the confines of audiovisual translator training, Desilla (2009, 2012) has used multimodal transcriptions to explore how **implicatures** evoked by the original film dialogue are mediated by subtitlers. Specifically, she examines whether, in those cases where subtitlers have failed to spell out the implicatures, whether deliberately or inadvertently, target language viewers are able to infer the implied meaning with the aid of the visual and acoustic resources deployed at that particular point of the film. Similarly, Mubenga (2009) uses a simplified version of multimodal transcriptions to gauge the impact of non-verbal semiotic modes on the subtitling of speech acts.

The analysis of audiovisual data can also benefit from the application of other software applications. **NVivo**,[1] for example, assists scholars with the organization and analysis of data held in a range of formats, including audio and video files. Once a given file has been imported into the NVivo interface, it is possible to organize, classify and code audiovisual material in different ways. It is possible to annotate content and insert links to other parts of the same project or to other files stored outside NVivo. As far as the actual manipulation of audiovisual files is concerned, this software application allows for the importing of existing transcripts of speech used in combination with non-verbal semiotics. By clicking on a given line of their transcript, analysts have immediate access to the section of the video that it relates to. Alternatively, users of NVivo can also opt to watch the transcript scroll in synchronization with the audiovisual text under scrutiny. More significantly, researchers using this tool are able to interrogate their data set using a range of query functions and to visualize the results of their investigation in a number of static and dynamic patterns, including word clouds, tree maps and word trees. Given the versatility of this tool, it is bound to be particularly useful in projects involving the deployment of different research methods (e.g. Li 2014), where there is an obvious need for cross-checking various sets of results.

Using multimodal concordances, multimodal corpora (Section 5.3.4) or other electronic platforms (e.g. NVivo) to analyse audiovisual data involves copying, digitizing and/or editing audiovisual material. While these processes are becoming ever easier to execute in the era of the digital culture, they are restricted by copyright and researchers should, in principle, obtain clearance from the copyright holder before using them. In the UK, however, there are some exemptions or **copyright exceptions** that

> fall within the scope of 'fair dealing'. Material reproduced for the purposes of non-commercial research or private study, for criticism or review or for the reporting of current events is included in this group. If material is reproduced for these purposes, provided it is genuinely and fairly used for the stated purpose, and is accompanied by a sufficient acknowledgement, it may be considered fair dealing and thus exempt from clearance. However, the test is subjective and will depend on the circumstances of each case.
>
> (Copyright Licensing Agency website)[2]

It is unclear what falls within the scope of fair dealing for criticism or review. As the UK's Intellectual Property Office acknowledges, what this means 'has been interpreted by the courts on a number of occasions by looking at the economic impact on the copyright owner of the use. Where the economic impact is not significant, the use may count as fair dealing'.[3] The complexity derived from the lack of clarity on 'fair dealing' is compounded by other issues, including (i) the similarities and differences between 'fair dealing' and other notions used outside the UK, such as 'fair use' in the US (Band and Gerafi 2013); (ii) the fact that researchers in our field often work on translated material, and it is often difficult to establish who holds copyright for the translated version. As far as audiovisual material is concerned, researchers may face additional hurdles to obtain clearance when the copyright is simultaneously held by different studios, actors and/or the latter's agents or estates.

In view of the regulations outlined above, extracting a number of frames from selected scenes of a film to produce a multimodal concordance of those excerpts may be interpreted to be within the scope of the fair dealing exception, as long as the images in question are not viewed or shared outside the context of the concordance. Obviously, consent should be secured before extended fragments of a film are added to a database or computer-held corpus of audiovisual material. Leaving these AVT-specific considerations aside, recommendations by translation scholars on how to obtain copyright permissions also apply in our field. Olohan (2004: 51), for example, notes that

> [w]hen asking for permission to use texts [as part of a computer-held corpus], it is essential to stress that they will be used for research purposes only, and to specify what other researchers will have access to (e.g. concordances but not the files themselves) and the degree of accessibility that other researchers may have, ranging from on-site access where the corpus is held to worldwide, unlimited access via the web.

Obtaining copyright permissions is not the only ethical consideration when investigating audiovisual translation phenomena. Much research is, by definition, an intrusive activity – whether it involves assessing the quality of the translation produced by an individual or a group of professionals, observing patterns of computer-mediated communication in an online network of amateur subtitlers, or monitoring the visual behaviour of viewers using eye-tracking technology, to give but a few examples. As a result, most UK institutions have developed procedures prompting postgraduate students and researchers to give serious consideration to the **ethical issues** that may arise when their work draws on/engages with humans and human-related data. The University of Manchester's *Code of Good Research Conduct*, for example, states that

> [a]ll projects conducted by University staff or students that involve human participants in a way that might harm, disturb or upset them (however slight the possibility) or where they can be deemed to be in a vulnerable or disadvantageous situation, must receive approval from a recognized research ethics committee.

Applying for ethical approval is thus becoming an increasingly common step in the execution of audiovisual translation research projects. Broadly speaking, research ethics committees will seek to establish whether the proposed project adheres to five basic principles:

- **Autonomy**: Will prospective participants in the study take part without coercion? Has the researcher made provisions to inform participants that they are free to withdraw at any time without having to justify their decision?
- **Non-maleficence**: Has the researcher taken robust precautions to avoid or mitigate any possible harm to participants?
- **Beneficence**: Are the aims of the proposed research worthwhile? Is the project likely to yield meaningful results? Will the potentially beneficial effects outweigh any risks involved in the study?
- **Integrity**: Is there sufficient evidence that the researcher will be open about any gains derived from the research?
- **Confidentiality**: Does the proposed project address the participant's right to anonymity? Has the researcher put in place mechanisms to ensure that participants' personal data and other confidential information derived from their participation in the project are adequately protected (unless the participants agree otherwise)?

For example, some institutions may find that research projects on activist subtitling communities operating in certain socio-political contexts may raise issues of risk for participants in the study. Similarly, institutional research ethics committees may have reservations about authorizing certain types of research on fansubbing networks, technically regarded as an illegal activity. Depending on the approval procedures in place in each institution, the researcher may be able to allay the committee's concerns in different ways. For example, they could secure ethical approval by showing they have made provisions to remove any record of the identities of participants responding to their online survey after the initial contact. By doing so, they would safeguard against having to release potentially sensitive information about participants to the authorities, or being drawn into criminal proceedings due to their indirect involvement with sensitive or illegal practices. Giving the committee members' assurances that they will use encryption to protect the security of data stored in institutional or personal computers will reinforce their commitment to the viability of their research project.

8.3 ORIENTATION FOR PRACTICAL DISSERTATIONS

Most UK universities allow students to write MA practical dissertations consisting of an extended audiovisual translation (e.g. a subtitling project) accompanied by a **critical analysis** or **commentary** – i.e. a theoretically informed and evidence-based reflection on the student's own translation.[4] If, as is often the case, students are allowed to choose a film, drama episode or documentary, they may be asked to opt for a text that has not yet been translated into the relevant target language. Also, they will normally be authorized to work with previously translated audiovisual texts, provided that they can put forward a convincing case for the production of yet another translation. On the other hand, in choosing a source text, students should ensure that the material allows for the discussion of one or several prominent themes as part of their critical analysis. In other words, their chosen text should feature elements that can be described and discussed productively from a translational perspective.

Of particular importance for the success of the project is the quality of the **translation brief**. Students will normally be encouraged to formulate a real or hypothetical translation situation and translation commission that fits the task they wish to undertake and is likely to influence their global and local translation strategies (see Boxes 8.8 and 8.9). The brief – which should be plausible and described precisely, whether it is real or imaginary – can be referred to in the discussion of translation choices when writing the

---

Box 8.8

Krawanja's (2009: 7–9) hypothetical brief for the production of a subtitled version of *The Royle Family* (1998–) in German (abridged):

The Austrian Broadcasting Cooperation ORF intends to broadcast the first three seasons of *The Royle Family* (all 18 episodes, each with a running time of 28 minutes) within its well-established Donnerstag Nacht ('Thursday Night') slot and has commissioned me to produce the first subtitled version in German.

Each edition of Donnerstag Nacht typically involves the broadcasting of a subtitled episode of a foreign series (predominantly from English-speaking countries). Although foreign TV series are usually dubbed in Austria, subtitled versions are often shown at off-peak times within arts programmes, such as Donnerstag Nacht.

This programme is geared at a young, well-educated audience, with a relatively good command of English, and hence willing to be exposed to foreign cultures. To some extent, the audience's expectations are comparable with those of anime fans who wish to access and become immersed in the unique imagery and connotational value of genre-specific cultural references.

Box 8.9

Piñero's (2010: 12–14) hypothetical brief for the production of a dubbed version of *The Inbetweeners* (2008–10) in Spanish (abridged):

> Following the commercial success of its first two seasons in the UK and the production and subsequent launch of a third season, award-winning comedy *The Inbetweeners* is set to be broadcast in Spain. The commissioner, Bwark Productions, is welcoming applications for a pilot dubbed episode of the series ('The Field Trip') in European Spanish, which might be broadcast by Spanish channel Cuatro.
>
> Cuatro is a private channel owned by Sogecable S.A. A leading pay television corporation in Spain and the third largest in Europe, Sogecable has pioneered the provision of digital, high definition and interactive television programmes in Spain. Cuatro describes itself as a 'young and new television channel whose bold, modern and diverse vision has contributed to enriching Spain's media marketplace'; it also presents itself as an 'ambitious alternative to current television with its original and occasionally risqué content'.
>
> With its culture-specific manifestations of humour comprised of foul language, and potentially offensive sexual references, *The Inbetweeners* neatly illustrates Cuatro's philosophy. The intended function of the TT is to offer its target audience an engaging, humorous foreign series that serves as an alternative to the standard viewer experience provided by costly mainstream American drama.

---

critical analysis. General considerations on the real/hypothetical translation brief may include the following:

- Who is commissioning the translation?
- Where/how will the translation be shown/broadcast?
- What special characteristics will the translation have (not only in terms of specialization and language, but also considering, for example, the layout and appearance of subtitles)?
- What function will the translation have?
- What kinds of features in the translation are required to help fulfil this function?
- What is the intended audience of the translation?

Before they begin working on their practical dissertations, students will normally have to submit a dissertation proposal. Tutors' feedback on dissertation proposals will address a number of key aspects:

- the overall **coherence** of the project design: Is the translation commission clear and plausible? Could the student be commissioned in real life to carry it out in this way?
- the **feasibility** of the proposed project: Will the student be able to complete the extended translation and critical analysis within the time frame proposed?
- the **credibility** of the proposed project: How well equipped is the student to carry out the project, both in terms of practical skills and of familiarity with relevant professional and academic literature? How much awareness does the student show of potential challenges or the difficulties that may arise during the execution of the project?

With an average word count between 7,000 and 10,000 words, critical analyses or commentaries normally consist of up to four sections. The introduction typically provides background information on the source material, including the title of the chosen film/series episode/documentary and the genre it belongs to; an overview of any distinctive characteristics and its intended function in the source culture; and an explanation of the role that verbal and non-verbal modes play to fulfil the said function. The introductory section is often followed by an account of the real/hypothetical translation brief for the project, and an overview of how the remainder of the critical analysis is organized.

The central section may consist of one or two chapters, each addressing one of the themes selected for analysis. Within each of these areas of focus (e.g. dialect or humour in subtitling), students will be expected to define the phenomenon under scrutiny and review previous work in the area, taking care to draw on relevant theoretical concepts. Once the relevant issues have been categorized and described, a range of examples should be discussed, using back-translations if/when appropriate.

The final section of the critical analysis, i.e. the conclusion, should provide evidence of the student's capacity for complex, original and relevant reflection on their own practice. The conclusion should also demonstrate that both the translation and reflection that accompanies it have considerably enhanced the student's critical understanding of professional practices in the field of audiovisual translation. Ultimately, this enhanced awareness of key issues in their chosen field of specialization will enable audiovisual translation students to confidently articulate professional strategies to translation difficulties as they arise.

NOTES

1   There are abundant online resources available to users interested in learning more about the affordances and features of NVivo, including printed guides (http://download.qsrinternational.com/Document/NVivo10/NVivo10-Getting-Started-Guide.pdf) and video tutorials (such as the dedicated YouTube playlist available at www.youtube.com/playlist?list=PL68DA95F8E2B15DD4). Both links were last accessed on 15 September 2013.

2   Further information is available at www.cla.co.uk/copyright_information/copyright_information (last accessed on 15 September 2013).

3   See www.ipo.gov.uk/types/copy/c-other/c-exception/c-exception-review/c-exception-fairdealing.htm (last accessed on 15 September 2013).

4   Much of the orientation delivered here is based on the dissertation guidelines issued by the Centre for Translation and Intercultural Studies, at The University of Manchester (UK).

CORE REFERENCES

Munday, Jeremy (2012) *Introducing Translation Studies*, 3rd edition, London and New York: Routledge (Chapter 12: Research and commentary projects).

Saldanha, Gabriela and Sharon O'Brien (2013) *Research Methodologies in Translation Studies*, Manchester: St Jerome.

Susam-Sarajeva, Sebnem (2009) 'The Case Study Research Method in Translation Studies', in Ian Mason (ed.) *Training for Doctoral Research*, special issue of *The Interpreter and Translator Trainer* 3(1): 37–56.

Williams, Jenny and Andrew Chesterman (2002) *The Map: A Beginner's Guide to Doing Research in Translation Studies*, Manchester: St Jerome.

Glossary

Note: This glossary contains only those terms that are either not accompanied by an explicit definition in the body of the book, or that pertain to the conceptual domain of film or media studies.

Words featuring in block letters in the body of a definition have their own entry in the glossary.

abusive subtitling: According to Nornes (1999, 2007), fansubbing is an abusive form of mediation. To resist the industry's demand for condensation and simplification of the original text, abusive subtitling deploys a range of experimental mediation practices. Although this may provide a more authentic experience of the source culture, it requires a bigger effort from audiences (cf. CORRUPT SUBTITLING).

academization: The process leading to the establishment and consolidation of audiovisual translation as a scholarly discipline.

adaptive dubbing: A variety of dubbing aiming at total domestication, occasionally involving the editing and reassembly of the non-verbal semiotic components of an audiovisual text.

aesthetic activism: In this book, the term designates a form of participatory, often interventionist, audiovisual translation that sets out to resist mainstream cultural and representation practices (e.g. fansubbing).

aesthetic subtitling: A form of AESTHETIC ACTIVISM.

aggregation site: An online environment that provides media consumers with direct access to torrent tracker engines and facilitates the rapid downloading of audiovisual content.

allochthonous model of translation: In the context of this book, this term refers to any THEORETICAL MODEL used to study audiovisual translation that has been imported from the wider field of translation studies and beyond (cf. AUTOCTHONOUS MODEL OF TRANSLATION).

assemblage: In multimodal theory, it designates the combination of different SCAPES or MODES.

autocthonous model of translation: In the context of this book, this term denotes any THEORETICAL MODEL used to study audiovisual translation that has been developed from within the domain of audiovisual translation studies (cf. ALLOCHTHONOUS MODEL OF TRANSLATION).

annotation: The process whereby consumers of media content in the era of the digital culture subtitle or incorporate other textual elements to the material they have APPROPRIATED, often with a view to RECIRCULATE it through video-sharing platforms.

appropriation (in reference to audiovisual material): The downloading of digital content for the purposes of ANNOTATING or editing it in a more comprehensive fashion, often followed by the RECIRCULATION of the appropriated material.

archiving: A specific form of RECIRCULATION, whereby media content is shared through an individual's or a group's main server or dedicated media player.

asynchronous consumption: Watching media content at a time chosen by the viewer (not while the film or series episode is being broadcast).

bricolage: The process of editing media content, by disassembling and re-assembling it in a different manner, often with a view to RECIRCULATE that material through video-sharing platforms.

cartelization: The grouping of European film companies into partnerships with a view to controlling the international distribution of their own films outside their borders as well as the inflow of films from other countries/companies to their own markets.

collective intelligence: In this book, this term designates the pool of linguistic or technological skills shared by networked communities involved in participatory practices of audiovisual translation.

commodification: The process whereby films, originally conceived as art works, become marketable products amenable to commercial exchange.

concretization: Each of the features through which culture systems, as conceptualized by Floros (2003), are realized (cf. HOLON).

convergence: Jenkins defines it as 'the flow of content across multiple media platforms, the cooperation between multiple media industries, and the migratory behavior of media audiences who would go almost anywhere in search of the kinds of entertainment experiences they wanted' (http://henryjenkins.org/).

co-creation: The involvement of media content consumers in the production and RECIRCULATION of audiovisual material for the enjoyment of fellow consumers.

corrupt subtitling: According to Nornes (1999, 2007), commercial subtitling is corrupt. By adhering to the industry's demand for condensation and simplification of the original text in different ways, commercial subtitling contributes to the commodification of subtitling and hampers viewers' experience of otherness (cf. ABUSIVE SUBTITLING).

crowdsourcing: In the context of this book, this term designates the outsourcing of an audiovisual translation job, traditionally performed by professionals, to an undefined, often large group of individuals in the form of an open call.

curation platform: Interactive online environments, such as wikis, where consumers discuss and review media content for the benefit of other potential consumers.

cyberculture: In the context of this book, this term denotes a culture that has emerged through, and been shaped by, advances in digital communication technology.

democratization of technology: Together with the TECHNOLOGIZATION OF DEMOCRACY, this is one of the two major contexts of cultural production shaped by the interplay between technology and democracy, as theorized by Foucault (1982). In the context of this book, this term refers to the involvement of ordinary citizens in amateur audiovisual translation as a form of cultural resistance, choosing their own technological tools and mediation conventions.

dependency theories (in reference to CO-CREATION): Theories that regard the involvement of ordinary media consumers in amateur co-creative practices as a form of exploitation by neo-liberal economic forces.

development theories (in reference to CO-CREATION): Theories that regard the involvement of ordinary media consumers in amateur co-creative practices as an empowering and democratizing phenomenon.

diegesis: A REPRESENTATIONAL mode that presents film characters as inhabiting their own fictional world, different from that of the audience.

diegetic film: Capitalizing on the advent of editing techniques, diegetic films construct linear narratives – thus avoiding the overlapping of action and the instances of temporal repetition that marred earlier 'single image' films.

dubbese: A derogatory term designating a linguistic variety developed for and used by characters in a dubbed film or TV series.

genre knowledge: The expertise that individuals gain through their involvement in participatory networks of amateur subtitling, both about the conventions of their favourite audiovisual genres and the expectations of fellow fans or network members.

doubling: An intralingual variety of dubbing, whereby the original dialogue is revoiced into the same language to improve the quality of outdoor recordings.

fansubbing: A form of participatory subtitling by fan networks with a particular interest in a given audiovisual genre, a specific television series, etc.

fandubbing: A form of participatory dubbing by fan networks with a particular interest in a given audiovisual genre, a specific television series, etc.

figure: In cognitive research, this term designates objects that are perceived as salient against its less salient counterparts (cf. GROUND).

genetic criticism: A strand of archival research where researchers are able to gain a better understanding of how a text came to be the way it currently is.

gestalt perception: Holistic processing of a visually complex object – as opposed to the successive processing of each of its individual constituents.

ground: In cognitive research, this term refers to elements of a scene that are perceived as less salient than their more prominent counterparts (cf. FIGURE).

headnotes: Snippets of text superimposed on the visuals to be read at the same time as traditional subtitles. Headnotes commonly feature at the top of the frame. Used normally in fansubbed material, headnotes are a prominent feature of CORRUPT SUBTITLING.

holon: A set of interrelated CONCRETIZATIONS through which culture systems, as conceptualized by Floros (2003), are realized.

hypersociability: In Deuze's (2006: 12) work, this term designates the process whereby individuals or networked communities build collective structures 'from the bottom up'.

idiographic interpretation: Approach to the study of social life that focuses on individual cases or events.

institutionalization: The embedding (of audiovisual translation) within universities, through the design and running of specialized degree programmes.

interpersonal pragmatics: The strand of pragmatics that studies communication between identified people, i.e. those who have picked each other out as co-interactants, whether in real or fictional encounters.

intersemiotic assistive mediation: A range of audiovisual translation modalities aimed at sensory impaired audiences, e.g. audio description and subtitling for the hard of hearing, including respeaking. These modalities of audiovisual translation transfer meaning across semiotic modes (from images to spoken languages, from speech to written language, etc.)

iterative consumption: Watching media content on more than one occasion.

landmark: A synonym of GROUND in cognitive theory.

linear models of communication: Traditional form of organization of the mass media industry, prior to the advent of digital communication technologies, under which viewers were unable to choose what to watch or when to watch media content.

living subtitle: A term proposed by Curti (2009) to articulate an alternative description of subtitles as a dynamic affective force within film semiotics.

media: The material means (e.g. screens and loudspeakers) required for semiotic resources used in MULTIMODAL texts to reach viewers' senses (cf. MODE).

mode: Each type of acoustic and optic semiotic sign involved in the creation of MULTIMODAL texts. Modes are also referred to in the literature as 'modality' (cf. MEDIA).

multilingual filming method: The production of several language versions of the same filmic narrative using different or multilingual casts.

multimediality: The combination of different MEDIA required for audio-visual texts to reach viewers' senses (cf. MULTIMODALITY).

multimodality: The combination of speaking, writing, visualization and music in a range of texts, including audiovisual ones (cf. MULTIMEDIALITY).

narrative location: In narrative theory, this term designates people's outlook on the world, as shaped by the narratives that circulate in their environment.

netnography: The study of CYBERCULTURES or networked communities through the online observation of the interaction between community members.

non-linear models of communication: A new form of organization of the mass media industry brought about by digital technologies, allowing for the ASYNCHRONOUS and ITERATIVE consumption of media content. Non-linear structures give audiences more power as to what to watch and when to watch it.

point-of-view shot: A shot that is meant to be seen from the point of view of a character within the scene.

political activism: In this book, the term designates a form of participatory, often interventionist, audiovisual translation that is intended as a form of resistance against global political and capitalist structures.

political subtitling: A form of POLITICAL ACTIVISM.

pop-up gloss: Sub-type of HEADNOTE.

presentationalism: The dominant REPRESENTATIONAL mode in the early stages in the history of cinema, involving the production of 'diagrammatic' abstractions of the real world – rather than realistic imitations.

rack focus: A shift of focus from a film's foreground to background or vice versa.

recirculation: Sharing media content by uploading the material to social networking sites, often after having ANNOTATED the original material.

reconstitution: In Deuze's (2006) work, this term designates the process whereby individuals or networked communities are able to process, engage with and 'make sense' of the digital media content circulating in their environment.

remediation: As used by Deuze (2006), remediation designates the process whereby old media content is combined with new material, including subtitles or a dubbed soundtrack, often with a view to RECIRCULATE it through video-sharing platforms.

re-narrativization: In the field of audio description, this term designates the process whereby a narrator verbalizes information conveyed through the film visuals, foregrounding narratively relevant information as s/he goes along.

representational practices: They contribute to the construction of selected aspects of reality – including ethnicity, nationhood, social class, gender, etc. – through films or other audiovisual narratives.

research method: As defined by Chesterman (2000: 16), it is a strategy for the collection of evidence in order to test a theory and/or interrogate a data set.

scape: Curti (2009) uses this term as a synonym of MODE.

self-mediation: The involvement of ordinary people in public culture through the APPROPRIATION, REMEDIATION and RECIRCULATION of media content and experiences.

spatial displacement: The RECIRCULATION of media flows, often by networked communities of media co-creators, outside the commercial circuits within which they were originally released.

spatializ(-e) (-ation): Adjustment of the volume of actors' voices on the basis of their relative position in the scene vis-à-vis that of the viewer.

synchronous diegetic sound: The delivery of film dialogue in a way that fully matches lip movements or sung vocals of actors on screen.

technologization of democracy: Together with the DEMOCRATIZATION OF TECHNOLOGY, this is one of the two major contexts of cultural production shaped by the interplay between technology and democratization, as theorized by Foucault (1982). In the context of this book, the term designates the phenomenon whereby ordinary citizens are provided with technological tools to carry out amateur audiovisual translation and adhere to the guidelines and restrictions imposed by the 'enabling' organizations.

telos: In systemic-functional linguistics, this is the organizing, completion-oriented principle of conversational encounters.

trajector: A synonym of FIGURE in cognitive theory.

translation model: Defined by Chesterman (2000: 15) as a 'preliminary, theoretical way of representing the object of research' (cf. TRANSLATION THEORY).

translation theory: Defined by Chesterman (2000: 15) as a 'set of concepts and statements (claims, hypothesis) that provides a systemic perspective on something, a perspective that allows us to understand it in some way, and hence perhaps to explain it' (cf. TRANSLATION MODEL).

Filmography

12 Angry Men (1957) Sidney Lumet. IMDb entry: www.imdb.com/title/tt0050083/

28 Days Later (2002) Danny Boyle. IMDb entry: www.imdb.com/title/tt0289043/

A Clockwork Orange (2005) Stanley Kubrick. IMDb entry: www.imdb.com/title/tt0066921/

Airplane! (1980) David Zucker and Jim Abrahams. IMDb entry: www.imdb.com/title/tt0080339/?ref_=nv_sr_1

Alles is Liefde (2007) Joram Lürsen. IMDb entry: www.imdb.com/title/tt0468644/

Annie Hall (1977) Woody Allen. IMDb entry: www.imdb.com/title/tt0075686/

Atonement (2007) Joe Wright. IMDb entry: www.imdb.com/title/tt0783233/

Avatar (2009) James Cameron. IMDb entry: www.imdb.com/title/tt0499549/

¡Ay, Carmela! (1990) Carlos Saura. IMDb entry: www.imdb.com/title/tt0101025/

Battle of the Planets (1978) Alan Dinehart and David E. Hanson. IMDb entry: www.imdb.com/title/tt0076983/

Battleship Potemkin (1925) Sergei Eisenstein. IMDb entry: www.imdb.com/find?q= Battleship+Pottemkin&s=all

Belle Époque (1992) Fernando Trueba. IMDb entry: www.imdb.com/title/tt0103791/?ref_ = fn_al_tt_1

Bienvenue chez les Ch'tis [Welcome to the Sticks] (2008) Dany Boon. IMDb entry: www.imdb.com/title/tt1064932/

Blood and Sand (1941) Rouben Mamoulian. IMDb entry: www.imdb.com/title/tt0033405/

Blotto (1930) James Parrott. IMDb entry: www.imdb.com/title/tt0020698/

Braveheart (1995) Mel Gibson. IMDb entry: www.imdb.co.uk/title/tt0112573/

Bridget Jones's Diary (2001) Sharon McGuire. IMDb entry: www.imdb.com/title/ tt0243155/

Bridget Jones: The Edge of Reason (2004) Beeban Kidron. IMDb entry: www. imdb.com/title/tt0317198/

Buffy the Vampire Slayer (1997–2003) Joss Whedon. IMDb entry: www.imdb. com/ title/tt0118276/

Burst Angel [Bakuretsu Tenshi] (2005) Kôichi Ôhata. Episode 1 ('Hell Comes Silently'), volume 1 ('In Death's Angel'). English fansubbed version by Lunar (www.lunaranime.org). IMDb entry: www.imdb.com/ title/ tt0409536/

Chacun cherche son chat [When the Cat's Away] (1996) Cédric Klapisch. IMDb entry: www.imdb.com/title/tt0115856/

College Chums (1907) Edwin S. Porter. IMDb entry: www.imdb.com/title/ tt0233471/

Cyrano de Bergerac (1990) Jean-Paul Rappeneau. IMDb entry: www.imdb.com/ title/tt0099334/?ref_ = fn_al_tt_1

Das Leben der Anderen [The Lives of Others] (2006) Florian Henckel von Donnersmarck. IMDb entry: www.imdb.com/title/tt0405094/

Dracula (1931) Tod Browning and Karl Freund. IMDb entry: www.imdb.com/ title/tt0021814/

Duck Soup (1933) Leo McCarey. IMDb entry: www.imdb.com/title/tt0023969/

Friends (1994–2004) David Crane and Marta Kauffman. IMDb entry: www. imdb.com/title/tt0108778/

Full Metal Jacket (1987) Stanley Kubrick. IMDb entry: www.imdb.com/title/ tt0093058/?ref_ = sr_1

Goodbye Lenin (2003) Wolfgang Becker. IMDb entry: www.imdb.com/title/ tt0301357/

Human Planet (2011) British Broadcasting Corporation. IMDb entry: www. imdb.com/title/tt1806234/

Il Postino [The Postman] (1994) Michael Radford. IMDb entry: www.imdb.com/ title/tt0110877/?ref_ = fn_al_tt_1

Israeli Apartheid 5 (2010) Available at: www.youtube.com/watch?v=ol-wFyQg32Y (last accessed 15 September 2013).

Jean de Florette (1986) Claude Berri. IMDb entry: www.imdb.com/title/ tt0091288/

Kagaku Ninjatai Gatchaman (1972–74) Masami Anô and Wataru Mizusawa. IMDb entry: www.imdb.com/title/tt0068792/

Kingdom Hearts 3D: Dream Drop Distance (2012) IMDb entry: www.imdb.com/ title/tt2125539/

Kung Fu Panda (2008) Mark Osborne and John Stevenson. IMDb: www.imdb. com/title/tt0441773/

La hora de los hornos [The Hour of the Furnaces] (1968) Octavio Getino and Fernando E. Solanas. IMDb entry: www.imdb.com/title/tt0063084/

La Lengua de las Mariposas [*Butterfly*] (1999) José Luis Cuerda. IMDb entry: www.imdb.com/title/tt0188030/?ref_ = nv_sr_1

La Reine Margot (1994) Patrice Chéreau. IMDb entry: www.imdb.com/title/tt0110963/

La Vida Nocturna (1930) James Parrott. IMDb entry: www.imdb.com/title/tt0211725/

Lost in Translation (2003) Sofia Coppola. IMDb entry: www.imdb.com/title/tt0335266/

M (1931) Fritz Lang. IMDb entry: www.imdb.com/title/tt0022100/

Millennium Actress [*Sennen joyû*] (2001) Kon Satoshi. IMDb entry: www.imdb.com/ title/tt0291350/

Naruto (2005–6) Yuuto Date and Hayato Date. Episode 178. English fansubbed version by Dattebayo (www.narutofan.com). IMDb entry: www.imdb.com/find?s=all&q= naruto

Nochnoi Dozor [*Night Watch*] (2004) Timur Bekmambetov. IMDb entry: www.imdb. com/title/tt0403358/

Ran (1985) Akira Kurosawa. IMDb entry: www.imdb.com/title/tt0089881/

Ridicule (1996) Patrice Leconte. IMDb entry: www.imdb.com/title/tt0117477/?ref_ = nv_sr_1

Secrets and Lies (1996) Mike Leigh. IMDb entry: www.imdb.com/title/tt0117589/

Shall We Dance? [*Shall We Dansu?*] (1996) Masayuki Suo. IMDb entry: www.imdb.com/title/tt0117615/?ref_ = sr_3

Sherlock (2010, season one) Mark Gatiss and Steven Moffat. IMDb entry: www.imdb.com/title/tt1475582/

Siete Vidas [*Seven Lives*] (1999–2006) Ricardo A. Solla *et al.* IMDb entry: www.imdb.com/title/tt0192877/

Snakes on a Plane (2006) David R. Ellis. IMDb entry: www.imdb.com/title/tt0417148/

Sound of Noise (2010) Ola Simonsson and Johannes Stjärne Nilsson. IMDb entry: www.imdb.com/title/tt1278449/

Surname Viêt Given Name Nam (1989) Trinh T. Minh-ha. IMDb entry: www.imdb.com/title/tt0098414/

Swallow the Sun [*Taeyangeul Ssamkyeora*] (2009) Soo-Won Cho and Yoo Chul Yong. IMDb entry: www.imdb.com/title/tt1567718/

Taxi Driver (1976) Martin Scorsese. IMDb entry: www.imdb.com/title/tt0075314/

Thank you for Smoking (2005) Jason Reitman. IMDb entry: www.imdb.com/title/ tt0427944/

The Arch of Triumph (1948) Lewis Milestone. IMDb entry: www.imdb.com/title/tt0040109/

The Artist (2011) Michel Hazanavicius. IMDb entry: www.imdb.com/title/tt1655442/

The Inbetweeners (2008–10) Ben Palmer, Gordon Anderson, Damon Beesley and Iain Morris. IMDb entry: www.imdb.com/title/tt1220617/

The Jazz Singer (1927) Alan Crosland. IMDb entry: www.imdb.com/title/tt0018037/

The Lummox (1930) Herbert Brenon. IMDb entry: www.imdb.com/title/tt0021105/

The Naked Gun: From the Files of the Police Squad (1988) David Zucker. IMDb entry: www.imdb.com/title/tt0095705/?ref_ = fn_al_tt_1

The Real Ghostbusters (1986–91) Will Meugniot, Richard Raynis, Stan Phillips and Masakazu Higuchi. IMDb entry: www.imdb.com/title/tt0090506/

The Royle Family (1998–) Caroline Aherne, Mark Mylod and Steve Bendelack. IMDb entry: www.imdb.com/title/tt0129711/fullcredits?ref_=tt_ov_st_sm

The Shining (1980) Stanley Kubrick. IMDb entry: www.imdb.com/title/tt0081505/

The Skin I Live In [*La piel que habito*] (2011) Pedro Almodóvar. IMDb entry: www.imdb.com/title/ tt1189073/

The Whole Dam Family and the Dam Dog (1905) Edwin S. Porter. IMDb entry: www.imdb.com/title/tt0235045/

The Woman in Black (2012) James Watkins. IMDb entry: www.imdb.com/title/tt1596365/

Train Pulling into a Station [*L'Arrivée d'un train en gare de La Ciotat*] (1896) Auguste Lumière and Louis Lumière. IMDb entry: www.imdb.com/title/tt0000012/

Un Chien Andalou (1929) Luis Buñuel. IMDb entry: www.imdb.com/title/tt0020530/

Une Nuit Extravagante (1930) James Parrott. IMDb entry: www.imdb.com/title/tt0211548/

Bibliography

Adams, Michael (2003) *Slayer Slang: A Buffy the Vampire Slayer Lexicon*, Oxford: Oxford University Press.

Agnew, Jeremy (2012) *The Old West in Fact and Film: History Versus Hollywood*, Jefferson, NC: McFarland.

Agost, Rosa (1999) *Traducción y doblaje: Palabras, voces e imágenes*, Barcelona: Ariel.

Ahlsén, Elisabeth (2011) 'Neurolinguistics', in James Simpson (ed.) *Routledge Handbook of Applied Linguistics*, London and New York: Routledge, 460–71.

Aitken, Stuart and Deborah P. Dixon (2006) 'Imagining Geographies of Film', *Erdkunde: Archiv für Wissenschaftliche Geographie* 60: 326–36.

Al-Adwan, Amer (2009) *Euphemisms as Politeness Strategy in Screen Translation in the Arab World*, Unpublished PhD Thesis, University of Manchester.

Alemán Bañón, José (2005) 'Propuesta de doblaje de un dialecto regional: *Billy Elliot*', *Puentes* 6: 69–75.

Ali, Novel (1997) 'Sulih Suara Dorong Keretakan Komunikasi Keluarga', in Deddy Mulyana and Ibi Subandy Ibrahim (eds) *Bercinta Dengan Televisi: Ilusi, Impresi, dan Imaji Sebuah Kotak Ajaib*, Bandung, Java: PT Remaja Rosdakarya, 338–46.

Antonini, Rachele (2005) 'The Perception of Subtitled Humour in Italy: An Empirical Study', *Humor, Journal of Humor Research* 18(2): 209–25.

—— (2008) 'The Perception of Dubbese. An Italian Study', in Delia Chiaro, Christine Heiss and Chiara Bucaria (eds) *Between Text and Image: Updating Research in Screen Translation*, Amsterdam and Philadelphia: John Benjamins, 135–48.

Antonini, Rachele and Delia Chiaro (2005) 'The Perception of Subtitled Humour in Italy: An Empirical Study', in Marina Bondi and Nick Maxwell (eds) *Cross-Cultural Encounters: Linguistic Perspectives*, Rome: Officina Edizioni, 33–44.

—— (2009) 'The Perception of Dubbing by Italian Audiences', in Gunilla Anderman and Jorge Díaz Cintas (eds) *Audiovisual Translation: Language Transfer on Screen*, Basingstoke: Palgrave MacMillan, 97–114.

Armstrong, Stephen, Andy Way, Colm Caffrey, Marian Flanagan, Dorothy Kenny and Minako O'Hagan (2006) 'Leading by Example: Automatic Translation of Subtitles via EBMT', *Perspectives: Studies in Translatology* 14(3): 163–84.

Asimakoulas, Dimitris (2004) 'Towards a Model of Describing Humour Translation: A Case Study of the Greek Subtitled Versions of *Airplane!* and *Naked Gun*', *Meta* 49(4): 822–42.

—— (2012) 'Dude (Looks Like a Lady): Hijacking Transsexual Identity in the Subtitled Version of *Strella* by Panos Koutras', *The Translator* 18(1): 47–75.

Baker, Mona (1993) 'Corpus Linguistics and Translation Studies: Implications and Applications', in Mona Baker, Gill Francis and Elena Tognini-Bonelli (eds) *Text and Technology: In Honour of John Sinclair*, Amsterdam and Philadelphia: John Benjamins, 233–50.

—— (1995) 'Corpora in Translation Studies: An Overview and Suggestions for Future Research', *Target* 7(2): 223–43.

—— (2006) *Translation and Conflict: A Narrative Account*, London and New York: Routledge.

—— (2014) 'The Changing Landscape of Translation and Interpreting Studies', in Sandra Bermann and Catherine Porter (eds) *A Companion to Translation Studies*, Oxford: Wiley-Blackwell, 15–27.

Baker, Mona and Braňo Hochel (1998) 'Dubbing', in Mona Baker (ed.) *Routledge Encyclopedia of Translation Studies*, 1st edition, London and New York: Routledge, 74–76.

Baker, Mona and Luis Pérez-González (2011) 'Translation and Interpreting', in James Simpson (ed.) *Routledge Handbook of Applied Linguistics*, London and New York: Routledge, 39–52.

Baldry, Anthony and Paul J. Thibault (2006) *Multimodal Transcription and Text Analysis*, London and Oakville: Equinox.

Ballester, Ana (1995) *La política del doblaje en España*, Valencia: Ediciones Episteme.

—— (2001) *Traducción y nacionalismo*, Granada: Comares.

Band, Jonathan and Jonathan Gerafi (2013) *The Fair Use/Fair Dealing Handbook*. Available online: http://infojustice.org/wp-content/uploads/2013/05/Fair-Use-Handbook-05072013.pdf (last accessed on 15 September 2013).

Banks, John and Mark Deuze (2009) 'Co-creative Labour', *International Journal of Cultural Studies* 12(5): 419–31.

Baños, Rocío, Silvia Bruti and Serenella Zanotti (2013) 'Corpus Linguistics and Audiovisual Translation: In Search of an Integrated Approach', *Perspectives: Studies in Translatology* 21(4): 483–90.

Barnes, Mike (2013) 'Mickey Knox, Actor and Sergio Leone Writer, Dies at 92', *The Hollywood Reporter*, 22 November. Available online: www.hollywoodreporter.com/news/mickey-knox-actor-writer-sergio-leone-dies-658437 (last accessed 15 September 2013).

Barra, Luca (2009) 'The Mediation is the Message: Italian Regionalization of US TV Series as Co-creational Work', *International Journal of Cultural Studies* 12(5): 509–25.

Bassnett, Susan (1980/1991) *Translation Studies*, revised edition, London: Methuen.

Baudrillard, Jean (1983) *In the Shadow of the Silent Majorities, or, the End of the Social and Other Essays*, translated by Paul Foss, Paul Patton, and John Johnston, New York: Semiotext(e).

Baumgarten, Nicole (2005) 'On the Women's Service?: Gender-conscious Language in Dubbed James Bond Movies', in José Santaemilia (ed.) *Gender, Sex and Translation. The Manipulation of Identities*, Manchester: St Jerome, 53–69.

Bean, Travis (2012) '*The Artist* or the Failed Use of Sound and Silence', 24 January. Available online at: http://cinemabeans.blogspot.co.uk/2012/01/artist-2011.html (last accessed 15 September 2013).

Benkler, Yochai (2006). *The Wealth of Networks: How Social Production Transforms Markets and Freedom*, New Haven, CT: Yale University Press.

Berlant, Lauren (2011) *Cruel Optimism*, Durham: Duke University Press.

Berliner, Todd (1999) 'Hollywood Movie Dialogue and the "Real Realism" of John Cassavetes', *Film Quarterly* 52(3): 2–16.

Bernal Merino, Miguel (2006) 'On the Translation of Video Games', JoSTrans: *Journal of Specialized Translation* 6: 22–36. Available online: www.jostrans.org/issue06/art_bernal.pdf (last accessed 15 September 2013).

Berthele, Raphael (2000) 'Translating African-American Vernacular English into German: The problem of 'Jim' in Mark Twain's *Huckleberry Finn*', *Journal of Sociolinguistics* 4: 588–613.

Blacking, John (2004) '"Let All the World Hear All the World's Music": Popular Music-Making and Music Education', in Simon Frith (ed.) *Popular Music*, vol. IV: Music and Identity, Critical Concepts in Media and Cultural Studies Series, London and New York: Routledge, 7–31. First published in 1987, *A Common Sense View of All Music*, Cambridge: Cambridge University Press, 121–49.

Blau, Andrew (2005) 'The Future of Independent Media', *Deeper News* 10(1). Available online: http://http://gbn.com/consulting/article_details.php?id=57 (last accessed on 15 September 2013).

Bloom, David (2002) 'Dubbing Biz Goes Modern', *Variety*, 22 September. Available online: http://variety.com/2002/digital/news/dubbing-biz-goes-modern-1117873084/ (last accessed on 15 September 2013).

Boellstorff, Tom (2003) 'Dubbing Culture: Indonesian *Gay* and *Lesbi* Subjectivities and Ethnography in an Already Globalized World', *American Ethnologist* 30(2): 225–242.

Bollettieri Bosinelli, Rosa Maria and Serenella Zanotti (2011) 'The Use of Translators Archives in Translation Research: A Multidisciplinary Approach', Paper delivered at the *Research Models in Translation Studies II Conference*, 29 April–2 May, University of Manchester.

Bosseaux, Charlotte (2008) 'Buffy the Vampire Slayer Characterization in the Musical Episode of the TV Series', *The Translator* 14(2): 343–72.

Bourdieu, Pierre (1977) *Outline of a Theory of Practice*, translated by Richard Nice, Cambridge: Cambridge University Press.

Bradshaw, Peter (2011) 'The Skin I Live In', *The Guardian*, 25 August. Available online: www.guardian.co.uk/film/2011/aug/25/the-skin-i-live-in-review?INTCMP=SRCH (last accessed on 15 September 2013).

Braun, Sabine (2007) 'AD from a Discourse Perspective: A Socially Relevant Framework for Research and Training', *Linguistica Antverpiensia* 6: 357–69.

Bridgeman, Bruce (1992) 'Conscious vs Unconscious Processes: The Case of Vision', *Theory and Psychology* 2(1): 73–88.

Brown, Penelope and Stephen Levinson (1987) *Politeness: Some Universals in Language Usage*, Cambridge: Cambridge University Press.

Bruns, Axel (2008) *Blogs, Wikipedia, Second Life, and Beyond: From Production to Produsage*, New York: Peter Lang.

Bruti, Silvia (2009) 'Translating Compliments and Insults in the *Pavia Corpus of Film Dialogue*: Two Sides of the Same Coin?', in Maria Freddi and Maria Pavesi (eds) *Analysing Audiovisual Dialogue: Linguistic and Translational Insights*, Bologna: CLUEB, 143–63.

Bucaria, Chiara and Delia Chiaro (2007) 'End User Perception of Screen Translation: The Case of Italian Dubbing', *Tradterm* 13(1): 91–118.

Byers, Michele (2003) 'Buffy the Vampire Slayer: The Next Generation of Television', in Rory Dicker and Alison Piepmeier (eds) *Catching a Wave: Reclaiming Feminism for the 21st Century*, Boston: Northeastern University Press, 171–87.

Caffrey, Colm (2009) Relevant Abuse? *Investigating the Effects of an Abusive Subtitling Procedure on the Perception of TV Anime Using Eye Tracker and Questionnaire*, Unpublished PhD Thesis, Dublin City University. Available online: http://doras.dcu.ie/14835/ (last accessed on 15 September 2013).

Caillé, Pierre-François (1960) 'Le traducteur devant l'écran', *Babel* 6(3): 103–9.

Camus, Carmen (2007) 'Translation, Censorship and Negotiation in Westerns'. Available online: www.port.ac.uk/departments/academic/slas/conferences/pastconferenceproceedings/translationconf2007/TranslationConference

2007files/filetodownload,138196,en.pdf (last accessed on 15 September 2013).

Cannon, Damian (1997) 'A review of 12 Angry Men (1957)'. Available online: www.film.u-net.com/Movies/Reviews/Twelve_Angry.html (last accessed 15 September 2013).

Cary, Edmond (1969) 'La traduction totale', *Babel* 6(3): 110–15.

Castells, Manuel (2001) *The Internet Galaxy: Reflections on the Internet, Business and Society*, Oxford: Oxford University Press.

Catford, John C. (1965) *A Linguistic Theory of Translation*, Oxford: Oxford University Press.

Cattrysse, Patrick (2004) 'Stories Travelling Across Nations and Cultures', *Meta* 49(1): 39–51.

Cavalcanti, Alberto (1939) 'Sound in Films', *Films* 1(1): 25–39. Available online: http://studio.berkeley.edu/coursework/moses/courses/185187WebPages/PRODUCTION/Theory%20Cavalcanti.htm (last accessed on 15 September 2013).

Cazdyn, Eric (2004) 'A New Line in the Geometry', in Atom Egoyan and Ian Balfour (eds) *Subtitles. On the Foreignness of Film*, Cambridge, MA and London: The MIT Press, 403–19.

Chafe, Wallace (1975) *The Pear Film*, University of California. Available online: www.linguistics.ucsb.edu/faculty/chafe/pearfilm.htm (last accessed on 15 September 2013).

—— (2002) 'Searching for Meaning in Language', *Historiographia Linguistica* 29: 245–61.

Chandler, Daniel (1998) 'Personal Homepages and the Construction of Identities on the Web', paper presented at *Aberystwyth Post-International Group Conference on Linking Theory and Practice: Issues in the Politics of Identity*, 9–11 September 1998, University of Wales, Aberystwyth. Available online: www.aber.ac.uk/media/Documents/short/webident.html (last accessed on 15 September 2013).

—— (2002) *Semiotics: The Basics*, London: Routledge.

Chaume Varela, Frederic (2002) 'Models of Research in Audiovisual Translation', *Babel* 48(1): 1–13.

—— (2004) *Cine y traducción*, Madrid: Cátedra.

—— (2012) *Audiovisual Translation: Dubbing*, Manchester: St Jerome.

—— (2013) 'Research Paths in Audiovisual Translation: The Case of Dubbing', in Carmen Millán-Varela and Francesca Bartrina (eds) *The Routledge Handbook of Translation Studies*, London and New York: Routledge, 288–302.

Chaves García, María José (2000) *La traducción cinematográfica: El doblaje*, Huelva: Servicio de Publicaciones de la Universidad de Huelva.

Chen, Chapman (2004) 'On the Hong Kong Chinese Subtitling of English Swearwords', *Meta* 49(1): 135–47.

Chesterman, Andrew (2000) 'A Causal Model for Translation Studies', in Maeve Olohan (ed.) *Intercultural Faultlines. Research Models in*

Translation Studies I: Textual and Cognitive Aspects, Manchester: St Jerome, 15–28.

—— (2006) 'Interpreting the Meaning of Translation', in Mickael Suominen, Antti Arppe, Anu Airola, Orvokki Heinämäki, Matti Miestamo, Urho Määttä, Jussi Niemi, Kari K. Pitkänen, and Kaius Sinnemäki (eds) *A Man of Measure. Festschrift in Honour of Fred Karlsson on his 60th Birthday*, Turku: Linguistic Association of Finland, 3–11.

Chiaro, Delia (2004) 'Investigating the Perception of Translated Verbally Expressed Humour on Italian TV', *ESP Across Cultures* 1: 35–52.

—— (2007a) 'The Effect of Translation on Humour Response: The Case of Dubbed Comedy in Italy', in Yves Gambier, Miriam Schlesinger and Radegundis Stolze (eds) *Doubts and Directions in Translation Studies: Selected Contributions from the EST Congress*, Lisbon 2004, Amsterdam and Philadelphia: John Benjamins, 137–52.

—— (2007b) 'Not in Front of the Children? An Analysis of Sex on Screen in Italy', *Linguistica Antverpiensia* 6: 255–76.

—— (2009) 'Issues in Audiovisual Translation', in Jeremy Munday (ed.) *The Routledge Companion to Translation Studies*, London and New York: Routledge, 141–65.

Chomsky, Noam (2006) 'On the US-Israeli Invasion of Lebanon'. Available online: www.chomsky.info/articles/20060819.htm (last accessed on 15 September 2013).

Chouliaraki, Lilie (2010) 'Self-mediation: New Media and Citizenship', *Critical Discourse Studies*, 7(4): 227–32.

—— (2012) 'Re-mediation, Inter-mediation, Trans-mediation', *Journalism Studies*, 14 (2): 267–83.

Chung, Sung-ill (2007) 'Four Variations on Korean Genre Film: Tears, Screams, Violence and Laughter', in Mee-hyun Kim (ed.) *Korean Cinema from Origins to Renaissance*, Seoul: Communication Books, 1–14.

Compaine, Ben (2005) 'The Media Monopoly Myth: How New Competition is Expanding our Sources of Information and Entertainment', *New Millennium Research Council*. Available online: www.thenmrc.org/archive/Final_Compaine_Paper_ 050205.pdf (last accessed on 15 September 2013).

Craigo-Snell, Shannon (2006) 'What Would Buffy Do? Feminist Ethics and Epistemic Violence', *Jump Cut: A Review of Contemporary Media* 48. Available online: www.ejumpcut.org/archive/jc48.2006/BuffyEthics/text.html (last accessed on 15 September 2013).

Crewe, Louise, Andrew Leyshon, Nigel Thrift and Pete Webb (2005) 'Otaku Fever? The Construction of Enthusiasm and the Coproduction of Markets'. Paper presented to the Royal Geographical Society Conference, London, 1 September 2005.

Crompton, Sarah (2012) 'The Timeless Appeal of Sherlock Holmes's Sexy Logic', *The Telegraph*, 1 January. Available online: www.telegraph.co.uk/

culture/tvandradio/bbc/8987577/The-timeless-appeal-of-Sherlock-Holmess-sexy-logic.html (last accessed on 15 September 2013).

Cronin, Michael (2003) *Translation and Globalization*, London and New York: Routledge.

—— (2009) *Translation Goes to the Movies*, London and New York: Routledge.

Cubbison, Laurie (2005) 'Anime Fans, DVDs, and the Authentic Text', *The Velvet Light Trap* 56: 45–57.

Cumbow, Robert C. (1985) *The Films of Sergio Leone*, Lanham, MD: Scarecrow Press.

Curti, Giorgio H. (2009) 'Beating Words to Life: Subtitles, Assemblage(s) capes, Expression', *GeoJournal* 74: 201–208.

Danan, Martine (1991) 'Dubbing as an Expression of Nationalism', *Meta* 36(4): 606–14.

Daniels, Joshua M. (2008) 'Lost in Translation: Anime, Moral Rights, and Market Failure', *Boston University Law Review* 88(1): 709–44.

de Grazia, Victoria (1989) 'Mass Culture and Sovereignty: The American Challenge to European Cinemas, 1920–60', *The Journal of Modern History* 61(1): 53–87.

Delabastita, Dirk (1989) 'Translation and Mass-Communication: Film and TV Translation as Evidence of Cultural Dynamics', *Babel* 35(4): 193–218.

—— (1990) 'Translation and the Mass Media', in Susan Bassnett and André Lefèvre (eds) *Translation, History and Culture*, London and New York: Pinter Publishers, 97–109.

—— (2013) 'B2B in Translation Studies: Business to Business, or Back to Basics?', *The Translator* 19(1): 1–23.

de Linde, Zoe and Neil Kay (1999) *The Semiotics of Subtitling*, Manchester: St Jerome.

De Marco, Marcella (2012) *Audiovisual Translation Through a Gender Lens*, Amsterdam and New York: Rodopi.

Denis, Claire (2004) 'Claire Denis interviewed by Atom Egoyan', in Atom Egoyan and Ian Balfour (eds) *Subtitles. On the Foreignness of Film*, Cambridge, MA and London: The MIT Press, 69–76.

Denison, Rayna (2011). 'Anime Fandom and the Liminal Spaces between Fan Creativity and Piracy', *International Journal of Cultural Studies* 14(5): 449–66.

Desilla, Louisa (2009) *Towards a Methodology for the Study of Implicatures in Subtitled Films: Multimodal Construal and Reception of Pragmatic Meaning Across Cultures*, Unpublished PhD Thesis, University of Manchester.

—— (2012) 'Implicatures in Film: Construal and Functions in Bridget Jones Romantic Comedies', *Journal of Pragmatics* 44: 30–53.

Desjardins, Renée (2008) 'Inter-Semiotic Translation and Cultural Representation within the Space of the Multi-Modal Text', *TranscUlturAl* 1(1): 48–58. Available online: http://ejournals.library.ualberta.ca/index.php/TC (last accessed on 15 September 2013).

Deuze, Mark (2006) 'Participation, Remediation, Bricolage: Considering Principal Components of a Digital Culture', *The Information Society* 22: 63–75.

—— (2009) 'Convergence Culture and Media Work', in Jennifer Holt and Alisa Perren (eds) *Media Industries: History, Theory, and Method*, Malden, MA: Wiley-Blackwell, 144–156.

Diab, Osama (2010) 'Egyptian Government Fears a Facebook Revolution', *The Guardian*, 21 October. Available online: www.guardian.co.uk/commentisfree/2010/oct/21/egypt-facebook-revolution?INTCMP=SRCH (last accessed on 15 September 2013).

Díaz Cintas, Jorge (2001) *La traducción audiovisual: el subtitulado*, Salamanca: Almar.

—— (2003) *Teoría y práctica de la subtitulación*, Barcelona: Ariel.

—— (2004), 'In Search of a Theoretical Framework for the Study of Audiovisual Translation', in Pilar Orero (ed.) *Topics in Audiovisual Translation*, Amsterdam and Philadelphia: John Benjamins, 21–34.

—— (2009) 'Introduction – Audiovisual Translation: An Overview of its Potential', in Jorge Díaz Cintas (ed.) *New Trends in Audiovisual Translation*, Bristol, Buffalo, Toronto: Multilingual Matters, 1–18.

—— (2013) 'Subtitling: Theory, Practice and Research', in Carmen Millán-Varela and Francesca Bartrina (eds) *The Routledge Handbook of Translation Studies*, London and New York: Routledge, 285–99.

Díaz Cintas, Jorge and Pablo Muñoz Sánchez (2006) 'Fansubs: Audiovisual Translation in an Amateur Environment', *JoSTrans: The Journal of Specialised Translation* 6: 37–52. Available online: www.jostrans.org/issue06/art_diaz_munoz.pdf (last accessed on 15 September 2013).

Díaz Cintas, Jorge and Aline Remael (2007) *Audiovisual Translation: Subtitling*, Manchester: St Jerome.

Dick, Bernard F. (1990) *Anatomy of film*. New York: St Martin's Press.

Di Giovanni, Elena (2008) 'The American Film Musical in Italy: Translation and Non-translation', *The Translator* 14(2): 295–318.

Dirks, Tim (1996) 'Review of 12 Angry Men (1957)'. Available online: www.filmsite.org/twelve.html (last accessed 15 September 2013).

Doane, Mary A. (1980) 'The Voice in the Cinema: The Articulation of Body and Space', *Yale French Studies* 60: 33–50.

Dreyer-Sfard, Regine (1965) *Die Verflechtung von Sprache und Bild: Sprache im Technischen Zeitalter* 13: 1034–39.

Duro Moreno, Miguel (2001) '"Eres patético": el español traducido del cine y de la televisión', in Miguel Duro Moreno (ed.) *La traducción para el doblaje y la subtitulación*, Madrid: Cátedra, 161–85.

Ďurovičová, Nataša (2003) 'Local Ghosts: Dubbing Bodies in Early Sound Cinema', in Anna Antonini (ed.) *Il film e i suoi multipli/Film and Its Multiples*, Udine: Forum, 1–22.

Dwyer, Tessa (2012) 'Fansub Dreaming on ViKi: "Don't Just Watch but Help when You Are Free"', in Sebnem Susam-Saraeva and Luis

Pérez-González (eds) *Non-professionals Translating and Interpreting: Participatory and Engaged Perspectives*, special issue of *The Translator*, 18(2): 217–43.

d'Ydewalle, Gery and Marijke Van de Poel (1999) 'Incidental Foreign-language Acquisition by Children Watching Subtitled Television Programs', *Journal of Psycholinguistic Research* 28: 227–44.

Ebert, Roger (2007) 'The Lives of Others', *Chicago Sun-Times*, 21 September. Available online: http://rogerebert.suntimes.com/apps/pbcs.dll/article? AID=/20070920/REVIEWS/70920002 (last accessed on 15 September 2013).

Edmonstone, Robert J. (2008) *Beyond 'Brutality': Understanding the Italian Filone's Violent Excesses*, Unpublished PhD thesis, University of Glasgow. Available online: http://theses.gla.ac.uk/608/ (last accessed on 15 September 2013).

Eguíluz, Federico, Raquel Merino, Vickie Olsen, Eterio Pajares and José Miguel (1994) (eds) *Trasvases culturales: literatura, cine, traducción*, Vitoria: Universidad del País Vasco.

Eisenstein, Sergei (1925) *Battleship Potemkin*. Available online at: www.youtube.com/watch?v=Bh2SuJrEjwM (last accessed on 15 September 2013).

Elley, Derek (2006) 'The Lives of Others: Das Leben der Anderen (Germany)', *Variety*, 11 June. Available online: www.variety.com/review/VE1117930778 /?categoryID=31&cs=1 (last accessed on 15 September 2013).

Ellis, Jack C. (1995) *A History of Film*, 4th edition, Boston and London: Allyn and Bacon.

Espasa, Eva (2004): 'Myths about Documentary Translation', in Pilar Orero (ed.) *Topics in Audiovisual Translation*, Amsterdam and Philadelphia: John Benjamins, 183–97.

Even-Zohar, Itamar (1979) 'Polysystem Theory', *Poetics Today* 1(1–2): 287–310.

Fawcett, Peter (1996) 'Translating Film', in Geoffrey T. Harris (ed.) *Translating French Literature and Film*, Amsterdam: Rodopi, 65–88.

—— (2003) 'The Manipulation of Language and Culture in Film Translation', in María Calzada Pérez (ed.) *Apropos of Ideology*, Manchester: St Jerome, 145–63.

Federici, Federico M. (ed.) (2011) *Translating Dialects and Languages of Minorities: Challenges and Solutions*, Bern: Peter Lang.

Fernández Costales, Alberto (2011) '2.0: Facing the Challenges of the Global Era', *Tralogy* 4, 19 March. Available online: http://lodel.irevues.inist.fr/ tralogy/index.php?id=120 (last accessed on 15 September 2013).

Fine, Elizabeth C. (1984) *The Folklore Text*, Bloomington, USA: Indiana University Press.

Floros, Georgios (2003). *Kulturelle Konstellationen in Texten: Zur Beschreibung und Übersetzung von Kultur in Texten*, Tübingen: Narr.

Fodor, István (1976) *Film Dubbing: Phonetic, Semiotic, Aesthetic and Psychological Aspects*, Hamburg: Helmut Buske.

Forbes, Jill and Sarah Street (2000) *European Cinema*, New York: Palgrave.

Foucault, Michel (1982) 'The Subject and Power', *Critical Inquiry* 8(4): 777–95.

Fox, Wendy (2013) 'Integrated Titles as an Alternative Solution to Traditional Subtitles', Paper presented at the *7th EST Conference. Translation Studies: Centers and Peripheries*, Germersheim (Germany).

Franco, Eliana, Anna Matamala and Pilar Orero (2010) *Voice-over Translation: An Overview*, Bern: Peter Lang.

Franzon, Johan (2008) 'Choices in Song Translation. Singability in Print, Subtitles and Sung Performance', *The Translator* 14(2): 373–99.

Freddi, Maria (2009) 'The Phraseology of Contemporary Filmic Speech: Formulaic Language and Translation', in Maria Freddi and Maria Pavesi (eds) *Analysing Audiovisual Dialogue: Linguistic and Translational Insights*, Bologna: Clueb, 101–23.

—— (2012) 'What AVT Can Make of Corpora: Some Findings from the Pavia Corpus of Film Dialogue', in Aline Remael, Pilar Orero and Mary Carroll (eds) *Audiovisual Translation and Media Accessibility at the Crossroads*, Amsterdam and New York: Rodopi, 381–407.

—— (2013) 'Constructing a Corpus of Translated Films: A Corpus View of Dubbing', *Perspectives: Studies in Translatology* 21(4): 491–503.

Freddi, Maria and Maria Pavesi (2009) 'The Pavia Corpus of Film Dialogue: Methodology and Research Rationale', in Maria Freddi and Maria Pavesi (eds) *Analysing Audiovisual Dialogue: Linguistic and Translational Insights*, Bologna: Clueb, 95–100.

Fresno, Nazaret (2012) 'Experimenting with Characters: An Empirical Approach to the Audio Description of Fictional Characters', in Aline Remael, Pilar Orero and Mary Carroll (eds) *Audiovisual Translation and Media Accessibility at the Crossroads*, Amsterdam and New York: Rodopi, 147–61.

Fuentes Luque, Adrián (2000) *La recepción del humor audiovisual traducido: estudio comparativo de fragmentos de las versiones doblada y subtitulada al español de la película* Duck Soup, *de los Hermanos Marx*, Unpublished PhD Thesis, Granada: Universidad de Granada.

—— (2003) 'An Empirical Approach to the Reception of AV Translated Humour. A Case Study of the Marx Brothers' *Duck Soup*', *The Translator* 9(2): 293–306.

Gamal, Muhammad Y. (2007) 'Audiovisual Translation in the Arab World: A Changing Scene', *Translation Watch Quarterly* 3(2): 78–95.

Gambier, Yves (1994) 'Audiovisual Communication: Typological Detour', in Cay Dollerup and Annette Lindegaard (eds) *Teaching Translation and Interpreting* 2, Amsterdam and Philadelphia: John Benjamins, 275–83.

—— (2003). 'Screen Transadaptation: Perception and Reception', *The Translator* 9(2), 171–89.

—— (2006a) 'Multimodality and Subtitling', in Mary Carroll, Heidrun Gerzymisch-Arbogast and Sandra Nauert (eds) *Proceedings of the Marie*

Curie Euroconferences MuTra: Audiovisual Translation Scenarios, Copenhagen 1–5 May 2006. Available online: www.euroconferences.info/proceedings/2006_Proceedings/2006_proceedings.htm (last accessed on 15 September 2013).

—— (2006b) 'Orientations de la recherche en traduction audiovisuelle', *Target* 18(2): 261–93.

—— (2008) 'Recent Developments and Challenges in Audiovisual Translation Research', in Delia Chiaro, Christine Heiss and Chiara Bucaria (eds) *Between Text and Image. Updating Research in Screen Translation*, Amsterdam and Philadelphia: John Benjamins, 11–33.

—— (2013) 'The Position of Audiovisual Translation Studies', in Carmen Millán-Varela and Francesca Bartrina (eds) *The Routledge Handbook of Translation Studies*, London and New York: Routledge, 45–59.

Gambier, Yves and Henrik Gottlieb (2001) (eds) *(Multi)Media Translation, Concepts, Practices and Research*, Amsterdam and Philadelphia: John Benjamins.

Garwood, Ian (2006) 'The Pop Song in Film', in John Gibbs and Deborah Pye (eds) *Close Up 1: Filmmakers' Choices/The Pop Song in Film/Reading Buffy*, London: Wallflower Press, 89–166.

Geertz, Clifford (1973) *The Interpretation of Culture*, New York: Basic Books.

Genette, Gerard E. (1983 [1980]) *Narrative Discourse: An Essay in Method*, translated by Jane E. Lewin, Ithaca, NY: Cornell University Press.

Gomery, Douglas (1980) 'Economic Struggle and Hollywood Imperialism: Europe Converts to Sound', *Yale French Studies* v: 80–93.

Gómez Capuz, Juan (2001) 'Diseño de análisis de la interferencia pragmática en la traducción audiovisual del inglés al español', in John D. Sanderson (ed.) *Doble o nada. Actas de las I y II jornadas de doblaje y subtitulación*, Alicante: Universidad de Alicante, 59–84.

Gottlieb, Henrik (1995) 'Establishing a Framework for a Typology of Subtitle Reading Strategies: Viewer Reactions to Deviations from Subtitling Standards', in Yves Gambier (ed) *Communication audiovisuelle et transferts linguistiques. Audiovisual Communication and Language Transfers*, Proceedings of the Forum held in Strasbourg, 22–24 June. Special Issue of *Translatio* (FIT) 14(3–4): 388–409.

—— (1997) *Subtitles, Translation and Idioms*, Copenhagen: University of Copenhagen.

—— (1998) 'Subtitling', in Mona Baker (ed.) *Routledge Encyclopedia of Translation Studies*, 1st edition, London and New York: Routledge, 244–48.

Govan, Fiona (2009) 'Lawsuit Filed against Spain's ex-PM over Iraq', *The Daily Telegraph*, 3 April. Available online. www.telegraph.co.uk/news/worldnews/europe/spain/5100640/Lawsuit-filed-against-Spains-ex-PM-over-Iraq.html (last accessed on 15 September 2013).

Green, Joshua and Henry Jenkins (2009) 'The Moral Economy of Web 2.0: Audience Research and Convergence Culture', in Jennifer Holt and Alisa Perren (eds) *Media Industries: History, Theory, and Method*, Malden, MA: Wiley-Blackwell, 213–25.

Grillo, Virgil and Bruce Kawin (1981) 'Reading at the Movies: Subtitles, Silence and the Structure of the Brain', *Post Script: Essays in Film and the Humanities* 1(1): 25–32.

Gronek, Agnieszka M., Anne Gorius and Heidrun Gerzymisch-Arbogast (2012) 'Culture and Coherence in the Pear Tree Project', *Perspectives: Studies in Translatology* 20(1): 43–53.

Gubern, Roman and Domènec Font (1975) *Un cine para el cadalso: 40 años de censura cinematográfica en España*, Barcelona: Euros.

Guidorizzi, Mario (1999) *Voci d'autore: storia e protagonisti del doppiaggio italiano*, Verona: Cierre.

Gutiérrez Lanza, Camino (1997) 'Spanish Film Translation: Ideology, Censorship and the Supremacy of the National Language', in Marian B. Labrum (ed.) *The Changing Scene in World Languages*, ATA Scholarly Monograph Series, vol. IX, Amsterdam and Philadelphia: John Benjamins, 35–45.

—— (2007) 'Traducción inglés-español y censura de textos cinematográficos: Definición, construcción y análisis del Corpus 0/Catálogo TRACEci (1951–81)', in Raquel Merino (ed.) *Traducción y censura en España (1939–1985). Estudios sobre corpus de cine, narrativa y teatro*, Vitoria y León: Universidad del País Vasco y Universidad de León, 97–240.

Harrod, Mary (2012) 'Linguistic Difference as Ontological Sameness in *Bienvenue Chez Les Ch'tis* (2008)', *Studies in French Cinema* 12(1): 75–86.

Hartley, John (2009) 'From the Consciousness Industry to the Creative Industries: Consumer-Created Content, Social Network Markets, and the Growth of Knowledge', in Jennifer Holt and Alisa Perren (eds) *Media Industries: History, Theory, and Method*, Malden, MA: Wiley-Blackwell, 231–44.

Hatcher, Jordan S. (2005) 'Of Otakus and Fansubs: A Critical Look at Anime Online in Light of Current Issues in Copyright Law', *SCRIPT-ed* 2(4): 514–42. Available online: www.law.edu.ac.uk/ahrc/script-ed/vol2–4/hatcher.asp (last accessed on 15 September 2013).

Hatim, Basil and Ian Mason (1997) *The Translator as Communicator*, London: Routledge.

Hay, Louis (2004) 'Genetic Criticism: Origins and Perspectives', in Jed Deppman, Daniel Ferrer, and Michael Groden (eds) *Genetic Criticism: Texts and Avant-textes*, Philadelphia: University of Pennsylvania Press, 7–27.

Heath, Stephen (1981) *Questions of Cinema*, London: Macmillan.

Heiss, Christine and Lisa Leporati (2000) 'Non é che ci mettiamo a fare i difficili, eh? Traduttori e dialoghisti alle prese con il regioletto', in Rosa

Maria Bollettieri Bosinelli, Christine Heiss, Marcello Soffritti, Silvia Bernardini (eds) *La traduzione multimediale: Quale traduzione per quale testo?*, Bologna: Cooperativa Libraria Universitaria Editrice Bologna, 43–66.

Heiss, Christine and Marcello Soffritti (2008) 'Forlixt 1 The Forlì: Corpus of Screen Translation: Exploring Microstructures', in Delia Chiaro, Christine Heiss and Chiara Bucaria (eds) *Between Text and Image. Updating Research in Screen Translation*, Amsterdam and Philadelphia: John Benjamins, 51–63.

Herbst, Thomas (1994) *Linguistische Aspekte der Synchronisation von Fernsehserien. Phonetik, Textlinguistik, Übersetzungstheorie*, Tübingen: Niemeyer.

—— (1997) 'Dubbing and the Dubbed Text – Style and Cohesion: Textual Characteristics of a Special Form of Translation', in Anna Trosborg (ed.) *Text Typology and Translation*, Amsterdam and Philadelphia: John Benjamins, 291–308.

Herman, David (2009) 'Cognitive Approaches to Narrative Analysis', in Geert Brône and Jeroen Vandaele (eds), *Cognitive Poetics: Goals, Gains, and Gaps*, Berlin and New York: Mouton de Gruyter, 79–118.

Hermans, Theo (2003) 'Cross-cultural Translation Studies as Thick Translation', *Bulletin of the School of Oriental and African Studies* 66 (3): 380–89.

Hills, Matt (2002) *Fan Cultures*, London: Routledge.

Holstein, James A. and Jaber F. Gubrium (2001) *The Active Interview*, Thousand Oaks, CA: Sega.

Ivarsson, Jan (2002) 'Subtitling Through the Ages. A Technical History of Subtitles in Europe', *Language International*, April: 6–10.

Iwabuchi, Koichi (2002) *Recentering Globalization: Popular Culture and Japanese Transnationalism*, Durham: Duke University Press.

—— (2010) 'Undoing Inter-national Fandom in the Age of Brand Nationalism', *Mechademia* 5 (Fanthropologies): 87–96.

Izard Martínez, Natàlia (1992) *La traducció cinematogràfica*, Barcelona: Centre d'Investigació de la Comunicació.

Jäckel, Anne (2001) 'The Subtitling of *La Haine*: A Case Study', in Yves Gambier and Henrik Gottlieb (eds) *(Multi) Media Translation: Concepts, Practices and Research,* Amsterdam and Philadelphia: John Benjamins, 223–35.

Jacobs, Lewis (1968) *The Rise of the American Film: A Critical History*, New York: Teachers College Press.

James, Meg (2001) 'Language Barrier Slows Movie Releases', *L.A. Times*, 25 August. Available online: http://articles.latimes.com/2001/aug/25/business/fi-38050 (last accessed on 15 September 2013).

Jenkins, Henry (2004) 'The Cultural Logic of Media Convergence', *International Journal of Cultural Studies* 7 (1): 33–43.

Jenkins, Henry, Katie Clinton, Ravi Purushotma, Alice J. Robison and Margaret Weigel (2006) *Confronting the Challenges of Participatory Culture: Media*

Education for the 21st Century, Chicago, IL: The MacArthur Foundation. Available online: www.digitallearning.macfound.org/atf/cf/%7B7E45C7E0-A3E0–4B89-AC9CE807E1B0AE4E%7D/JENKINS_WHITE_PAPER.PDF (last accessed on 15 September 2013).

Jennett, Charlene, Anna L. Cox, Paul Cairns, Samira Dhoparee, Andrew Epps, Tim Tijs and Alison Walton (2008) 'Measuring and Defining the Experience of Immersion in Games', *International Journal of Human-Computer Studies* 66(9): 641–61.

Jensema, Carl J. (1998) 'Viewer Reaction to Different Television Captioning Speeds', *American Annals of the Deaf* 143(4): 318–24.

Jensema, Carl J., Ramalinga Sarma Danturthi and Robert Burch (2000a) 'Time Spent Viewing Captions on Television Programs', *American Annals of the Deaf* 145(5): 464–68.

Jensema, Carl J., Sameh El Sharkawy, Ramalinga Sarma Danturthi, Robert Burch and David Hsu (2000b) 'Eye Movement Patterns of Captioned Television Viewers', *American Annals of the Deaf* 145(3): 275–85.

Jiménez Hurtado, Catalina and Claudia Seibel (2012) 'Multisemiotic and Multimodal Corpus Analysis in Audiodescription: TRACCE', in Aline Remael, Pilar Orero and Mary Carroll (eds) *Audiovisual Translation and Media Accessibility at the Crossroads*, Amsterdam and New York: Rodopi, 409–25.

Kalaian, Sema A. and Rafa M. Kasim (2008) 'Research Hypothesis', in Paul J. Lavrakas (ed.) *Encyclopedia of Survey Research Methods*, Thousand Oaks, CA: SAGE, 732–34.

Karamitroglou, Fotios (1998) 'A Proposed Set of Subtitling Standards for Europe', *Translation Journal* 2(2). Available online: www.bokorlang.com/journal/04stndrd.htm (last accessed on 15 September 2013).

—— (2000) *Towards a Methodology for the Investigation of Norms in Audiovisual Translation*, Amsterdam and Atlanta: Rodopi.

Karlin, Fred and Rayburn Wright (2004) *On the Track: A Guide to Contemporary Film Scoring*, 2nd revised edition, London and New York: Routledge.

Kawin, Bruce F. (1992) *How Movies Work*, Berkeley and Los Angeles, University of California Press.

Kayahara, Matthew (2005) 'The Digital Revolution: DVD Technology and the Possibilities for Audiovisual Translation Studies', *JoSTrans: The Journal of Specialised Translation* 3: 64–74. Available online: www.jostrans.org/issue03/art_kayahara.pdf (last accessed on 15 September 2013).

Kendrick, James (2012) 'The Woman in Black', *QNetwork Entertainment Portal*. Available online: www.qnetwork.com/index.php?page=review&id=2715 (last accessed on 15 September 2013).

Kirchner, Jesse Saba (2006) 'And in Some Language That's English? Slayer Slang and Artificial Computer Generation', *Slayage: The Online International Journal of Buffy Studies* 20 (5.4). Available online: http://

slayageonline.com/PDF/Kirchner.pdf (last accessed on 15 September 2013).

Koskinen, Kaisa (2010) 'On EU Communication 2.0: Using Social Media to Attain Affective Citizenship', in Mona Baker, Maeve Olohan and María Calzada Pérez (eds) *Text and Context*, Manchester: St Jerome, 139–56.

Kozinets, Robert V. (2010). *Netnography: Doing Ethnographic Research Online*. Thousand Oaks, CA: Sage Publications.

Kozloff, Sarah (2000) *Overhearing Film Dialogue*, Berkeley, Los Angeles, London: University of California Press.

Kozoulyaev, Alexey (n.d.) '3D Subtitling – A New Deal Beyond', *DVD and Beyond*. Available online: www.dvd-and-beyond.com/features/feature.php?feature=126 (last accessed 15 September 2013).

Krawanja, Angelika (2009) *Subtitling into German One Episode of the Television Sitcom* The Royle Family *on the Lives of a Working Class Manchester Family*, Unpublished MA Dissertation, University of Manchester.

Kress, Gunther and Theo van Leeuwen (2001) *Multimodal Discourse: The Modes and Media of Contemporary Communication*, London: Arnold.

—— (2006) *Reading Images: The Grammar of Visual Design*, 2nd edition, London and New York: Routledge.

Kruger, Jan-Louis (2012) 'Making Meaning in AVT: Eye Tracking and Viewer Construction of Narrative', *Perspectives: Studies in Translatology* 20(1): 67–86.

Kumar, Shanti (2005) *Gandhi Meets Primetime*, Champaign: University of Illinois Press.

Lambert, José and Dirk Delabastita (1996) 'La traduction de textes audiovisuels: modes et enjeux culturels', in Yves Gambier (ed.) *Les transferts linguistiques dan les médias audiovisuels*, Villeneuve d'Ascq: Presses Universitaires du Septentrion, 33–58.

Landow, George P. (1992) *Hypertext: The Convergence of Contemporary Critical Theory and Technology*, Baltimore: Johns Hopkins University Press.

Lang, Brent (2010) 'James Cameron: Yes, *Avatar* is Political', *The Wrap*, 13 January. Available online: www.thewrap.com/movies/article/james-cameron-avatars-political-message-12929 (last accessed on 15 September 2013).

Lång, Juha, Jukka Mäkisalo, Tersia Gowases, Sami Pietinen (2013) 'Using Eye Tracking to Study the Effect of Badly Synchronized Subtitles on the Gaze Paths of Television Viewers', *New Voices in Translation Studies* 10. Available online: www.iatis.org/images/stories/publications/new-voices/Issue10–2013/articles/article-long-2013b.pdf (last accessed on 15 September 2013).

Langacker, Ronald W. (1987) *Foundations of Cognitive Grammar*, Stanford, CA: Stanford University Press.

Leavis, Frank R. (1930) *Mass Civilisation and Minority Culture*, Cambridge: Minority Press.

Lecuona Lerchundi, Lourdes (1994) 'Entre el doblaje y la subtitulación: la inter-pretación simultánea en el cine', in Federico Eguíluz, Raquel Merino, Vickie Olsen, Eterio Pajares and José Miguel (1994) (eds) *Trasvases culturales: literatura, cine, traducción*, Vitoria: Universidad del País Vasco, 279–86.

Leonard, Sean (2005) 'Progress Against the Law: Anime and Fandom, with the Key to the Globalization of Culture', *International Journal of Cultural Studies* 8(3): 281–305.

Leuzinger-Bohleber, Marianne and Tamara Fischmann (2006) 'What is Conceptual Research in Psychoanalysis?', *International Journal of Psycho-analysis* 87(5): 1355–86.

Levi, Dennis M., Stanley A. Klein and A. P. Aitsebaomo (1985) 'Vernier Acuity, Crowding and Cortical Magnification', *Vision Research* 25(7): 963–77.

Levy, Pierre (2000) *Collective Intelligence: Man's Emerging World in Cyberspace*, New York: Perseus.

Lewin, George (1931) 'Dubbing and its Relation to Sound Picture Production', *Journal of the Society of Motion Picture Engineers* 16(1): 38–48.

Li, Dang (2014) *Amateur Translation and the Development of a Participatory Culture in China: A Netnographic Study of* The Last Fantasy *Fansubbing Group*, Unpublished PhD Thesis, University of Manchester.

Li, Xiaochang (2009) *Dis/Locating Audience: Transnational Media Flows and the Online Circulation of East Asian Television Drama*, Unpublished MA Dissertation, Massachusetts Institute of Technology.

Lindgren, Simon (2013) 'Sub*culture: Exploring the Dynamics of a Networked Public', *Transformative Works and Cultures* 14. Available online: http://journal.transformativeworks.org/index.php/twc/article/view/447/359 (last accessed on 15 September 2013).

Lippi-Green, Rosina (1997) *English with an Accent: Language, Ideology, and Discrimination in the United States*, London and New York: Routledge.

Littau, Karin (1997). 'Translation in the Age of Postmodern Production: From Text to Intertext to Hypertext', *Forum for Modern Language Studies* 33: 81–96.

—— (2006) *Theories of Reading: Books, Bodies and Bibliomania*. Cambridge: Polity Press.

Loiperdinger, Martin (2004) 'Lumière's Arrival of the Train: Cinema's Founding Myth', *The Moving Image* 4(1): 89–118.

Lorefice, Michael (2001) '12 Angry Men (1957)'. Available online: www.metalasylum.com/ragingbull/movies/angrymen.html (last accessed 15 September 2013).

Lúcia Santiago Araújo, Vera and Celia M. Magalhães (2009) 'Multimodal Transcription as Tool for Training Novice Audio Describers', Paper delivered at the *3rd International Conference Media for All: Quality Made to Measure*, 22–24 October, Antwerp.

Luyken, Georg-Michael, Thomas Herbst, Jo Langham-Brown, Helen Reid and Hermann Spinhof (1991) *Overcoming Language Barriers in Television. Dubbing and Subtitling for the European Audience*, Manchester: European Institute for the Media.

McChesney, Robert and Dan Schiller (2003) 'The Political Economy of International Communications: Foundations for the Emerging Global Debate about Media Ownership and Regulation', *Technology, Business and Society Programme*, Paper Number 11, October 2003, United Nations Research Institute for Social Development.

McClarty, Rebecca (2013) 'In Support of Creative Subtitling: Contemporary Context and Theoretical Framework', *Perspectives: Studies in Translatology*, DOI: 10.1080/0907676X.2013.842258.

MacDonald, Scott (1995) 'Introduction', in Scott MacDonald (ed.) *Screen Writings. Scripts and Texts by independent Filmmakers*, Berkeley, Los Angeles and London: University of California Press, 1–14.

McDonald, Keiko I. (2006) *Reading a Japanese Film: Cinema in Context*, Honolulu: University of Hawai'i Press.

McFarlane, Brian (2008) 'Watching, Writing and Control: *Atonement*', *Screen Education* 49: 8–16.

Macintyre, Donald and Eric Silver (2006) 'UK calls Israeli Attacks "Disproportionate"', *The Independent*, 24 July 2006. Available online: www.independent.co.uk/news/world/middle-east/uk-calls-israeli-attacks-disproportionate-409087.html (last accessed on 15 September 2013).

McNair, Brian (2006) *Cultural Chaos: Journalism, News and Power in a Globalised World*, London and New York: Routledge.

Mangirón, Carmen and Minako O'Hagan (2006) 'Game Localisation: Unleashing Imagination with "Restricted" Translation', *JoSTrans: The Journal of Specialized Translation* 6. Available online: www.jostrans.org/issue06/art_ohagan.php (last accessed on 15 September 2013).

Mann, Thomas (1928/1978) 'Über den Film', in Anton Kaes (ed.) *Kino-Debatte: Texte zun Verhältnis von Literatur und Film 1909–1929*, Tubingen: Max Niemayer, 164–66.

Manovich, Lev (2001) *The Language of New Media*, Cambridge, MA: MIT Press.

Martí Ferriol, José Luis (2006) *Estudio empírico y descriptivo del método de traducción para doblaje y subtitulación*, Unpublished PhD Thesis, Castelló de la Plana: Universitat Jaume I. Available online: www.tdx.cat/bitstream/handle/10803/10568/marti.pdf;jsessionid=C94DD56B8359EB0D9C38F9 9CFB16792B.tdx2?sequence=1 (last accessed on 15 September 2013).

Mason, Ian (1989) 'Speaker Meaning and Reader Meaning: Preserving Coherence in Screen Translation', in Henry Prais, Rainer Kölmel and Jerry Payne (eds) *Babel. The Cultural and Linguistic Barriers between Nations*, Aberdeen: Aberdeen University Press, 13–24.

—— (2001) 'Coherence in Subtitling: The Negotiation of Face', in Frederic Chaume Varela and Rosa Agost (eds) *La traducción en los medios audiovisuales*, Castelló de la Plana: Servei de Publicacions de la Universitat Jaume I, 19–32.

Matthews, Bob and Liz Ross (2010) *Research Methods: A Practical Guide for the Social Sciences*, Edinburgh: Pearson Education.

Mayoral, Roberto, Dorothy Kelly and Natividad Gallardo (1988) 'Concept of Constrained Translation. Non-linguistic Perspectives of Translation', *Meta* 33(3): 356–67.

Mereu, Carla (2012) 'Censoring Interferences in the Dubbing of Foreign Films in Fascist Italy: 1927–43', *Meta* 57(2): 294–309.

Merino Álvarez, Raquel (ed.) (2008) *Traducción y censura en España (1939–1985). Estudios sobre corpus TRACE: cine, narrativa, teatro*, Bilbao: Servicio Editorial de la Universidad del País Vasco. Available online: www.ehu.es/argitalpenak/images/stories/libros_gratuitos_en_pdf/Humanidades/Traduccion%20y%20censura%20en%20Espana%20(1939–85).pdf (last accessed on 15 September 2013).

Mével, Pierre-Alexis (2007) 'The Translation of Identity: Subtitling the Vernacular of the French *cité*', *MHRA Working Papers in the Humanities* 2, 49–56. Available online: www.mhra.org.uk/ojs/index.php/wph/article/viewFile/56/50 (last accessed on 15 September 2013).

Minh-ha, Trinh T. (1992) *Framer Framed*, New York: Routledge.

—— (2005) *The Digital Film Event*, London: Routledge.

Molina Foix, Vicente (2005) 'El Director Exquisito', *El País*, 6 March. Available online: http://elpais.com/diario/2005/03/06/eps/1110094011_850215.html (last accessed on 15 September 2013).

Montreal Film Journal (1998) 'Review of Annie Hall (1977)'. Available online: www.montrealfilmjournal.com/review.asp?R=R0000019 (last accessed on 15 September 2013).

Morgan, Jason (2007) 'Battleship Potemkin'. Available online: www.filmcritic.com/reviews/1925/battleship-potemkin/ (last accessed on 15 September 2013).

Morris, Julia (2009) *An Investigation into Subtitling in French and Spanish Heritage Cinema*, Unpublished MPhil Dissertation, University of Birmingham. Available online: http://etheses.bham.ac.uk/1026/1/Morris10MPhil.pdf (last accessed on 15 September 2013).

Mowitt, John (2004) 'The Hollywood Sound Tract', in Atom Egoyan and Ian Balfour (eds) *Subtitles. On the Foreignness of Film*, Cambridge, MA and London: The MIT Press, 382–401.

Mubenga, Kajingulu Somwe (2009) 'Towards a Multimodal Pragmatic Analysis of Film Discourse in Audiovisual Translation', *Meta* 54(3): 466–84.

Munday, Jeremy (2012) *Introducing Translation Studies*, 3rd edition, London and New York: Routledge.

Murray, Terence P. (2012) *Diglossia in Taiwanese Screen Translation: Measuring Formality in Translated Mandarin and Tai-gi*, Unpublished MA Dissertation, The University of Manchester.

Musser, Charles (1991) *Before the Nickelodeon: Edwin S. Porter and the Edison Manufacturing Company*, Berkeley: University of California Press.

Nadiani, Giovanni (2004) 'Dialekt und filmische Nicht-Übersetzung: Der Einzig Mögliche Weg?', in Irmeli Helin (ed.) *Dialektübersetzung und Dialekt in Multimedia*, Bruxelles, Bern, Berlin, Frankfurt am Main, New York, Oxford, and Vienna: Peter Lang, 53–74.

Naficy, Hamid (2001) *An Accented Cinema. Exilic and Diasporic Filmmaking*, Princeton and Oxford: Princeton University Press.

—— (2003) 'Theorizing "Third World" Film Spectatorship: The Case of Iran and Iranian Cinema', in Anthony R. Guneratne and Wimal Dissanayake (eds) *Rethinking Third Cinema*, London: Routledge, 183–201.

—— (2004) 'Epistolarity and Textuality in Accented Films', in Atom Egoyan and Ian Balfour (eds) *Subtitles. On the Foreignness of Film*, Cambridge, MA and London: The MIT Press, 131–51.

Napier, Susan J. (2007) *From Impressionism to Anime: Japan as Fantasy and Fan Cult in the Mind of the West*, New York: Palgrave Macmillan.

Nedergaard-Larsen, Birgit (1993) 'Culture-bound Problems in Subtitling', *Perspectives* 2: 207–41.

Negroponte, Nicholas (1991) 'Multimedia', *Hightech*, August: 68.

Neves, Joselia (2005) *Audiovisual Translation: Subtitling for the Deaf and Hard-of-Hearing*, Unpublished PhD Thesis, University of Roehampton, UK. Available online: http://roehampton.openrepository.com/roehampton/bitstream/10142/12580/1/neves%2520audiovisual.pdf (last accessed on 15 September 2013).

Nichols, Bill (1991) *Representing Reality: Issues and Concepts in Documentary*, Bloomington and Indianapolis: Indiana University Press.

Nornes, Abé M. (1999) 'For an Abusive Subtitling', *Film Quarterly* 52(3): 17–33.

—— (2007) *Cinema Babel: Translating Global Cinema*, Minneapolis and London: University of Minnesota Press.

Novell-Smith, Geoffrey (1998) 'Introduction', in Geoffrey Novell-Smith and Steven Ricci (eds) *Hollywood and Europe: Economics, Culture, National Identity 1945–1995*, London: British Film Institute, 1–16.

Novell-Smith, Geoffrey and Steven Ricci (eds) (1998) *Hollywood and Europe: Economics, Culture, National Identity 1945–1995*, London: British Film Institute.

O'Brien, Charles (2005) *Cinema's Conversion to Sound: Technology and Film Style in France and the U.S.*, Bloomington: Indiana University Press.

O'Connell, Eithne (1998) 'Choices and Constraints in Screen Translation', in Lynne Bowker, Michael Cronin, Dorothy Kenny and Jennifer Pearson (eds) *Unity in Diversity? Current Trends in Translation Studies*, Manchester: St Jerome, 65–71.

—— (2007) 'Screen Translation', in Piotr Kuhiwczak and Karin Littau (eds) *A Companion to Translation Studies*, Clevedon, Buffalo and Toronto: Multilingual Matters, 120–33.

O'Hagan, Minako (2003) 'Can Language Technology Respond to the Subtitler's Dilemma? – A Preliminary Study', in *Translating and the Computer 25*, Conference Proceedings of the 2003 ASLIB Conference, London: ASLIB. Available online: www.mt-archive.info/Aslib-2003-OHagan.pdf (last accessed 15 September 2013).

—— (2008) 'Fan Translation Networks: An Accidental Translator Training Environment?', in John Kearns (ed.) *Translator and Interpreter Training: Issues, Methods and Debates*, London: Continuum, 158–83.

—— (2012) 'From Fan Translation to Crowdsourcing: Consequences of Web 2.0 User Empowerment in Audiovisual Translation', in Aline Remael, Pilar Orero and Mary Carroll (eds) *Audiovisual Translation and Media Accessibility at the Crossroads*, Amsterdam and New York: Rodopi, 25–41.

O'Sullivan, Carol (2011) *Translating Popular Film*, Basingstoke: Palgrave Macmillan.

Olohan, Maeve (2004) *Introducing Corpora in Translation Studies*, London and New York: Routledge.

Olohan, Maeve and Mona Baker (2009) 'Coherence and Clarity of Objectives in Doctoral Projects. A Research Design Workshop', *The Interpreter and Translator Trainer* 3(1): 143–64.

Orero, Pilar (2008) 'Three Different Receptions of the Same Film', *European Journal of English Studies* 12: 179–93.

—— (2012) 'Audio Description Behaviour: Universals, Regularities and Guidelines', *International Journal of Humanities and Social Science* 2(17): 195–202.

Orero, Pilar and Anna Vilaró (2012) 'Eye Tracking Analysis of Minor Details in Films for Audio Description', in Rosa Agost, Pilar Orero and Elena di Giovanni (eds) *MONTI 4: Multidisciplinarity in Audiovisual Translation*: 295–319.

Ortabasi, Melek (2006) 'Indexing the Past: Visual Language and Translatability in Kon Satoshi's Millennium Actress', *Perspectives: Studies in Translatology* 14(4): 278–91.

Panofsky, Erwin (1934/1999) 'Style and Medium in the Motion Pictures', in Leo Braudy and Marshall Cohen (eds) *Film Theory and Criticism*, New York and Oxford: Oxford University Press, 279–92.

Pavesi, Maria (2005) *La traduzione filmica. Aspetti del parlato doppiato dall'inglese all'italiano*, Rome: Carocci.

—— (2009a) 'Dubbing English into Italian: A Closer Look at the Translation of Spoken Language', in Jorge Díaz Cintas (ed.) *New Trends in Audiovisual Translation*, Bristol: Multilingual Matters, 197–209.

—— (2009b) 'Referring to Third Persons in Dubbing: Is There a Role for Source Language Transfer?', in Maria Freddi and Maria Pavesi (eds)

Analysing Audiovisual Dialogue. Linguistic and Translational Insights, Bologna: Clueb, 125–41.

Pavesi, Maria and Maria Freddi (2009) 'Introduction', in Maria Freddi and Maria Pavesi (eds) *Analysing Audiovisual Dialogue. Linguistic and Translational Insights*, Bologna: Clueb, 11–16.

Perego, Elisa (2004) 'Subtitling Culture by Means of Explicitation', in Maria Sidiripoulou and Anastasia Papaconstantinou (eds) *Choice and Difference in Translation*, Athens: University of Athens, 145–68.

Pérez-González, Luis (2006) 'Fansubbing Anime: Insights into the "Butterfly Effect" of Globalisation on Audiovisual Translation', *Perspectives: Studies in Translatology* 14(4): 260–77.

—— (2007a) 'Appraising Dubbed Conversation: Systemic Functional Insights into the Construal of Naturalness in Translated Film Dialogue', *The Translator* 13(1): 1–38.

—— (2007b) 'Intervention in New Amateur Subtitling Cultures: A Multimodal Account', *Linguistica Antverpiensia* 6: 67–80.

—— (2009) 'Audiovisual Translation', in Mona Baker and Gabriela Saldanha (eds) *The Routledge Encyclopedia of Translation Studies*, 2nd edition, London and New York: Routledge, 13–20.

—— (2010) '"Ad-hocracies" of Translation Activism in the Blogosphere: A Genealogical Case Study', in Mona Baker, Maeve Olohan and María Calzada-Pérez (eds) *Text and Context: Essays on Translation and Interpreting in Honour of Ian Mason*, Manchester: St Jerome, 259–87.

—— (2012) 'Amateur Subtitling and the Pragmatics of Spectatorial Subjectivity', *Language and Intercultural Communication* 12(4): 335–53.

—— (2013a) 'Amateur Subtitling as Immaterial Labour in Digital Media Culture: An Emerging Paradigm of Civic Engagement', *Convergence: The International Journal of Research into New Media Technologies*, 19(2): 157–75.

—— (2013b) 'Co-creational Subtitling in the Digital Media: Transformative and Authorial Practices', *International Journal of Cultural Studies* 16(1): 3–21.

—— (2014a) 'Multimodality in Translation Studies: Theoretical and Methodological Perspectives', in Sandra Bermann and Catherine Porter (eds) *A Companion to Translation Studies*, Wiley-Blackwell, 119–31.

—— (2014b) 'Translation and New(s) Media: Participatory Subtitling Practices in Networked Mediascapes', in Juliane House (ed.) *Translation: A Multidisciplinary Approach*, Basingstoke: Palgrave Macmillan.

Pérez-González, Luis and Sebnem Susam-Saraeva (2012) 'Non-professionals Translating and Interpreting: Participatory and Engaged Perspectives', *The Translator* 18(2): 149–65.

Pettit, Zoë (2004) 'The Audio-Visual Text: Subtitling and Dubbing Different Genres', *Meta* 49(1): 25–38.

Piñero, Neil J. (2010) *The Inbetweeners: A Proposed Spanish Dubbed Version and Analysis of the Translation of Humour*, Unpublished MA Dissertation, The University of Manchester.

Planalp, Sally (1999) *Communicating Emotion: Social, Moral, and Cultural Processes*, Cambridge: Cambridge University Press.

Podhoretz, John (2009) 'Avatarocious: Another Spectacle Hits an Iceberg and Sinks', *The Weekly Standard*, 28 December. Available online: www.weeklystandard.com/Content/Public/Articles/000/000/017/350fozta.asp (last accessed on 15 September 2013).

Popovič, Anton (1970) 'The Concept "Shift of Expression" in Translation Analysis', in James S. Holmes (ed.) *The Nature of Translation: Essays on the Theory and Practice of Literary Translation*, The Hague and Paris: Mouton, 78–87.

Pulver, Andrew (2009) '*Avatar* Review: James Cameron Just got Slack', *The Guardian*, 11 December. Available online: www.guardian.co.uk/film/2009/dec/11/avatar-james-cameron-film-review (last accessed on 15 September 2013).

Punathambekar, Aswin (2008) 'Audiences: Unimaginable Communities', *C3 Weekly Update*. Available online: http://mit.edu/samford/www/weekly-update_20080410.html (last accessed on 15 September 2013).

Queen, Robin (2004) '"Du hast jar keeneAhnung": African American English Dubbed into German', *Journal of Sociolinguistics* 8(4): 515–37.

Quinn, Anthony (2013) 'The Collaboration: Hollywood's Pact with Hitler by Ben Urwand', *The Guardian* 16 October. Available online: www.theguardian.com/books/2013/oct/16/collaboration-hollywood-hitler-ben-urwand (last accessed 15 September 2013).

Radford, Ceri (2011) 'Human Planet, BBC One, review', *The Telegraph*, 14 January. Available online: www.telegraph.co.uk/culture/tvandradio/8258258/Human-Planet-BBC-One-review.html (last accessed on 15 September 2013).

Rajendran, Dhevi J., Andrew T. Duchowski, Pilar Orero, Juan Martínez and Pablo Romero-Fresco (2013) 'Effects of Text Chunking on Subtitling: A Quantitative and Qualitative Examination', *Perspectives: Studies in Translatology* 21(1): 5–21.

Ranzato, Irene (2012) 'Gayspeak and Gay Subjects in Audiovisual Translation: Strategies in Italian Dubbing', *Meta* 57(2): 369–84.

Ray, Rebecca and Nataly Kelly (2011) *Crowdsourced Translation: Best Practices for Implementation*, Lowell: Common Sense Advisory.

Reiss, Katharina (1971/2000) *Möglichkeiten und Grenzen der Übersetzungskritik*, Munich: Max Hüeber, translated by Erroll F. Rhodes (2000) *Translation Criticism: Potential and Limitations*, Manchester: St Jerome and the American Bible Society.

Remael, Aline (2001) 'Some Thoughts on the Study of Multimodal and Multimedia Translation', in Yves Gambier and Henrik Gottlieb (eds)

(Multi) Media Translation: Concepts, Practices and Research, Amsterdam: John Benjamins, 13–22.

—— (2003) 'Mainstream Narrative Film Dialogue and Subtitling', *The Translator* 9(2): 225–47.

—— (2004) 'A Place for Film Dialogue Analysis in Subtitling Courses', in Pilar Orero (ed.) *Topics in Audiovisual Translation*, Amsterdam and Philadelphia: John Benjamins, 103–26.

—— (2007) 'Sampling Subtitling for the Deaf and the Hard-of-Hearing in Europe', in Jorge Díaz Cintas, Aline Remael and Pilar Orero (eds) *Media for All*, Amsterdam: Rodopi, 23–52.

—— (2010) 'Audiovisual Translation', in Yves Gambier and Luc van Doorslaer (eds) *Handbook of Translation Studies* (Volume 1), Amsterdam and Philadelphia: 12–17.

Rich, B. Ruby (2004) 'To Read or not to Read: Subtitles, Trailers, and Monolingualism', in Atom Egoyan and Ian Balfour (eds) *Subtitles. On the Foreignness of Film*, Cambridge, MA and London: The MIT Press, 153–69.

Richardson, Kay (2010) 'Multimodality and the Study of Popular Drama', *Language and Literature* 19(4): 378–95.

Rodgers, Scott (2010) *Level Up! The Guide to Great Video Game Design*, John Wiley and Sons.

Romero-Fresco, Pablo (2006) 'The Spanish Dubbese: A Case of (Un)idiomatic *Friends*', *JoSTrans* 6: 134–52. Available online: www.jostrans.org/issue06/art_romero_fresco.pdf (last accessed on 15 September 2013).

—— (2009) 'Naturalness in the Spanish Dubbing Language: A Case of Not-so-close *Friends*', *Meta* 54(1): 49–72.

—— (2011) *Subtitling Through Speech Recognition: Respeaking*, Manchester: St Jerome.

—— (2012) 'Respeaking in Translator Training Curricula. Present and Future Prospects', *The Interpreter and Translator Trainer* 6(1): 91–112.

Romney, Jonathan (2006) 'Filtered for Extra Smoothness', *ABC: The Arts, Books and Culture Magazine from The Independent*, 16 June, 10.

Rosenberg, Grant (2007) 'Rethinking the Art of Subtitles', *Time*, 15 May. Available online: www.time.com/time/arts/article/0,8599,1621155,00.html (last accessed on 15 September 2013).

Ross, Andrew (2009) *Nice Work If You Can Get it: Life and Labour in Precarious Times*, New York: New York University Press.

Ruh, Brian (2010) 'Transforming U.S. Anime in the 1980s: Localization and Longevity', *Mechademia* 5 (Fanthropologies): 31–49.

Saldanha, Gabriela and Sharon O'Brien (2013) *Research Methodologies in Translation Studies*, Manchester: St Jerome.

Salmon Kovarski, Laura (2000) 'Tradurre l'etnoletto: Come doppiare in italiano l'accento ebraico', in Rosa Maria Bollettieri Bosinelli, Christine Heiss, Marcello Soffritti, Silvia Bernardini (eds) *La traduzione multimediale:*

Quale traduzione per quale testo?, Bologna: Cooperativa Libraria Universitaria Editrice Bologna, 67–84.

Salway, Andrew (2007) 'A Corpus-based Analysis of Audio Description', in Jorge Díaz Cintas, Pilar Orero and Aline Remael (eds) *Media for All. Subtitling for the Deaf, Audio Description and Sign Language*, Amsterdam and New York: Rodopi, 151–74.

Sato, Kenji (2002) 'More Animated than Life', *The Kyoto Journal. Media in Asia* 56. Available online: www.kyotojournal.org/media/animated.html (last accessed on 15 September 2013).

Scandura, Gabriella (2004) 'Sex, Lies and TV: Censorship and Subtitling', *Meta* 49(1): 125–34.

Scholte, Jan Aart (2005) *Globalization: A Critical Introduction*, 2nd edition, Basingstoke: Palgrave Macmillan.

Scholz, Trebor (2008) 'Market Ideology and the Myths of Web 2.0', *First Monday* 13(3). Available online: http://firstmonday.org/htbin/cgiwrap/bin/ojs/index.php/fm/article/view/2138/1945 (last accessed on 15 September 2013).

Schudson, Michael (1995) *The Power of News*, Cambridge, MA: Harvard University Press.

Schwarzbaum, Lisa (2007) 'The Lives of Others', *Entertainment Weekly*, 7 February. Available online: www.ew.com/ew/article/0,20010660,00. html (last accessed on 15 September 2013).

Shackman, Jessica E. and Seth D. Pollac (2005) 'Experiential Influences on Multimodal Perception of Emotion', *Child Development* 76(5): 1116–26.

Shafik, Viola (2007) *Arab Cinema. History and Cultural Identity*, new revised edition, Cairo and New York: The American University in Cairo Press.

Shohat, Ella and Robert Stam (2006) 'The Cinema after Babel: Language, Difference, Power', in Ella Shohat, *Taboo Memories, Diasporic Voices*, Durham and London: Duke University Press, 106–38.

Shuttleworth, Mark and Moira Cowie (1997) *Dictionary of Translation Studies*, Manchester: St Jerome.

Silverman, David (1993) *Interpreting Qualitative Data: Methods for Analysing Talk, Text and Interaction*, London, Thousand Oaks and New Delhi: Sage.

Sinha, Amresh (2004) 'The Use and Abuse of Subtitles', in Atom Egoyan and Ian Balfour (eds) *Subtitles: On the Foreignness of Film*, Cambridge, MA and London: The MIT Press, 172–90.

Skretvedt, Randy (1987) *Laurel and Hardy: The Magic Behind the Movies*, Beverly Hills: Moonstone Press.

Smith, Adam (2006) '12 Angry Men', Radio Times, 7–13 October, 47.

Smith, Susan (2007) 'Voices in Film', in John Gibbs and Douglas Pye (eds) *Close-Up 02*, London and New York: Wallflower Press, 159–238.

Snell-Hornby, Mary (1988/1995) *Translation Studies: An Integrated Approach*, Amsterdam and Philadelphia: John Benjamins.

Sotelo Dios, Patricia (2011) 'Using a Multimedia Parallel Corpus to Investigate English-Galician Subtitling', in Bente Maegaard (ed.) *Proceedings of the Supporting Digital Humanities Conference*, Copenhagen 17 – 18 November 2011. Available online: http://crdo.up.univ-aix.fr/SLDRdata/doc/show/copenhagen/SDH-2011/submissions/sdh2011_submission_46.pdf (last accessed on 15 September 2013).

Sotelo Dios, Patricia and Xavier Gómez Guinovart (2012), in Alberto Simões, Ricardo Queirós and Daniela da Cruz (eds) *Proceedings of the 1st Symposium on Languages, Applications and Technologies SLATE 2012*, Schloss-Dagstuhl: OASIcs, 255–66. Available online: http://drops.dagstuhl.de/opus/volltexte/2012/3527/pdf/20.pdf (last accessed on 15 September 2013).

Stöckl, Hartmut (2004) 'In Between Modes: Language and Image in Printed Media', in Eija Ventola, Cassily Charles and Martin Kaltenbacher (eds) *Perspectives on Multimodality*, Amsterdam and Philadelphia: John Benjamins, 9–30.

Susam-Sarajeva, Sebnem (2009) 'The Case Study Research Method in Translation Studies', in Ian Mason (ed.) *Training for Doctoral Research*, special issue of *The Interpreter and Translator Trainer* 3(1): 37–56.

Szarkowska, Agnieszka (2009) 'The Audiovisual Landscape in Poland at the Dawn of the 21st Century', in Angelika Goldstein and Biljana Golubovi (eds) *Foreign Language Movies – Dubbing vs. Subtitling*, Hamburg: Verlag Dr. Kova , 185–201.

Talmy, Leonard (2000) *Toward a Cognitive Semantics*, Cambridge, MA and London: MIT Press.

Taylor, Chris (2003) 'Multimodal Transcription in the Analysis, Translation and Subtitling of Italian Films', *The Translator* 9(2): 191–205.

Taylor, Richard (2000) *Battleship Potemkin*, London and New York: I.B. Tauris.

Terranova, Tiziana (2004) *Network Culture: Politics for the Information Age*, London: Pluto Press.

Testa, Bart (2002) 'Early Cinema and the Avant-Garde'. Available online: www.sixpackfilm.com/archive/veranstaltung/festivals/earlycinema/symposion/symposion_testa.html#1 (last accessed on 15 September 2013).

Thibault, Paul (2000) 'The Multimodal Transcription of a Television Advertisement: Theory and Practice', in Anthony Baldry (ed.) *Multimodality and Multimediality in the Distance Learning Age*, Campobasso: Palladino Editore, 311–85.

Thomson, David (2006) 'And the Oscar should have gone to . . . Bernard Herrmann', *ABC: The Arts, Books and Culture Magazine from The Independent*, 18 June, 17.

Titford, Christopher (1982) 'Subtitling: Constrained Translation', *Lebende Sprachen* 27(3): 113–16.

Toury, Gideon (1995) *Descriptive Translation Studies and Beyond*, Amsterdam and Philadelphia: John Benjamins.

Tyler, Andrea and Vyvyan Evans (2003) *The Semantics of English Prepositions*, Cambridge: Cambridge University Press.

Tymoczko, Maria (2005) 'Trajectories of Research in Translation Studies', *Meta* 50(4): 1082–97.

—— (2007) *Enlarging Translations, Empowering Translators*, Manchester: St Jerome.

Ulrych, Margherita (2000) 'Domestication and Foreignisation in Film Translation', in Christopher Taylor (ed.) *Tradurre il cinema*, Trieste: Università degli studi di Trieste, 127–44.

Urwand, Ben (2013) *The Collaboration: Hollywood's Pact with Hitler*, Cambridge, MA: Harvard University Press.

Valentini, Cristina (2006) 'A Multimedia Database for the Training of Audiovisual Translators', *JoSTrans: The Journal of Specialised Translation* 6. Available online: www.jostrans.org/issue06/art_valentini.php (last accessed on 15 September 2013).

—— (2008) 'Forlixt 1: The Forlì Corpus of Screen Translation: Exploring Macrostructures', in Delia Chiaro, Christine Heiss and Chiara Bucaria (eds) *Between Text and Image. Updating Research in Screen Translation*, Amsterdam and Philadelphia: John Benjamins, 37–51.

—— (2009) *Creazione e Sviluppo di Corpora Multimediali: Nuove Metodologie di Ricerca Nella Traduzione Audiovisiva* [Creation and Development of Multimedia Corpora: New Research Methods in Audiovisual Translation], Unpublished PhD Thesis, Università di Bologna. Available online: http://amsdottorato.cib.unibo.it/2125/1/Valentini_Cristina_Tesi.pdf (last accessed on 15 September 2013).

—— (2013) 'Phrasal Verbs in Italian Dubbed Dialogues: A Multimedia Corpus-based Study', *Perspectives: Studies in Translatology* 21(4): 543–62.

Van Leeuwen, Theo (2011) *The Language of Colour*, London and New York: Routledge.

Vandaele, Jeroen (2012) 'What Meets the Eye: Cognitive Narratology for Audio Description', *Perspectives: Studies in Translatology* 20(1): 87–102.

Vanoye, Francis (1985) 'Conversations publiques', *Iris* 3(1): 99–188.

Van Waes, Luuk, Mariëlle Leijten and Aline Remael (2013) 'Live Subtitling with Speech Recognition: Causes and Consequences of Text Reduction', *Across Languages and Cultures* 14(1): 15–46.

Vasey, Ruth (1992) 'Foreign Parts: Hollywood's Global Distribution and the Representation of Ethnicity', *American Quarterly* 44(4): 617–42.

Ventola, Eija, Cassily Charles and Martin Kaltenbacher (eds) (2004) *Perspectives on Multimodality*, Amsterdam and Philadelphia: John Benjamins.

Venuti, Lawrence (2008) 'Translation, Simulacra, Resistance', *Translation Studies* 1(1): 18–33.

Vercauteren, Gert (2012) 'A Narratological Approach to Content Selection in Audio Description: Towards a Strategy for the Description of

Narratological Time', in Rosa Agost, Pilar Orero and Elena di Giovanni (eds) *MONTI 4: Multidisciplinarity in Audiovisual Translation*: 207–31.

Vercauteren, Gert and Pilar Orero (2013) 'Describing Facial Expressions: Much More than Meets the Eye', *Quaderns: Revista de Traducció* 20: 187–99.

Vilaró, Anna, Andrew T. Duchowski, Pilar Orero, Tom Grindinger, Stephen Tetreault and Elena di Giovanni (2012) 'How Sound is the Pear Tree Story? Testing the Effect of Varying Audio Stimuli on Visual Attention Distribution', *Perspectives: Studies in Translatology* 20(1): 55–65.

Vinay, Jean-Paul and Jean Darbelnet (1958/1995) *Comparative Stylistics of French and English: A Methodology for Translation*, translated and edited by Juan C. Sager and Marie-Josée Hamel, Amsterdam and Philadelphia: John Benjamins.

Volk, Martin, Rico Sennrich, Christian Hardmeier and Frida Tidstrom (2010) 'Machine Translation of TV Subtitles for Large Scale Production' in Ventsislav Zhechev (ed.) *Proceedings of the Second Joint EM+/CNGL Workshop. Bringing MT to the User: Research on Integrating MT in the Translation Industry (JEC'10)*, Denver, CO, 53–62. Available online: www.diva-portal.org/smash/get/diva2:420760/FULLTEXT01.pdf (last accessed 15 September 2013).

Von Hippel, Eric (2005) *Democratizing Innovation*, Cambridge, MA: MIT Press.

Waxman, Sharon (2006) 'After Hype Online, "Snakes on a Plane" is Letdown at Box Office', *The New York Times*, 21 August. Available online: www.nytimes.com/2006/08/21/movies/21box.html?ref=arts (last accessed on 15 September 2013).

Weizman, Elda and Shoshana Blum-Kulka (1987) 'Identifying and Interpreting Translated Texts: On the Role of Pragmatic Adjustment', in Gideon Toury (ed.) *Translation Across Cultures*, New Delhi: Bahri Publications, 61–73.

Wellman, Barry (2002) 'Little Boxes, Glocalization, and Networked Individualism', in Makoto Tanabe, Peter Van den Besselaar and Toru Ishida (eds) *Digital cities II: Computational and Sociological Approaches*, New York: Springer, 10–25.

Whitakker, Tom (2012) 'Locating "La Voz": The Space and Sound of Spanish Dubbing', *Journal of Spanish Cultural Studies*, 13(3): 292–305.

Whitman-Linsen, Candace (1992) *Through the Dubbing Glass*, Frankfurt: Peter Lang.

Widler, Brigitte (2004) 'A Survey Among Audiences of Subtitled Films in Viennese Cinemas', *Meta* 49(1): 98–101.

Wilcox, Rhonda (2005) *Why Buffy Matters: The Art of Buffy the Vampire Slayer*, London: I.B. Tauris.

Williams, Jenny and Andrew Chesterman (2002) *The Map: A Beginner's Guide to Doing Research in Translation Studies*, Manchester: St Jerome.

Wilson, Deirdre and Dan Sperber (2004) 'Relevance theory', in Laurence R. Horn and Gregory Ward (eds) *The Handbook of Pragmatics*, Oxford: Blackwell, 607–32.

Wood, Michael (2011) 'At the Movies', *London Review of Books*, 28 April, p. 25. Available online: www.lrb.co.uk/v33/n09/michael-wood/at-the-movies (last accessed on 15 September 2013).

Woźniak, Monika (2012) 'Voice-over or Voice-in-between? Some Considerations About the Voice-over Translation of Feature Films on Polish Television', in Aline Remael, Pilar Orero and Mary Carroll (eds) *Audiovisual Translation and Media Accessibility at the Crossroads*, Amsterdam and New York: Rodopi, 209–28.

Wray, Alison (2002) *Formulaic Language and the Lexicon*, Cambridge: Cambridge University Press.

Wurm, Svenja (2007) 'Intralingual and Interlingual Subtitling: A Discussion of the Mode and Medium in Film Translation', *Sign Language Translator and Interpreter* 1(1): 115–41.

Xin, Shuang, John Tribe and Donna Chambers (2013) 'Conceptual Research in Tourism', *United Kingdom Annals of Tourism Research* 41: 66–88.

Yau, Wai-Ping (2012) 'Power, Identity and Subtitling in a Diglossic Society', *Meta* 57(3): 564–73.

Yin, Robert K. (1994) *Case Study Research: Design and Methods*, 2nd edition, Applied Social Research Methods Series, vol. 5, Thousand Oaks, London and New Delhi: Sage.

Yin Yuen, Cheong (2004) 'The Construal of Ideational Meaning in Print Advertisements', in Kay O'Halloran (ed.) *Multimodal Discourse Analysis: Systemic Functional Perspectives*, London and New York: Continuum; 163–95.

Zabalbeascoa, Patrick (2008) 'The Nature of the Audiovisual Text and its Parameters', in Jorge Díaz Cintas (ed.) *The Didactics of Audiovisual Translation*, Amsterdam and Philadelphia, John Benjamins, 21–37.

Zhang, Xiaochun (2012) 'Censorship and Digital Games Localisation in China', *Meta* 57(2): 338–50.

Subject index

Terms and page references in *italics* refer to text within boxes and figures.

Name index

Page references in *italics* refer to text within boxes and figures.

Film/drama index

Page references in *italics* refer to text within boxes and figures. Page references in **bold** relate to material within a table.